AIA Guide 1

"If you plan to explore Boston and Cambridge, by all means take Michael and Susan Southworth along! Their guide is surely the best of its kind on this continent. It tells you not only what you ought to know about America's most remarkable and varied collection of buildings, but also about the people and the culture that shaped these buildings and that these buildings, in turn, helped to shape.

P. T. Barnum, Jenny Lind ("the Swedish Nightingale"), Benjamin F. Keith (who invented "vaudeville"), Edgar Allan Poe, Louisa May Alcott, and Jane Jacobs are quite rightly as much part of the Southworths' story, as the Cabots and the Lowells and the Lodges, Paul Revere, Charles Bulfinch, H. H. Richardson, Walter Gropius, and I. M. Pei.

The Southworths manage to be highly informative without the solemn pedantry that makes most architectural guidebooks such a bore. They manage to be entertaining and yet strictly to the point. Most of all, in a quiet, unobtrusive way, they present Boston from their own, personal point of view. One must have a point of view if one really wants to see anything."

—Wolf Von Eckardt, design critic, *Time* magazine

"The most comprehensive guide to Boston architecture ever published. . . . Yet for all its useful information, the *AIA Guide to Boston* is no dry, dense tome. The authors enliven their material with fascinating bits of history, culture, humor, and sharp opinion."

—Janice Harayda, *Boston Business Journal*

"There is no more thorough nor entertaining guide to the notable landmarks [of Boston]. . . ."

—F.Y.I. Eastern Airlines Review

"It is addictive . . . a marvelously readable and informative book, which I read endlessly, go right through and then start over. Boston is a unique city of a sort rare in America, and [the AIA Guide has] done it full justice."

—Nash Kerr Burger, the *New York Times Book Review*

"Architectural buffs will here find a wealth of information on distinctive Bostonian structures and their histories."

—*Midwest Book Review*

"In this readable volume, the authors include anecdotes, social history commentary, and lucid building descriptions that will be useful to the professional and of interest to the informed layperson."

—*Library Journal*

"This guidebook certainly provides a rich source of possibilities to build upon. Over 500 of the city's notable landmarks are highlighted; there's an abundance of photographs and enough information about each place to make the excursions pleasantly educational."

—*Daily Hampshire Gazette*, Northampton, MA

"A truly great 'opus,' and *very* useful."

—Charles F. Mason, Jr., curator of prints, Boston Athenaeum

"Not only fun to read, this one would be fun to *do* . . . and there are several really neat walking tours outlined in it. Boston is a walking town anyhow; this is just a new and pleasurable angle."

—Book Bag, *Courier-Gazette*, Rockland, ME

THE BOSTON SOCIETY OF ARCHITECTS'

AIA Guide to BOSTON

Second Edition

by SUSAN and MICHAEL SOUTHWORTH

A Voyager Book

OLD SAYBROOK, CONNECTICUT

Library of Congress Cataloging-in-Publication Data

Southworth, Michael.
    The AIA guide to Boston / by Michael and Susan Southworth. — 2nd ed.
        p.   cm.
    Rev. ed. of: The A.I.A. guide to Boston. c1984.
    Includes bibliographical references and index.
    ISBN 0-87106-188-0
    1. Architecture—Massachusetts—Boston—Guide-books. 2. Boston
(Mass.)—Buildings, structures, etc.—Guide-books. 3. Boston
(Mass.)—Description—Guide-books. I. Southworth, Susan.
II. Boston Society of Architects. III. Southworth, Michael. A.I.A.
guide to Boston. IV. Title: AIA guide to Boston.
NA735.B7S69 1992
720'.9744'61—dc20   91-40261
                                                                            CIP

Manufactured in the United States of America
Second Edition/Third Printing

The Boston Society of Architects (BSA) is the American Institute of Architects (AIA) chapter in eastern Massachusetts. It is the regional professional association of about 2,000 architects and 1,000 Affiliate Members and is one of the largest and most active chapters of the AIA. The BSA's Affiliate Members include developers, contractors, public officials, other allied professionals, students, and laypeople.

As a service organization, the BSA is committed to excellence in architecture and service to the public. It sponsors many efforts such as the Boston Foundation for Architecture to support public education, a monthly lecture series, tours of local architecture firms, design awards programs, an annual design and construction trade show, and professional development programs.

Membership is open to everyone—architects, allied professionals, and laypeople. BSA members enjoy the many benefits of membership, including the BSA's delightfully informative Chapter Letter, discounts on BSA programs, career services, educational services, and the opportunity to serve on more than sixty BSA committees and task forces.

Since its establishment in 1867, the BSA has been committed to uniting the profession in fellowship, promoting the value of architecture, and encouraging public awareness of the impact of design on our lives and the public service roles architects play.

THE BOSTON SOCIETY OF ARCHITECTS
52 Broad Street
Boston, Massachusetts 02109
Telephone 617–951–1433
Facsimile 617–951–0845

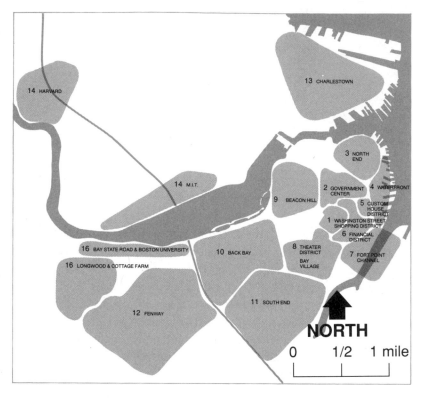

The following labels appear on the map:

14 HARVARD
14 M.I.T.
13 CHARLESTOWN
3 NORTH END
2 GOVERNMENT CENTER
4 WATERFRONT
9 BEACON HILL
5 CUSTOM HOUSE DISTRICT
1 WASHINGTON STREET SHOPPING DISTRICT
6 FINANCIAL DISTRICT
16 BAY STATE ROAD & BOSTON UNIVERSITY
16 LONGWOOD & COTTAGE FARM
10 BACK BAY
8 THEATER DISTRICT
BAY VILLAGE
7 FORT POINT CHANNEL
11 SOUTH END
12 FENWAY

NORTH

0   1/2   1 mile

Maps

Contents

Introduction

The architecture of Boston is extraordinary in America for both the quality and the variety of buildings of every era, from the city's seventeenth-century beginnings through the twentieth century. Founded in 1630 and one of the oldest American cities, Boston dominated the colonies throughout the pre-Revolutionary era. Even today Bostonians tend to see their city as the "hub of the universe"—the center of learning, art, science, and commerce. But one must not take this pride in their quaint ways too seriously, for they have always been quick to adopt new ideas from throughout the world. Perhaps it is this combination of proud tradition with innovation—the ability to cherish the past while looking ahead—that has made the city unique. Boston's love of art and learning, combined with Yankee practicality and determination, have made it a fertile ground for the development of a fascinating city and a significant architectural tradition.

Since it had a head start in everything, it is not surprising that Boston has scored a number of architectural firsts. Beginning with the earliest Colonial structures of wood and continuing with the later Georgian and Federal buildings of brick and stone, one can trace the history of this small peninsula through its architecture and its architects. Charles Bulfinch, one of the most important American architects of the eighteenth and early nineteenth centuries, was born in Boston and had a long and productive career in architecture and planning here, as well as in Washington, D.C., where he served as one of the architects of the new Capitol. Alexander Parris and other Boston architects developed the unique "Boston granite style," making use of the abundant granite in the region for the warehouses and commercial buildings of the city's thriving commerce. In the nineteenth century the Back Bay, the South End, and downtown were showcases for the eclectic Victorian designs of many nationally prominent Boston firms, including those of the most influential American architect of the century, Henry Hobson Richardson. Frederick Law Olmsted, the revered landscape architect, relocated his firm here from New York because he found Boston more sympathetic to his progressive ideas; some of his most important projects are here, including the remarkable string of parks known as the Emerald Necklace. And it was in Boston that Louis Sullivan, leader of the Chicago School, was born and spent his formative years. Even Frank Lloyd Wright, Sullivan's devoted student, spent three years of his boyhood, from 1874 until 1878, outside Boston in Weymouth, where his father was a Baptist minister.

Boston's leadership in architecture has continued into this century with innovations in all areas of design. Besides work of locally and nationally known architects, several important international architects are represented, including Alvar Aalto, Le Corbusier, Walter Gropius, Eero Saarinen, and José Luis Sert. With its three schools of architecture—MIT, Harvard, and the Boston Architectural Center—Boston has also been a leader in design education and probably has more architects and architecture students per capita than any other American city.

But Boston's most significant achievements in this century may have been in urban design and planning. Like European cities, Boston is highly accessible by foot, bicycle, or subway, with many residential neighborhoods within delightful walking distance of places for work, shopping, and entertainment. A long tradition of providing livable outdoor public places has produced a fine-grained network of parks and squares that range from the large and informal seventeenth-century Common and the formal nineteenth-century Public Garden, to linear public spaces like Commonwealth Avenue Mall, the Esplanade, Harbor Walk, and Southwest Corridor Park, to the many intimate and varied spaces of the financial and shopping districts. Boston has been notable for integrating new architecture with that of the past and at the same time maintaining an emphasis on the human scale. More than any other American city, it has retained or adapted its physical past while allowing new landmarks to take root.

This happy coexistence came to an end in the later 1980s, however, with the boom mentality that allowed development to pose serious threats to some of the most cherished districts—and to the rich and varied street scene that Bostonians had come to expect. Especially threatened were the labyrinthine old financial district and the curious little streets of older commercial areas.

Nevertheless, the city has survived and benefited from major transformations in the past. The Quincy Market, the filling of the South End and the Back

Bay, the construction of the Emerald Necklace of parks, and the damming of the Charles River were all large-scale projects that had positive impacts on the entire city. The tradition of big thinking continues. In the 1980s the massive Southwest Corridor Park and its related transit facilities were built. During the 1990s the Fitzgerald Expressway is to be put underground in an attempt to knit back together the city torn apart by this 1950s highway. The new land on top of the highway offers a major urban design opportunity for the next century, an opportunity worthy of the best urban design thought in the world today.

Many mistakes have been made, too. The environmental low point was the dawning of the era of simplistic urban renewal in the 1950s. At this time the City Planning Department was abolished and its functions absorbed into the new Redevelopment Authority, an action that compromised the objectivity and equity of planning by placing development in the forefront. In the 1950s construction of the elevated Fitzgerald Expressway cut off the North End from the rest of the city with a devastating impact on the urban landscape. The destruction of the old West End is still a scandal decades after it happened, and the obliteration of the old Madison Park neighborhood of Roxbury was no more sensitive. The developments that replaced these bulldozed neighborhoods have not been successful additions to the city in architectural or urban design terms. Yet it was during the same era that the landmark Boston City Hall design by Kallmann, McKinnell, and Knowles won a national competition as the centerpiece for another massive but more successful renewal project, Government Center. The pioneering renewal and transformation of the waterfront was also begun

During the long administration of Mayor Kevin White (1968–1984), Boston's development took a new direction. Departing from the bulldozer-style megadevelopment approach of his predecessors, White attempted to build consciously on Boston's social and physical resources. The complexity of Boston was treated as a resource, not a cancer to be destroyed, an approach that was also politically astute. Although numerous office buildings, hotels, and mixed-use projects were built, they rarely involved the razing of more than one or two existing structures, and many of them were relatively small in scale and closely related to their surroundings. Such qualities have not generally been valued by developers, yet Boston attracted many of them despite some unusual and rather stringent constraints. For example, developers were required to retain small, winding historic street patterns or outdoor fruit and vegetable markets in their plans for new hotels or shopping centers. The Faneuil Hall Marketplace reuse project became the symbol of the Boston development philosophy of those years.

In the later 1980s developers built megaprojects that compromised the skyline and sacrificed some of Boston's urban delight. John Powers of the *Boston Globe* (December 31, 1990) wrote, "In those giddy years between Reaganomics and reality, it seemed that everybody with a $10,000 line of credit, a lawyer, and an 'Etch-A-Sketch' wanted to build something big in Boston." Some small, irregular parcels laid out in the city's first century disappeared into superblocks. Glitzy lobbies of marble and shiny metal facade details became the norm. Regrettably, in the construction craze some of the nooks and crannies, the odd "only in Boston" charms, disappeared along with eccentric shops on narrow Dickensian alleyways. Important landmarks like the Custom House Tower lost their significance on the skyline when they were upstaged by new towers. For much of a decade and a half, development rules had been created precisely for each site to preserve and to enhance views, old street patterns, whatever was most important. The new administration consciously rejected this approach in favor of simpler rules that would apply to all sites in a district. But after the boom came the bust, with foreclosures and distress sales of underoccupied new towers.

In the late 1980s and early 1990s Boston was inundated with "retro-Deco"–style buildings, a passion impossible to explain. At the same time, the "Boston contextual style" flourished. Many new buildings tried to pay homage to their surroundings through related materials, height of street facades, window styles, or stylistic details. Some architects who were asked to fit huge new structures into fine-grained and fragile historic settings experimented with the "facade wrap" and "historic skirt" approaches to contextual design. Today Boston probably exhibits more examples of contextual design—good and bad—than any other city in the country.

While the development programs may have been misguided, architectural designs by Boston architects have frequently been more sensitive to the Boston setting than those by outside architects, who too often created massive inappropriate blocks that ignored the surrounding context and became a blot on the skyline. This should not be an excuse to avoid importing outstanding architectural talent to design projects in Boston; there is a long tradition of seeking out the best from around the world. But it is essential that architects unfamiliar with the city be challenged to relate their architectural concepts to the unique circumstances of Boston.

Boston is not a case study to be copied verbatim. Each city has its own personality. Only out-of-date thinking attempts to force identical development concepts on vastly different environments—what is good for Dallas or Atlanta is not necessarily desirable for Kalamazoo or St. Louis, too. Is there an approach that is replicable? Experience to date suggests that no process in itself guarantees architecturally satisfactory results. Each process is largely dependent upon the knowledge and concerns of the individuals involved. The greatest hope is in design awareness of public officials and citizens alike.

As a virtual textbook of American architecture, landscape architecture, and urban design, Boston offers the interested observer a firsthand "touch it, feel it, see it" education on work of over three centuries. This book is part of a wide-ranging effort of the authors and of the Boston Society of Architects to help people see and understand this legacy of environmental design. Neither a history book nor a theoretical treatise, this guide is intended to give the reader a quick understanding of a large number of buildings and urban spaces. We have written the guide for laypeople and architects, visitors and residents, anyone who wishes to know more about Boston and its fascinating architectural history. Our brief discussion of each site emphasizes its design significance but also considers the social and historical background. Being a cultural endeavor, architecture is more than mere construction and gains significance in its cultural context. We have emphasized facts rather than opinions. Our purpose has been to expose the reader to Boston's best architecture from all eras and styles in a lively but organized fashion that can be enjoyed in the armchair or firsthand on the street.

The guide is based on extensive historical research, field surveys of every site, and interviews with dozens of architects, landscape architects, planners, community leaders, and citizens. Looking critically at each building has been a labor of love that has left us more awed than ever by Boston and simultaneously more worried about its future. Boston is a national treasure. Can all of its best qualities be retained and enhanced for future generations?

Using the Guide

We have selected sites primarily because of their architectural and urban design significance. Many are the work of eminent architects, have won various design awards, are Boston Landmarks or National Historic Landmarks, are on the National Register of Historic Places, or are buildings that Boston architects regard as important and influential. While the guide focuses on the most accessible central Boston neighborhoods, it also covers several outlying sites, including Harvard and MIT. Of course, space limitations forced us to exclude many interesting buildings and districts that readers will enjoy discovering for themselves.

Since this is a topographic guide, sites and neighborhoods are arranged by their geographic proximity as much as possible. Beginning with the old center of town and commerce—the Washington Street shopping district—neighborhoods radiate out from the center of the Boston peninsula.

Within each district or subdistrict, sites are generally presented alphabetically by street and numerically by address. The address is the only site identification used on the maps, so the confusion of multiple numbering systems is avoided. For each site the architect and construction dates are given following the name and address of the building, except in the handful of cases where this information was not available. All sites can be found in the index under architect, building name, address, and often style. Sites of outstanding architectural interest are indicated with a 🏛, and landmark status is noted.

Guide maps introduce each district or subdistrict and show the location of many sites and their addresses. In addition, a recommended tour of architectural highlights is delineated on the map and described for each area. Nearly all of the sites are within easy reach of MBTA transit stations, which are noted on the maps with the symbol Ⓣ. At the end of the guide, several theme tours are presented. Adjacent to many transit stations, walkers will notice kiosks with large pictorial neighborhood maps by the authors. These maps illustrate some of the sites from this book and are a helpful guide.

Acknowledgments

We are grateful to the many architects and photographers who have provided information and photographs for the guide. The encouragement and cooperation of the Boston Society of Architects were important to the project. The Boston Athenaeum and Boston Public Library have been essential in the research, and the Boston Landmarks Commission and Boston Redevelopment Authority have provided useful information. In particular we thank Lowell Erickson, Richard Fitzgerald, Earl Flansburgh, Polly Flansburgh, Carol Huggins, Alexandra Lee, Rose Marston, Judy McDonough, Tom Payette, Sally Pierce, Homer Russell, Peter Steffian, Paul Sun, Anthony Tappé, Kathleen Tritchler, Will Watkins, and Sally Withington. In addition, we are indebted to Charles Everitt, Linda Kennedy, Jay Howland, Kevin Lynch, Bruce Markot, and their associates at The Globe Pequot Press.

ONE

Washington Street Shopping District

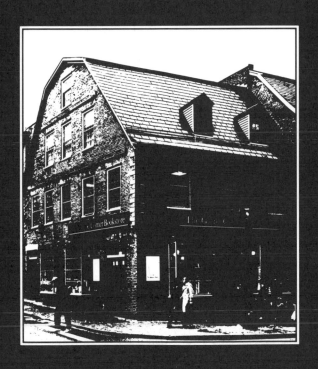

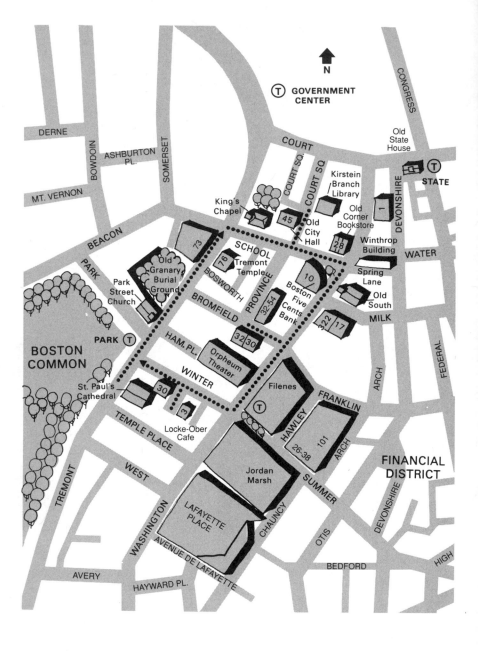

Washington Street Shopping District

Washington Street is the ancient thoroughfare linking the Old State House with the town gate at the neck of the Shawmut peninsula. Its original names—Cornhill, Marlborough, Newbury, and Orange streets—were changed in honor of Washington's visit to Boston in October 1789. Since its earliest history the street has been an important focus of activity, and historic landmarks still line it. Province House, the official residence of the royal governors, fronted on Washington Street, but all that remains today are its garden steps next to Cafe Marliave on Province Street.

Throughout much of the nineteenth century the section near the Old Corner Bookstore and Old South Meeting House was Boston's Fleet Street, a concentration of publishers, booksellers, and newspapermen. Since Boston's earliest shops were here, it is fitting that the street remains the commercial center of the city, with major department stores drawing shoppers to the many smaller stores along the narrow street. The inns and taverns that lined the lane in early Boston have unfortunately disappeared, but housing is returning in the form of luxury towers.

While Washington Street has always been the busy commercial street, nearby Tremont Street was more ceremonial, with the Royal Custom House, the King's Chapel, Royal Governor John Endicott's house, and the Old Granary Burial Ground. In Victorian times the Boston Museum, a rather gaudy multimedia display of curiosities, attracted throngs of people—including the awestruck young P. T. Barnum—to its building on Tremont Street between Court and School streets. Another Tremont Street attraction was Papanti's Dance Hall, an elegant gilt-mirrored and chandeliered ballroom with America's first dance floor built on springs. Here Bostonians first danced the waltz under the tutelage of Lorenzo Papanti, whose successful dance academy operated from 1837 until 1899.

Washington Street Shopping District Tour

For a walking tour of the Washington Street shopping district, begin in the **Boston Common** (**449**) near Park Street station. Facing Tremont Street is **St. Paul's Cathedral** on your right (**13**). Walk up Tremont Street past the **Park Street Church, Old Granary Burial Ground,** and **Tremont Temple** (**11**). The old **Orpheum Theater** is off Tremont Street in Hamilton Place (**11**). In the distance you will see a corner of the new **City Hall** and beyond that the spire of **Old North Church.** After visiting **King's Chapel** (**9**), proceed down School Street past the **Old City Hall** (**7**) to the **Boston Five Cents Savings Bank** (**6**), **Old Corner Bookstore, Winthrop Building,** and **Old South Meeting House** (**14, 16**). At City Hall Avenue you may take a short side trip to the **Kirstein Business Branch** of the Boston Public Library (**7**). Walk down the **Washington Street** pedestrian mall but take a side trip up **Bromfield Street** to see two fine old granite buildings at **30–32** (**5**), then return to Washington Street until you reach **Filene's** and **Jordan Marsh** (**19**), at "**Downtown Crossing.**" Walk up Winter Street with a glance at **Locke-Ober's** at Winter Place (**20**), then return to the Boston Common.

BROMFIELD STREET

Originally called Rawson's Lane, this was the site of the stage house for horse-drawn stagecoaches. In the nineteenth century the name was changed to Bromfield Street in honor of Edward Bromfield, who built his house in the open fields near Beacon Street and had a large yard with terraces and a gazebo overlooking the harbor from a point near Rawson's Lane. Today the street is a haven from the glitzy new Boston and contains a variety of shops, including several specializing in cameras, antique coins and stamps, and stationery.

30–36 Bromfield Street

🏛 30 Bromfield Street

1847–1848
Boston Landmark

The great popularity of granite buildings in Boston during the first half of the nineteenth century is represented here by an outstanding refined example. Two smooth granite stylized Doric pilasters define the windows in a facade of enormous vitality and simplicity. The attic has bold and unusual dormers with windows facing three directions.

Hutchinson Building, 32–54 Province Street

Wesleyan Association Building

32–36 Bromfield Street
HAMMET AND JOSEPH BILLINGS, 1870

Next door to the extraordinary granite building at 30 Bromfield Street is this more conventional but fine French Second Empire five-story building, also of granite. The central pavilion has a roof projecting above the mansard roof.

The second floor has bracketed lintels over segmental arch windows. Both buildings face Province Street and the Hutchinson Building, where the official residence of the royal governor of the Massachusetts Bay was built in 1679. After the Revolution the residence was renamed Government House and was occupied until 1796. Its garden steps still survive at the entrance to Cafe Marliave.

🏛 Boston Five Cents Savings Bank
10 School Street
KALLMANN AND McKINNELL, 1972

One of several award-winning buildings by Kallmann and McKinnell, architects of the new Boston City Hall, this addition to the Boston Five Cents Savings Bank was the winner of a limited competition. The problem was challenging, but the solution solves most of the difficulties. The site is odd-shaped and small, lending itself to no regular geometry, and it faces two eighteenth-century landmarks, Old South Meeting House and the Old Corner Bookstore.

Boston Five Cents Savings Bank

A brawny concrete structural skeleton radiates from the center, following the curve of the site, while a tall wall of glass, set back behind the columns, exposes the full interior to the street. In no way does the form attempt to emulate its older neighbors, yet it does them no harm. In fact, its bold and simple openness provides a good setting for their solid and decorated masses. The cutting away of the corner of School Street speci-

fied by the competition program was a fine urban design gesture that opens views to Old South Meeting House from School Street while creating a pleasant pedestrian space on crowded and narrow Washington Street. Recent interior alterations on the main floor of the bank, however, were unsympathetic to the architecture.

Old City Hall

45 School Street

GRIDLEY J. FOX BRYANT AND ARTHUR
GILMAN, 1862–1865;
RENOVATION: ANDERSON, NOTTER
ASSOCIATES, 1969–1970
National Historic Landmark

The Boston Public Latin School, the first public school in America, was erected on this site in 1635 and gave School Street its name. The elaborate French Second Empire City Hall is dominated by the exuberant central pavilion, which rises several floors above the basic mass. The base of banded rustication supports two levels of pilasters and arched windows. A fine cast-iron gate and fence stands at the property line, while statues of Benjamin Franklin and Josiah Quincy dominate the lawn.

Old City Hall

Many Bostonians remember the opulent interiors, with black-and-white marble floors and grand staircases of iron and oak on the first floor. The second-floor hall of aldermen, forty-four feet square with a twenty-six-foot ceiling, had noteworthy ornamentation and magnificent proportions. On the fourth floor the Common Council Chamber, forty-four feet square with a twenty-seven-foot ceiling, was surrounded by ornamented galleries on three sides. Unfortunately, all of these were removed when the building was recycled as modern offices and a restaurant.

Kirstein Business Branch

Boston Public Library
School Street at 20 City Hall Avenue
PUTNAM AND COX, 1930

Despite its broad-sounding name, City Hall Avenue is a pleasant narrow pedestrian lane that connects School Street with Court Street and the Government Center beyond. At the center is the Kirstein Business Branch of the Public Library, a Georgian Revival brick box that is very sympathetic in scale to the pedestrian lane it faces.

The facade is based on the central pavilion of Bulfinch's fine Tontine

Kirstein Business Branch, Boston Public Library

Crescent, built on Franklin Street in 1793–1794 and demolished about 1858. The central Palladian window is framed by pairs of Ionic pilasters and engaged columns that support the entablature. The segmental arch in the Tontine Crescent was an open passageway, and the rooms above it were presented by Bulfinch to the Boston Library Society and the Massachusetts Historical Society. Bulfinch acted as both architect and developer in the Tontine Crescent project, which proved financially disastrous to him and his family.

Kennedys

26–38 Summer Street, 1874
101 Arch Street
HOSKINS SCOTT TAYLOR & PARTNERS, INC., 1989

Kennedys was one of the "commercial palaces" built to house dry-goods and clothing businesses shortly after the great fire of 1872. Constructed of red brick with sandstone trim and decorative terracotta, it is an elaborate example of the Panel Brick style. In the 1980s it was the focus of a heated preservation controversy when it was slated for demolition to make way for a new tower. The result was a compromise that set the direction for several other Boston projects: The new tower would be built mid-block with an "historic skirt" projecting out at its base to define the street space. The old structure was encased in an elaborate steel frame and entirely gutted to make way for the tower. Although architectural preservation was compromised, the historic scale and character of Summer and Arch streets can still be sensed, and the restored facades of the brownstone Gothic Revival 101 Arch Street and cast-iron Long's building enhance the street.

In addition to the Summer Street entrance, the developers gave the new tower an entrance at 101 Arch Street by eliminating a narrow street, Bussey Place, and then enclosing the space to create an escalator lobby. The rough brick exterior wall of Long's 1873 building with its old five-story cast-iron spiral fire escape now forms one wall of the lobby. Although not easily seen at street level, the tower can be identified on the skyline by its

Kennedys building and 101 Arch Street

giant clock and "postmodern" pediment and Deco Revival surface motifs. The "odd-top" concept was the focus of San Francisco's urban design efforts for a decade; the idea was that putting eye-catching devices on the tops of new towers would create a wonderful skyline. San Francisco ended up with a real menagerie of knickknacks on the tops of new buildings.

🏛 King's Chapel
58 Tremont Street
PETER HARRISON, 1749–1754
National Historic Landmark
Open to the Public

From King's Chapel one can see Old North Church in the North End as well as the corner of the new City Hall. The vista linking these three important Boston landmarks was created intentionally as part of the urban design plan for Government Center. King's Chapel, founded in 1686 to serve British officers, first occupied a small wooden structure on the same site. The first Angelican church in Puritan Boston, it was quite unpopular with the colonists.

In 1749 the present building, designed by Peter Harrison, an architect from Newport, Rhode Island, was begun. Construction was financed largely by Charles Bulfinch's grandfather, who wanted to strengthen the Church of England in Boston. Other notable works by Harrison include the Redwood Library, Touro Synagogue, and Brick Market in Newport, and Christ Church in Cambridge (see 0 Garden Street, p. 412). Harrison, who was known as a loyalist, later became a crown official in New Haven, where his house was wrecked by the Connecticut equivalent of the Sons of Liberty.

A fine example of American Georgian architecture, King's Chapel was conceived as a James Gibbs type of church such as St. Martin's in the Fields in London. It was intended to have an elaborate steeple, but because of lack of funds this was never built. In order to avoid disrupting services, the new building was built around the old one, which was then dismantled and tossed out the windows! Built of dark Quincy granite, the church has four-foot-thick walls, surmounted by a hipped roof. The rectangular mass has two stories of arched windows on the north and south and a Paladian window on the east. The wood colonnade of Ionic columns, also by Harrison, was added around the square tower in 1785–1787.

Inside, pairs of large Corinthian columns, each carved from a single tree, project in front of the galleries. The main floor is divided into family pews that were owned or rented and were originally decorated according to the tastes of their owners. One pew was reserved for the royal governors and later for important Americans such as George Washington. Slaves sat in the rear gallery on the cemetery side of the church, and condemned prisoners had a special pew to the right of the main entrance where they came to hear a sermon before being hanged on the Common. The fine tracker-action organ was built by Charles Fisk in 1963 and looks much like the church's 1756 English organ, said to have been played by Handel.

After the evacuation of Boston by the British, few Angelican families remained.

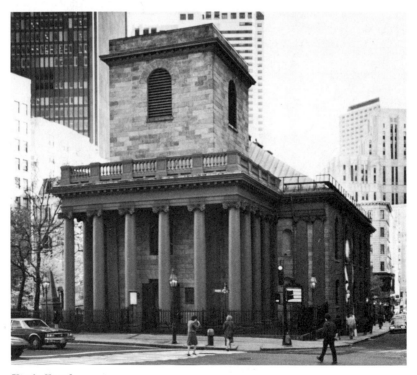

King's Chapel

Under the leadership of James Freeman, a lay reader, King's Chapel (called Stone Chapel after the Revolution) became the first Unitarian church in America in 1789. The cemetery adjacent to the church, dating from 1631, is the oldest in the city. Governors John Winthrop and John Endicott lie buried here.

73 Tremont Street

WINSLOW WETHERELL, 1896; RENOVATION: CHILDS, BERTMAN, TSECKARES, 1990

An important element in the improvement of Tremont Street was the renovation of this prominent office building. During the renovation the original large outdoor light court was filled in and the interior was completely rebuilt with a new two-story lobby. The architects were sensitive to the building's surroundings; no historic narrow streets were eliminated and no tower was shoehorned in.

Tremont Temple

76 Tremont Street
CLARENCE H. BLACKALL, 1896

The famous early Boston theater, Tremont Temple, was built here in 1828. Many well-known actors and orators were seen here, including Charlotte Cushman, Fanny Kemble, Daniel Webster, and Edward Everett. Jenny Lind sang here during her celebrated American tour. The current office and church complex carries a reminder of that temple at the top of its facade, which also has Venetian aspirations in its diamond-patterned stonework. Another

example of the temple-topped tall building may be found in the Danker and Donohue parking garage at 341 Newbury Street, which uses a simple suggestion of the Greek prototype.

Tremont Temple

Orpheum Theater

Hamilton Place, off Tremont Street
SNELL AND GREGERSON, 1852; ALTERATIONS: LITTLE AND BROWNE, 1900, ARTHUR VINAL, 1904, AND THOMAS LAMB, 1915

The Old Music Hall, now the Orpheum Theater, was an important center in Boston's musical history. The New England Conservatory began here, the Handel and Haydn Society performed here for decades, the Tchaikovsky first piano concerto received its world premiere here, and the Boston Symphony Orchestra played their first concert here in 1881. Among the Orpheum's premieres was the American premiere of the Second Symphony by Brahms, which provoked concert goers to walk out. Many prominent Bostonians, however, stayed to hear all of this outrageous new music and were accused of being

"Brahmins." The name stuck. This is one explanation for the origin of the term "Boston Brahmin." The two thousand-seat theater was extensively altered in the early twentieth century, and in 1915 it was converted to Boston's first cinema. In the last few decades it has reverted to a performance theater, and it served as the home of the Opera Company of Boston for a number of years.

Granite detail, Old Granary Burial Ground

🏛 Old Granary Burial Ground
Tremont Street near Park Street
1660

Passing through the Egyptian-style granite gateway designed by that multitalented man, Solomon Willard (see Bunker Hill Monument, p. 372), one enters one of the most illustrious cemeteries in the country nestled among the tall nineteenth-century buildings that surround it. Not only Paul Revere, but Samuel Adams, Governor John Hancock, Benjamin Franklin's parents, Peter Faneuil, and Robert Treat Paine lie buried here, along with many other Patriots and victims of the Boston Massacre. The cemetery is named after the granary that once stood next to it on the site of the Park Street Church.

Old Granary Burial Ground and Park Street Church

🏛 Park Street Church
Tremont Street at Park Street
PETER BANNER, 1810

To make way for the church, it was necessary to demolish the 1738 granary, a long wooden structure designed to hold twelve thousand bushels of grain in case of scarcity. Next to it on Park Street was the Workhouse, a two-story 120-foot-long building that accommodated idlers, tramps, and vagabonds and kept them busy working.

The English architect Peter Banner adapted a Christopher Wren design for the steeple, which rises 217 feet. The church has always emphasized evangelism and missions; it founded the Hawaiian church that was responsible for the establishment of many other churches in the remote Pacific islands beginning in 1819. Several Boston families sent sons there to make their fortunes or serve as missionaries. It was in Park Street Church that William Lloyd Garrison gave his first speech against slavery and where "America" was first sung. The location of the church came to be known as "brimstone corner" because of the zeal of its Congregational preachers. Also contributing to the name was the fact that gunpowder was stored in its basement during the War of 1812.

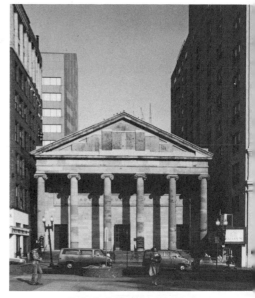

Cathedral Church of St. Paul

Cathedral Church of St. Paul
Tremont Street near Winter Street
ALEXANDER PARRIS, 1820
National Historic Landmark

Facing "brimstone corner" of the Boston Common is Alexander Parris's dignified gray granite Greek temple with Ionic portico of Potomac sandstone, the Episcopalian Cathedral. The bas-relief figures were never carved in the tympanum; the blocks have patiently waited while the temple has become overshadowed by the commercial buildings that now tower over it. The interiors are equally austere and commanding. The chancel was remodeled along Classical lines by Ralph Adams Cram in 1913–1927. Parris designed St. Paul's five years before Quincy Market, where he also saw fit to employ a temple facade, despite the utilitarian function of the market building.

The Devonshire
Washington Street and
1 Devonshire Place
STEFFIAN BRADLEY ASSOCIATES, 1980–1983

The Devonshire, a forty-two-story tower, includes 478 apartments on the top thirty-two floors, seven floors of office space, ten thousand square feet of retail space at the street level, and 242 parking spaces, making it one of the largest mixed-use buildings in Boston. Two offset masses with beveled corners are organized around a central elevator core. The exterior expresses the windows as unbroken horizontal bands, separated by smooth bands of aluminum curtain wall. A pedestrian and vehicular passage through the building connects Washington and Devonshire streets.

Spring Lane
off Washington Street

Spring Lane, an intimate pedestrian way, is defined by the Winthrop Building on one side. For more than two centuries Bostonians obtained water from the spring that was here. Mary Chilton and her husband, John Winslow, had a house on Spring Lane where she died in 1679. Mary was the only Mayflower passenger to leave Plymouth to live in Boston; the Chilton Club was named after her (see 152 Commonwealth Avenue, p. 257).

🏛 Winthrop Building
276–278 Washington Street
CLARENCE H. BLACKALL, 1893
National Register of Historic Places

The unusual slender curving form of the Winthrop Building was dictated by the ancient Spring Lane and Water Street and makes a wonderful object in its context. The elegant ornamentation of the narrow office building includes egg-and-dart moldings, pateras, and terra-cotta bands in the spur pattern on the third and fourth floors. This is reputed to be Boston's first entirely steel-framed office building. For the best view of the Winthrop Building, stand on Water Street across from the Post Office, looking uphill toward its narrow end and curving side.

Winthrop Building and Spring Lane

🏛 Old Corner Bookstore
formerly Thomas Crease House
285 Washington Street
C. 1718; RENOVATION AND REAR ADDITION
1828; RESTORATION: FRANCIS N. CUMMINGS, JR., 1960–1964
National Register of Historic Places

The house of William and Anne Hutchinson formerly stood on this site. It was here that the dynamic Anne Hutchinson tended the sicknesses of neighbors and held religious meetings in which she encouraged Bostonians to seek salvation through improvement of their spiritual

Old Corner Bookstore

state, not just through good works. In 1637 Anne Hutchinson was excommunicated and banished by a court in Cambridge for religious heresy. She, her husband, and their fourteen children left for Rhode Island, where her husband died. Anne and all her children were killed by Indians on Long Island in 1643.

The large Hutchinson home was destroyed in the fire of 1711, and several years later (probably in 1718), an apothecary named Thomas Crease built the present house of rose red brick with a deep gambrel roof. The main room at street level was his apothecary shop, entered from Washington Street. A garden on the School Street side of the

property gave access to his residence above. Several subsequent owners carried on their business in the shop and lived upstairs until it became the Old Corner Bookstore in 1828. A young publisher renovated the house, adding shop windows similar to those now present and the rear extension where the garden had been. He put his presses in the extension and a bookshop in the original apothecary shop.

Never again was the house lived in, but it had various commercial enterprises associated with publishing, most notable of which was that of Ticknor and Fields, the publishers of Longfellow, Lowell, Whittier, Holmes, Hawthorne, Thoreau,

Emerson, Tennyson, Browning, Thackeray, Dickens, and Harriet Beecher Stowe. It was also here that the *Atlantic Monthly* became the most famous periodical of the day. The decision of the *Boston Globe* to occupy this venerable publishing landmark with the Globe Corner Bookstore made possible the restoration of one of Boston's most important early-eighteenth-century commercial structures.

🏛 Old South Meeting House
Washington Street at Milk Street
JOSHUA BLANCHARD, BUILDER, 1729
National Historic Landmark
Open to the Public

A handsome spire of wood surmounts the balustraded square brick tower of the

Old South Meeting House

Forged iron gate next to Old South Meeting House by artist-blacksmith Albert Paley

Wren-influenced Old South Meeting House, Boston's second oldest church. (The oldest is Old North Church.) Originally, this was the site of the garden of John Winthrop. It was here that the town meetings leading to the Boston Tea Party and the Revolution were held. In 1670 the first meeting house of the South Church was built on the site, and Benjamin Franklin was baptized there in 1705 across the street from his birthplace at 17 Milk Street. After the British occupation, the church was left in such poor condition that the congregation was unable to use it for five more years. It narrowly escaped destruction in the great fire of 1872, which stopped just short of it. Again in 1876 it came close to demolition for commercial development, but was saved in the nick of time through a public appeal for funds to purchase the property. The Old South Association has operated Old South Meeting House as a monument and a museum of its role in American history since that time. The congregation has met in the New Old South Church in Copley Square since 1875 (see 645 Boylston Street, p. 230).

Boston Transcript Building

322–328 Washington Street
GRIDLEY J. FOX BRYANT, 1873

In the later nineteenth century, "booksellers' row" was in this area and had the atmosphere of London's Fleet Street.

Two newspaper publishers stood side by side, the Boston Transcript and the Boston Post, at 17 Milk Street. The Boston Transcript Building is a mansard-roof granite structure with corner quoins and the suggestion of end pavilions on its Milk Street facade. Each floor is defined by projecting string courses.

Boston Post Building

Washington Street off 17 Milk Street
PEABODY AND STEARNS, 1874

This building occupies the site of Benjamin Franklin's birthplace, which stood here until 1810, when it was destroyed by fire. The architects integrated a memento of that fact into the elaborate cast-iron facade, made to resemble stone.

Boston Post Building

Washington Street Mall, Downtown Crossing

Washington Street between Milk Street
and Temple Place

ARCADE AND STREET IMPROVEMENTS:
ARROWSTREET, 1975–1978

Fires plagued downtown Boston from
the early days. Finally in 1803 a law was
enacted requiring all buildings ten feet or
more in height to be made of brick or
stone and roofed in slate or tile.
Nevertheless, there were still fires, the
most spectacular being the great fire of
November 1872, which destroyed a huge
area bounded by Washington, Broad,
Milk, and Summer streets. Nearly all of
the Washington Street district was built
after the 1872 fire.

Boston Transcript Building

Several centuries of change on this
pre-Revolutionary street eliminated
almost every convenience for the throngs
of shoppers on foot. By the 1970s the
shopping area had become architecturally complex and the simplistic, homogeneous suburban shopping centers
seemed awesome competition. The creation of the Washington Street pedestrian
mall was motivated by the need to
accommodate pedestrians on narrow
Washington Street as part of the downtown renewal program. The designers
worked with merchants, building owners,
and business organizations to accommodate individual needs and to develop

support for the plan. Such support was
essential in obtaining the cooperation of
city agencies.

The elimination of through traffic
and provision of a well-paved walking
surface with street furniture has made
the old downtown far more usable for
shoppers. The individualistic facades
remain above the first-story level and
deserve close scrutiny. The designers
also created special pedestrian and
vehicular signs for Downtown Crossing.
The project was a joint effort of the
Massachusetts Bay Transportation
Authority and the Boston Redevelopment Authority.

Filene's

426 Washington Street

DANIEL BURNHAM AND COMPANY, 1912

National Register of Historic Places

This was the last major building by the outstanding Midwestern city planner and architect of the early 1900s, Daniel Burnham. The basically simple facade organization of corners, cornice, and base outlining the mass and providing a frame for the window infill reflects the influence of the Chicago School. The design emphasis was on bringing light into the store interior through the plentiful windows, although later alterations have blocked most of them. Burnham's gray-and-green terra-cotta ornamentation is far more traditional than his design conception. The subtle curve of the Summer Street facade enriches the street space.

Filene's and Downtown Crossing

Jordan Marsh

450 Washington Street

PERRY, SHAW, AND HEPBURN, 1948–1951

Although built during the reign of the International Style, the Jordan Marsh department store displays distinct postmodernist tendencies in its medley of

Jordan Marsh

themes. Federalist window frames separated by roundels are plastered on the steamshiplike brick mass. The delightful corner at Summer and Chauncy streets is the best part of the building. A three-story cylindrical window made up of small panes penetrates the concave brick corner wall. The concave corner is repeated at a smaller scale in the set-back mass and top band of windows. All is unified by the canopy as it sweeps around the corner.

🏛 Locke-Ober Cafe

3 Winter Place off Winter Street
FOUNDED MAY 1875
National Register of Historic Places

In the mid-nineteenth century Winter Place was lined with attractive row houses, parts of which remain. Louis Ober took over a new restaurant at number 4 in 1868. After arriving here with his parents, Ober, a French Alsatian, had tried many occupations including barbering, taxidermy, and bookselling—but never before had he been associated with a restaurant. In 1875 he purchased the house where his restaurant occupied the cellar and the adjacent 3 Winter Place, renovated them both, and expanded his restaurant. Eben Jordan, founder of Jordan Marsh and a regular patron of the restaurant, loaned him the money, and the new restaurant was opened under the name of Ober's Restaurant Parisien. Ober and his family took up residence in the upper floors of the two houses. The restaurant prospered and grew in reputation, and a second renovation was undertaken in 1886, when all of the grandeur of the first floor that remains today was installed—the carved mahogany, the extraordinary German silver tureen and platter covers on counterweights, the brass fittings, and the leather-upholstered chairs.

In 1892 a competitor, Frank Locke, opened a restaurant at numbers 1 and 2 Winter Place. Two years later Ober abruptly sold his restaurant to liquor dealers and devoted himself to his many real-estate holdings. Locke's new restaurant was lavish in its decoration and furnishings—mirrors, glass, myriad electric lights twinkling everywhere, paintings, carved mahogany, plush and damask, and a waterfall! Over the entrance hung a large, intricately scrolled lock with the name Frank on it, which inspired the lock-shaped sign of today. Just two years later Frank Locke died, and the same liquor merchants who had taken over Louis Ober's restaurant now bought the extravagant competition next door and combined the two. A Parisian manager, Emil Camus, was hired but left Boston in 1896, only to return in 1901 and buy Locke-Ober's. He ran the restaurant in his imperious, taciturn style until 1939, establishing many of the menus still enjoyed today.

Locke-Ober Cafe main dining room in 1876

TWO

Government Center

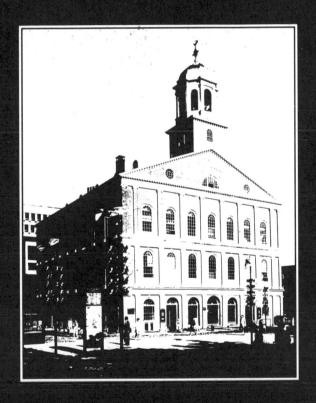

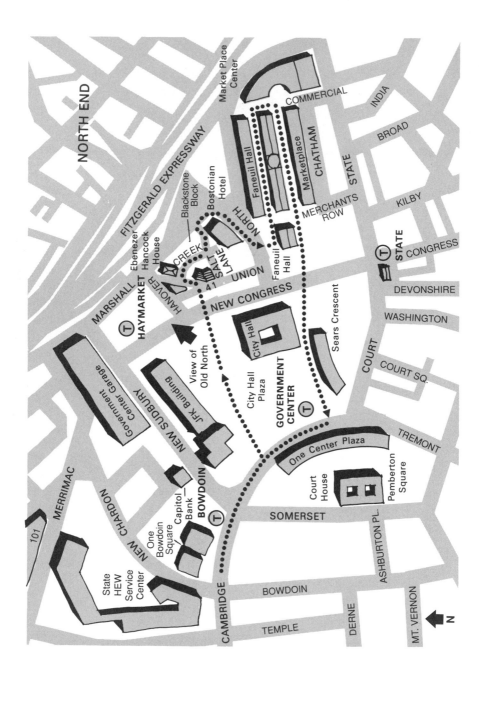

Government Center

T his compact district connects the downtown area with the waterfront and North End and juxtaposes some of Boston's oldest landmarks with contemporary examples of architecture and urban design. The Boston Stone, Ebenezer Hancock house, and Faneuil Hall are a stone's throw from the new government center of the 1960s that replaced the seedy lanes of old Scollay Square. Here, in the original market area of the city, one still finds meat shops and lively street markets as well as the delightful "old Boston"-style restaurants, Durgin-Park and the Union Oyster house. More recent additions to the food scene are the dozens of eateries in the recycled Quincy Market buildings.

Government Center Tour

Sites in Government Center are organized topographically rather than alphabetically, since many of the buildings lack street addresses. Beginning in **City Hall Plaza** near the MBTA station, proceed clockwise, from **City Hall (27)** and the **Sears Crescent (28)** to **One Center Plaza**, the **Court House**, and the **JFK Building (29–30)**. The **Capitol Bank** and **State Health, Education, and Welfare Building** are an optional side trip **(31–32)**. In the distance you can see the **Government Center Garage (32)**. Continue from City Hall Plaza to the **Blackstone Block** and **Bostonian Hotel (32, 35)** and then to **Faneuil Hall** and the **Marketplace (37–39)**. Return to the City Hall Plaza.

Government Center Master Plan

I. M. Pei and Partners, 1960

The master plan for Government Center has shaped development of the area for two decades. Carved out of the historic but decidedly seedy Scollay Square section of Boston, the fifty-six-acre site integrates city, state, and federal offices along with private office and retail space, parking, and public transit.

Several historic landmarks and views were retained as part of the redevelopment plan. Thus, preservation of the Sears Crescent, the 227-gallon steaming teakettle, and the views from various points on the plaza of Faneuil Hall, the Old State House, Old North Church, and the U.S. Custom House Tower were specified. New buildings were subject to development controls including height, bulk, setbacks, open space, and spatial relations between buildings. The focus of the development was to be the new City Hall, the placement and massing of which were part of the master plan and served as the framework for the national competition for its design.

Pedestrian access and amenity are emphasized throughout the plan. The large brick plaza has pedestrian links to Washington and State streets via Washing-

© Aerial Photos International

Government Center

ton Mall, to the arcaded One Center Plaza, and to Faneuil Hall and the market area, which was intended to be an elevated pedestrian link above Congress Street, the beginning of the "walk to the sea."

Government Center makes an abrupt change in the scale and character of the historic city center. While the architects Paul Rudolph and Kallmann and McKinnell created strong twentieth-century statements that may justify the destruction of the past they replace, the concept of high-density, low-rise building form that served Boston so well for centuries is inadequately expressed in the site planning for the new government offices. Many have felt the plaza as built is too large and undefined for the scale and texture of Boston. The preliminary site plan developed by Adams, Howard, and Greeley with Kevin Lynch and John Myer, the basis for Pei's plan, called for a considerably smaller plaza (but did not preserve the Sears Crescent). City Hall Plaza does not have a form or design that makes it appear inevitable as the great Italian piazzas do. The expanses of the plaza cry out for the judicious application of appropriately scaled infill to form and define the space and its gateway functions.

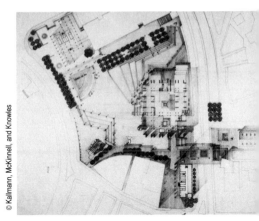

Plan, Boston City Hall

© Kallmann, McKinnell, and Knowles

🏛 Boston City Hall

City Plaza

KALLMANN, McKINNELL, AND KNOWLES
WITH CAMPBELL, ALDRICH, AND NULTY,
1961–1968

The powerful expressionist form of the Boston City Hall communicates symbolically the organization of city government. The vast plaza flows into the brick base of the building where the public functions are clustered on several levels. Monumental gathering spaces both inside and outside provide the setting for celebrations, performances, ceremonies, exhibitions, and political rallies. Looming over the entrances are the dramatic concrete forms of the mayor's office and council chambers, and above these, the pigeonholes of city bureaucracy. The top-heavy massing and overhanging sun screens recall the handsome form of Le Corbusier's convent at La Tourette and won for the architects the national competition that established their reputation. The rugged interiors of concrete, brick, and glass seem indestructible, as they should be for public buildings, but have considerable architectural interest throughout the building. After its completion the City Hall inspired similar buildings across the country.

Sears Crescent

City Hall Plaza
1816
RENOVATION: DON STULL ASSOCIATES, 1969
National Register of Historic Places

The most successful edge of City Hall Plaza hugs the Sears Crescent and its small granite neighbor, the Sears Block, along the old street line. The curving brick facade forms a perfect backdrop and is compatible with its aggressive neighbor, the City Hall, while recalling the historic form of the area. The six-story central brick building is flanked by a pair of five-story wings with wooden attics above their brick machicolation and cornice. The facade rests on an open base of granite posts and lintels, providing generous light, view, and access to the ground floor. Next door the small Sears Block (1848) sports the famous steaming 227-gallon teakettle, the most beloved sign in Boston, which was retained from old Scollay Square as a

part of the urban design plan. The style of the windows in both buildings was altered in the renovation.

The steaming teakettle

Sears Crescent

One Center Plaza

City Hall Plaza
WELTON BECKETT AND ASSOCIATES,
1966–1969

One Center Plaza, although architecturally unremarkable, performs the urban design functions it was appointed to do, namely, to echo the curved facade of the Sears Crescent and to link Tremont and Cambridge streets with a neutral backdrop for City Hall Plaza. It also accommodates a pedestrian shopping arcade, which is pierced at the center with a stairway and escalator connection to the higher-level Pemberton Square Plaza and the Suffolk County Court House. Unfortunately, the visual link between Government Center Plaza and Pemberton Square is weak because the opening is far too small for a view of the Court House.

View of Pemberton Square, 1885

Boston Athenaeum

Suffolk County Court House

behind One Center Plaza in
Pemberton Square
GEORGE A. CLOUGH 1896, ENLARGED
1906–1909; ADDITION: DESMOND AND LORD,
1936–1939
National Register of Historic Places

Old Pemberton Square, developed in the
1830s, was an attractive residential
square of brick row houses surrounding
a small park much like Louisburg Square
(see Louisburg Square, p. 171). Construction of the Court House in 1895 dealt the
first blow to one side of the square. The
remaining houses survived into the
1960s, when Government Center was
developed.

The grand French Second Empire
Court House has a facade that is articulated to suggest a smaller building of
three or four stories plus attic. Above the
rough granite base smooth-faced arches
and pilasters rise to a heavy cornice and
entablature. The pale green two-story
mansard roof, a later addition, has three
different styles of dormers. The central
entrance pavilion relates to the end
pavilions in form and features a Roman-
numeral clock surmounted by a broken
pediment with cartouche in the tympanum. Inside, a grand space decorated
with allegorical figures by Domingo
Mora provides a common focus for the
different floors. The Art Deco tower
addition seems bland by comparison,
but its entrance deserves a look.

Suffolk County Court House

John F. Kennedy Federal Office Building

City Hall Plaza
THE ARCHITECTS COLLABORATIVE AND
SAMUEL GLASER ASSOCIATES, 1967

Defining one side of City Hall Plaza and
providing a background for the City Hall
is the one-million-square-foot Kennedy
Building, composed of a twenty-six-story
tower and a long, low four-story building. Both are clad in quartz-studded precast concrete panels. The tower is
actually made up of two offset rectangles
joined by the elevator core; this solution
broke down the mass and brought more
light into the offices. Windows are oper-

able to provide office workers with control over their microclimate and for cleaning. A mural by Robert Motherwell is located in the connector link between the two buildings, and a bronze sculpture by Dimitri Hadzi stands on the outdoor plaza. The building is more successful at close quarters than as a backdrop for the enormous plaza, and it is incompatible with the style, massing, and materials of the City Hall.

Capitol Bank and Trust Company
New Sudbury Street at
One Bulfinch Place
ANDERSON AND NOTTER, 1972

Were it not for an attention-getting corner, this would be a conservative brick box. A giant bite has been taken out of its most visible corner, revealing the insides of three floors through the jagged glass walls. The cantilevered mass looms over the entrance, defying gravity. Is it

an architectural pun on the nearby City Hall, which has pulled the same stunt on a larger scale? In any case, it is a bit of whimsy suited to its rather stodgy surroundings.

🏛 State Health, Education, and Welfare Service Center
Cambridge Street at New Chardon
PAUL RUDOLPH; SHEPLEY BULFINCH RICHARDSON AND ABBOTT; PEDERSEN AND TILNEY; M. A. DYER; DESMOND AND LORD; 1970

In a tour de force demonstrating the sculptural possibilities of concrete, Paul Rudolph created his own landscape for a large government complex using his trademark corduroy concrete. The long stretches of terracing, deep overhangs,

© Randolph Langenbadr

Capitol Bank and Trust Company

State Health, Education, and Welfare Service Center

and cylindrical towers form a twentieth-century evocation of a European piazza. It establishes its own strong vocabulary without attempting to relate to its diverse neighbors. Sunscreens mask the endless office windows, stairways become sculptural flights, and paving swirls in sinuous curves of small terraces. For lack of funds the focal tower was never built, leaving a gaping wound in the plaza that reveals a cross-section of the subsurface parking and opens the courtyard to view from New Chardon Street.

101 Merrimack Street
THE ARCHITECTS COLLABORATIVE; MURAL: RICHARD HAAS, 1990

The focus of this contextual office building is a six-story trompe l'oeil mural by Richard Haas. Most of one wall of the multilevel central interior space is a mural suggesting a domed glass pavilion filled with palms, while real falling water at the base provides sound to reinforce the image. Haas's painted details enhance the central space, producing a winter garden effect without the chore of maintaining real palm trees and tropical plants.

Government Center Garage
New Sudbury Street
KALLMANN AND MCKINNELL WITH SAMUEL GLASER AND PARTNERS, 1970

This must be one of the most dramatic garages ever built. It carries on the brutalist concrete style started with the City Hall by the same architects, but with completely different means. Built of precast concrete components stacked up almost

© 1990 Nick Wheeler

Richard Haas mural at 101 Merrimack Street

like Lincoln Logs, bold sun-catching elements are juxtaposed with deep voids. At the northeast end, which crosses over Congress Street, the lower floors of the garage step back to shelter and accommodate access to Haymarket Station and bus service, recalling at the same time the stepped-back form of the City Hall. Two floors of offices were added on top in the late 1980s.

⛫ Blackstone Block
Boston Landmark
National Register of Historic Places

The seventeenth- and early-eighteenth-century street pattern of old Boston survives in the Blackstone Block. Its

Government Center Garage

winding lanes include Marshall Street, Scott Alley, Salt Lane, Marsh Lane, and Creek Square. Benjamin Franklin spent much of his boyhood in the neighborhood near here, where his father had a chandlery shop. In 1633 a small stream ran where Blackstone Street is and was used by the area's butchers for disposing of waste. The area has been a center for meat marketing throughout Boston's his-

Boston Stone

tory, and the tradition continues today. Three centuries of Boston architecture are to be found in the block, from the early-eighteenth century Capen House to the recent Bostonian Hotel. At Creek Square the Boston Stone, the marker from which distances to and from Boston were measured, can be seen. The stone was originally used for grinding paint pigments, but was placed here as a marker in 1737.

Union Oyster House
originally Capen House
41 Union Street
c. 1713–1717

An oyster house has been here since 1826. Before then it had been the dry-goods shop and home of the Capen family, and in 1798 the home of James Amblard, tailor, above whose shop the

Duke of Chartres lodged and taught French to Boston merchants. (He returned to London in 1800, later to assume the French throne as Louis Philippe.) On the second floor Isaiah Thomas printed the *Massachusetts Spy*, an early newspaper of the Whig Party, from 1771 to 1775. The three-story building has a gambrel roof with dormers. The Union Street facade is of Flemish bond brick with dentil cornice, string course, and segmental arch windows at the second floor.

🏛 Ebenezer Hancock House
10 Marshall Street

c. 1767

Boston Landmark

Ebenezer Hancock, John Hancock's brother, may have built this house, since he was a mason and bricklayer. During the Revolution Ebenezer was paymaster for the Continental army, which was paid here in 1779. In style the house is similar to the Union Oyster House at 41 Union Street, with Flemish bond brick, second-floor string course, and segmental arch windows. The first floor was remodeled as a store before the close of the eighteenth century.

Union Oyster House

The Bostonian Hotel
North Street
MINTZ ASSOCIATES, 1980–1982

The major twentieth-century contribution to the Blackstone Block is a new hotel of one hundred fifty rooms. To put a hotel on this small remnant of seventeenth-century Boston might seem a disastrous idea, yet the result is surprisingly successful. All of the old streets have been retained, including the narrow Scott Alley, Salt Lane, Marsh Lane, and Creek Square, which afford various views into the hotel as they wind through the block. The impact of the hotel is small-scale, and it has the appearance of several buildings. A three-story curving brick facade along North Street conceals the off-street vehicle entrance and courtyard. The narrow six-story 1889 building by Peabody and Stearns at 24 North

Scott Alley

Ebenezer Hancock house

Street was retained and integrated into the plan and contributes to the sense of small old plots of land. The feeling really is that of a small European hotel. The unornamented treatment of the brick is appropriate to the simple commercial structures that have always been associated with the block. The striped canvas awnings over the windows add a bit of frivolity that relates directly to the traditional awnings of the produce markets.

James Michael Curley Statues
Park between Union Street and City Hall
LLOYD LILLIE, SCULPTOR, 1980

Boston has never forgotten its beloved Mayor James Michael Curley, and in these sculptures he becomes a permanent part of the street life. It was about his Irish political machine that Francis W.

Hatch, a Yankee of poetic bent, quipped: "Vote often and early for James Michael Curley."

James Michael Curley statues

Bostonian Hotel

© Sam Sweezy

🏛 Faneuil Hall

JOHN SMIBERT 1740–1742; REBUILT 1762;
REBUILT AND ENLARGED 1805–1806,
CHARLES BULFINCH; RESTORED 1898–1899;
GROUND FLOOR AND BASEMENT ALTERED
1979; RESTORATION: GOODY, CLANCY &
ASSOCIATES, INC., 1992

National Historic Landmark
Open to the Public

John Smibert, an artist, designed the original Faneuil Hall in the style of an English country market, with an open ground floor and an assembly room above. The building was a gift of French Huguenot merchant Peter Faneuil (probably pronounced "Funnel" in his time). After a fire the building was rebuilt in 1762 along the same lines.

By Bulfinch's time Faneuil Hall was becoming too cramped for the rapidly growing city, so Bulfinch prepared a clever design that retained its Colonial character but doubled its width and added a third floor. This increased the height of the assembly hall and provided space for the Ancient and Honorable Artillery Company in the attic. Four bays were added to the original three, the

Italian market

cupola was moved to the Dock Square end of the building, and the open arcades on the ground floor were enclosed. The original dormers were changed to barrel-shaped ones, relating to the bull's-eye windows in the pediments. Brick pilasters in the Doric order are on the first two floors, and the new third floor was given the Ionic order. Pilasters are paired at each corner. Inside, Bulfinch added galleries on three sides of the meeting hall and numerous decorative elements, including the swag panels between the old and new windows on the east and west walls. In 1898–1899 the hall was entirely rebuilt using noncombustible materials.

🏛 Faneuil Hall Marketplace

ORIGINAL BUILDINGS BY ALEXANDER PARRIS,
1824–1826; REUSE: BENJAMIN THOMPSON
AND ASSOCIATES, 1976–1978

National Historic Landmark
(Quincy Market)

Quincy Market, named after Mayor Josiah Quincy, who conceived it as an extension to the Faneuil Hall markets, was the largest single development yet undertaken in Boston. Today it is the centerpiece of Faneuil Hall Marketplace. In Mayor Quincy's own words: "A granite market house, two stories high, 535 feet long, covering 27,000 feet of land, was erected at a cost of $150,000. Six new streets were opened, and a seventh greatly enlarged, including 167,000 feet of land, and flats, docks and wharf rights obtained to the extent of 142,000 square feet. All this was accomplished in the center of a populous city, not only with-

Faneuil Hall

out any tax, debt or burden upon its pecuniary resources, but with large permanent additions to its real and productive property."

Architect Alexander Parris, like many of his contemporaries, had a penchant for the Greek Revival style. He had also designed St. Paul's Cathedral (see Tremont Street near Winter Street, p. 13) in the same idiom. When built, the handsome structures of Quincy granite were at the harbor's edge at the town dock. Meat and produce merchants' stalls lined the long market halls, and at the center was a rotunda. Despite the traditional style, the original structure employed several innovations, including cast-iron columns, iron tension rods, laminated wood ribs for the copper-covered dome, and the first large-scale use of granite and glass in the manner of post-and-beam construction.

The enormously successful restoration-recycling of the old markets as Faneuil Hall Marketplace, which has been widely admired and emulated, did not come about easily. For a while it appeared that the old buildings might even be pulled down, but the architects worked for several years trying to persuade the Boston Redevelopment Authority, financiers, and developers that their concept for the

© Steve Rosenthal

Faneuil Hall Marketplace

Marketplace was viable. Architect Benjamin Thompson's marketing experience as founder of Design Research helped his firm work out marketing plans for the Marketplace and communicate them to businessmen. Finally, after approaching several developers, the architects convinced James W. Rouse, chairman of the Rouse Company, to take on the project. Rouse had become interested in downtown development, but until then had not found the right project. After considerable encouragement and negotiation, the enterprise went ahead and became the Rouse Company's biggest success. Later, they used a similar approach on Baltimore's waterfront, New York's South Street Seaport, New Orleans's River Walk, and elsewhere.

The Marketplace illustrates the architects' belief that renovation should not attempt to recreate the past artificially. Instead, they wished to retain elements of the past and combine them with the new. In order to preserve the genuineness of historic parts, however, they considered it essential to distinguish, however subtly, new repairs, replacements, or additions from the originals. Their precepts extended into the realm of style, where new elements such as windows, lighting, greenhouse additions, and signing are obviously late twentieth century and stand in sharp contrast to the historic granite structures.

Happily, the markets still function in much the way they did when they were built, with individual merchants lined up in stalls displaying and selling their merchandise, though there is certainly more variety and intensity of activity today than ever before. The pushcarts, too, follow the historic precedent of the Italian market across the street and give small merchants a chance. Selection of merchants, signing, displays, and interior treatments are carefully controlled by the developer. The city still owns the buildings and the Rouse Company has a ninety-nine-year lease.

Marketplace Center
115 State Street
WZMH GROUP, 1983–1985

Marketplace Center terminates South Market Street, the Faneuil Hall Marketplace outdoor space, and masks the intrusive elevated expressway. At the same time it provides an inviting gateway that leads pedestrians on the "walk to the sea" from the Marketplace and under the expressway to the waterfront. The three-story retail base contains shops and offices. Offset on a portion of the base is a tower, whose awkward location was dictated by the desire to minimize its visibility from Faneuil Hall Marketplace. Its height was limited to sixteen stories to maintain the visibility and dominance of the Custom House Tower in the district.

Marketplace Center

North End

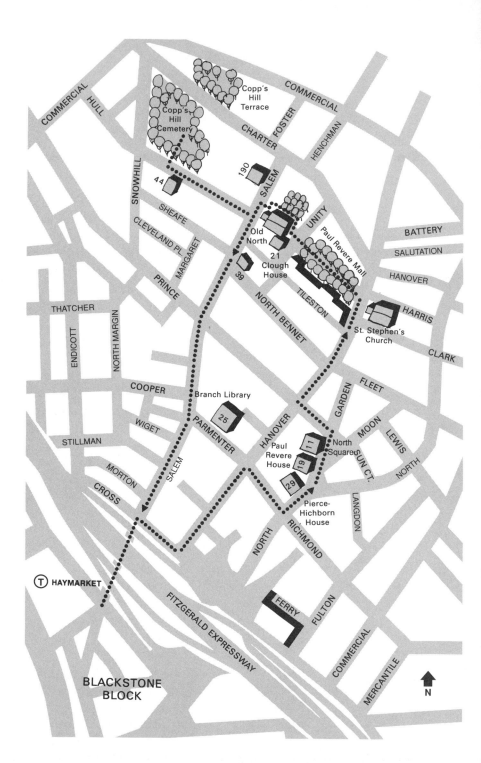

North End

Before the Revolution the North End was the fashionable area of Boston and the site of the mansions of Lieutenant Governor Hutchinson, Sir Henry Frankland, and Governor Phips. Nearly an island, it was connected to the mainland by bridges over the Mill Creek. Although it had only a few houses and a windmill in the early 1700s, by the end of the century it was the most densely populated section of Boston. Wharves had been built in every possible location, all but obliterating the original shoreline.

The area never really recovered its earlier status after the Revolution, however, since a number of Loyalists who had been among its leading residents were forced to abandon their property and fled to Halifax. Although most of the early settlers were Puritans, a settlement of Afro-Americans on Copp's Hill had given that area the nickname "New Guinea." Throughout the nineteenth and early twentieth centuries successive waves of immigrants moved into the North End, and later to the West End and Beacon Hill. Beginning with the potato famine in 1824 the Irish came, followed in the 1860s and later by Jews of eastern Europe, then Portuguese and Italians. In this context Eben Jordan founded his department-store chain and John Fitzgerald ("Honey Fitz") began his career in politics.

Today the North End is an explorable labyrinth of narrow activity-filled streets with attentive residents and laundry hanging out of upper windows. This is the area Jane Jacobs praised in the early 1960s for its street life and sense of community, when urban renewal was destroying other such neighborhoods across the country. It is a close-knit Italian community with strong traditions and fierce pride, despite creeping gentrification. Streets are lined with shops selling fine Italian imported foods, cafes with delicious gelati and cappuccino, pasta and pastry shops, and fresh-produce markets. Storefront social clubs, some of which are funeral brotherhoods, play an important part in the life of the neighborhood. Each club has a patron saint, usually the patron saint of the members' home town in the old country, and sponsors a summer street *festa* honoring the patron. These colorful street festivals are famous North End events that attract admiring participants from all parts of the city. Confetti, balloons, and dollar bills are thrown down on the processions from windows above the decorated streets as the statue of the honored saint is carried on the shoulders of the club members. From the statue hang streamers to which people pin money for charity in the name of the saint. The street life, social traditions, and political sentiments of the North End create a strong and vital community.

North End Tour

If you begin your tour of the North End starting in Government Center, walk under the Fitzgerald Expressway and turn right onto Cross Street, then left onto **Hanover Street (47)**. Turn right again at Richmond Street, then left to **North Square** and the **Pierce-Hichborn house, Paul Revere house,** and **Mariners' House (50–51)**. From North Square, return to Hanover Street and continue to **St. Stephen's Church** and the **Paul Revere Mall (48–49)**. Look at the **Clough house** on Unity Street **(56)**, then approach **Old North Church** from behind, passing the Washington Memorial Garden **(54)**. A short side trip up Hull Street to **Copp's Hill** is recommended **(54)**. Return to the Old North Church and walk down **Salem Street,** passing the **North Bennet Street School** and Italian street life **(52–53)**, arriving back at your starting point.

Ferry Street, birthplace of "Honey Fitz"

FERRY STREET,

birthplace of "Honey Fitz"

John F. Fitzgerald, "Honey Fitz," grandfather of John Fitzgerald Kennedy, was born on Ferry Street in 1863. He spoke so frequently and fondly of the "dear old North End" that the neighborhood's residents came to be called the "Dearos." The name was adopted by the Irish political and social organization led by Fitzgerald. Rose Fitzgerald Kennedy, daughter of Honey Fitz and mother of President Kennedy, was born at 4 Garden Street a few blocks away.

HANOVER STREET

From the settlement of Boston until recently, Hanover Street was the road that linked the North End with the rest of the Boston peninsula. Today it is the commercial spine of the neighborhood, lined with Italian shops and restaurants. The Union Oyster House and Boston City Hall may be viewed beyond the elevated expressway. Two department-store tycoons started business on Hanover Street. Eben Jordan, who came to Boston from Danville, Maine, with $1.25 in his pocket, opened a small dry-goods store at 168 Hanover Street that eventually became the Jordan Marsh Company. A few years later Rowland H. Macy of Nantucket opened a similar store on the

street, the predecessor of the R. H. Macy
Company in New York City.

North End Branch Library

off Hanover Street
at 25 Parmenter Street
CARL KOCH AND ASSOCIATES, 1965

In his design for the library, Carl Koch
considered the cultural background of
the Italian residents of the North End.
The interior is treated as a courtyard or
piazza, a common element in the architecture of Italy. The stone-paved central
space is landscaped with large plants,
comfortable furnishings, and a pool. The

North End Branch Library

roof, composed of concrete hyperbolic
paraboloids supported on nine columns,
is raised to form a clerestory that lights
the space. The brick exterior is ornamented with brick and colored glass
ceramics that recall Frank Lloyd Wright's
geometric ornamentation. An iron fence

composed of flat strips defines the edge
of the garden. Inside the library visitors
may see a well-executed fourteen-foot-
long model-diorama of the Doge's Palace
in Venice, modeled in plaster by Miss
Henrietta Macy, a North End kindergarten
teacher who spent much of her life in
Europe and died in Venice in 1927.

🏛 St. Stephen's Church

originally New North Church
Hanover Street
CHARLES BULFINCH, 1802–1804;
RESTORATION, CHESTER F. WRIGHT,
1964–1965
National Register of Historic Places
Open to the Public

Of the five churches Bulfinch built in
Boston, only this one remains. It features
an elaborate facade. The entrance, set
within a three-story recessed brick arch,
is flanked by pairs of two-story stone
pilasters, originally painted white to sim-
ulate marble, with Ionic capitals and an
entablature of wood. The side aisles and
galleries are expressed on the facade by
the lower set-back side masses with inset
brick arches that frame the two windows.
A balustrade defines the top of this mass.
The central block rises a story higher,
with another set of pilasters supporting
an entablature, which in turn supports
the elaborate tower and two side urns on
pedestals with scroll brackets. As in the
churches of the English architect James
Gibbs, the tower is at the front and is an
elaborate assemblage of pediments,
arches, engaged columns, and urns, all
supporting an octagonal cupola.

The Reverend Francis Parkman,
father of the noted historian, was minis-

St. Stephen's Church

ter here from 1813 until 1849. With the influx of Catholic immigrants into the North End in the mid-nineteenth century, the Unitarian church was sold to the Roman Catholic diocese in 1862. It was renamed St. Stephen's, and the religious change was further expressed by removal of the weathervane and construction of a spire over the cupola. In 1870, when Hanover Street was widened, the church was moved back sixteen feet and raised more than six feet. When the church was restored in 1964 it was lowered to its original level.

🏛 Paul Revere Mall

("The Prado") off Hanover Street across from St. Stephen's
ARTHUR SHURTLEFF, 1933

One of the city's finest urban spaces, the Paul Revere Mall is carved out of the densely built-up North End and links two landmarks, Bulfinch's St. Stephen's Church and the Old North Church (see Hanover Street, p. 47, and 193 Salem Street, p. 53). The irregularly shaped space is effectively defined by brick walls, above which rise the back sides of apartment buildings. The bronze plaques on the walls tell about some of the people and places of the North End. Two rows of trees strengthen the linear space and provide shade and visual relief from the hard surfaces of the narrow brick streets. Year round the Prado, as it is called by North Enders, bubbles with activity. Children play while their mothers or grandmothers look on, men huddle over tables playing checkers or cards, boys play frisbee, and tourists parade through.

This mall is the best pedestrian approach to Old North Church. One passes Cyrus Dallin's 1885 (not cast until 1940) equestrian statue of Paul Revere amidst the outdoor life of today's North End. At the head of the mall is the restored Clough house (see 21 Unity Street, p. 56) and a good view of the back of Old North or Christ Church. As one ascends the stairs the space squeezes in, presenting views of small contained gardens and the side of the church. Then it pinches in again at the church's front entrance, tight against narrow Salem Street. Certainly the mall's designer, Arthur Shurtleff, had in the back of his mind the wonderful spatial sequences of Venice and other Italian cities when he conceived this.

NORTH SQUARE

North Street

The triangular granite plaza is rich in history and still has some of the flavor of Colonial Boston in the Revere and Hichborn houses, blended with the nineteenth-century Mariners' House and the apartments of today's Sicilian and Italian residents. In the eighteenth century Boston's two grandest houses were on North Square, called Clark's Square then. William Clark, merchant, had a three-story brick house with twenty-six lavish rooms, and nearby, facing the garden court, was John Foster's house, later occupied by Governor Hutchinson. On Moon Street just off the square was the house of the Reverend Samuel Mather. At the head of the square was the church of the Mathers, the Second Church of Boston, dating from 1677, called "Old North." It was destroyed by the British for firewood in 1776. There is substantial evidence that this was in fact the church from which Paul Revere was warned of the approaching British, but the matter has never been settled conclusively.

Across from the Paul Revere House is the Rachel Revere Park, a playground named after Paul Revere's second wife, the mother of eight of his sixteen children. A bit farther down North Street at Richmond Street is the oldest sign in Boston, dating from 1694. It is at the third-story level of the northeast corner and is inscribed with the initials "W, T, S." They are the initials of Timothy

Wadsworth and his wife Susannah, granddaughter of Nicholas Upsall, who owned the Red Lyon Inn at this corner. North Street was originally called Anne Street, and by the early nineteenth century it had become a rowdy place, known for "the nymphs of Ann Street." In the 1850s it was cleaned up and renamed North Street.

Mariners' House
11 North Square
1838

The Mariners' House is dedicated to the service of seamen. The dignified structure of four stories plus dormered attic is in the Federal style. On its roof is an octagonal lantern or cupola, presumably built so the seafaring residents of the

North Square, Mariners' House

house could keep their eyes on the sea. The six-over-six-pane windows have granite lintels and sills.

🏛 Paul Revere House
19 North Square
C. 1677, EXTENSIVELY REBUILT MID-
EIGHTEENTH CENTURY; RESTORATION: JOSEPH
E. CHANDLER, 1907–1908
National Historic Landmark
Open to the Public

Paul Revere, descendant of Huguenots named Revoire, purchased his house in 1770, when it was already nearly one hundred years old, and owned it until 1800, fathering a family of sixteen children at a rate of one every two years. Revere was a gold- and silversmith as well as a copper engraver, and a maker of cannons and church bells as well as false teeth.

The oldest frame house in Boston, it was built shortly after the great Boston fire of 1676 and provides a good sense of homes of the period. Like many houses of the day, it was a small frame structure, close to the street, with an overhanging second floor or jetty. The low-ceilinged dark rooms cluster about the massive central chimney. Small leaded windows provide light and view. Several of the Reveres' furnishings may be seen inside. The land behind it was large enough for a garden or stable and had the unsanitary combination of well and privy, the cause of much disease. Rear lots were often sold off and built upon, with the small back houses linked to the main streets by a maze of tiny passageways.

Paul Revere house

🏛 Pierce-Hichborn House
29 North Square
1710; RESTORED 1950
National Historic Landmark
Open to the Public

Nathaniel Hichborn, Paul Revere's cousin, lived next door to the Reveres in this brick house built in 1710 by Moses Pierce, a glazier. The three-story house is laid in the early-American bond of three stretcher courses for every header course. String courses separate the floors. Windows are framed with brick relieving arches. On the ground floor are the kitchen and parlor, each with a large fireplace. The floors have the original pine boards of varying widths up to twenty inches. Walls are papered in a reproduc-

tion of the original early eighteenth-
century English wallpaper discovered
during restoration beneath seventeen
layers of paper. Behind the house is an
attractive garden with pump.

Salem Street, Italian street market

ers, and bakeries. Happily, it has
changed little in recent decades. Sophie
Tucker lived at 22 Salem Street as a child.

Pierce-Hichborn house

SALEM STREET

Beginning in the 1850s, Salem Street was
the center of the North End community
of eastern European immigrants, mainly
Jewish. The song "My Name Is Solomon
Levi" tells of a man who has a clothing
store on Salem Street. This was the Washington Street of the North End, with
many clothing, tailoring, fabric, and lace
shops. Today the street is demonstrably
ethnic, with Italian grocery stores, butch-

Doorway, 18 Cooper Street

North Bennet Street School
Salem Street at 39 North Bennet Street
1881

In 1881, educator and social worker Pauline Aggassiz Shaw established the North Bennet Street Industrial School in this mansard-roofed three-story brick structure to help the North End's immigrants develop job skills. Today the school offers courses in cabinet making, carpentry, watch repair, piano tuning and regulation, and several other fields.

🏛 Christ Church ("Old North")
193 Salem Street
WILLIAM PRICE, 1723
National Historic Landmark
Open to the Public

Christ Church or Old North is the oldest church building and the second Angelican parish in Boston. Built of brick in the style of Sir Christopher Wren, it is thought to have been modeled after St. Andrew's-by-the-Wardrobe in Blackfriars, London. Its bricks were made in Medford and the timber came from the area of York, Maine. The 175-foot, three-tier steeple houses a peal of eight bells, cast by Abel Rudhall of Gloucester, England, in 1744. They are the oldest church bells in America and are still rung today. At age fifteen Paul Revere formed a guild of bell ringers with six friends. The steeple has twice been toppled by hurricanes, first in 1804, after which it was rebuilt from a drawing by Charles Bulfinch, and again in 1954. The original weathervane by Deacon Shem Drowne, a Colonial craftsman, still tops the spire.

Inside, the bright airy space, painted

Christ Church (Old North)

white since 1912, offers tranquility and purity contrasting sharply with the complex and animated maze of shadowed brick streets outside. The high box pews were owned by parishioners and were designed to keep the warmth of hot coals or bricks placed on the floor on wintry days. The gleaming brass chandeliers were gifts of Captain William Maxwell and were first lighted on Christmas Day, 1724. At the rear gallery ticks a clock made by two parishioners, Avery and Bennett, in 1726.

Each year on the eve of Patriots' Day, lanterns are hung in the belfry by descendants of Paul Revere or Robert Newman to commemorate the night of April 18, 1775, when Revere rode on horseback to warn Lexington and Concord of the approaching British forces. Eighteen years earlier, the steeple had been the launching pad for the first flying man in America, John Childs, who in 1757 leaped from the tower with an umbrella-like contraption strapped to his back and landed safely several hundred feet away. The controversy over whether this is the real Old North Church or whether it was in fact Second Church on North Square, referred to as "The North" or "The Old North," has never been fully put to rest.

Several peaceful small gardens cluster about the back of the church, including the Washington Memorial garden

and an herb garden. The ironwork was made by inmates of the old state prison in Charlestown.

🏛 Copp's Hill Burial Ground
off Salem at Hull and Snowhill streets
National Register of Historic Places

From Copp's Hill Cemetery one has excellent views of the Boston Harbor, Charlestown, Bunker Hill, the Navy Yard, and the USS *Constitution*. The cemetery is the oldest in the North End, the first burial probably having occurred in 1660. It is estimated that there have been over ten thousand burials here, including one thousand blacks. Boston's first black colony, called "New Guinea," was located on Copp's Hill at the northeastern base. The western portion of the cemetery was reserved for blacks, slave and free, and has a monument to them placed in that section by the Masons. Among the many notables buried here

Copp's Hill Burial Ground

are the Mathers—Increase, Cotton, and Samuel—as well as Thomas Hutchinson and John and Andrew Eliot. Strolling among the old slate gravestones, the visitor will find some stones scarred by the British soldiers who used them for target practice during the siege of Boston. Copp's Hill Terrace, a fine granite promontory off Charter Street at the edge of the cemetery, leads down to Commercial Street and the waterfront. Nearby Jackson Avenue, a charming pedestrian lane, also leads down to the waterfront.

44 Hull Street
off Salem Street
c. 1800

This house has the as yet uncontested distinction of being the narrowest house in Boston. Since it has a width of about ten feet and only one window per floor on the front, this reputation is not difficult to believe. According to popular legend, the house was built solely to spite a neighbor in another house behind it by blocking its light and view.

44 Hull Street

Copp's Hill Terrace
off Salem Street across from Copp's Hill Burial Ground
National Register of Historic Places

Climbing the ramparts of Copp's Hill Terrace, one finds views of the Bunker Hill Monument, USS *Constitution* and Charlestown Navy Yard, Boston Harbor, and Copp's Hill Cemetery. It was near here that the famous molasses disaster occurred in 1919. A huge 2 ½-million-gallon tank of molasses burst, releasing a tidal wave of molasses that took with it buildings and people. Twenty-one people were killed in the spill and the area smelled of molasses for decades. Nearby, at the corner of Commercial and Foster streets, Paul Revere had a foundry where he cast church bells. The USS *Constitution* (Old Ironsides) was built at Constitution Wharf at 409 Commercial Street. Its keel was laid in 1794 and it was launched in 1797. Near 379 Commercial Street the North Battery was erected in 1646 to defend Boston.

Dodd House

190 Salem Street

1804

The Dodd house was built on land that was part of Sir William Phips's estate and originally overlooked Governor Phips's garden. The Dodds were the last of the old North End families to remain in their family home. They were also the last to do their cooking in the fireplace. When stoves replaced fireplaces, the Dodds went up to Hanover Street and ordered a stove, but after returning home and thinking about it, they decided the new gadget was not for them and canceled the order. The basement contains a bricked-up archway that is said to have connected with a mysterious tunnel to Copp's Hill. Possibly it connected with the legendary tunnel of Captain Gruchy, a smuggler and privateer and deacon of Old North Church who used the tunnel to avoid taxation on goods he stole at sea. Gruchy lived in the old Phips home.

Clough House

21 Unity Street

c. 1715

National Register of Historic Places

Ebenezer Clough, a master mason and one of the Sons of Liberty who participated in the Boston Tea Party, built this house and was one of two masons who laid the brick of Old North Church. The house is one of the few early eighteenth-century houses remaining in Boston. Originally, the house was two stories

Clough House

with a gambrel roof and dormers, but over the years the roof was raised to make a full third story. By 1962 the property was in poor condition and had been divided into six apartments with a butcher shop on the ground floor. Old North purchased and restored the house in 1972, cleaning the original brick and restoring the fireplaces, wainscoting, and English oak staircase with pendant acorn drops. Window and door lintels are finely executed in brick, with raised brick panels over the first-floor windows and carved brick detail over the door.

The house next door, one of a row of six built by Clough, was owned by Benjamin Franklin and occupied by his two sisters. It was demolished when the Mall was built.

FOUR

Waterfront

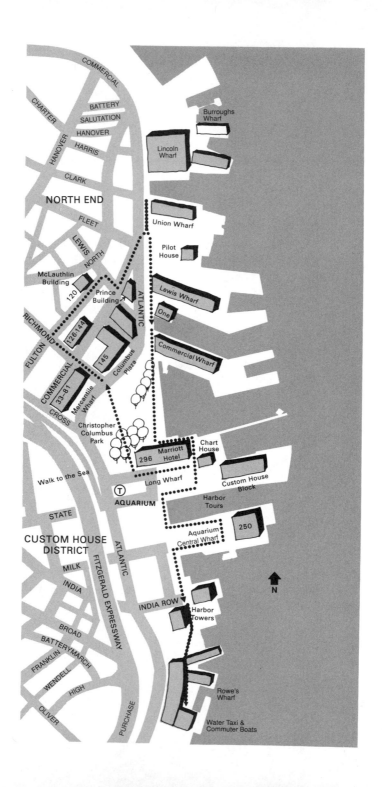

Waterfront

Too often the American city has turned its back on its waterfront, leaving it to industrial and warehouse uses. This was the case with the Boston waterfront, too, until the 1960s, when several architects began renovating the wharf buildings as apartments. The rebirth was further advanced by the Government Center and Faneuil Hall Marketplace projects, which strengthened links to the harbor. The current design is based on the plan of Kevin Lynch and John Myer that rerouted Atlantic Avenue to accommodate a waterfront park. Today Boston has the most accessible, visible waterfront of any major American city. Cities from San Francisco to New York could benefit from the model. After decades of planning, continuous pedestrian walkways lined with diverse activities now define the water perimeter of downtown Boston and several neighborhoods as well. Despite massive buildings along the water side of the waterfront, one constantly sees the harbor and feels in contact with it, because the finger piers are perpendicular to the street with no interruption in the pedestrian frontage. A substantial population lives or works in the renovated wharf buildings with nearby restaurants, shops, parks, museums, boat tours, and other activities. On a nice day thousands of people come to enjoy the area for sightseeing, lunches, and recreation.

Waterfront Tour

Beginning near the Aquarium MBTA station, walk through the **Waterfront Park** toward the large granite **Mercantile Wharf Building** and **Christopher Columbus Plaza** elderly housing (**63, 69, 72**). Walk up Richmond Street, passing the granite **Commercial Block** and **Commercial Street** (**69**), to Fulton Street. Turn right, passing the cast-iron **McLauthlin Building** (**71**); turn right again onto Commercial Street, walking toward **Union Wharf** (**70**) and the **Pilot House** (**60**). Proceed down Atlantic Avenue, passing **Lewis Wharf, Commercial Wharf, Waterfront Park, Long Wharf Marriott,** and the **Custom House Block** and **Chart House** (**60–65**). Continue along East India Row to the **New England Aquarium** (**66**), **Harbor Towers** (**66**), and **Rowe's Wharf** (**67**).

Pilot House

1–10 Atlantic Avenue

1863; RENOVATION: CARL KOCH, 1971

This small brick wharf building with arched windows was built by the Eastern Railroad during the Civil War. It has been renovated as apartments and a restaurant.

Pilot House

One Lewis Wharf

off Atlantic Avenue

SKIDMORE, OWINGS & MERRILL, 1982

This office building is oriented to the harbor with primarily glass facades on the south and east. Cantilevered sun-screens permit solar heat gain in winter but shade the offices from the summer sun, while providing visual interest on an otherwise solid mass. A brick screen wall with tinted precast-concrete bands faces the street. Corner offices of the three partners of the law firm that owns the building have views of the harbor and Lewis Wharf and open out onto the third-floor deck.

One Lewis Wharf

Lewis Wharf

28–32 Atlantic Avenue

RICHARD BOND, 1836–1840;
RENOVATION: CARL KOCH AND
ASSOCIATES, 1965–1969, 1971

Lewis Wharf, one of the first wharf buildings to be renovated for residential use, is constructed of Quincy granite and heavy timber. The original gabled roof has been greatly altered and now accommodates two floors of apartments. Until about 1868 the building extended west as far as the site of today's brick flower shop, formerly a Sunoco station,

designed by Anderson, Notter. In the eighteenth century, John Hancock's warehouses were located on Hancock Wharf on the north side of Lewis Wharf. Opposite the head of the wharf was the North End Coffee House until 1783. Edgar Allan Poe's macabre tale "The Fall of the House of Usher" is said to be based upon actual events that took place on the site of Lewis Wharf in the eighteenth century. Two lovers—a sailor and the young wife of an elderly man—were trapped in their trysting place, a mysterious underground tunnel, by the avenging husband. Years later, when the old Usher house was torn down in 1800, it has been said that two embracing skeletons were found at the foot of some steps behind a rusty iron gate.

Prince Building

formerly Prince Macaroni Company
45–69 Atlantic Avenue

RENOVATION: ANDERSON, NOTTER, FEINGOLD,
1966–1969

Originally the Prince Macaroni factory, this structure was one of Boston's first conversions of industrial space into apartments. The simple reinforced-concrete structural system is clearly expressed on the exterior with new recessed window balconies defined by white fins. A variety of unit types has been worked into the irregular building plan.

Lewis Wharf

Prince Building

Commercial Wharf

84 Atlantic Avenue

ISAIAH ROGERS, 1832–1834;
RENOVATION, EAST SECTION: HALASZ AND
HALASZ, 1968–1969; WEST SECTION:
ANDERSON, NOTTER, FEINGOLD, 1971

Isaiah Rogers, a leader in the design of monolithic granite buildings, had worked for Solomon Willard, another influential designer in granite. Rogers is also remembered as architect in 1828 of Boston's first luxury hotel, the Tremont House, which impressed Charles Dickens during his visit to Boston. This fine wharf building uses Quincy granite both decoratively and structurally. Window and door lintels and jambs and a string course above the first floor are of smooth cut granite, while the walls are rough with more massive blocks on the first floor. The building is now in two parts, one on each side of Atlantic Avenue, which cut through its middle about 1868. The mansard roof on the eastern section was added at that time. A dignified classical entrance with an inset clock above it is centered on the narrow end of the western half of the building.

Commercial Wharf

The two doors flanking the entrance have simple carved lintels with stylized pediments cut into them. These are now unfortunately obscured by signs and window alterations. The simplified pediment form appears on all the lintels of the upper floors. Both buildings have been subjected to roof and facade alterations, but the strength of the original design is still apparent.

Christopher Columbus Waterfront Park

Atlantic Avenue

SASAKI ASSOCIATES, 1976

When Atlantic Avenue was rerouted from the water's edge, space was created for a 4½-acre park, designed to complete the "walk to the sea" that commences at City Hall Plaza. The focus of the park is a cobblestone plaza at the water edge, extending from the rebuilt sea wall to the waterfront promenade. A 340-foot-long arched trellis of wood, 20 feet high, defines the main space and connects the sub-areas of the park, including a grove area of honey locust trees and a children's play area with a timber play structure resembling a ship. Materials were chosen to reflect the waterfront character of the area—brick, granite, cobblestones, and wood. The furniture continues the nautical theme with bollards linked by anchor chain, lighting resembling ship's lanterns, and sturdy wood benches. The park is intensely used by neighborhood residents of all ages, as well as by tourists and workers in the area.

© Hillel Burger

Christopher Columbus Waterfront Park

🏛 Long Wharf

202 Atlantic Avenue
at the end of State Street
1710
National Historic Landmark

Long Wharf originally extended from near the Old State House along what is now State Street into the harbor. At the wharf's head was the Bunch of Grapes Tavern, on the site of the old Boston Stock Exchange (see 53 State Street, p. 103).

Long Wharf was the focus of Boston's great harbor and was constructed beginning in 1710 by Captain Oliver Noyes. Early maps show it running far out into the harbor, by far the longest wharf, lined with warehouses and ships. Nineteenth-century land-filling projects, however, cut its length in half, and the construction of the central artery in the 1950s dealt another blow. The painter John Singleton Copley spent his childhood on the wharf, where his mother had a tobacco shop.

Custom House Block
off Atlantic Avenue on Long Wharf
ISAIAH ROGERS, 1845–1847; RENOVATION: ANDERSON, NOTTER, FEINGOLD, 1973

As in his earlier Commercial Wharf building (see 84 Atlantic Avenue, p. 62), Isaiah Rogers designed the Custom House Block primarily of granite. The forceful ground level is constructed of massive posts and lintels of single chunks of stone. A central block with pyramidal roof rises one story above the four-story building to define the arched center entrance. The brick rear facade is of utterly different character, with several gabled windows. It was here that Nathaniel Hawthorne served as customs inspector.

Gardner Building and Custom House Block

Chart House Restaurant

formerly Gardiner Building
off Atlantic Avenue on Long Wharf
1763, 1812;
RENOVATION: ANDERSON, NOTTER, FEINGOLD,
1973

Long Wharf was originally built up with Colonial-style brick warehouses similar to this one, the only remaining building. The simple but solid structure has a slate roof and six-over-six-paned windows with shutters and granite lintels and sills.

south and east sides to open views to the Chart House from Waterfront Park and Atlantic Avenue. The lower floors of the building contain function rooms and a 225-car garage. On the main floor, three five-story spaces serve as lobbies, lounges, and public function areas. The building rests on about five hundred precast, prestressed concrete piles, fourteen inches square and with an average length of ninety feet, that bear on bedrock. Its bolted steel frame is designed for earthquake loads.

Long Wharf Marriott Hotel

Atlantic Avenue at 296 State Street
COSSUTTA AND ASSOCIATES, 1980–1982

The linear form of the Long Wharf Marriott Hotel relates to the thrust of the original wharf, and its simple massing and use of brick vaguely recall the early warehouse buildings. The stepped form rises to heights that vary from 49 to 104 feet, relating in scale to its neighbors, the smaller Chart House and the larger Custom House Block. It is set back on the

Long Wharf Marriott Hotel

Site plan, Long Wharf area

New England Aquarium and Central Wharf

250 Atlantic Avenue

CAMBRIDGE SEVEN, 1969, 1973, 1979

Open to the Public

Charles Bulfinch designed the original Central Wharf buildings, completed in 1817, a row of four-story brick structures nearly thirteen hundred feet long. A small fragment of this handsome wharf survives on the other side of the express-way (see 146–176 Milk Street at India Street, p. 80). Today the Aquarium occu-pies part of the site. The core of the Aquarium complex is a discreetly sculpted concrete box housing a dra-matic three-story, forty-foot-diameter tank surrounded by a ramp that rises through the four-story central space. The visitor is guided in a one-way sequence past beautifully illuminated tanks, inset into the walls, that give a real sense of underwater life.

Harbor Towers

off Atlantic Avenue at 65–85 East India Row

I. M. PEI AND PARTNERS, 1971

One of the most ambitious projects in the country at that time, India Wharf included more than one-half mile of wharves, warehouses, and stores running from India Wharf along India Street to State Street. Bulfinch's fine 1807 India Wharf buildings stood here until the last section was razed in 1962 to make way for the Harbor Towers. In contrast to the historic long low forms of brick, granite, and timber extending like fingers into the harbor, Pei's towers introduced a new form and scale to the Boston water-front. Apartments in the forty-story tow-ers of cast-in-place concrete are organized pinwheel fashion about a cen-tral core and offer dramatic views of the city on one side and the harbor on the other. Concrete balconies stack up to

New England Aquarium

Harbor Towers

create a zipperlike sculptural relief against the flat grid of the facade. The stainless-steel sculpture at the base is by David von Schlegell (1972). Fine views of the harbor and waterfront may be had from the terrace beyond the sculpture.

CENTRAL ARTERY,

Fitzgerald Expressway
1954

This was one of the first urban expressways to be built under the federal highway program of the 1950s, and nearly every mistake possible was made in its design. The Central Artery mercilessly cut through the historic core of Boston, separating the North End and the waterfront from the rest of the city. No attempt was made to mitigate the intrusive structure through design. Now there is a plan to correct some of the problems. The Central Artery project may be the begin-

ning of a new national direction if the Conservation Law Foundation of New England is successful in convincing or coercing the Federal Highway Administration to mandate public transit as a part of any new highway construction in the country. The idea would be to expand and improve regional public transit in conjunction with the construction of the larger new underground highway through downtown Boston. Ideally most of the public transit improvements would be in place before the completion of the new Central Artery around the year 2000. Planning and urban design leadership is increasingly leaving the hands of responsible local governments, with activist citizens and public interest groups taking their viewpoints to the courts. Urban design by lawsuit is generally unsatisfactory, but it is sometimes the only option.

If the Central Artery project is realized, the forty acres of new land on top of the highway will offer an opportunity for urban design comparable to the major achievements of the past.

🏛 Rowe's Wharf

Atlantic Avenue near Harbor Towers
SKIDMORE, OWINGS & MERRILL, CHICAGO, 1987

The success of Rowe's Wharf is due in large part to the strict and site-specific design rules developed by the city before a 1982 competition for the site. The rules included a fifteen-story height limitation, the preservation of various views, continuous public pedestrian frontage along the water, and public

Rowe's Wharf

water shuttle and commuter boat facilities in a prominent part of the site. Such juxtapositions and requirements are rare in most American cities; luxury hotels generally would not consider giving up their prime water frontage to public facilities serving people who are not using the hotel, but the requirements work beautifully in Boston. Water taxis from here reach the airport in seven minutes, and commuter and regional boats connect with other points along the coast.

The development accommodates a hotel, condominiums, and offices in a vaguely traditional red brick complex of three eight-story stepped structures resembling finger piers, a massive arched gateway building symbolizing the water travelers' arrival in Boston, and connected midrise office towers. The arch recalls on a grand scale that of Bulfinch's 1807 India Wharf. An octagonal domed glass pavilion serves as an elegant waiting room for the water shuttle. The promenade along the water on two levels links water commuters to financial district destinations and to the continuous pedestrian waterfront walk.

Commercial Block

126–144 Commercial Street

ATTRIBUTED TO GRIDLEY J. FOX BRYANT,
1856; RENOVATION: MINTZ ASSOCIATES, 1978

A dignified granite facade rises from a simple trabeated first floor. Rusticated pilasterlike verticals strengthen the corners, while string courses and a bracketed cornice organize the facade horizontally. Architectural historians have praised Boston's granite warehouses. Sigfried Giedion felt the Commercial Block in particular was an important influence on the work of H. H. Richardson.

Commercial Block

Christopher Columbus Plaza Housing for the Elderly

145 Commercial Street

MINTZ ASSOCIATES, 1977

Sponsored by the Ausonia Knights of Columbus of the North End, this 151-unit elderly housing project was developed with the participation of community groups and the Massachusetts Historical Commission. Its unpretentious brick volumes, penetrated by simply detailed large windows, relate in height to the surrounding buildings and allow the animated rooflines of the North End and St. Stephen's and Old North churches to be seen from the Waterfront Park. Because of the very different scale on each of the streets surrounding the project, an effort was made to relate each facade to the character and scale of its particular street.

Commercial Street

© Sam Sweezy

Christopher Columbus Plaza

As in the North End, the building hugs the street, but a semiprivate courtyard is created in the center. On the ground floor there are crafts, games, and meeting rooms opening onto the inner courtyard, and a library-lounge with a terrace opens onto Atlantic Avenue with views of Waterfront Park and the Great Cove. The entrance area, also opening onto the courtyard, has a covered outdoor sitting area and an inside area with views of activity on Commercial Street and the inner court. Three lounges on each of the upper floors provide for viewing and socializing, and on the fifth floor a greenhouse and solarium overlook the park.

Union Wharf

323 Commercial Street

C. 1846; RENOVATION: MORITZ BERGMEYER, 1979

National Register of Historic Places

The somber dignity of Boston's granite warehouses is nowhere better expressed than in Union Wharf. Its rough granite is

© Steve Rosenthal

Union Wharf

utterly straightforward and without artifice. The building's masonry walls with iron- shuttered windows speak for themselves and its name is boldly set in granite in the pediment. The stone blocks of the ground floor are of a larger scale than in the upper floors. Unfortunately, brick dormers were added when the building was still a warehouse, seriously compromising the original form. A string of new brick row houses has been added to the wharf by the same architect who did the renovation.

Lincoln Wharf Condominiums

357 Commercial Street

1901; RENOVATION: THE ARCHITECTURAL TEAM, 1987

This former MBTA power plant has been converted to low- and moderate-income housing. Units are organized around an interior atrium.

Lincoln Wharf Condominiums

🏛 McLauthlin Building

120 Fulton Street

POSSIBLY DANIEL BADGER, C. 1864;

RENOVATION: MORITZ BERGMEYER, 1979

The first cast-iron-facade building in New England, the McLauthlin Building is reminiscent of the work of James Bogardus in New York. Besides being fire resistant and easily fabricated, cast-iron facades made possible large windows for interior lighting. The facade is divided into six bays, and on the second through fourth floors each bay holds two arched windows with fanlights. Pilasters and small columns alternate across the facade. Each floor is defined by a projecting string course. The fifth floor is topped by a cornice, and the sixth floor is awkwardly squeezed into a mansard roof. Until recently the building was occupied by its original owner, the McLauthlin Elevator Company. It is now condominiums. Compare this with another famous cast-iron building, the Richards Building (see 114 State Street, p. 81).

McLauthlin Building

beneath the windows of each floor, while a substantial bracketed cornice defines the top of the mass. Each three-window bay is expressed by rusticated verticals, similar to pilasters but without capitals. The ground floor with its large arched openings is particularly impressive. The shallow arches with keystones rest on slender granite posts, supporting the facade.

Ships' chandlers, sail makers, and riggers were the original occupants of the building, but today it has been recycled as a shopping galleria with apartments surrounding a six-story space. The exterior has been well preserved, the major change being the windows, which were originally six-over-six-paned sash. It is admirable that this wharf conversion has maintained the rooflines, whereas most others have added decks and dormers.

Mercantile Wharf

33–81 Mercantile Street
GRIDLEY J. FOX BRYANT, 1856;
RENOVATION: JOHN SHARATT AND ASSOCIATES, 1976

Architect Gridley Bryant, son of the builder of the Bunker Hill Monument, also designed the State Street Block opposite the Custom House (see 177-199 State Street at 1 McKinley Square, p. 83). Mercantile Wharf is an example of the late "Boston granite style" and closely resembles the nearby Commercial Block built one year later (see 126–144 Commercial Street, p. 69). String courses run

Detail, Mercantile Wharf

FIVE

Custom House District

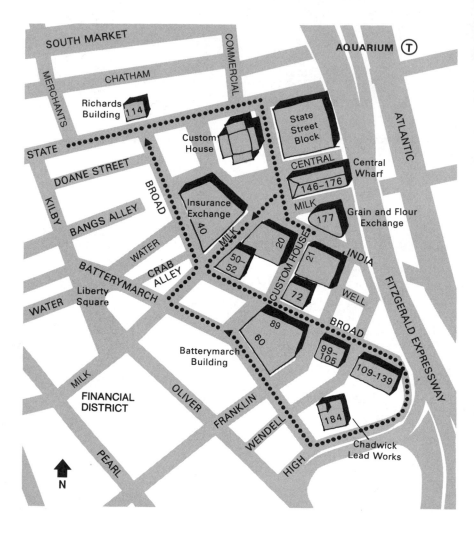

Custom House District
National Historic District

I n the early nineteenth century, the Custom House was at the center of Boston economic life. Situated at the head of Long Wharf (now State Street), it looked directly out over the harbor, which was then bordered by India Street. A few reminders of Boston's mercantile past survive in the district, including parts of Charles Bulfinch's rows of brick warehouses and stores on Broad Street and Central Wharf, as well as several outstanding examples of granite warehouses. While the Custom House tower dominated the Boston skyline for many decades, it has been upstaged by megaprojects of the 1980s.

Custom House District Tour

Walk down State Street from State Street station, passing the cast-iron **Richards Building** on your left (**81**). Pass the Classical Revival **Custom House** (**82**) and turn right at the **State Street Block** (**83**), passing the remains of **Central Wharf** (**80**) and the **Grain and Flour Exchange Building** at the corner of Milk and India streets (**80**). Turn right on Milk Street, then left on Broad Street. The next few blocks of **Broad Street** are lined with outstanding brick and granite buildings making up one of the most important surviving early nineteenth-century mercantile environments in the country (**76**). At the expressway turn right onto High Street to reach the **Chadwick Lead Works** (**80**). Then turn right on Batterymarch Street to contrast the facade of the **Batterymarch Building** with the facade previously seen on Broad Street (**78**). At the intersection with Milk Street continue on Broad Street to arrive back at your starting point.

🏛 BROAD STREET

Broad Street was laid out by the Broad Street Association according to the plans of Charles Bulfinch shortly after 1805. Several of the Federal-style 4½-story buildings from that development survive. The Broad Street Association included Harrison Gray Otis, Francis C. Lowell, and Rufus G. Amory, under the leadership of the indefatigable developer Uriah Cotting. Today this is one of the most impressive but fragile historic streets in Boston, an important remnant of early nineteenth-century commerce. Its future is uncertain.

The Architects Building

50–52 Broad Street
CHARLES EDWARD PARKER; 1853; RENOVATION: KEN DeMAY, PETER FORBES, DENNIS RIESKE, BRIGID WILLIAMS, 1989
Boston Landmark

One of the few structures to survive the great fire of 1872, this handsome granite building with mansard roof has rock-faced rustication on the second, third, and fourth floors. Windows of the upper

The Architects Building

floors have bracketed lintels, while those of the ground floor have semicircular arches with prominent keystones. Originally the building was used as a warehouse, and later it held offices and various businesses. Granite-faced buildings began replacing the Federal brick buildings on Broad Street in the mid-nineteenth century, significantly changing the scale of the street and dwarfing the remaining Federal architecture. In

Insurance Exchange Building (Coolidge and Shattuck, 1923) 40 Broad Street

1988 the building was purchased and renovated by the Boston Society of Architects, with the financial backing of Jung/Brannen Associates and the entire building industry, for use as the headquarters for the BSA and the building industry.

72 Broad Street

FROM DESIGNS OF CHARLES BULFINCH, 1805–1807

Boston Landmark

This is one of the early nineteenth-century remnants of Bulfinch's plan for new warehouses and stores to replace the old wharves that had developed here in a rather helter-skelter fashion during the seventeenth century. The brick structures

72 Broad Street

have flared lintels with small square windows on the top floor in the Federal manner. Beneath the hipped roofs were brick dentil courses, and string courses of granite separated the floors. Other buildings of the Bulfinch development survive, although several have been extensively altered, at 5, 7–9, 63–65, 64–66, 67–73, 68–70, and 102 Broad Street.

Batterymarch Building

89 Broad Street and
60 Batterymarch Street
HENRY KELLOGG, 1928

An early Art Deco building that both breaks and makes the rules, the Batterymarch Building has the solid block mass at street level, but instead of carrying sheer walls up ten or fifteen stories before terracing in with typical Art Deco giant steps, the base is an unintimidating two stories. The third-story open arcade is a decorative device for defining and framing the open courts as it connects the three elegant, narrow brick towers, which are actually connected at the back. The verticality of the towers is emphasized by vertical dividers projecting between ranks of windows. At the top, the forms of the towers change, with chamfered corners and stepped end bays. The building suggests New York's Beekman Tower (originally the Panhellenic Hotel), built about the same time, which even employs the same two-story-plus-arcade base.

One of the most intriguing design innovations of the Batterymarch Building is its use of color. The brick is shaded from dark at the base to progressively lighter tones toward the top, thus increas-

Batterymarch Building

99–105 Broad Street
1854

Here is an important example of early slab-granite construction. The smooth granite facade of these large warehouse buildings is highlighted by prominent string courses and a deep bracketed cornice.

99–105 Broad Street

ing the building's impression of height. If one stands near the base and gazes directly up at one of the towers, it seems to recede into the sky. It is surprising the client agreed to have his facade vary from brown to buff brick! Architects' renderings of Art Deco buildings frequently showed the tops of towers ringed with clouds, so tall were they considered to be. The color shading of the Batterymarch Building is a literal realization of the shading and coloring used on these drawings, although inappropriate masonry repairs have weakened the effect.

109–139 Broad Street
1870

Segmental arches cut from single slabs of granite form the lintels for both the large ground-floor windows and doors and the upper windows. Rock-faced rustication has been used, with each story defined by a string course of smooth granite. The top floor is an attic with three-sided dormer windows. Between

109–139 Broad Street

115 Broad Street

numbers 105 and 109, old Half Moon Lane leads past a sensuously curved brick wall to the Chadwick Lead Works and its brick tower, which was used to make lead shot (see 184 High Street).

20 and 21 Custom House Street

BRUNER/COTT & ASSOCIATES, INC., 1988, 1989

These two buildings were the first to be developed in response to the Boston Redevelopment Authority's 1986 guidelines. Modest in size, style, and design, they are built of granite like many of their notable neighbors. A one-block pedestrian-scaled street passes between them.

© 1989 Peter Vanderwarker

20 and 21 Custom House Street

Chadwick Lead Works
184 High Street
WILLIAM PRESTON, 1887

From the square tower attached to the rear of the Chadwick Lead Works, molten lead was dropped, forming shot in the course of its fall. The front facade is notable for its bold three-story arches topped by a cornice of closely spaced windows and corbeled parapet. Spandrels between the arches are treated decoratively, the lower one of herringbone brickwork bulging out along with the windows, the top one dotted with bumps.

Chadwick Lead Works

Central Wharf Buildings
146–176 Milk Street at India Street
ATTRIBUTED TO CHARLES BULFINCH, 1816–1817

Central Wharf was built in 1816–1817 following designs of Bulfinch. Originally it contained fifty-four buildings, as well as a seamen's chapel, and extended beyond the expressway to the wharf where the Aquarium now stands. Only eight of the original wharf buildings survive, in various degrees of alteration. The original Federal-style buildings were four stories tall and three windows wide and had hipped roofs.

🏛 Grain and Flour Exchange Building
177 Milk Street
SHEPLEY, RUTAN, AND COOLIDGE, 1891–1893

Richardson's successors designed the Grain and Flour Exchange using many of the ideas he had employed in his wholesale store for Frederick L. Ames, built in 1882 at Kingston and Bedford Streets. The rounded corner of the site is dramatized by the conical roof surrounded by a string of pointed dormers topped by finials. The sixth and seventh floors are suspended from the roof structure and are now used as an architectural office. The Milford granite exterior is organized into several tiers with two ranges of arches, the large lower order encompassing three floors. The small clustered arches of the top floor act as a cornice.

© Shepley Bulfinch Richardson and Abbott

Grain and Flour Exchange Building

Richards Building

114 State Street

c. 1867

Because Boston was well developed by the opening of the nineteenth century, cast-iron architecture never achieved the popularity here that it did in some younger cities. During the era of cast-iron construction, there were still far more granite than cast-iron buildings built in Boston. Since the 1820s, granite had seemed to suit the city's need for solidity and permanence. Cast iron was, however, used extensively for ornament in the newly developing South End during the 1850s and 1860s.

This cast-iron facade was fabricated in Italy and bolted together after it reached Boston. Four stories of Italianate arcades are surmounted with a pair of two-story oriel windows in an ornate example of cast-iron design.

Next door at 126 State Street, the Cunard Building makes deft use of ornamentation to express the nautical nature of the business. Between the second and third floors a Vitruvian scroll band strongly suggests waves and has a head of Neptune at each end. Bronze anchors support the lighting brackets at the entrance.

Richards Building

🏛 Custom House

State Street at India Street
AMMI BURNHAM YOUNG, 1837–1847;
TOWER ADDITION: PEABODY AND STEARNS,
1913–1915
Boston Landmark

Built at the nineteenth-century water edge, the new Custom House was ideally situated on State Street, which had long served as the primary route from the wharves to the Old State House, the banks, and Washington Street. (State Street, called King Street until the Revolution, was the most important street in

Custom House

152 State Street

seventeenth-century Boston.) The original Custom House was a four-faced Greek temple with fluted Doric columns of granite weighing forty-two tons each. A skylit dome was over the interior rotunda, but the tower was built over this in 1913. Although Boston had a 125-foot height restriction, the federally owned Custom House property was not subject to city height limits. Thus Boston's first skyscraper was built, a peculiar sixteen-story landmark that was a shock to the city. The entrance lobby is worth a visit, and fine views of the harbor and financial district may be had from the small observation balcony of the tower.

🏛 State Street Block

177–199 State Street at
1 McKinley Square
GRIDLEY J. FOX BRYANT, 1858

McKinley Square is dominated by the
enormous dark granite mass of the mid-
nineteenth-century State Street Block,
which originally was much longer,
stretching down to the waterfront. The
rockfaced rustication of the upper floors
is ornamented by the contrasting smooth
granite string courses between floors and
by segmental arches with keystones over
the windows. The central pavilion displaying the carved name of the building
has a massive broken segmental pediment in front of the two-story mansard
roof. A granite globe is centered in the
window framed by the pediment.
Assorted additions have been made
above the cornice, including the mansard.

State Street Block

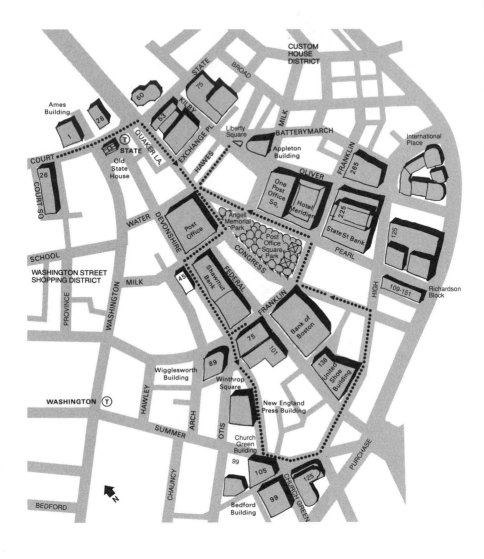

Financial District

T he financial district is the old center of financial wisdom for the entire country. In the early nineteenth century, most of the banks in Boston were located on State Street, where Boston's commerce was first conducted. The conservative trust funds of New England fortunes have been managed on these streets since the seventeenth century. Unlike the old commercial centers of most American cities, Boston's financial district has not experienced wholesale destruction. It was particularly difficult for us to select sites for this book from the old mercantile, financial, and government areas, where many fine buildings represent two centuries of history. But one of the most significant assets of the district is its complex pattern of streets based on those laid out in the seventeenth and eighteenth centuries.

The narrow, irregular streets focus on "squares" (usually triangular in shape) such as Winthrop, Church Green, Post Office, or Liberty Square. Instead of following an abstract geometric concept such as a rectangle, the pre-Bauhaus architecture hugs the streets, creating odd-shaped buildings and wonderful street spaces. It is exciting just to wander through the area, following one's intuition, enjoying spatial sequences that are full of surprises. Some of the newer buildings have failed to understand this architecture of the street, employing inappropriate setbacks, plazas, or rigid massing. Enough of the old survives, however, to maintain the character. Let us hope that future development will respect this tradition.

Financial District Tour

Start at Government Center station and the steaming teakettle. Turn left onto Court Street, passing the **Old Boston City Hall Annex** and **28 State Street (93, 103)**. Turn right at the **Old State House, 60 State Street,** and **Exchange Place (101–4)** onto Congress Street and walk toward **Angell Memorial Park, Post Office Square Park,** and the **Post Office (90–92).** Turn right on Milk Street for one block, then left on Devonshire Street between the **International Trust Company**

Building and **Shawmut Bank** (**98, 100**). Continue toward **Winthrop Square,** passing the **Wigglesworth Building** on the right, and don't miss the lobby of the Art Deco **State Street Trust Building** on the left (**93–95**). Walk through the square to the left of the **New England Press Building** (**94**). Turn left onto Summer Street and pass through **Church Green** (**89**) noting the **Church Green** and **Bedford buildings** and **125 Summer Street** (**106**). Continue on High Street past the Art Deco **United Shoe Machinery Building** (**96**), then turn left onto Congress Street walking past the **Bank of Boston** (**96**). Turn right on Franklin Street toward the **Hotel Meridien** in the former Federal Reserve Bank (**100**) and the **State Street Bank** (**96**). Turn left on Pearl Street passing the hotel and **One Post Office Square** tower (**100**). After **Post Office Square Park** and **Angell Memorial Park,** turn right on Water Street and go one block to **Liberty Square,** noting the **Appleton Building** and the view of the **Batterymarch Building.** From here you may continue into the Custom House district and waterfront or return to the starting point.

CHURCH GREEN

Church Green Building

105–113 Summer Street

ATTRIBUTED TO JONATHAN PRESTON, C. 1873

Boston Landmark

Bedford Building

99 Bedford Street

CUMMINGS AND SEARS, 1875–1876;

RENOVATION: BAY-BEDFORD COMPANY, 1983

National Register of Historic Places

The triangular intersection of Summer and Bedford streets acquired the name of Church Green because of the fine granite church designed by Charles

Detail, Bedford Building

Church Green Building

Bulfinch that stood from 1814 until 1868 where the Church Green Building is today. In 1838 E. C. Wines of Philadelphia voiced his impression of Summer Street: "Another pleasant feature of Boston is the many green and shady front yards which relieve and refresh the eye, as you wander through its winding streets. More or less of these are met with in every part of the city; but Summer Street, on both sides, is lined with them from one end to the other. This, to my taste, is decidedly the handsomest street in Boston. Town and country seem here married to each other. . . ."

After the 1872 fire, residents moved out of the Church Green and Summer Street area and it became the center of the leather and shoe business. All of the buildings in the district date from after the fire. The Bedford Building, built in 1875–1876, is a fine example of Ruskin Gothic style and is executed in red granite, white Tuckahoe marble, and terra-cotta panels.

Angell Memorial Park
Congress Street
EARL R. FLANSBURGH AND ASSOCIATES AND CITY LIFE BOSTON, 1982

The primary focus of the redesigned Post Office Square continues to be the Angell Memorial Fountain, designed by architects Peabody and Stearns as a watering spot for horses in 1912. The fountain is a

memorial to George Thorndike Angell, a founder of the Society for the prevention of Cruelty to Animals. A new secondary focus is a "creature pond" made up of assorted bronze animals. Circular bands of paving radiate from the two foci, framed by a circle of inward-looking granite benches. The outer edges are bordered by greenery and long benches formed of steel rods, which are oriented to face the streets. The park is the result of several years' work by artists, designers, and the city. It is maintained by four real-estate companies that own property surrounding Angell Memorial Park.

© Warren Jagger

Angell Memorial Park

🏛 Post Office Square Park

LANDSCAPE DESIGN: THE HALVORSON
COMPANY, INC., 1991; PARK STRUCTURES AND
GARAGE: ELLENZWEIG ASSOCIATES, INC., 1990

Although a fifty-story tower designed by Edward Larrabee Barnes was proposed here, Post Office Square Park instead became one of Boston's most successful new public spaces on the site of a dismal old parking garage. Seven levels of underground parking accommodating 1,400 cars are buried beneath the park; the discreet narrow entry ramps have retaining walls topped with cast iron fencing. The garage excavation, 80 feet below grade, holds the record as the deepest building excavation in Boston.

Escalator access to the garage is in glass gazebos that look almost too delicate to withstand the fierce Boston winters. Other glass and lattice gazebos shelter a cafe and flower stand. No avant-garde minimalist tortured landscape here; people felt at home in the park from the day it opened. Among the plants are six specimen trees about thirty feet tall on permanent loan from the Arnold Arboretum. An open pergola, manicured grass, and precise border plantings create a light-hearted domestic style that is decidedly welcoming. The design gives special attention to accommodating users at peak lunchtime hours and offers a variety of seating arrangements for both individuals and groups. The builders used an unusual "top-down" construction technique, as in a mining operation. After they completed the top level, they excavated and built the subsequent levels below.

Post Office Square Park

© 1991 Peter Vanderwarker

🏛 Post Office

Congress Street at Angell Memorial Park
CRAM AND FERGUSON WITH JAMES A.
WETMORE, 1929–1931

One of Boston's best Art Deco buildings, the Post Office exhibits several features typical of the style. Its windows are organized vertically into recessed slits between granite strips that soar skyward. As the top stories are approached, the hard mass of light gray granite softens with elaborate geometric steps and ornament. The ornamentation is a combination of geometric devices and stylized plant forms. The Art Deco style originated in Paris, the term deriving from the French *Arts Decoratifs*, and was the conscious rejection of all historic style and form. Its practitioners restricted themselves primarily to surface features and did not rethink the entire basis for architecture, as did the founders of the International Style.

Window grille, Post Office

🏛 Ames Building

1 Court Street
SHEPLEY, RUTAN, AND COOLIDGE, 1889
National Register of Historic Places

The massive and solid appearance of the Ames building is a reflection of its masonry bearing-wall construction. It is the second tallest such structure in the world, and for several years it dominated the Boston skyline. The Romanesque Revival motifs made famous by H. H. Richardson dominate the facade of this building carried out by his successors, Shepley, Rutan, and Coolidge, after Richardson's death in 1886. Three three-story Romanesque arches organize the lower stories, which form a base for the upper levels. The middle five stories are unified by four arches that have no relation to the rhythm of the large arches below. The top two stories form a massive cornice, with a string of arched windows that almost create the effect of corbeling.

Post Office

Ames Building

Boston School Committee Building
originally Old Boston City Hall Annex
26 Court Street
EDWARD T. P. GRAHAM, 1914

Banded rustication provides a base of suitable scale for the monumental Classical Revival office building. Enormous six-story engaged fluted Corinthian columns of the entrance facade become pilasters on the side facade and support an equally gigantic architrave, frieze, and dentil cornice. Atop the cornice four amazons in flowing Greek drapery by sculptor Roger Noble Burnham once stood.

🏛 Wigglesworth Building
89–93 Franklin Street
at Winthrop Square
N. J. BRADLEE AND W. T. WINSLOW, 1873;
RENOVATION: SHEPLEY BULFINCH
RICHARDSON AND ABBOTT, 1984
National Register of Historic Places

The five stories of this brick building curve and turn to follow the complex

Old Boston City Hall Annex

Wigglesworth Building

form of the bordering streets, creating a beautiful and dynamic form for the public space. The undulations are emphasized by the string courses of the second, third, and fourth floors.

New England Press Building
off Franklin Street at
1 Winthrop Square
WILLIAM RALPH EMERSON AND CARL FEHMER, 1873; RENOVATION: CHILDS, BERTMAN, TSECKARES ASSOCIATES, 1974

In the mid-nineteenth century Winthrop Square was an important center of dry-goods merchandising. Not only was Beebe located at 1 Winthrop Square, but in the 1860s Eben Jordan and his partner had a six-story wholesale and warehouse

building on Devonshire Street in the square. Henry Cabot Lodge was born in his grandfather's house on Winthrop Square in 1850. In 1872 the great fire started just behind the Beebe store on Summer and Otis streets. After the fire, Beebe immediately hired Ralph Waldo Emerson's architect nephew and Carl Fehmer to design his new store on the same site.

The granite-faced result is quite unusual in its use of corner pavilions, which entirely overwhelm the low pediment marking the center of the facade. The cornice above the third story almost comes as a separation between two entirely different buildings, so dramatically do the two parts differ. The top two floors recall the visual tricks Emerson

© Hutchins Photography, Inc.

New England Press Building

played with "the house of odd windows" and the Boston Art Club (see 24 Pinckney Street, p. 186, and Newbury Street at 270 Dartmouth Street, p. 284). The bracket falling down over the top edge of the pediment is extremely odd, and the low mansard roof behind it, which crouches between the taller hipped-roof pavilions, stranger still. The center column is almost unheard of. Emerson's work was daringly unconventional, and his playful attitude toward architectural traditions astonishingly contemporary.

State Street Trust Building
Franklin Street at 75 Federal Street
THOMAS M. JAMES, 1929

101 Federal Street
KOHN PEDERSON FOX, 1988

The 1929 Art Deco jewel at 75 Federal Street presented a striking profile against the sky, a skewed stepped mass crowned by a gilded pyramid. It was an example of the willingness of developers to work effectively with the odd-shaped sites of Boston's financial district. But in the late 1980s the Boston Redevelopment Authority permitted the elimination of narrow streets such as Snow Street to create larger parcels. An L-shaped parcel was assembled here to accommodate the tower at 101 Federal Street, conceived as three crenellated shafts and joined on the first eleven floors to 75 Federal Street. The fenestration of the limestone facade of 101 Federal Street takes its cues from its distinguished neighbor. The surface

© Cervin Robinson

101 Federal Street

appliqué of raised circles and linear ocean-liner motifs in brushed aluminum does not compete with the low-relief figurative and floral bands concentrated between the second, third, and fourth floors of 75 Federal Street. Inside, the original Art Deco lobby of 75 Federal remains the star. Golden yellow and black marble are coupled with stunning gold and black elevator doors, with elevator control panels and signs lettered in the Broadway Engraved style.

State Street Bank Building

225 Franklin Street

PEARL STREET ASSOCIATES
(HUGH STUBBINS AND ASSOCIATES, F.A. STAHL AND ASSOCIATES, LE MESSURIER ASSOCIATES), 1966

The cruciform cantilevered thirty-four-story tower stands on a low base that relates to the older and smaller buildings in the area. The high-relief precast concrete window units also reflect the scale of the surroundings and create a highly textured facade unlike the sleek surfaces of many high-rise buildings of the late 1960s and the 1970s.

United Shoe Machinery Building

🏛 United Shoe Machinery Building

High Street at 138–164 Federal Street

PARKER, THOMAS, AND RICE, 1928–1930

Boston Landmark
National Register of Historic Places

The house in which Trinity Church rector Phillips Brooks was born stood on this land before the large trapezoidal Art Deco building was built. It was the first Art Deco skyscraper in Boston and influenced the design of subsequent buildings in both New York and Boston. Sitting on a base of limestone and black granite, the complex mass is clad in brick, stone, and metal. The various vertical blocks step back progressively toward a central tower capped by a truncated pyramid of tile. Boston's height-restriction law was revised in 1928 to allow taller buildings, provided they were stepped back in this fashion to allow more sun to reach street level. The elaborate Art Deco metalwork still survives in the lobby.

Bank of Boston

99 High Street at Congress Street

CAMPBELL, ALDRICH, NULTY, 1971

One of many Boston buildings that gets larger as it rises up, following the lead of the City Hall, this one surprises us by getting slimmer again toward the top, making it a building with a belly. Presumably program requirements necessitated the not very comely bulge. Although pedestrians get generous ground space as a result, the heavy dark granite slabs hang ominously over the entrances and the ground-level setbacks do nothing to strengthen the street space.

Bank of Boston and "Art Moderne" Telephone Building (Cram and Ferguson, 1947)

125 High Street

JUNG/BRANNEN, 1991

This building meets the sky with a stepped top and the ground with an exterior arcade. The twin towers echo the Art Deco style, from the interior lighting fixtures and stair rails to the variations on diamonds and squares in the granite and gray-green metal facade decorations. Between the towers is an eight-story skylit atrium with space frame glass roof and retail shops. A superblock development that doesn't look like one, 125 High

Street includes an Alexander Graham Bell Museum, renovated nineteenth-century buildings on Purchase and Oliver streets, and a new fire station.

International Place

High Street at Fort Hill Square

PHILIP JOHNSON AND JOHN BURGEE, 1985, 1992

The site of these buildings is significant in Boston history, for beginning in 1632 and to the end of the eighteenth century, this was the location of one of the forts that defended the city from attack by sea. In the early 1800s the site developed into an attractive square surrounded by brick rowhouses, much like Monument Square in Charlestown today. From the park atop the hill merchants such as Thomas Handasyd Perkins and Harrison Gray Otis enjoyed watching ships enter the harbor. By the 1850s, in response to the demand for housing from immigrant workers, property owners subdivided their homes into rooming houses and apartments. Conditions became so crowded and unhealthful that in 1866 the city began clearing the entire area for redevelopment for commercial use, and by 1872 the eighty-foot-high Fort Hill itself was leveled.

Today International Place stands on an irregular 2.6-acre site that was part of Fort Hill. Crammed onto one of Boston's most historic sites, this two-million-square-foot complex is a highly visible representative of the worst of the overdevelopment of the 1980s. Although the architects attempted to break down the mass into smaller units, a great failure was in not understanding the street space and how to humanize the buildings at the ground level. The facade of endlessly repeated Palladian windows with false mirror-glass arched tops is a travesty of the form. The project stimulated so much opposition and debate in the later 1980s that zoning and design review for downtown Boston were eventually modified.

International Trust Company Building

45 Milk Street

WILLIAM GIBBONS PRESTON, 1893; ENLARGED 1906

Boston Landmark
National Register of Historic Places

The fire of 1872 stopped at the intersection of Milk and Devonshire streets but burned part of the five-story iron building that stood on this site. The founda-

International Trust Company Building

tion and internal structure left standing were used in this new building of 1893. The third, seventh, and eighth floors are horizontally organized by means of a series of arched windows, while the fourth, fifth, and sixth floors are unified vertically by attenuated engaged columns and decorative trim around the window groups. At the center is a shallow inset bay window of three stories. The eclectic facade is further decorated by Beaux Arts–style figures representing Commerce, Industry, Security, and Fidelity carved by Max Bachman.

Liberty Square

EARL R. FLANSBURGH AND ASSOCIATES, 1989

Appleton Building

110–114 Milk Street

COOLIDGE AND SHATTUCK, 1924–1926;
RENOVATION: IRVING SALSBERG, 1981

Liberty Square is a prime spatial asset of the old financial district, a human-scaled space tightly defined by historic buildings. The buildings form a charming ensemble framing this tiny intersection of six narrow seventeenth- and eighteenth-century streets. The old winding streets provide a sense of enclosure and create unexpected vistas such as the view of the Batterymarch Building.

The Appleton Building's rounded corner between Batterymarch and Kilby streets dominates the square. The building is named for Samuel Appleton, a leader in the Boston insurance industry. The Classical Revival facade is appealing in its simplicity. Window openings are organized into tiers, and three bands of small windows function as friezes and

© 1991 Cymie Payne

Liberty Square

subdivide the facade. The largest window openings encompass two floors and add variety to the treatment.

Liberty Square was named at the end of the eighteenth century when a sixty-foot liberty pole was set up to commemorate the Stamp Act riots that took place here in 1765. The area had been a center of Tory businesses, including the London Bookstore and British Coffee House, so it was a natural choice as the location of the new office for the King's stamp master. While the pre-Revolutionary era is no longer apparent, Liberty Square today retains a sense of its nineteenth-century character and a suggestion of its long importance in the financial and political concerns of the nation. In the 1980s the Flynn administration decided this was the place to memorialize the October 1956 Hungarian Revolution and added a new eighteen-foot figural sculpture by Gyuri Hollosy to the tiny 1,300-square-foot triangular park. The Hungarian revolutionaries tore the communist insignia out of the flag, leaving the hole represented in the sculpture. The brick paving and granite seating, planting walls, sculpture base, and bollards reflect the character of the district.

Shawmut Bank

Milk Street at 1 Federal Street
THE ARCHITECTS COLLABORATIVE, 1975

The eight-story base follows the oblique edges of the site, reinforcing the irregular street pattern of the area. Deep undercuts in this mass add street-level interest and provide much-needed pedestrian space in the crowded financial district. A crisply detailed thirty-story tower rises above the base. The steel-framed building is faced in precast exposed-aggregate concrete. The architects also designed the interiors and the signing system for the building.

Hotel Meridien

formerly Federal Reserve Bank
Pearl Street at Franklin Street
R. CLIPSTON STURGIS, 1922;
RENOVATION: JUNG, BRANNEN ASSOCIATES, 1981

Boston Landmark

One Post Office Square

Pearl Street at Milk Street
JUNG, BRANNEN ASSOCIATES, 1981

The Federal Reserve board specified that the developer of the former Federal Reserve Bank site provide varied activities to bring new life to the old financial district. A 330-room hotel has been worked into the shell of the Renaissance Revival bank, preserving and restoring selected spaces and elements such as marble door frames and mantelpieces, bronze-arched windows on the lower level, the painted dome ceiling and gold-leaf vaults in the foyer, and murals by N. C. Wyeth. Four extra floors of hotel rooms were added within a sloping mansard roof form of glass.

Next door, the new forty-story office tower at One Post Office Square maximizes corner offices—prime rental spaces—by making double jogs at each corner, and gives these spaces larger windows. The multilevel lobby features Carrara marble.

Richardson Block

109–151 Pearl Street
WILLIAM G. PRESTON, 1873
National Register of Historic Places

Even though each building in this row was built by different owners, the entire block was designed as a unit. Built shortly after the great fire of 1872 that destroyed much of downtown Boston, it is a rare example of a marble-facade commercial block. The storefronts consisted of cast-iron piers with granite lintels but have been mistreated. Each of the upper stories is treated in a different

Richardson Block

manner; all feature incised ornament. The block was built for use by the leather industry. Preston designed several other Boston buildings, including the Museum of Natural History (now Louis), the oldest section of the Hotel Vendome, and the International Trust Company Building. Until 1872 Pearl Street was a world center for the boot and shoe industry.

🏛 Old State House

State Street at Washington Street
1712–1713; REBUILT, 1748;
ALTERATIONS: ISAIAH ROGERS, 1830;
RESTORATION: GEORGE A. CLOUGH,
1881–1882; RENOVATION: GOODY, CLANCY
& ASSOCIATES, INC., 1991
National Historic Landmark

From the mid-seventeenth century onward, the old Town House and the State House that replaced it were the center of business and political life for the colony. The earliest marketplace of Boston was established on this site even before the building of the old Town House, which housed the market in its open first floor. As early as 1634 the stocks and whipping post of Puritan Boston were here. In 1772, just two years after the Boston Massacre occurred in front of the building, the first stage coach to New York left from this important focus of Boston activity.

Despite the pack of towering office buildings that has grown up around it, the fine Old State House remains the focus of State Street. Its gambrel roof is concealed from the end elevations by the stepped and pedimented end facades. The lion and unicorn, symbols of the crown from pre-Revolutionary times, ornament the State Street gable

© 1991 by Peter Vanderwarker

Old State House

above the bull's-eye windows. From the ceremonial balcony with segmental pediment over Corinthian pilasters, the Declaration of Independence was first read to Bostonians on July 18, 1776. An ornate three-tier windowed tower rises above the slate roof.

28 State Street

EDWARD LARRABEE BARNES WITH
EMERY ROTH AND SONS, 1969

The first of Boston's sleek, ultra-simple office towers, this one stands on a prominent site between the Old State House and the new Boston City Hall. The program—an office building with a bank at the bottom and a club, restaurant, and executive offices on top—is expressed in the design. The base and top of the granite-faced structure are sculpted with shadowed openings, terraces, and arcades to express the special requirements of their prime tenants. The shaft of the building is the foil, severely simple, with glass and stone elegantly detailed as a taut skin.

© Gorchev and Gorchev

28 State Street

Stock Exchange Building and Exchange Place

53 State Street

PEABODY AND STEARNS, 1889–1891
FACADE RESTORATION AND TOWER ADDITION:
WZMH GROUP, 1981–1984

Boston Landmark

The Stock Exchange Building stands on the site of the historic Bunch of Grapes Tavern, which was at the head of Long Wharf in the eighteenth century, the water edge being near Kilby Street then. The tavern was the favorite meeting place of the Patriots before the Revolution and was reputed to serve the best bowl of punch in Boston. The first Masonic Lodge in the country was formed there in 1733, and in 1786 the Marietta Company, pioneer in the development of the Midwest, was organized there. Nearby was the first Boston house of John Winthrop (1588–1649), who was governor of Massachusetts for twelve years.

The main floor of the Boston Stock Exchange Building by Peabody and Stearns was a replica of the old counting house. When developers bought the site with intentions to demolish the Exchange Building and replace it with a one million square-foot tower, preservationists protested, but succeeded in rescuing only a sixty-foot L-shaped portion of the pink granite facade facing State and Kilby streets. The new tower, sheathed in a grid of reflective glass, is linked to the remains of the old building by a five-story climate-controlled greenhouse-atrium. An existing monumental marble staircase from the ground to the second floor is the focus of the restored space.

Stock Exchange Building and Exchange Place

60 State Street

The project is an example of a nationwide wave of facade preservation, often at the expense of the substance of the building. The battle between the most profitable use of land and the retention of strong visible links with the past will continue to be fought.

60 State Street

SKIDMORE, OWINGS & MERRILL, 1977

The focal position of 60 State Street across from the Old State House, opposite Edward Larrabee Barnes's 28 State Street and at the Congress Street entrance to the financial district from Government Center, demanded sculptural treatment of the tower. Clad in a ribbed granite grid, the mass is composed of two connected beveled prisms that meet the sky at an angle. At the top of the tower is the Bay Tower Room, a club for business lunches by day and a restaurant by night, offering splendid harbor views from its multi-leveled dining room.

75 State Street

DESIGN ARCHITECTS: GRAHAM GUND ARCHITECTS AND SKIDMORE, OWINGS & MERRILL, CHICAGO; ARCHITECTS AND ENGINEERS: SKIDMORE, OWINGS & MERRILL, 1988

Sometimes called "the painted lady" or "the Tammy Faye Bakker of architecture" (Robert Campbell), this exuberantly decorated building dominates its immediate surroundings—Faneuil Hall Marketplace and the Custom House district—which are much smaller in scale. The building is clad in five types of granite decorated with 3,600 square feet of gold leaf. The designers tried hard to break up, even to conceal, the massiveness of the building through setbacks, projecting bays, surface decoration, and even color. In the end the building fails to fit in; instead it is bright and brassy. Although the facade design at the street level relates in scale to its neighbors, there is no way the great size of the structure could have been hidden. Nor should it be hidden. But why call attention to it? Be sure to take a look inside at the six-story Great Hall, a glittering domed space of almost Roman

grandeur finished in seven types of marble with mahogany and bronze details. Although it has a shop-lined semipublic lobby, 75 State Street lacks a sense of activity and vitality. It is the first close neighbor of the Custom House Tower allowed to overwhelm it, eliminating a long-standing urban design function of one of Boston's major landmarks. This represents a significant change in the city's philosophy about its skyline.

99 Summer Street
GOODY, CLANCY & ASSOCIATES, INC., 1986

This is one of many 1980s high-rise buildings that have tried to respect the historic scale and character of the street facades by setting the high-rise mass in the center of the block. The gray granite facade was

75 State Street

99 Summer Street

inspired by that of the older buildings, as were the window proportions and the granite cornice lines. Even the hugely exaggerated pedimented dormers encompassing the upper floors derive from those of the historic five-story buildings at the base. But here the analogy is lost because of the enormous jump in scale. When 99 Summer Street is seen together with the old Church Green Building (p. 86), the older structure is exceedingly refined, elegant, and comfortable in comparison with its overfed cousin.

125 Summer Street

KOHN, PEDERSON, FOX, 1990

This highly visible tower is a prime example of the "historic skirt" style of preservation and is one of the best arguments for it. The new tower takes its architectural cues from the restored historic facades at its ankles and tries to sit primly behind them by retaining enough roof over each facade for verisimilitude. And the four five-story brick and granite commercial buildings dating from the 1870s were well worth saving. Each of the faces of the tower responds differently to its surroundings. Most striking is the eighty-foot-diameter apsoidal form facing South Station. The granite and cast stone facade is liberally decorated with pediments, pilasters, cornices and moldings, and bay windows. While one nor-

mally experiences culture shock when entering a "facade wrap" or "historic skirt" lobby, the designers of 125 Summer Street happily settled on a nineteenth-century European–style interior arcade lined with shops.

125 Summer Street

SEVEN

Fort Point Channel

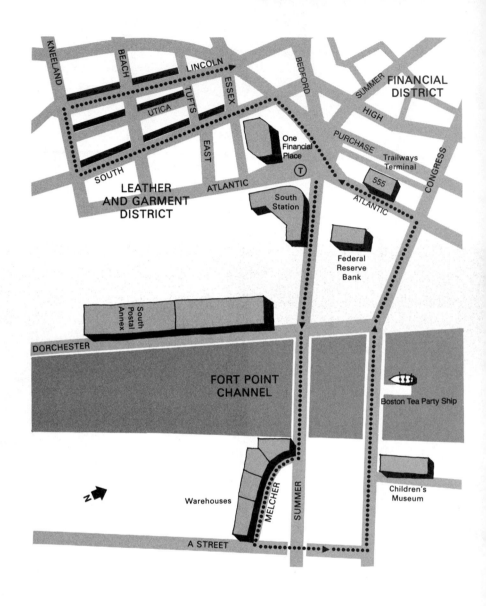

Fort Point Channel

For most of its history, the Fort Point Channel area has been an industrial district, particularly for the leather and garment industries, as well as for printing and general warehousing. In the beginning it was water-oriented, and finger piers wrapped completely around the peninsula. With the coming of railroads in the 1830s, however, commerce shifted to rail, and a new compact industrial area with substantial buildings of brick and stone developed on the South Boston side of the Fort Point Channel. This district survives nearly intact, but today many of the industrial structures are seeing new life as offices, galleries, museums, and loft apartments or studios.

Fort Point Channel Tour

Start at **South Station** and the **Federal Reserve Bank** (**111**) and walk down Summer Street past the **South Postal Annex** (**113**) and over the bridge to the **Summer Street warehouses** (**114**). To reach the **Children's Museum** (**115**) on foot, walk down Summer Street and take the stairway to the A Street underpass. Take A Street to Congress Street and turn left to reach the Museum. Crossing the Congress Street Bridge, notice the replica of the brig *Beaver*, a reminder of the Boston Tea Party, which took place near here. Continue on Congress Street and turn left on Atlantic Avenue, noting the **Trailways Bus Terminal** on the right (**110**). Now that you have returned to **South Station,** you can visit the old leather and garment district by proceeding for one block from **One Financial Place** to **South** and **Lincoln streets** (**115**).

Trailways Bus Terminal

Trailways Bus Terminal
555 Atlantic Avenue
SKIDMORE, OWINGS & MERRILL, 1980

The Trailways Bus Terminal is strategi-
cally located in the heart of one of
Boston's transportation centers, providing access to commuter bus and rail,
Amtrak, the subway system, and major
interstate highways. Its low, long-span
steel-truss roof floats above walls of
ground-face concrete block. Skylights
and a continuous band of windows
between the walls and roof create an
airy and open public area. It is built on
air rights over the Dewey Square Tunnel.

One Financial Place

One Financial Place
Dewey Square
JUNG, BRANNEN ASSOCIATES, 1983

Offices, shops, restaurants, cinemas, and
parking space are combined in this forty-
six-story six-sided tower at the juncture
of the financial district and the Fort Point

Channel area. A ninety-foot-high atrium
opens onto Dewey Square and serves as
the major entrance to the building. The
base of the building is granite, relating to
South Station, while the upper floors are
of cast stone and glass. It is the only struc-

ture in Boston clad with a precast-concrete rain-screen system (developed in Canada) that uses the pressure-equalization principle to minimize water penetration.

Federal Reserve Bank of Boston
600 Atlantic Avenue
HUGH STUBBINS AND ASSOCIATES, 1977

Boston's Federal Reserve Bank is a structural tour de force. The long-span floors of the tower are supported on tall and slender end pylons, which in turn straddle a low U-shaped mass housing public areas and high-security banking operations. The top of the low-rise block contains recreation and employee facilities, which have access to a landscaped roof garden. The aluminum skin was selected in part to reduce solar heat gain. The projecting aluminum spandrels of the tower both serve as sunshades and help

Federal Reserve Bank

reduce the downdraft problem characteristic of tall buildings, thus making the ground level more comfortable for pedestrians. The entrance area features a "water court" with a pool and an 18-foot-high, 140-foot-long waterfall running along the gallery-exhibition area. The bank sponsors fine art exhibitions and concerts that are open to the public without charge.

South Station
Atlantic Avenue at Summer Street
SHEPLEY, RUTAN, AND COOLIDGE, 1899;
REDEVELOPMENT CONCEPT: SKIDMORE,
OWINGS & MERRILL; RESTORATION: HUGH
STUBBINS & ASSOCIATES; PUBLIC SPACE AND
OFFICE AREAS: STULL AND LEE, INC.; CONSULT-
ING RETAIL ARCHITECT: PRELLWITZ/CHILINSKI,
1989
National Register of Historic Places (South Station Headhouse)

South Station stands on the site of the Bull Inn, built as a private frame house in 1668 but converted to an inn in 1689. South Station has been a landmark and the focus of Dewey Square since its construction. Its curved corner facade of Classical aspirations nicely joins Summer Street and Atlantic Avenue. Above the two-story entry arches rise three-story Ionic columns topped by a balustrade and entablature with center pediment. The eagle and clock provide a final flourish.

One of the most significant civic accomplishments of the 1980s was the renewal of South Station. With the advent of mass air and auto travel, the station declined, becoming one of the most decrepit transit stations in the Northeast. That has all changed, and today the sta-

© Edward Jacoby, APG

South Station

South Station concourse

© Steve Rosenthal

tion is a celebration of public transit, providing convenient connections between rail, subway, and bus in a pleasant public setting that is within walking distance of Boston's historic core. The old structure was restored on the outside and completely renovated on the inside, and a new west wing was added in the style of the original building, even incorporating pink granite from the same quarry in Connecticut that had been used ninety years earlier. The spacious and high-ceilinged concourse is entirely new, replacing the old squat space that was too deteriorated to restore.

The new Food Court, with shops and express food stands, has the sophistication and excitement bustling train stations must have had before airlines and cars became the primary ways to travel. It is a solution for the big old empty train station, because it brings people from the surrounding office buildings into the station to reinforce and support the transportation function. Having lunch while watching the trains arrive and depart just outside the expansive glass wall and listening to the train announcements can prompt diners to try a train journey.

South Postal Annex

Summer Street at 15 Dorchester Avenue
RENOVATION: PERRY, DEAN, ROGERS AND PARTNERS, 1980

Facing Boston Harbor, the metal-clad South Postal Annex recalls in appearance the streamlined ocean liners of the 1920s. Until 1980 this 1934 general mail facility was faced with brick. Refaced with insulating metal panels, it now is energy efficient and relates visually to the adjacent postal-service building built in the 1960s. A new covered pedestrian walkway provides passage to South Station. The 560,000-square-foot interior has been reorganized to provide an efficient work environment. The rehabilitation project extended the building's useful life for at least twenty years.

South Postal Annex

Brig *Beaver*, the Boston Tea Party ship, Congress Street Bridge

Melcher Street warehouses

🏛 Summer Street Warehouses

Now in the process of becoming Boston's Soho, the substantial, richly formed turn-of-the-century warehouses of this district, including nearby Congress Street, are largely the work of M. D. Safford. Particularly appealing is the curving Melcher Street, which dips down one full level to cross under Summer Street at A Street, leaving its imprint on the wonderful curved forms of 253 and 259 Summer Street.

🏛 Children's Museum, Boston

Museum Wharf
Congress Street at Fort Point Channel
M. D. SAFFORD, 1889; RENOVATION:
CAMBRIDGE SEVEN AND DYER BROWN
ASSOCIATES, 1975

This former warehouse works well in its new role as a museum for children. The large, simple open spaces with rough character easily absorb many large groups of children, with no ill effects on the building or restraints on the behavior of the children. The entrance is from a long raised boardwalk. The large glass-enclosed elevator is the major exterior change. New floor-to-ceiling openings in the brick facade provide views out, and bring light in. The giant milk bottle functions as a sign alerting people to the unexpected location of the museum and prepares visitors for the kind of imaginative play they will find inside.

Children's Museum

Leather and Garment District

South and Lincoln streets
National Historic District

The great fire of 1872 destroyed almost eight hundred buildings, many associated with merchandising and manufacturing centers in Boston such as the old leather and garment district. Lincoln and South streets are lined with five- and six-story warehouse and factory buildings constructed over three decades after the fire. Artifacts of the old New England leather and garment companies can be seen in some of the bracketed shop windows. Some of the buildings are handsome compositions of Romanesque arches and carved stone ornamentation. The strength of the district lies in the continuity of the brick facades and the handsome rhythm of the windows, as well as the uniformity of building height, massing, material, and frontage line. The old home of the shoemaking and leather tanning industries experienced a renaissance in the 1980s and is now the center of a number of serious galleries. The huge old warehouse spaces are ideal to accommodate the widest range of art, as well as artist's lofts. High-style restaurants have arrived to cater to the artists and collectors hanging out in what has become Boston's Soho. One on Kneeland Street is a classic deep blue and silver diner with corrugated metal and glass block. Another, the Loading Zone, is an industrial-style restaurant behind three industrial overhead doors and a loading-dock ramp. Inside, each table is a work of art by Ross Miller with hand truck–style chairs and exposed-conduit construction lighting.

EIGHT

Theater District

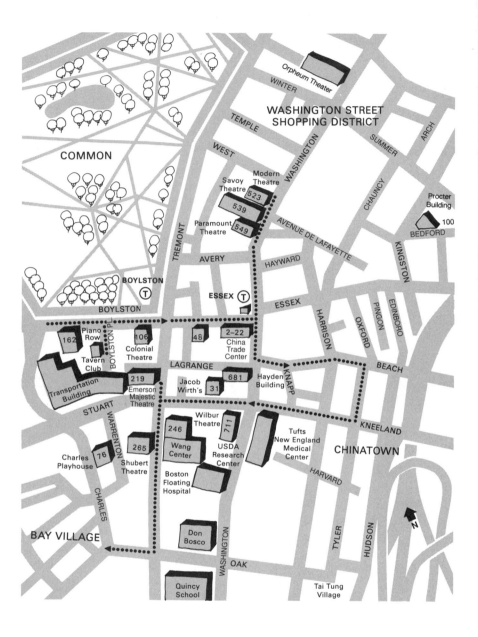

Theater District

National Register of Historic Places

A s New York systematically demolishes all its best old theaters, Boston remains in possession of the most outstanding group of early theaters in the country. Most of them are clustered on Tremont and Washington streets near Boylston and Stuart streets. For more than a century this has been the theater district, but in the eighteenth century this area of Washington Street was lined with wharves. In fact, Josiah Knapp's wharf at the intersection of Washington and Stuart streets was so close to the street that pedestrians complained about the bowsprits of his vessels obstructing the highway.

Boston has had many theaters and a distinguished theater history, with famed actors from England and the continent regularly appearing on stages here. The first theaters were built near where the 1852 Orpheum Theater still stands (see Tremont Street at Hamilton Place, p. 11). The district expanded when a dozen theaters were built several blocks south of the Orpheum on Tremont, Washington, and Boylston streets. The district was so well identified and densely populated with theaters that there was a connecting network of underground passages and lobbies. In bad weather patrons could walk from theater to theater without ever going out of doors. In 1900 there were thirty-one theaters in Boston with a total of 50,000 seats, but they were threatened by competition from coin-operated video machines or "nickelodeons," the forerunners of movies that launched the careers of Sam Goldwyn and the Warner brothers in Boston. The nickelodeon ultimately meant the demise of many theaters not only in Boston but across the country. With the closing of theaters, Boston actors began the flight to Hollywood in the 1920s. Some legitimate theaters, such as the Majestic, Plymouth, and Copley, were turned into movie houses, and D. W. Griffith's *Birth of a Nation* premiered in 1915 in the Tremont Theatre.

Today the theater district is active, with full seasons of plays, operas, and ballet in a number of historically and architecturally significant theaters, but the district character is not yet strong and cohesive. Design of the large-scale environment could reinforce the important role Boston's playhouses perform in the contemporary city. Restoration of several of the old theaters now in the hands of low-grade movie houses and elimination of the "combat zone" will be important steps in the district's rebirth.

Theater District Tour

Starting at Boylston station on the corner of the **Common (449)**, visit **Piano Row (122)**, including **Boylston Place (123)** and the **Colonial Theatre (122)**. Continue on Boylston Street past the **Young Men's Christian Union (121)** and the **Boylston Building (121)**. Turn left at the metal-and-glass **Essex Station (130)** if you wish to make a side trip to visit three **Washington Street theaters (128–30)**. Otherwise, turn right on Washington Street for one block of squalid entertainment before turning left at H. H. Richardson's **Hayden Building (131)** onto Beach Street to reach **Chinatown (134)**. After one block of Tyler Street, turn right onto Kneeland Street and proceed past **Tufts New England Medical Center,** the **Human Nutrition Research Center, Boston Floating Hospital (131–32)**, and the venerable **Jacob Wirth's (124)**. The large curved brick building in view at the end of the street is the **Transportation Building (124)**. At the **Emerson Majestic Theatre (124)** turn left onto Tremont Street to visit the **Wilbur** and **Shubert theaters**, the **Wang Center for the Performing Arts (125–27)**, and the **Don Bosco** and **Josiah Quincy schools (132)**. At this point one may return up Tremont Street to the starting point or turn right onto Oak Street to begin the Bay Village tour.

Procter Building
100–106 Bedford Street
WINSLOW AND WETHERELL, 1897
Boston Landmark

Certainly this is the most exuberant commercial building in Boston! It would almost be simpler to list the ornamental elements that are absent. The small cream-colored building is decorated with a frieze, cornice, arches, finials, and lovely cresting along the roof line, forming a delightful small composition that is entirely unified despite the complex mixture. The familiar top of the Custom House Tower pops into view from this location.

Procter Building

Boylston Building/China Trade Center
2–22 Boylston Street
CARL FEHMER, 1887; RENOVATION: THE ARCHITECTURAL TEAM, 1987
Boston Landmark
National Register of Historic Places

The sandstone facade of this handsome six-story building is dominated by Romanesque arches in three sizes. Now renovated, it improves the character and image of this rather threatening area.

Boylston Building/China Trade Center

Young Men's Christian Union
48 Boylston Street
NATHANIEL J. BRADLEE, 1875
Boston Landmark
National Register of Historic Places

Boston once had many more of these Ruskin Gothic buildings, but most of them have been demolished. The tiers of pointed arches are accentuated with stone voussoirs and moldings in alternat-

Young Men's Christian Union

ing colors. The gable over the complex entrance composition is ornamented with crockets. The building originally had a tall clock over the entrance.

Piano Row

Boylston Street between Tremont and Charles streets
National Register of Historic Places

"Piano Row" was the center for piano building and music publishing in Boston,

indeed in the entire country, in the nineteenth and early twentieth centuries. Besides the Steinert Building, other piano buildings include the E. A. Starck Piano Company Building at 154–156, the Vose and Sons Piano Company at 158–160, and the Wurlitzer Company at 100 Boylston Street. The Mason and Hamlin Building at 146 Boylston Street has been demolished.

Colonial Theatre
106 Boylston Street
CLARENCE H. BLACKALL, 1889–1900;
INTERIOR DECORATION: H. B. PENNELL

The prestigious Colonial Theatre, Boston's oldest theater to survive intact under the same name, has been the setting for countless theatrical debuts, from Sigmund Romberg and Irving Berlin to the Ziegfeld Follies and Rodgers and Hammerstein. The combination of a theater with an office building was a sophisticated idea that beautifully integrates prime street frontage for use as shops and lobbies for the theater and offices. Beyond the rather narrow street entrance are lavish gold theater interiors combining elaborate paneling and bas-reliefs executed by the John Evans Company with ceiling and wall murals.

Clarence H. Blackall (1857–1942) made many important and lasting contributions to Boston architecture, including his fourteen theaters, the fine Winthrop Building (see 276–278 Washington Street, p. 14), and several other buildings. Blackall was a senior partner in the Boston firm of Blackall, Clapp, and Whittemore.

Steinert Hall

162 Boylston Street
WINSLOW AND WETHERELL, 1896

Piano showrooms, offices, studios, and a concert hall are contained behind the six-story limestone and brick Beaux Arts–style facade with terra-cotta ornament and a copper cornice. The concert hall, Steinert Hall, now in poor condition because of water damage, was a restrained Adam-style auditorium with fluted Corinthian pilasters separating round arches.

Boylston Place and the Tavern Club

4 Boylston Place, 1819;
5–6 Boylston Place, 1844

Tavern Club, Boylston Place

Boylston Place is a remnant of the mid-nineteenth century that finds itself at the end of the twentieth century a heavily used pedestrian access to the Transportation Building. A tablet in the Common identifies Boylston Place as the location "where football was born." A student of Mr. Dixwell's Private School organized the first game in 1860, using for a ball a rubber sphere that is now in the collection of the Society for the Preservation of New England Antiquities.

The venerable Tavern Club has occupied its charming and historic quarters in three brick row houses connected by a stucco structure over a carriage way since 1887. Number 4 is a Federal house with fanlight and side lights at its entry door, and numbers 5 and 6 are early Victorian row houses with oriel windows and dormered attics. The club's private performances of musicals and hilarious plays with club members as cast and backstage crew have been famous among generations of Bostonians. The presence of the club in this extremely urbane little corner of the district reinforces the character and special nature of the theater district. The unusual brick building at 3 Boylston Place, built in 1888, has cast-iron ornaments on its arches and shallow copper oriel windows.

An iron gateway by artist-blacksmith Dmitri Gerakaris provides a fitting entry to the world of theater, music, and fantasy. A bronze frieze includes the musical dog, cat, rooster, and donkey from the tale of the Bremen Town Musicians. The arch is spanned by lyres with a keystone of piano keys and theater masks. A four-foot Tavern Club bear in top hat, tails, and evening cape stands at the gate holding back the folds of a steel curtain. Other motifs include the Swan Boats and bridge from the Public Garden, as well as ducklings from *Make Way for Ducklings.*

Transportation Building
Park Square
GOODY, CLANCY & ASSOCIATES, 1983

The best thing about the Transportation Building is the way it hugs the bend of Stuart Street. In many other areas Boston's unique street pattern has been negated by insensitive development that has imposed regular geometry onto the irregular fabric. The facade of the 880,000-square-foot mixed-use building is architecturally unengaging, however, and ignores the texture of older buildings in the area in its lack of detail. Two interior pedestrian malls connect Stuart Street to the Park Plaza area and Boylston Street to the theater district. A high atrium at the intersection of the malls is overlooked by the public offices of transportation agencies. The provision of retail space in a public building is unusual in Massachusetts and provides activity to the theater district both day and night.

🏛 Jacob Wirth's
31 Stuart Street
GREENLEAF C. SANBORN, 1844–1845
Boston Landmark
National Register of Historic Places

These simple dormered bowfront row houses are an important reminder of the

Jacob Wirth's

mid-nineteenth-century architectural context now largely gone from this area. The restaurant and bar, a Boston institution, seemingly offer the same German sausage and sauerkraut menu and service in the same atmosphere as when they opened their doors in 1868. It is a rare opportunity to experience a genuine nineteenth-century restaurant interior that makes no compromise for the sake of modernity.

Emerson Majestic Theatre
219 Tremont Street
JOHN GALEN HOWARD, 1901–1903
Boston Landmark

The Majestic Theatre was particularly known for musicals and light opera. A lobby of Numidian marble was buried beneath an unfortunate redecoration, but the grand Rococo theater interior survives. Above the marquee, the exterior is extravagant and elaborate gray terra-cotta. Fluted engaged columns with

Emerson Majestic Theatre

composite capitals dominate the facade. Festooned windows are surmounted by oculi and high-relief masked faces as keystones. Beneath the balustrade a Vitruvian scroll band is executed in terracotta. The interiors were the first to use electric lighting creatively. Glass globes are integrated into the richly sculpted arches of garlands that enclose the auditorium. The architect, John Galen Howard, founded the University of California School of Architecture. He had studied at MIT and at the Ecole des Beaux Arts and worked under H. H. Richardson and McKim, Mead, and White. Eben Jordan, son of the founder of Jordan Marsh, built this theater as well as Jordan Hall (see 290–94 Huntington Avenue, p. 343) and the Boston Opera House, now demolished. The theater is being restored by Emerson College.

Wilbur Theatre

246 Tremont Street
CLARENCE H. BLACKALL, 1914
Boston Landmark
National Register of Historic Places

The Wilbur Theatre is a good example of Colonial Revival design and incorporates Georgian, Federal, and Greek Revival motifs. The freestanding mass is topped by a cornice and balustrade with discreet Adam-style bas-relief and name panels. Three tall arched windows with iron balconies and carved tympanums appear on the second floor above the three Classical pedimented entrances with Ionic columns *in antis*. The intimate one-thousand-seat theater has had its share of important premieres, including the pre-Broadway trials of Thornton Wilder's *Our Town* and Tennessee Williams's *A Streetcar*

Wilbur Theatre

Named Desire with the young Marlon Brando and Jessica Tandy. The interior makes economical use of space with an attractive lower lobby that now serves as a cafe. Only the marquee needs improvement on this fine building.

Shubert Theatre
265 Tremont Street
HILL, JAMES, AND WHITAKER, 1908–1910
National Register of Historic Places

The small, elegant facade is beautifully proportioned and detailed with a Palladian window, carved tympanum, and modillion cornice. The wrought-iron and glass marquee was reinstalled when the original marble facade was replaced with

Shubert Theatre

limestone at the time of the 1925 widening of Tremont Street. The theater was named after Sam S. Shubert, eldest of three brothers in the theater business. He is often called "the founder of the independent theater movement." This theater's illustrious dramatic history has included performances by Sir Laurence Olivier, John Barrymore, Maurice Evans, and John Gielgud.

Wang Center for the Performing Arts

originally the Metropolitan Theater
268 Tremont Street
BLACKALL, CLAPP, AND WHITTEMORE, 1923–1925; EXPANSION JUNG/BRANNEN, 1982

Boston Landmark (interior)
National Register of Historic Places

The Music Hall, originally called the Metropolitan Theater, was conceived and built as a true movie palace several years before Radio City Music Hall in New York City. The intention was to attract well over four thousand people to each of four variety and film showings every day. Four lavish Louis XIV marble lobbies organized the flow of ticket holders and departing patrons, keeping them entertained all the while. Besides gazing at the opulent rose jasper pillars, marble doorways, and eighteen-hundred-pound gold-plated chandeliers, patrons could amuse themselves with bridge games, Ping-Pong, dancing, billiards, and other activities until the next show began.

In 1932 a stylish Art Deco restaurant called The Platinum Salon was added. The theater was a miniature city that even had its own medical station in case of emergency. An immense Wurlitzer organ, a grand orchestra that rose out of the pit on an elevator, a corps de ballet, a one-hundred-voice chorus, and stars such as Jack Benny and Burns and Allen provided stunning reviews prior to the film showing, all for thirty-five cents, seventy-five cents on weekends.

Today the theater has been upgraded, with special attention to enlarging the stage and improving the technical facilities for use by national and international opera, ballet, and theater companies.

Charles Playhouse

76 Warrenton Street
ASHER BENJAMIN, 1838–1839;
RENOVATION: CAMBRIDGE SEVEN, 1957–1966
National Register of Historic Places

Built as the Fifth Universalist Church in 1839 and later used by the Hebrew Tem-

Charles Playhouse

ple Ohabei Shalom and the Scotch Presbyterian Church, this Greek Revival
structure took up a theatrical life only in
the late 1950s. The pediment is supported on brick pilasters and two central
Ionic columns on the second and third
levels. The granite ground floor was built
as two stores to provide rental income to
the church.

Modern Theatre
523 Washington Street
CLARENCE H. BLACKALL, 1913; ORIGINAL
BUILDING: LEVI NEWCOMB AND SON, 1876

The Modern Theatre, one of Boston's
first movie theaters, was inserted into an

Modern Theatre

already existing Victorian Gothic furniture store and warehouse built thirty-
seven years earlier. The small theater
seated eight hundred. It had no stage
and was designed with special concern
for its acoustics with the assistance of
Wallace Sabine, the Harvard professor
who first applied scientific principles to
the study of sound and space. The interiors were executed in the Renaissance
style. The entrance facade featured a
large entry arch, originally open, framed
by Corinthian pilasters with entablature.
The first talking film, *The Jazz Singer,*
was premiered at the Modern Theatre in
the late 1920s.

Savoy Theatre
originally the B. F. Keith Memorial
Theatre
539 Washington Street
THOMAS LAMB, 1928

Benjamin F. Keith, for whom this theater
was originally named, introduced the
term "vaudeville" and the notion of continuous, wholesome entertainment at
low prices. By the time of his death he
had a chain of over four hundred theaters. Part of Keith's success was in his
opulent theaters, which attracted
respectable society and later became the
model for movie theaters. The flamboyant Spanish Baroque facade in terra-cotta
is only a taste of what follows in the vast
high-ceilinged lobby with its several levels of galleries and sixteen Italian marble
columns weighing seven tons each. The
auditorium is equally impressive and
quite well preserved. The theater was
used for a number of years by the Opera
Company of Boston.

Savoy Theatre

Paramount Theatre
549 Washington Street
ARTHUR BOWDITCH, 1930–1932
Boston Landmark

The facade of Boston's best Art Deco theater is dominated by its "Moderne" sign, which was particularly effective when illuminated at night. Much of the Deco marquee has been removed or covered over. The theater was built exclusively for films but had a large Wurlitzer organ that could be raised to stage level for entertainment before the film. The Art Deco interiors have inlaid woodwork of polished Oriental walnut and African ebony with geometric aluminum and gold decorations. Many of the design motifs were used in other Paramount theaters across the country.

Essex Street MBTA Station and Headhouse
Washington Street at Essex Street
EARL R. FLANSBURGH AND ASSOCIATES, 1969, 1974

Part of the MBTA station modernization program, the Essex Street Station is constructed of stainless steel tubing and bulletproof glass. It was assembled away from the site, delivered on a Sunday morning, and installed in one day. The design provides maximum visibility of the interior, day and night. Although the headhouse is currently adjacent to a building, it is designed to be freestanding when the structure is demolished as part of the renewal plan. Essex Street Station was the first in Boston to include a work of art in the design. A competition was held, and the winner, George Greenameyer, created a large sculpture for the space.

Essex Street MBTA Station

Paramount Theatre marquee

Hayden Building

681 Washington Street at
La Grange Street
HENRY HOBSON RICHARDSON, 1875–1876
Boston Landmark
National Register of Historic Places

This little-known five-story office building by Richardson is in his characteristic
Romanesque Revival style using rusticated masonry. A broad segmental arch
on the second floor contains three windows, while narrow but tall arches unite
the third and fourth floors. The use of
simple stone slabs on the top floor is
reminiscent of the "Boston granite style."

Hayden Building

Human Nutrition Research Center

U. S. Department of Agriculture
711 Washington Street
SHEPLEY BULFINCH RICHARDSON AND
ABBOTT, 1982

Part of the Tufts–New England Medical
Center, this high-rise research facility contains a unique combination of laboratories, housing for twenty-eight volunteers
who will live at the center for six- to
twelve-month periods, recreational facilities including a swimming pool, and
extensive animal-research areas. The first
two floors of the granite-faced building
form an open arcade together with a
lobby, reception areas, and an auditorium. The long face of the building was
beveled to open up the street space.

Health Services Building and School of Dental Medicine Tufts–New England Medical Center

Washington Street at Kneeland Street
THE ARCHITECTS COLLABORATIVE, 1973

TAC's long-range development plan for
the Tufts–New England Medical Center
provided for the merging of three separate hospitals and the Tufts schools of
medicine and dentistry into one area and
helped revive a deteriorating section of
downtown Boston. The plan included
use of air rights to link all components of
the complex. The horizontal layout and
modular construction allowed for phased
growth. The Health Services Building is a
forty-two-bed teaching hospital with

diagnostic and treatment facilities, and the School of Dental Medicine has an additional forty-eight beds.

New England Medical Center, Boston Floating Hospital

Washington Street near Kneeland Street

PERRY, DEAN, ROGERS AND PARTNERS, 1982

The Reverend Rufus Tobey conceived the Boston Floating Hospital in 1892. Tobey had noticed how mothers fled the hot tenements and took their young children to the harbor to refresh them in cool ocean breezes. By 1894 he had raised enough money to launch a ship that would cruise about the harbor in the summer, exposing the children to sunshine and sea air and providing them with free medical care. Besides the young patients, the Floating Hospital had

New England Medical Center, Boston Floating Hospital

on board doctors, nurses, and often parents. The Floating Hospital has been a leader in pediatric medicine since its founding and originated the concept of family participation in the care of the hospitalized child, as well as play programs in treatment and the "whole child" approach to hospitalization.

Although the new hospital no longer floats, it appears to, supported by four truss arches spanning Washington Street at an angle and connecting it with the Proger Health Services Building. Part of the seventh floor is semicircular and provides close visual and physical access between patients and staff. Above the patient floor there is a two-story playroom where play therapy and medical care are combined.

Josiah F. Quincy School and Community Center

885 Washington Street

THE ARCHITECTS COLLABORATIVE, 1976

This innovative elementary school is conceived like an urban village on its small site. Its terraced rooftops form piazzas for play areas while a "pedestrian street" runs diagonally through the site, linking two neighborhoods. All of the community and shared facilities are located along this path. The school's four open-plan subschools are clustered around a media center and central support facilities. A porcelain enamel frieze derived from children's drawings decorates the exterior.

Josiah F. Quincy School and Community Center

**Addition, Don Bosco Techni-
cal High School (Halasz and
Halasz, 1975)**

Gateway, Chinatown

🏛 Chinatown

Beach, Hudson, Oxford, and Tyler streets

National Register of Historic Places

A large Chinese gate is the formal entrance to Chinatown on Beach Street. Other signs of Asian culture can be found in the district's architectural motifs: look for fu dogs, decorative posts on upper floors, and a pagoda roof terrace on the top of the Chinese Merchants Association Building at the corner of Hudson and Stuart streets. The Chinese restaurants on Tyler Street have flamboyant facades, and on the other streets many shops display Chinese groceries, fresh fish, spices, produce, pots and pans, and colorful clothing. Chinatown has grown geographically and culturally and is now a focus for a variety of Asian cultures. Vietnamese grocery stores and the China Trade Center have changed the atmosphere of Washington Street in the former "combat zone," and Asian decorative arts shops have spread into the leather district.

Bay Village

Boston Architectural Conservation District

The mud flats of the Bay Village area became buildable in 1825 with the construction of a dam near Fayette Street. The neighborhood's streets were laid out in the 1820s and 1830s, but it took more than a decade for them to become built up. The name Bay Village is recent, as the area was long known as the Church Street district after the Presbyterian Church built in 1827 on Church Street between Piedmont and Winchester streets.

In the late 1860s the filling of the Back Bay caused sanitary problems for Bay Village, making it necessary to raise the level of the entire neighborhood. In a mammoth undertaking, almost five hundred houses and commercial buildings were raised, the first floors to eighteen feet above sea level and the backyards to twelve feet.

Bay Village is able to claim a major literary figure among its residents, since Edgar Allan Poe was born here in 1809 while his parents were boarding in the house of H. Haviland at 62 Carver Street, demolished in the late 1960s. (Some have claimed incorrectly that 15 Fayette Street was Poe's birthplace.) Other residents of the neighborhood included Ephraim Marsh, a prominent developer of the early nineteenth century, who built many houses here and on Beacon Hill. In fact, many carpenters and artisans for Beacon Hill homes built their own modest but finely crafted homes in the neighborhood. The original inhabitants of the area included housewrights, painters, ink makers, harness and rope makers, blacksmiths, surrey makers, sail makers, paperhangers, salt merchants, tin workers, toll gatemen, cabinetmakers, and musical instrument makers. The world-renowned Haynes Flute and Piccolo Company at 12 Piedmont Street is a twentieth-century continuation of the tradition of artisans in the area.

The colorful history of the area was enhanced during the 1920s, when there were known to be many speakeasies located here. As the adjacent area to the north became a thriving theater district, actors and musicians and entertainment-related activities flocked to the neighborhood. While the neighborhood has

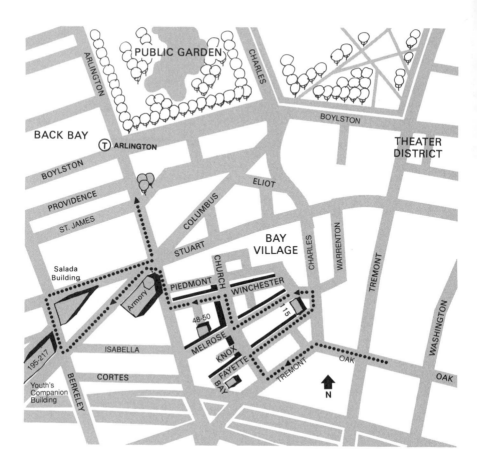

PUBLIC GARDEN

ARLINGTON

CHARLES

BOYLSTON

BACK BAY

Ⓣ ARLINGTON

THEATER
DISTRICT

BOYLSTON

PROVIDENCE

ST. JAMES

ELIOT

COLUMBUS

BAY
VILLAGE

STUART

CHARLES

WARRENTON

TREMONT

Salada
Building

Armory

PIEDMONT

CHURCH

WINCHESTER

115

WASHINGTON

48-50

195-217

ISABELLA

MELROSE

KNOX

FAYETTE

BERKELEY

CORTES

BAY

TREMONT

OAK

OAK

Youth's
Companion
Building

N

remained primarily residential, it has been a center for film distribution companies and has several office and light industrial buildings. Today the neighborhood has retained its pleasant short streets of small brick houses, but many of these now house three or four flats or condominiums.

Bay Village Tour

The Bay Village tour is an extension of the theater district tour and begins at Oak and Charles streets. Take Tremont Street to **Church Street** and walk one block to **Fayette Street (138)**. Note the Art Deco details at **115 Broadway (138)** and turn the corner to **Melrose Street.** Turn right and you are once more on Church Street for a block before leaving the Bay Village residential area by turning left on Winchester Street to Arlington Street and the **First Corps of Cadets Armory (139)**. Turning left at the Armory, pass its drawbridge entrance on Columbus Avenue. Turn right onto Berkeley Street to reach the **Youth's Companion Building** and the **Salada Tea Building (141)** and right again to view the bronze doors of the Stuart Street entrance. You may continue on Berkeley Street to the Back Bay Copley Square tour or to the Arlington MBTA station.

1 Bay Street
1830s

The only remaining house on Bay Street
is this tiny but charming ivy-covered two
and one-half story house. Built on land
once owned by Ephraim Marsh, it is a
good example of carpenters' work of the
1830s. This small street inspired the new
name of Bay Village after the historic
name, Church Street district, had lost its
appeal. Originally there were four brick
houses on the east side of the street and
six wood houses on the west.

1 Bay Street

Art Deco details, 115 Broadway,
Bay Village

Fayette Street row houses

🏛 First Corps of Cadets Armory

130 Columbus Avenue at Arlington Street
WILLIAM G. PRESTON, 1891–1897
Boston Landmark
National Register of Historic Places

The First Corps of Cadets, which financed and built the Armory, was a private military organization founded in 1741 to guard the governor of the Massachusetts Bay Colony. Reorganized in 1776, the corps was commanded by John Hancock, and its members served valiantly as Patriots in a number of battles in the Revolution. During the Civil War and the First World War they continued to serve as a unit, and in 1940 they were inducted into the National Guard. In its new role as a National Guard unit, the First Corps of Cadets no longer focused its activities on the Armory. It stopped using the building altogether in the late 1960s, when the Armory was taken over by the University of Massachusetts and used as a library.

The imposing and quite convincing rusticated granite castle dominates the intersection and in fact was located for its strategic military position in the center of the city population, near the railroad lines, and with visual communication to the State House for signaling. The structure is outfitted with the necessities of medieval defense, which must have fascinated the Victorians, considering the number of castlelike armories across the country. It has a six-story crenellated tower with machicolation and loop windows for arrows. A drawbridge crosses the "moat," actually a light well for the basement, into the drill hall, which is

First Corps of Cadets Armory

wisely provided with corbel towers for "flank defense." After a period of neglect, the Armory served as the setting for the Bicentennial exhibit on Victorian Boston. Now it functions successfully as a convention and exhibition hall for the Park Plaza Hotel.

48–50 Melrose Street

1915; RENOVATION AND ADDITION; WILLIAM RAWN ASSOCIATES, 1985

This is an outstanding example of contextual design, executed by one of Boston's best architects working in that mode. The original 1915 structure was built as a two-story film studio at a time when Bay Village was the center of the film industry in Boston. The renovation added two floors in a very sympathetic way, with window size, placement, and

48-50 **Melrose Street**

© Steve Rosenthal

style very similar to the original facade. Imaginative and subtle surprises were introduced, however, in the small balcony and the grouping of arched windows that illuminate an interior two-story space. The facade contributes to the entire street without trying to imitate its Federal-style neighbors. The resulting building is better than the original. The basement and ground floor are now office space, and the upper floors are apartments.

Youth's Companion Building

195–217 Columbus Avenue and
140–144 Berkeley Street
HARTWELL AND RICHARDSON, 1982
National Register of Historic Places

Built of brick and red sandstone, this building is in the Richardson Romanesque style. The facade is organized in tiers and the windows are grouped in bays. The monumental entry portal with a deeply recessed entry beneath a coffered archway is reminiscent of similar entrances in Louis Sullivan's Chicago

Youth's Companion Building, 195–217 Columbus Avenue

the Gorham Company from a design by Henry Wilson, an English artist, and depict scenes from the tea trade. The doors won a silver medal at the Paris Salon in 1927. Elephant heads project in bas-relief from the capitals of the pilasters, and elephants in profile form the frieze above the doors. These were carved in stone by Caesar Caira, a French sculptor. Above the frieze is a broken pediment with cyma reversa (double curve) molding. The classically inspired building appears to be a massive square block, but in fact it is triangular in plan.

Salada Tea Building, Stuart Street entrance

work. The *Youth's Companion,* founded in 1827, was published here. It was a weekly illustrated publication intended to entertain young people and to instill the values of education, work, thrift, and morality.

Salada Tea Building
Stuart Street at Berkeley
DENSMORE, LE CLEAR, AND ROBBINS, 1929

The elephants on the bronze doors of the Stuart Street entrance to the Salada Tea Building have long delighted children and adults alike. They were cast by

NINE

Beacon Hill

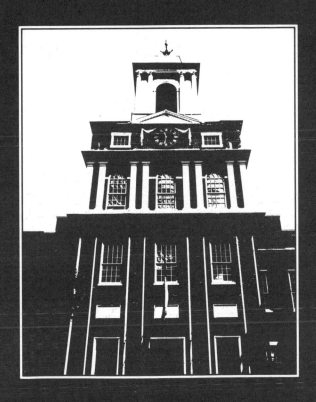

Beacon Hill
National Historic District

A h, Beacon Hill . . . what visions those words connote in New England and beyond. For nearly two centuries it has been the seat of state government in Bulfinch's gold-domed capitol building. To many urban romantics who move to Boston, Beacon Hill is the only place they dream of living. It seems not a part of contemporary America, so thoroughly does it express another era, one that is out of reach in most American communities. On the hill where Boston's first settler, the Reverend William Blaxton, made his home in 1625, thousands of people live today in an environment that is almost entirely early to mid-nineteenth century.

Until the late eighteenth century, the south slope was pasture and grassy slopes owned by the painter John Singleton Copley. The topography then was strikingly different, consisting of three odd hills called the Trimountain. One of these was Mount Vernon, which towered sixty feet above the present-day Louisburg Square. Pemberton or Cotton Hill rose eighty feet above Pemberton Square, where the Suffolk County Court House now stands, and Sentry Hill was sixty feet above what is now the State House parking lot. These three summits were leveled in the process of developing the south slope, the fill going to make new land in the marshes beyond Charles and Cambridge streets. The filled area beyond Charles Street was built up with stables and carriage houses. In this century many of them have been recycled as charming houses on Lime, Byron, Chestnut, and Mt. Vernon streets and Beaver Place.

Charles Bulfinch designed fine houses on the south slope that remain distinguished residences today. The other Beacon Hill developers built at a rapid pace, and by 1848 the entire hill was covered with row houses. Nearly all are of brick and generally of three or four stories. The Federal, Georgian, Greek Revival, and Victorian styles predominate. The streetscape is one of narrow streets with houses often directly next to the brick sidewalks. Rather than front yards, there are often stoops with wrought-iron railings, boot scrapers, and the occasional hitching post.

Many houses have tunnellike passageways to rear gardens as a result of an 1830s building restriction requiring a passage between houses wide enough for a cow and high enough for a boy with a basket on his head. Although the basic street pattern is a grid, it is an interesting one that planners and urban designers should study. Streets vary in both width and length, and several have slight bends, adding considerable interest. Since there are only three through streets, traffic is discouraged.

Many people associate Beacon Hill with the wealthy "Boston Brahmins," yet it has always had a diverse population. Through accidents of development, the north and south slopes have had very different characters. The south slope is epitomized by Louisburg Square, the quiet and lovely Chestnut Street, and the large and busier but immensely dignified Mount Vernon Street, so revered by Henry James. The north slope shares many of the amenities and has its splendid views but has managed to retain its own characteristic population, which today is a blend of Bohemian elements with aspiring young professionals and students.

The Hill was the fashionable place to live until the 1870s and 1880s, when the Back Bay was developed on a grander scale. Families left Louisburg Square, Chestnut Street, and Mount Vernon Street houses for French-influenced boulevards and mansard-roofed houses that were larger, lighter, and airier than the basically English style of Beacon Hill. The period of decline on the south slope was reversed in the mid-twentieth century, and Beacon Hill was suddenly the place to be once more. Each year the neighborhood holds a window-box competition and a tour of the tiny walled gardens behind many of the row houses, where shade gardening is pursued with determination and enthusiasm.

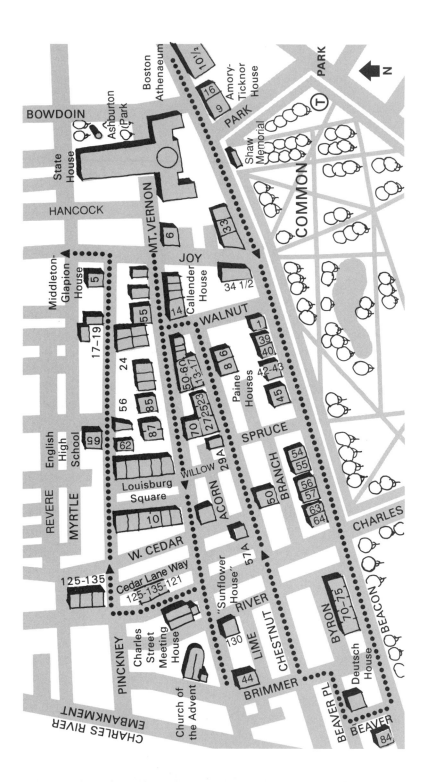

The South Slope

Beacon Hill—South Slope Tour

Start at the **Boston Athenaeum** and head toward the **State House,** passing the **Amory-Ticknor house, Shaw Memorial,** and several other sites on your right between the **George Parkman house** and **75 Beacon Street,** until you reach the bottom of the Hill (**148**). Turn right onto Beaver Street and then Beaver Place at the **Deutsch House** (**161**). Turning left on Brimmer Street and right on Chestnut Street (**164**), pass the small shops and restaurants and walk up the hill past many noteworthy sites until you reach the **Swan houses** (**165**). Turn left onto Walnut Street and then right on Mount Vernon Street at **John Callender's house** (**177**). At the intersection of Joy Street you will see the **Lyman-Paine house** (**175**).

Turn around and walk down Mount Vernon Street past the **Nichols House Museum,** the **second Harrison Gray Otis house, Louisburg Square,** and several other sites (**171, 179, 181**). Cross Charles Street to see the **Charles Street Meeting House,** the **"Sunflower" house,** and the **Church of the Advent** (**163, 183**), then return to Charles Street, turn left, and walk up Pinckney Street. You will pass Louisburg Square again, as well as the **hidden houses, English High School,** the **"house of odd windows,"** the **Middleton-Glapion house,** and several other charming sties (**185**). Turn left onto Joy Street to begin the North Slope tour. To return to your starting point, turn right onto Joy Street and walk to Beacon Street.

ACORN STREET

This cobblestone street is a charming remnant of early nineteenth-century life and one of the narrowest streets in Boston. The flat-facade brick row houses fronting the narrow brick sidewalk have foundations and door and window lintels of granite. These very desirable small homes were originally the residences of coachmen who served families in the nearby mansions and fine homes on Chestnut and Mount Vernon streets.

Acorn Street

BEACON STREET

Beacon Street has had such a long and proud history that it is surprising to learn that its seventeenth-century name was "Poor House Lane," no doubt because it was adjacent to the old almshouse near Park Street. It was a quiet and undeveloped area in early Boston where Boston's first settler, the Reverend William Blaxton, developed the first named variety of apple in America, "Blaxton's Yellow Sweeting." When the Reverend was not tending his orchard near present-day Charles Street, he might be seen riding about Boston on the saddled bull he had trained.

It was not until 1708 that the street was formally laid out and given the name of Beacon Street after the signal lantern atop a pole at the summit of the hill. Construction of the stately row houses followed the building of the State House at the end of the eighteenth century.

🏛 Boston Athenaeum

10½ Beacon Street
EDWARD CLARKE CABOT, 1847–1849
ENLARGED AND REBUILT: HENRY FORBES
BIGELOW, 1913–1914
National Historic Landmark

The Boston Athenaeum is a proprietary library founded in 1807. Before moving to its present location overlooking the Old Granary Burial Ground, it changed locations several times. Edward Clarke Cabot, who won a competition for its design in 1846, based his scheme on Palladio's Palazzo da Porta Festa in Vicenza, a work which was illustrated in a book

© Boston Athenaeum

Reading Room, Boston Athenaeum

held by the Athenaeum at that time, *Le Fabbriche e i Disegni di Andrea Palladio* by Ottavoi Bertotti Scamozzi. For years prior to this venture, Cabot had raised sheep in Vermont and Illinois! After his success in architecture, he served as the first president of the Boston Society of Architects from 1867 until 1869.

The dignified facade of gray sandstone with rich patina is visually organized into two stories. Corinthian pilasters define the window bays, with double pilasters around the window of the central projecting bay in which the entrance is situated. Pedimented windows are set within the slightly recessed arches. The first floor is treated as a more massive basement story with rusticated arches framing its windows.

The wonderfully varied and serene high-ceilinged interiors and labyrinthine

stacks have provided the perfect setting for several generations of scholars and esthetes. The cathedrallike fifth-floor reading room was added in this century by Henry Forbes Bigelow. Especially appealing is its large central space under a coffered, vaulted ceiling with many small sun-filled alcoves amidst stacks of books and odd little stairways to the upper stacks. As David McCord wrote, it "combines the best elements of the Bodleian, Monticello, the frigate *Constitution*, a greenhouse and an old New England sitting room." In earlier decades literary spinsters and old gentlemen went in the afternoon to the Athenaeum for tea of bouillon with cheese sandwiches or sweet crackers, a tradition which remained unchanged for a century, as did the original charge for tea of three cents.

An early Athenaeum librarian, Charles Ammi Cutter, developed an early and influential book classification system for the library (1874–1882), and much of the Athenaeum's collection is still organized by it, much to the bafflement of many readers. The library houses many important historical collections, including George Washington's personal library.

Chester Harding House
16 Beacon Street
1808
National Historic Landmark

This four-story brick Federal house was built by Thomas Fletcher in 1808 and now serves admirably as the headquarters of the Boston Bar Association, the

Chester Harding house

oldest legal organization in the country. Its most famous resident was the artist Chester Harding.

Amory-Ticknor House,

"Amory's Folly"
Beacon at 9 Park Street
CHARLES BULFINCH, 1803–1804;
ALTERED C. 1815 AND AFTER 1885

Bulfinch's progressive design notions and relentless concern for the good of the town over many decades were remarkable. As a member of the Board of Selectmen, he had persuaded the city to enact a town ordinance regulating building height *and* style in the European manner at the east end of the Common. When this house was built for Thomas Amory, a merchant, it was the largest house of its period in Boston.

Built on the site of the old almshouse, it was intended to set the standard for future development in the area. Unfortunately, Amory lost many of his ships at sea and went bankrupt shortly before the housewarming. Since no one could afford to purchase the house, it became a boardinghouse for politicians, and in 1806 it was divided in half. The northern half on Park Street was occupied for many years by George Ticknor, Harvard professor and historian.

Today the once great mansion stands sadly altered and barely recognizable, although the basic brick volume and Adam entrance portico with fanlight and curving granite steps (one half is missing) are more or less intact. Many ground-floor shop extensions have been added, along with Queen Anne–style oriel windows and dormers on the upper floors.

Claflin Building (William G. Preston, 1884), 20 Beacon Street

Amory-Ticknor house

Union Club (c. 1830–1840, remodeled, 1896), Park Street near Beacon Street

Staircase and entrance, Amory-Ticknor house

🏛 State House

Beacon Street
CHARLES BULFINCH, 1795–1797
RESTORED 1896–1898; REAR ANNEX: CHARLES
E. BRIGHAM, 1889–1895; WINGS: CHAPMAN,
STURGIS AND ANDREWS, 1914–1917; RENO-
VATION: SHEPLEY BULFINCH RICHARDSON AND
ABBOTT, 1993
National Historic Landmark
Open to the Public

Charles Bulfinch, self-taught and foremost architect in America in the first
decades after the Revolution, was born
in 1763 into one of Boston's wealthiest
families and was the son of a physician.
As a boy he had gone to Boston Latin
School and had watched the Battle of
Bunker Hill from the roof of his family's
home on Bowdoin Street. Between 1778
and 1781 he attended Harvard College,
where he lived in number 11 Hollis Hall.
Then in 1785 he went to Europe for a
grand tour of two years. He admired the
new English architecture, especially the
neoclassic styles of Robert Adam and Sir
William Chambers.

Returning to Boston, Bulfinch described the next several years as a "season
of leisure, pursuing no business, but giving gratuitous advice in architecture." It
was during this period that he designed
two state capitols, three churches, two
public monuments, a theater, a hotel, and
twelve private homes! Although he was
never well off financially during his
Boston career, his contributions to the
city were enormous. Besides his numerous fine buildings and ideas for civic
improvement, he was Chief of Police and
head of the Board of Selectmen for many
years. Mayor Josiah Quincy wrote of
Bulfinch: "During the many years he

presided over the town government, he
improved its finances, executed the laws
with firmness, and was distinguished for
gentleness and urbanity of manners,
integrity and purity of character. . . . Few
men deserve to be held by the Citizens
of Boston in more grateful remembrance
than Charles Bulfinch."

One of his great contributions to the
city, the state, and the country—for it
was the most outstanding public building in America for decades after its construction—was the Massachusetts State
House. Bulfinch prepared his first plan
for it on his return from Europe in 1787,
when he was but thirty-four years old.
His design was in the style of Sir William
Chambers's 1778 Somerset House in
London. Although Worcester, Plymouth,
and the South End had been considered
as a site, John Hancock's steep and
rough pasture near the summit of Beacon Hill was purchased for the new State
House. The design of the south (front)
facade features a central projecting portico with colonnade of Corinthian
columns (originally of solid Maine pine,
but replaced by cast iron in 1960) supported on an arcade of brick arches. The
gilded dome rests on a higher central
pediment with brick pilasters beneath.
Atop the dome is a lantern topped with
a gilded pinecone, symbol of the abundant forests of Massachusetts. The north
facade was similar to this, except
pilasters were used instead of a portico
colonnade.

The dome was originally white-
washed wood shingles. In 1802 the shingles were replaced with copper painted
gray, installed by Paul Revere and Sons.
This remained until 1861, when the

State House

dome was gilded; it has remained so ever since, except during World War II when it was blackened again. Brick for the State House and most Boston buildings of the period came from Charlestown. In 1825 the red brick walls were painted white and thirty years later yellow, then white again in 1918 to match the new marble wings. (In Bulfinch's time it had been common to paint the brick of more pretentious buildings, if granite or marble could not be used.) Finally in 1928 the paint was removed, exposing the red brick. Inside, one can still see most of Bulfinch's work in the Doric Hall of the first floor under the dome and in the Senate Chamber (originally the House of Representatives)

and Reception Room (originally the Senate) on the second floor. The building has suffered numerous alterations, including a long rear extension built in 1889–1895. Six times the size of the original building, of yellow brick with gray trim, the extension must have looked absurd until the marble wings added 1914–1917 obscured the view.

Bulfinch also designed state houses for Connecticut (1793–1796) and Maine (1829–1832). President Monroe, impressed with Bulfinch's Massachusetts State House and his other Boston buildings, as well as by his administrative skills, appointed Bulfinch as Architect of the Capitol in 1817. He and his wife moved to Washington and spent the

next twelve years supervising completion of the first Capitol building and
designing the west front. For Bulfinch
these were the happiest years of his life.
For the first time he felt well paid for his
services, receiving $2,500 per year. In
1829 he returned to Boston but did no
more work in the city. He died in 1844
at the age of eighty-one.

State House Annex

Shaw, the twenty-six-year-old son of an
old Boston family, died while leading his
regiment in the assault on Fort Wagner,
South Carolina, in 1863. The bas-relief
memorial was dedicated in 1897 after
thirteen years' work in the studio of
Saint-Gaudens. The monument was
beautifully sited by McKim, Mead, and
White across from the State House
between two grand elms on a small
plaza with granite balustrade overlooking the Boston Common. Broad steps on
each side lead down to the Common.

Shaw Memorial

Shaw Memorial

Beacon Street at Park Street

AUGUSTUS SAINT-GAUDENS, SCULPTOR IN
COLLABORATION WITH McKIM, MEAD, AND
WHITE, COMPLETED 1897

The first regiments of freed blacks in the
Civil War were formed in Boston. This
memorial by Augustus Saint-Gaudens
honors the very first black regiment,
which was led by Robert Gould Shaw.

George Parkman House

33 Beacon Street

CORNELIUS COOLIDGE, BUILDER, 1825

The flat brick facade of this four and one-
half–story house has been modified with
the later addition of a delicate cast-iron
verandah. George Francis Parkman lived
here after the death of his father, Dr.
George Parkman, who was murdered in
the 1850s by Harvard Professor John
White Webster in one of the grisliest and

George Parkman House

John Phillips House

Beacon Street at 1 Walnut Street
CHARLES BULFINCH, 1804–1805;
ALTERED C. 1830

John Phillips was Boston's first mayor. Originally, the entrance was on Beacon Street, at the center of a five-bay Georgian facade resembling that of the Amory-Ticknor house at the corner of Beacon and Park streets. The entrance was moved to Walnut Street about 1830, greatly compromising the architectural integrity of the house. Wendell Phillips, reformer, abolitionist, and lecturer, was born here.

most publicized murders of the nineteenth century. Parkman—along with his mother and sister—withdrew from the public eye and lived in solitude in this house from 1859 until his death in 1908. Parkman felt a strong commitment to the public parks and in his will left to the city his house and five and one-half million dollars for maintenance of the Boston Common, which the house overlooks. It has been renovated for use by the city as a conference and reception center.

The publisher Little, Brown and Company is headquartered next door at number 34 in a brick house that closely resembles 33 Beacon Street. Number 25 is also an office building, but only the first-floor facade is original to the house; the rest was built in 1926.

John Phillips house

Rippling facade, Tudor Apartments (S. J. F. Thayer, 1885–1887), 34½ Beacon Street at Joy Street

Appleton-Parker Houses

39–40 Beacon Street

ALEXANDER PARRIS, 1818;

ADDITION: HARTWELL AND RICHARDSON, 1888

National Register of Historic Places

This handsome pair of early Greek Revival bowfront row houses were for many years the home of the Women's City Club, which continues to use part of the space. The houses have Ionic porticoes, and wrought-iron balconies run across the facade on the upper floors. It was here that Henry Wadsworth Longfellow courted and married Fanny Appleton. In 1888 a fourth floor was added to both houses above the original cornice line; now there are two cornices. Later

the bow of the Appleton house was altered by the addition of an extra middle window on each of the four floors. In 1983 number 39 was renovated as condominiums.

Entrance, Appleton-Parker houses

Somerset Club

42–43 Beacon Street

ALEXANDER PARRIS, 1816–1819

National Register of Historic Places

The famous Boston painter John Singleton Copley had a house on this site and lived here until 1774, when he went to England. Four decades later Colonel David Sears built the two-story bowfront granite house that is the basis of the right half of the present structure. In 1832 the left half was added by Sears.

Since 1872 it has been the Somerset Club, an exclusive private club (until recently for men only). It was after they acquired the building that the third floor was added. The bows project more than the typical Boston bow and rise above the cornice line to create a separate volume. The rusticated garden wall distances the building from the street, increasing its monumentality.

Somerset Club

Gate, Somerset Club

🏛 Third Harrison Gray Otis House,

American Meteorological Society

45 Beacon Street

CHARLES BULFINCH, 1805–1808

Harrison Gray Otis built three notable houses, all designed by Bulfinch. Remarkably, all three are still standing today. This house in the Federal style was the last and largest of the three, and Mr. Otis remained here until his death in 1848. At the age of eighty, despite forty years of gout, he was said to breakfast on pâté de foie gras. Each afternoon ten gallons of punch were consumed from the Lowestoft bowl hospitably placed on the stair landing for those en route to the drawing room upstairs.

Samuel Eliot Morison, the Boston historian, wrote: "My great-grandmother, Emily Marshall Otis, died in childbirth in 1836. Her two little girls, Emily, my grandmother, Mary, who became Mrs. Alexander H. Stevens, and George (a childhood friend of Henry Adams), then lived in their grandfather Otis's mansion at 45 Beacon Street, where they were brought up under the care of a widowed aunt. My grandmother assured me that there was no plumbing of any description in that great house; all water had to be brought in from a well in the yard. She, Mary, and George were marched to the Tremont House once a week for a tub bath." Bathtubs were prohibited in Boston as late as 1842 because medical authorities said cockroaches lived in dirty water and died in fresh water; thus, bathwater was considered a menace.

The house was built on a foundation of stone taken from a neighboring pow-

Third Harrison Gray Otis house

Common on three sides and the courtyard on the fourth. The Blue Hills were visible across the waters of Back Bay, which came to within two hundred yards of the front door. These green surroundings were lost in 1831, when Otis built a house for his daughter. The new house stood in his garden directly to the east and wrapped around his former bow window on the second floor.

The building is now owned and occupied by the American Meteorological Society. The interior has been altered but the exterior is largely intact.

Headquarters House
55 Beacon Street
National Register of Historic Places

54–55 Beacon Street
ASHER BENJAMIN, 1808

der house. The four-story facade is organized into five bays, and the center entrance is defined by a portico with pairs of Ionic fluted columns. The ground floor originally had recessed brick arches, like most Bulfinch houses. The tall triple-hung windows of the second floor are ornamented with classical lintels supported on console brackets and with Chinese fretwork balconies, also used in the second Otis house at 85 Mount Vernon Street. A fine cobblestone courtyard leads to the carriage house, which is joined to the main house by a large servant's ell.

When the house was built, it was surrounded by English gardens and the

Asher Benjamin added considerable distinction to this pair of bowfront brick row houses by his extensive use of Greek architectural motifs, notably the three-story wooden pilasters, the first-story colonnade with delicate columns, and the balustrade atop the cornice, now missing from the house on the right. The houses have fanlight doors and ornamental iron balconies on three floors. The tall slender second-floor windows are triple-hung sash.

The left-hand house, 55 Beacon Street, is "Headquarters House" for the National Society of Colonial Dames in the Commonwealth of Massachusetts. Between 1845 and 1849 it was the residence of William Prescott, who entertained the British author William

54–55 Beacon Street

57 Beacon Street

Makepeace Thackeray as his houseguest. The house inspired Thackeray's setting for his novel *The Virginians.*

56–57 Beacon Street

EPHRAIM MARSH, 1819

These houses may have been the first built on Beacon Street with bathrooms— which were rather inconveniently located in the front room of the cellar. The construction contract specified that "in the cellar there is to be a bathing room in front into which the aqueduct is to be led" and that "the pump in the back yard is to have a box to hang meat in." The pair of bowfront row houses should be compared with those at 63–64 Beacon Street designed by the same architect a few years later. The paired entrances in this earlier set have flat Federal-style doorways, each with a fanlight and sidelights framing the door. The Victorian oriel window with decorative iron filigree on the second floor of number 57 is a later addition.

King's Chapel Parish House and Rectory

63–64 Beacon Street

EPHRAIM MARSH, 1820s

A short time after completing the very similar bowfront pair of houses at 56–57 Beacon Street, Ephraim Marsh designed

King's Chapel Parish House and Rectory

this pair with the newer Greek Revival–style portico entrances at the extreme ends of the houses rather than adjacent. To further emphasize the individuality of the houses, the portico on the right has Ionic capitals and full sidelights framing the door, while the entrance on the left has Doric capitals and a triglyph motif ornamenting the frieze. The houses are notable for the purple colored glass in their windows. Between 1818 and 1824 a glass manufacturer in England shipped glass with this unusual hue caused by the transformation of the manganese oxide. Today authentic colored windowpanes survive

only on these two houses and at 39 and 40 Beacon Street and 29A and 70B Chestnut Street.

70–75 Beacon Street
ATTRIBUTED TO ASHER BENJAMIN, 1828

Facing the Public Garden is a handsome row of light gray granite-front houses. The original pattern of three-story facades plus attic has been broken by three of the houses, and a picturesque small Victorian oriel was added to the second floor of number 70. The rusti-

70 Beacon Street

Wrought iron stair rails, 72–73 Beacon Street

The Bull & Finch Pub in the basement of the Hampshire House at 84 Beacon Street is the setting for the long-running television program "Cheers."

cated ground floor of each house has three arches with prominent voussoir patterns. Ornamental iron stair rails enhance the street scene. Distinguished though these houses now appear, when the Mount Vernon Proprietors built them on the Mill Dam they were very near the city dump. The common sewer emptied into the bay at what is now the corner of Beacon and Arlington streets, and wharf rats made their home on the west side of the Public Garden.

Deutsch House

Beaver Street at Beaver Place
GRAHAM GUND ASSOCIATES, 1983

On a street of former stables and carriage houses, this small corner house seems to grow out of the garden wall and has the air of a garden pavilion with its stucco walls clad in trellis and playful diamond and circle windows under the

Deutsch House

© Steve Rosenthal

small gables. The second-floor addition was actually built above a tiny existing house. A two-story stair hall organizes the interior space. As one moves through the hall the entire length and height of the house up to the loft in the roof can be seen, giving a sense of space despite its modest size. The materials and basic forms are traditional and familiar on Beacon Hill, but the ensemble is surprising in its context.

BRANCH STREET

This narrow lane contains a unique mix of garages, carriage-house residences, and small private gardens glimpsed through gates. It was originally known as Kitchen Street because it served the rear entrances of the houses on Beacon and Chestnut streets.

CEDAR LANE WAY

The charm of Beacon Hill lies not only in its historic architecture but also in its street pattern. The intimate pedestrian scale is as rewarding as it is rare in late twentieth-century America. Cedar Lane Way is a fine example of the benefits of high-density, low-rise residential site planning, which does not depend on outstanding architecture to create a delightful small neighborhood. This may be the narrowest street in Boston. The tiny houses and gardens are entirely consistent with the diminutive scale of the site yet provide charming interior spaces.

Cedar Lane Way

CHARLES STREET

Originally residential, Charles Street is now a pleasant shopping and service area for the adjacent neighborhood.

Many of the houses retain residential uses on one or two upper floors, while the street level and often the old cellars have been converted to shops, restaurants, or offices. In keeping with its historic character, Charles Street has been noted for its antique shops. Several of the small specialty shops have a long tradition of serving Beacon Hill families. The curve of the street around the base of Beacon Hill contributes greatly to the sense of the enclosed small-scale shopping street. The greatest alteration to Charles Street occurred in the 1920s, when it was widened. Some of the buildings on the west side lost a front portion and acquired new facades at that time, while the east side retained most of its nineteenth-century architecture. Between Revere and Cambridge streets are two groups of Greek Revival row houses (81–85 and 121, 125–135 Charles Street).

🏛 Charles Street Meeting House
70 Charles Street
ASHER BENJAMIN, 1804; RENOVATION: JOHN SHARRATT ASSOCIATES, 1982

Asher Benjamin designed this church two years before his Old West Church was built. The two brick Federal-style churches are similar, but this one is simpler. Both have rectangular towers serving as the primary facade and ceremonial entrance. The Charles Street Meeting House cupola is eight-sided and sits on a square projection above the tower.

The original congregation was the Third Baptist Church, which used the adjacent Charles River bank for its baptism ceremonies. Important antislavery

Charles Street Meeting House

Beacon Hill, so the building was sold to the Unitarian-Universalist church. It has now been converted to a mixture of office and commercial uses but retains its essential external character.

121, 125–135 Charles Street
1820s

These three-story Greek Revival brick row houses show the character of Charles Street in the early nineteenth century. Today the houses have small shops on the first floor and in the basements and apartments on the upper floors.

125–135 Charles Street

speakers were heard from the pulpit, including William Lloyd Garrision, Wendell Phillips, Frederick Douglass, Harriet Tubman, and Sojourner Truth. In 1876 it became the African Methodist Episcopal Church, conveniently located for the black population on the north slope of Beacon Hill. When Charles Street was widened in 1920, the church was moved ten feet west while its neighbors lost their facades. After the Depression the black congregation no longer lived on

CHESTNUT STREET

Starting midway up the hill at Walnut Street and running down to the Charles River and Storrow Drive, Chestnut Street epitomizes the qualities for which Beacon Hill is noted. Houses have been orna-

© John Sharratt Associates

mented to express the tastes of their owners. Ornamental iron balconies, kitchen yard gates, fences, a cast-iron hitching post, and early wrought-iron boot scrapers integrated into the delicate stair rails on several of the houses provide interest for the passing pedestrian. Altogether, it is an urban design lesson in the harmonious use of varying ornamentation on row houses of restrained but excellent architecture. Without the thoughtful embellishments so splendidly illustrated on Chestnut Street it might almost become monotonous. It is informative to compare the street with those of similar architecture in Charlestown, which in general lack these embellishments.

🏛 Charles Paine Houses, the Society of Friends

6–8 Chestnut Street

ATTRIBUTED TO CHARLES BULFINCH, 1803–1804

Few changes have been made to this pair of mirror-matched houses, which share an entrance portico with curved steps similar to those of the Amory-Ticknor house at the corner of Beacon and Park streets. Originally each house had a side garden, but when Cornelius Coolidge, merchant and architect, purchased them twenty years later, he built houses in the side lots. The brown sandstone lintels over the first- and second-floor windows are in the reed pattern. The houses are now owned by the Society of Friends.

Charles Paine houses

🏛 The Swan Houses

13, 15, and 17 Chestnut Street

CHARLES BULFINCH, 1804–1805

National Historic Landmark (number 13)

Hepzibah Swan, a Boston heiress, built these Federal houses and the stables at 50, 56, and 60 Mount Vernon Street as gifts to her three daughters upon their marriages in 1806, 1807, and 1817. Her first daughter to be married was Mrs. John Turner Sargent, who moved into number 13 Chestnut Street in 1806. The deeds carry Mrs. Swan's restriction that

The Swan houses

the roofs of the stables never be higher than thirteen feet above the street, to retain the views of Mount Vernon Street from the Chestnut Street houses. A further restriction provides a maintenance in perpetuity of a steeply sloped cattleway almost nine feet wide from the stable yards to Mount Vernon Street so that the carriages and cattle of the three houses could go in and out. This survives intact.

Although Mrs. Swan had a Boston town house, she preferred to live in her elegant country house in Dorchester overlooking Dudley Street. Also designed by Bulfinch and built about 1796 (demolished c. 1890), the house had a two-story round drawing room. Mrs. Swan's husband, Colonel James Swan, was involved in shaky financial dealings in Europe and in 1798 returned to France, where he was put in debtors' prison for the remaining twenty-two years of his life.

The houses are twenty-five feet wide, fifty feet deep, and four stories tall, plus basement and dormered attic. The simple brick facades are adorned with shuttered windows that reduce in height from the second story upward. The entry level of each house, defined by a granite foundation and a sandstone string course at ceiling height, employs recessed arches around the ground-floor windows, a favorite Bulfinch treatment that serves to set off the more important second story of the house. The entrance in the Adam style is defined by four slender fluted columns and a simple entablature. The door has sidelights. A front stair leads directly to the basement from the sidewalk.

Typical of Bulfinch, the interiors are simple, with ornament focused on the ceilings and mantels. In the original plan, still retained in number 13, the low-ceilinged entry level contains reception hall with handsome stair on the left, a front dining room, and a large rear kitchen that overlooks the spacious garden. High-ceilinged double living rooms with classic but simple detailing and fine proportions are on the *piano nobile,* the second floor, which has windows ornamented with wrought-iron railings. An arch with sliding double doors connects the double living rooms. The third floor contains two bedrooms, and the fourth floor has four servants' rooms with an attic space above. No Bulfinch house had a bathroom, but the pipeless privy was common. The introduction of the service stairway was in part to service the commode chairs in bedrooms or dressing rooms.

Julia Ward Howe, author of "Battle Hymn of the Republic," lived in number 13 for a short time and held meetings of the noted Radical Club there.

23–25 Chestnut Street

1809

A charming house typical of Chestnut Street was built at number 23 together with its neighbor at 25 by Jeremiah Gardner in 1809. The Federal-style doorway with fanlight and sidelights is recessed within a portico *in antis* framed by fluted columns supporting Ionic capitals, architrave, frieze, and cornice. The Greek inspiration for the entrance is repeated in the cast-iron corner posts of the fence, which feature the Greek key-and-anthemion motif. The balcony on the second story uses an alternating pattern of anthemion, lotus buds, and an unusual star in circle for its cast-iron ornamentation.

23–25 Chestnut Street

27 Chestnut Street

27 Chestnut Street

BELLOWS, ALDRICH, AND HOLT, 1917–1918;
RENOVATION: BULLERJAHN ASSOCIATES, 1965

An architectural oddity, this massive four-story Gothic Revival building is surprisingly compatible with the rest of Chestnut Street. Originally built as a theological school, it now houses contemporary condominiums designed by Bullerjahn in 1965. While the setback limestone facade is an interruption of the brick context, the buttresses meet the facade line of the older Chestnut Street houses.

Detail, Chestnut Street

29A Chestnut Street
CHARLES BULFINCH, 1799–1800;
REMODELED C. 1818

The noted actor Edwin Booth, brother of John Wilkes Booth, lived here at one time. The Mount Vernon Proprietors, the wealthy developers of the south slope of Beacon Hill, began by building this house and sold it to Benjamin Joy. Like that of 55 Mount Vernon Street, also by Bulfinch, its facade is perpendicular to the street and overlooks a small side garden. The mid-Georgian design may be based on a similar house built by Thomas Leverton in 1769 in London's Bedford Square. The bow front has masonry unlike the rest of the facade and is thought to have been added after 1817 by Charles R. Codman. The extension at

Ironwork, Chestnut Street

29A Chestnut Street

the back of the garden, now a separate dwelling, was built for Hopkinson's Boys' School, which occupied the buildings for a time.

Francis Parkman House
50 Chestnut Street
CORNELIUS COOLIDGE, 1830s
National Historic Landmark

In the 1830s Cornelius Coolidge was actively involved as architect and builder of a number of Chestnut Street houses on the south side of the street, of which this is one. The noted American historian, Francis Parkman, lived here from 1865 until 1893.

Window, Chestnut Street

Francis Parkman house

Harvard Musical Association
57A Chestnut Street
WEST CEDAR STREET SECTION, 1827

In 1837 several Harvard graduates founded the Harvard Musical Association to provide a focus for musical gatherings and to encourage Harvard College to establish a department of music. In 1900 the organization purchased this building for its musical men's club. Many of the members formerly had been in the Harvard University Band. On the second floor is a fine concert hall for their musical evenings. Baked beans and beer followed by Welsh rarebit (no dessert) make up the traditional menu for the substantial pre-concert suppers. The first music library in the country was established by the Association. Note the ornamental iron lyre inset in the brick wall on West Cedar Street.

Harvard Musical Association

JOY STREET

Joy Street is one of the oldest streets in Boston and dates from 1661. It was originally two streets, Belknap's Lane on the north slope and George Street on the south slope. Not until 1803 were they joined across Myrtle Street when the ropewalks (see p. 205) were dismantled. In 1851 the George Street section was renamed after an apothecary, Dr. John Joy, who had acquired two acres of land on George Street in 1791 and was thus the primary property owner. Dr. Joy's third house was built in 1822 on his George Street property but facing Mount Vernon. This house, number 32 Mount Vernon, was purchased by Dr. Samuel Gridley Howe and his wife Julia Ward Howe in the 1870s.

🏛 Louisburg Square

PLAN: S. P. FULLER, 1826;
HOUSES BUILT 1834–1848

For many people Louisburg Square is the epitome and heart of Beacon Hill. It demonstrates the enormous impact of thoughtful site planning at the neighborhood scale. Its cobblestone street and green center park defined by a tall iron fence are flanked by facing rows of dignified and varied red brick row houses.

The Mount Vernon Proprietors had a plan drawn by S. P. Fuller for this development area, but the first house was not built on the Square until almost a decade later. The notion of the private elongated oval park in the center with common ownership by all the property owners fronting on it was an innovation in the United States. The Louisburg Square Proprietors were the first home association in the country and had the responsibility of taxing the various owners for the maintenance of the park. When the trees were trimmed, the wood was divided into twenty-two stacks and delivered to the twenty-two houses for the owners to burn in their fireplaces. The statues of Aristides and Columbus were donated in 1850 by a Greek merchant, Joseph Iasigi, of number 3 Louisburg Square. When boys vandalized the statues, the Proprietors voted that no outsiders should be allowed within the park and built the fence of iron bars with cast-iron ornaments and posts.

The tradition in America of Christmas Eve caroling and candles in windows started here in the late nineteenth century. It continues in Louisburg Square today as groups gather in the snow to hear the famous bell ringers and to enjoy the special flavor that Beacon Hill imparts to Christmas.

Louisburg Square

1 and 3 Louisburg Square
1846–1847

This pair of bowfront houses is ornamented with elaborate cast-iron balconies at the second story. Noteworthy
wrought-iron serpents have twisted
tongues and tails forming flagpole holders. Number 2, across Louisburg Square,
was built at the same time as this pair.

4 and 6 Louisburg Square
1842

In contrast to the rest of the west side of
the Square, numbers 2, 4, and 6 are flat-
facade buildings with number 2 the
largest of all. The pair built at 4 and 6
are in the restrained Federal Revival style
with tall windows and cast-iron balcony
on the second level. William Dean How-
ells lived at number 4 while he was edi-

Entrance, 8 Louisburg Square

1 and 3 Louisburg Square

tor of the *Atlantic Monthly.* Number 6 was the original home of the elite Number Six Club for MIT undergraduates.

Louisa May Alcott House

10 Louisburg Square

1835

After Louisa May Alcott's literary success, she purchased this house and moved her penniless parents and sisters here from 20 Pinckney Street. Her imaginative but impecunious father, Bronson Alcott, died in the house just before Louisa herself succumbed. Like numbers 8–22, the

Alcott house is a three-story bowfront plus dormered attic. Originally all these houses had dining rooms in the basement kitchen level with windows looking up toward the sidewalk. Most of the houses have now been considerably altered inside.

14–20 Louisburg Square

1836

On February 15, 1852, Jenny Lind, the "Swedish Nightingale," was married at 20 Louisburg Square to her accompanist, Otto Goldschmidt. The house belonged to Samuel Ward, the representative of Jenny Lind's London bankers and the brother of Julia Ward Howe. The marriage marked the completion of an American tour that earned P. T. Barnum a half-million-dollar profit. The ever resourceful Barnum had neither seen nor heard the Swedish soprano when he signed her to an American tour at fees that were enormous for those days. For a year before the tour, Barnum ran a national publicity blitz based largely on his imagination. By the time Jenny Lind arrived in America, Barnum had succeeded in arousing the American public to a frenzy of excitement about this unknown singer.

🏛 MOUNT VERNON STREET

Henry James said of Mount Vernon Street that it was "the only respectable street in America." Originally called Olive Street, it sweeps majestically from the Bowdoin Street side of the State House, through the passage beneath the Annex, past the fine residences built by the Mount Vernon Proprietors, and down the hill toward the Charles River. The group of wealthy investors included Harrison Gray Otis, Jonathan Mason, Charles Bulfinch, Benjamin Joy, and Mrs. James Swan. Harrison Gray Otis had wangled eighteen acres of pasture from John Singleton Copley's agent for the bargain price of $1,000 per acre, despite Copley's horrified but tardy protests from England. The Proprietors began building in 1799 and did not complete the development of the land until 1848.

Like many developers after them, they demolished fine buildings, large old Federal mansions in this case. Bulfinch designed a few of the houses built by the group and has a total of twelve houses remaining on Beacon Hill. For

more than three decades after Bulfinch, Greek Revival was the predominant style of Beacon Hill architecture, creating a beautiful blend with the older Federal row houses and a harmonious neighborhood that is widely admired.

Beacon Hill Memorial Column

Mount Vernon Street behind the State House

CHARLES BULFINCH, 1790–1791; REBUILT 1865

Ashburton Park

CAROL R. JOHNSON & ASSOCIATES, INC., 1990

The summit of Beacon Hill, first called Sentry Hill, was originally sixty feet higher than it is today and was roughly in the area of the State House Annex. In 1634 a beacon on a wooden pole was placed at the top of the hill by the general court "to give notice of any danger." It remained there until one windy November night in 1789 when it blew down. The young Charles Bulfinch proposed to replace it with a monument to the American Revolution, a classical column such as those he had seen in Europe, and proceeded on his own to solicit donations for its construction. The sixty-foot monument was composed of a gilded eagle atop a Doric column made of plaster on brick, set on a stone pedestal that had four commemorative plaques.

Because of poor construction, the column began to deteriorate after only two years. It was finally taken down in 1811 by John Hancock's money-hungry heirs, who had purchased the hill at a

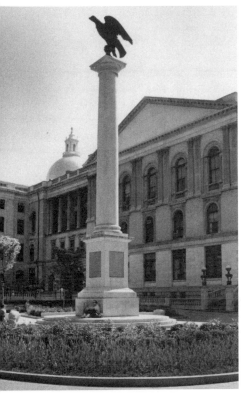

Beacon Hill Memorial Column

versial but is hardly inspired by this historic setting.

Lyman-Paine House
Mount Vernon Street at 6 Joy Street
ALEXANDER PARRIS, 1824

At the busy intersection of Mount Vernon and Joy streets is this solid four and one-half–story house with lovely private garden bordered by an unusual wrought-iron fence with wavy bars. Its unpretentious facade with some asymmetrical elements is pleasing but unusual for this period on Beacon Hill. Exterior ornament is largely focused on the Greek Revival entrance on Joy Street.

Lyman-Paine house

public auction. By leveling the summit they made almost fifty acres of new land in the old millpond at the foot of the hill. In 1898 the column was reconstructed, sixty feet lower and one hundred feet to the east of its original position. Until 1990, when a new underground garage was built, the column stood awkwardly in the State House parking lot. Atop the garage is a park enclosed by a stone balustrade and iron fence. The design focus is the column on its central pedestal, surrounded by quarter-circle flower beds and grass with flower borders. The design is certainly noncontro-

With neighbors such as the State House, Little, Brown, and Company, and the Appalachian Mountain Club, the serenity within the house is a surprise. The garret apartment has wonderful views over Beacon Hill and the Boston Common. This house and the one next door at 18 Mount Vernon Street were interconnected and owned by the same family from the time of construction until 1943.

28, 30, 32, and 34 Mount Vernon Street

1822

Number 32, Dr. John Joy's house, was sold to Dr. Samuel Gridley Howe and his wife Julia Ward Howe, author of "The Battle Hymn of the Republic," in the 1870s. They entertained notable people on a regular basis, among them General Ulysses S. Grant and the writer Bret Harte, who was served a hearty breakfast that included broiled chickens, English bacon, and buckwheat cakes.

Dr. Howe is best remembered as the founder of the Perkins Institution for the Blind. Less well known is his role as the organizer of the Committee of Vigilance to protect fugitive slaves. On September 26, 1846 Dr. Howe wrote to forty abolitionist acquaintances informing them that they had been selected as members of the Committee to prevent the return of any fugitive slaves who had sought safety in Massachusetts. The Committee had a distinguished career, with records of aid given to more than three hundred fugitive slaves, most of whom were men. The money for all the activities of the Committee came from its prominent Boston members. Often the Committee paid for railroad and boat fares to take the fugitives to safety in the Maritime Provinces. Not only did the Committee aid runaway slaves who had taken the initiative to escape, but if word came to them of slaves being held in any ship in the harbor, a daring rescue was sometimes undertaken. The Committee also printed and circulated abolitionist sermons, provided legal defense for any fugitive slave in jeopardy, and pressed for legal changes within the government.

28–34 Mount Vernon Street

37 Mount Vernon Street
1805

Flemish bond brickwork, rarely used after the early nineteenth century, is found in this four-story house with brownstone string course and granite foundation. A "header" brick—the short end of the brick—is laid alternating with the long side—the "stretcher" side of the brick. Each row is identical, but the order is offset so that an interesting pattern results.

John Callender's "small house for little money"

🏛 John Callender's "Small House for Little Money"
Mount Vernon Street at 14 Walnut Street
1802

John Callender's "small house for little money" was built on land purchased from Dr. Joy and was one of the first houses on Mount Vernon Street. The lot cost Mr. Callender $2,155, and he spent between $5,000 and $7,000 on the construction of the house in 1802. Its Federal-style brick sheathed in butt-joined boards is typical of the period. The Mount Vernon Street side was the original entry facade of the house, but in 1821 the elevation of Walnut Street was lowered by the city, so a fine large retaining wall had to be built for the garden. Mr. Callender decided to move the entrance to Walnut Street at the lower level, leaving an uncharacteristic Federal facade on Mount Vernon Street. Someone later added the curious oriel window near the corner of the Mt. Vernon Street facade. The wonderful large garden in the rear has street access through an arched passageway.

40–42 Mount Vernon Street
1850

Augustus Hemenway demolished an 1822 mansion in order to build this large brownstone pair in 1850. For many years it served as the World Peace Foundation but is now condominium apartments.

44, 46, and 48
Mount Vernon Street
1820s

These dignified smaller houses typify much of the fabric of the south slope of Beacon Hill. In each house a fine detailed recessed entry with fanlight and leaded sidelights around the door provides a gracious entry into the first-floor hallway, parlor, and dining room. The basements have inconspicuous front entries with steep descending steps and dwarf-size doors.

Swan Stables
50–60 Mount Vernon Street
CHARLES BULFINCH, 1804–1805

The stables, now converted to dwellings, were built by Hepzibah Swan to accompany the houses for her three daughters at 13, 15, and 17 Chestnut Street. They are restricted by deed to a height of thirteen feet (see 13, 15, 17 Chestnut Street, p. 165). The cattle ramp remains in its original condition, ready to serve as carriage and cattle access for the Swan houses.

Swan stables

Entrance, 46 Mount Vernon Street

Mason Houses
51–57 Mount Vernon Street

🏛 Nichols House Museum
55 Mount Vernon Street
CHARLES BULFINCH, 1804
Open to the Public

Jonathan Mason, one of the Mount Vernon Proprietors, commissioned Bulfinch to design this series of houses for his daughters. Originally both 55 and 57, which stepped back, faced Mason's gardens and his Bulfinch-designed mansion to the west (demolished). Number 57 had a side entrance like that of 55, but when a house was built directly to the west in 1837, cutting off its view, the entrance was moved to face the street and the eight-foot space between the houses was filled with an extension.

Daniel Webster lived in 57 from 1817 to 1819 and Charles Francis Adams lived there from 1842 to 1886. His sons, Charles Francis Adams II and Henry Adams, author of *Mont St. Michel and Chartres*, spent their boyhoods here.

Except for 55, all of the houses have been greatly altered; in 55 only the entrance portico is not original. Miss Rose Nichols, writer, landscape architect, niece of Augustus Saint-Gaudens, and true Beacon Hill eccentric, was the last resident of 55. Her sister, Mrs. Arthur Shurcliff, started Beacon Hill's Christmas Eve tradition of hand bell ringing in Louisburg Square. When Rose Nichols died at eighty-eight in 1960 she left her house and furnishings to the public as a museum, the only private house museum on Beacon Hill.

Nichols House Museum

59–83 Mount Vernon Street
1836–1837 (NOS. 61 & 65 REBUILT)

59 Mount Vernon Street
EDWARD SHAW, 1837

Jonathan Mason built a large stone mansion designed by Bulfinch on the north side of Mount Vernon Street with stables behind it on Pinckney Street. When he died in 1836, both the mansion and the stables were torn down and the Greek Revival houses numbered 59 through 83 were built on the vacated land. The gra-

59 Mount Vernon Street

61 Mount Vernon Street

Mount Vernon Proprietor Harrison Gray Otis had agreed to maintain this setback on their adjoining properties.

Number 59 has the restrained dignity of the Greek Revival style in its four-story bow front plus attic with handsome Ionic portico *in antis* supported on Ionic columns. Number 61 has a flamboyant and impressive cast-iron fence of large scrolled vines with anthemion-and-lotus motifs supported on massive lotus posts. The gate, largely of cast iron, is designed to fit within the carved granite posts. Number 77 houses the venerable Club of Odd Volumes, whose small membership is limited to distinguished book collectors, publishers, and writers. Sir Winston Churchill was given a luncheon here by his American publishers, the Boston firm of Houghton Mifflin.

70–72 Mount Vernon Street

RICHARD UPJOHN, 1847;
RENOVATION: BULLERJAHN ASSOCIATES, 1965

John and Nathaniel Thayer left their rural life in Lancaster, Massachusetts, where their father was a minister, to make their fortune as Boston bankers. Needing houses, they commissioned Richard Upjohn to design this massive adjoining pair for them. After their deaths the buildings served for many years as the Boston University Theological School and were connected to the Gothic Revival structure at 27 Chestnut Street. In 1965 the Mount Vernon and Chestnut Street buildings were renovated as apartments and are now condominiums. Preservation-conscious Beacon Hill residents prevented the buildings from being

cious thirty-foot setback distinguishes this block from any other on Beacon Hill. Jonathan Mason and his fellow

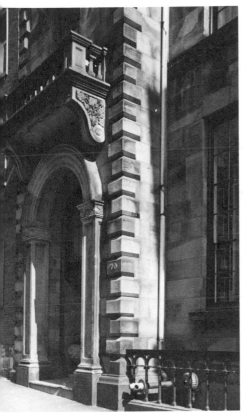

70–72 Mount Vernon Street

razed by a developer who planned to erect a new apartment building.

Everything about these brownstone houses is large and different in scale from the rest of the street. The first-floor windows are twice the height of those of the neighboring houses, and the first two floors could contain nearly three floors of a typical Beacon Hill house. Projecting entrance bays with quoins, tall recessed round arches, and projecting balconies on brackets define each end of the facade. Third-floor windows have heavy

projecting stone lintels on brackets. The large second-floor windows appear to be later alterations, replacing narrow windows like those on the other floors. The interiors are completely contemporary.

🏛 Second Harrison Gray Otis House

85 Mount Vernon Street
CHARLES BULFINCH, 1800–1802
National Register of Historic Places

In this second house designed for Otis, Bulfinch attempted to establish the character he hoped would prevail for the rest of the development by the Mount Vernon Proprietors on the land formerly owned by John Singleton Copley, the painter. Bulfinch's vision of Mount Vernon Street lined with grand freestanding mansions on spacious landscaped grounds obviously did not materialize. This house remains the exception to Beacon Hill's dense development.

As in many other Bulfinch works, the ground-floor windows are set within recessed arches, but in this case the tall windows, ornamented with iron railings of Chinese fretwork, are those of the principal rooms of the house. In contrast, the third-story windows are small squares. Several strong ornamental features enliven the facade. Two-story Corinthian pilasters resting on a string course define the ends of the four-bay facade. The cornice is surmounted by a balustrade and on the roof is an octagonal cupola.

A cobblestone drive leads to the entrance and to the rear stable, now a separate dwelling. The original entrance

Second Harrison Gray Otis house

was on the other end of the house, where the bow window is now located. Otis lived here only until 1806, when he sold the house to the widow of a Salem merchant for $22,984. One twentieth-century owner was an elderly lady who occupied the entire house, but she spent most of her time living frugally in a single third-story room, its floor covered with linoleum, heated by a small freestanding gas heater.

Stephen Higginson House
87 Mount Vernon Street
CHARLES BULFINCH, 1804–1809

Between 1804 and 1806 Bulfinch was involved in at least eighteen building projects, in addition to being head of the Board of Selectmen and chief of police for Boston.

Bulfinch bought this property and that next door at 89 Mount Vernon and built twin houses on it, which he then sold to Stephen Higginson, Jr., a banker (number 87), and to David Humphreys, a Connecticut mill owner (number 89). The houses were set back to conform with the thirty-

Cobblestone drive, 85 Mount Vernon Street

foot setback of the Otis house at 85 Mount Vernon Street. Elaborate tall windows grace the second-floor parlors. Placement of the entrance in the second bay of the first floor allowed creation of two rooms in addition to the entrance hall.

More than twenty craftsmen were involved in the Mount Vernon Street houses, including ornamental plasterer Daniel Raynerd and woodcarver Simeon Skillin, who also carved the State House capitals. The ornamental plaster and woodwork are most evident in the parlors on the second floor. Number 87 was for many years the home of General Charles J. Paine, America's Cup defender and yachtsman. It is now headquarters for the Colonial Society of Massachusetts. Number 87 has been altered beyond recognition and is now twentieth-century Georgian.

🏛 "Sunflower House"
130 Mount Vernon Street
1840; RENOVATION: CHARLES LUCE, 1878

Charles Luce had some fun when he transformed a small 1840 house into a whimsical Tudor (some use the more general category of Queen Anne) cottage. The stuccoed first floor and garden wall are painted bright yellow in gay contrast with the red English-style tiles on the second floor. The huge carved sunflower under the half-timber gable is hardly the traditional Tudor flower. The projecting entrance is centered beneath the Tudor Revival jetty supporting the overhanging second story on the Mount Vernon Street facade. A large ornamented dormer penetrates the roof of the River Street side.

"Sunflower House"

🏛 Church of the Advent
Mount Vernon Street at Brimmer Street
STURGIS AND BRIGHAM, 1875–1888;
LADY CHAPEL INTERIOR: CRAM AND
GOODHUE, 1894

The congregation of the Church of the Advent was founded in 1844 in the old West End to bring the Oxford Movement to Boston and has always been considered very high church. In 1883 they moved into this brick and stone Gothic Revival church with Perpendicular influence. Its art and liturgy caused a sensation in Puritan Boston and made it something of a tourist attraction in the later nineteenth century. The tower has angle buttresses and a spire of brick and stone with gablet-topped lucarne windows on each face. It houses one of the finest sets of carillon bells in the country. At the base of the tower are clustered chapels, forming a delightfully complex frontage along Mount Vernon Street.

The highly ornamented interior spaces were designed for religious ceremony. Tall striped Gothic arches rest on striped columns, while several rows of

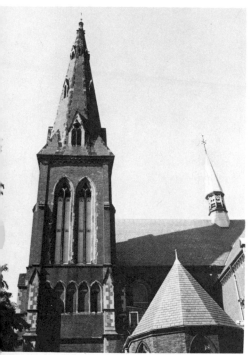

Church of the Advent

Cram and Bertram Goodhue and illustrate Cram's concern with making ornament serve the larger purposes of the architecture and its ceremonial functions. The attractive garden of the church rectory is sometimes open to the public.

Samuel Eliot Morison House
Mount Vernon Street at
44 Brimmer Street
1850s

This Victorian house was continually inhabited by the family of historian Samuel Eliot Morison until his death in 1976.

light-colored string courses accentuate the form of the apse. The high altar, designed by Sturgis, and the screen above it by Sir Ernest George and Harold Peto, were both given to the church by Isabella Stewart Gardner ("Mrs. Jack"), one of the more colorful parishioners. It is told that as penance for one of her more flamboyant escapades she was required to scrub the church steps during Lent. The stained-glass windows include work by the English makers Kempe, Clayton and Bell, and Christopher Whall. The Lady Chapel interiors, executed in 1894, were the first important religious interiors by Ralph Adams

Samuel Eliot Morison House

PINCKNEY STREET

Along with Myrtle Street, Pinckney acts as a dividing line between the dignified south slope and the Bohemian north slope of Beacon Hill. The difference is that Pinckney Street has always been a part of the south slope because in its earliest history Pinckney was cut off from the north slope by the Myrtle Street ropewalks. The street is named for Charles E. Pinckney, who said, "Millions for defense, but not one cent for tribute" when it was suggested that Talleyrand be offered a bribe to receive the American ministers. With its steep slope diving toward Charles Street and the Charles River and its frontage on Louisburg Square, it has always been known for its fine views. The repeating bow fronts cascading down the hill have awed many visitors and residents with their beauty, particularly at sunset.

Middleton-Glapion House

🏛 Middleton-Glapion House

5 Pinckney Street

c. 1795

George Middleton, a black coachman and Revolutionary War soldier, and Louis Glapion, a mulatto barber, built this house at the end of the eighteenth century. A two-story clapboard house, it has had an attic dormer added, but otherwise remains among the oldest and least changed buildings on Beacon Hill.

Hidden Houses

9½ and 74½ Pinckney Street

These houses are hidden from the street, being located in the middle of the block. They are entered through tunnels or "sally ports." Number 9½ Pinckney has a tunnel that leads to a courtyard on which there are three hidden houses.

17–19 Pinckney Street

This Federal-style three-story framehouse stands perpendicular to the street, like many houses of the period (including number 21 next door), and faces an intimate courtyard that it shares with its clapboard neighbor at the rear of the site. Number 17 has prominent corner quoins, flat Federal entrance with fanlight and sidelights, and a Victorian oriel on its narrow street facade.

17 Pinckney Street

20 Pinckney Street

This modest house was the first Beacon Hill home of Bronson Alcott, Louisa May Alcott's father, and his family. Later they moved to Louisburg Square (see 10 Louisburg Square, p. 173).

🏛 House of Odd Windows

24 Pinckney Street

RENOVATION: WILLIAM RALPH EMERSON, 1884

Ralph Waldo Emerson's nephew, William, designed this house with extraordinary individuality. From its rooftop eyelid window to the small square window sharing the door lintel, every window in the house is different but exquisitely proportioned and placed. Emerson predated Robert Venturi by almost a century in his "complex and contradictory" renovation of this former carriage house.

Pie-Shaped House

56 Pinckney Street

Although this house has a typical and very attractive bay-front street facade suggesting no less spaciousness and grandeur than its neighbors, the interior reveals a

Pie-shaped house

House of odd windows

surprise that is quite charming. Because it is squeezed between its neighbors, the house gradually narrows to a point!

House with Hidden Chamber for Fugitive Slaves
62 Pinckney Street
1846

A number of houses on Beacon Hill were stopping points on the Underground Railroad, including this brick row house built for George S. Hillard. Beginning in the 1850s many white abolitionists in Boston provided secret quarters for fugitive slaves,

since it frequently became too hazardous to board them among black Bostonians. Since Hillard was an ardent Webster Whig, it would be most unlikely to suspect him of harboring runaway slaves in his own home. It is unclear whether he knew they were there, but his wife was an enthusiastic abolitionist and her friends knew she helped the "underground" people. While making repairs to the house in the 1920s, workmen discovered a small attic space in the ell accessible through a concealed trap door in a closet. Although the space had no windows, it had provisions for ventilation and was large enough to hold several people. Two tin plates and two iron spoons were found, perhaps remains of the last meal eaten there.

Boston English High School
now condominiums
Pinckney Street at 65 Anderson Street
1824; RENOVATION: GRAHAM, MEUS, 1983–1984

This cruciform school building was influenced by the work of Charles Bulfinch and Asher Benjamin and uses relieving arches above the second-story windows. It served as the first building of the English High School until 1844, when the Phillips School, a grammar school named after the first mayor of Boston, John Phillips, moved in. The school accepted both black and white boys and was the first integrated school in Boston. In 1861 the Phillips School moved, to be replaced by the Sharp School, a public school. Today the building has been recycled as twelve condominium units.

English High School

7, 9, and 11 West Cedar Street
ASHER BENJAMIN C. 1825

These restrained brick row houses by Asher Benjamin contribute enormously to the elegance of West Cedar Street. Benjamin designed and built number 9 as his own residence. The tall second-story windows of numbers 7–9 are beautifully ornamented by a cast-iron balcony railing with beveled scrolls and ribbed leaves.

Ironwork, 7–9 West Cedar Street

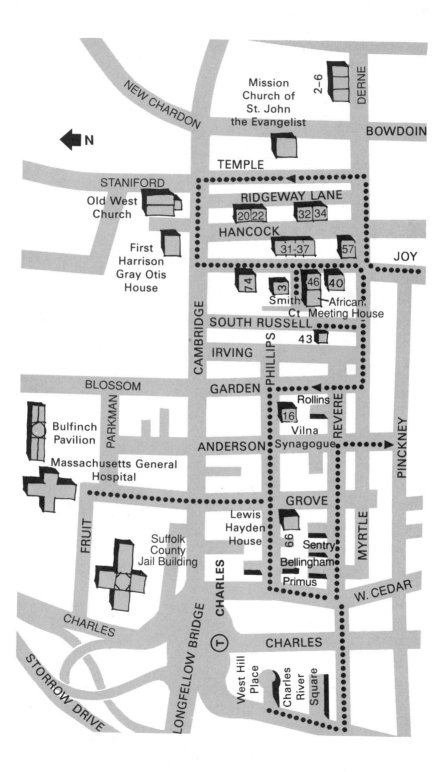

The North Slope

Beacon Hill—North Slope Tour

Begin the tour at the corner of Joy and Myrtle streets behind the **State House** (**152**). Walk on Derne Street to **Temple Walk,** a pedestrian street (**209**). Proceed down it toward the **Old West Church** and **first Harrison Gray Otis house** (**196–97**) and then walk back up the hill on Joy Street, passing **74 Joy Street, Smith Court** and the **African Meeting House,** and the **old Joy horse stables** (**201**). Turn right onto **Myrtle Street** (**205**), the site of ropewalks in the eighteenth century.

Turn right onto South Russell Street to see one of the oldest houses on Beacon Hill, the **Ditson house** (**209**), then return to Myrtle Street and turn right on Garden Street, then left onto Phillips Street. Here you will find the **Old Historic Vilna Synagogue,** the **Lewis Hayden house,** and **Primus Avenue** and **"flower lane"** (**206–7**). A side trip may be taken down Grove Street to **Massachusetts General Hospital** and the **Bulfinch Pavilion and Ether Dome** (**195**). Turn left onto West Cedar Street and consider a side trip down Revere Street to **Charles River Square** and **West Hill Place** (**197**) and to the **Longfellow Bridge** and the **Suffolk County Jail** (**193**). Otherwise, complete your tour by turning left up Revere Street past many charming **cul-de-sacs** (**207**) and return to Myrtle Street.

Mission Church of St. John the Evangelist

🏛 Mission Church of St. John the Evangelist
35 Bowdoin Street
SOLOMON WILLARD, 1831

A harmonious row of brick bowfront houses along Bowdoin Street forms a solid boundary defining the northeast side of historic Beacon Hill. The focus is this English Gothic Revival church of handsome rough dark granite blocks. The back side seen from Temple Street is almost as striking as the front. The heavy square crenellated tower has quatrefoil windows. Originally the church was built for the Congregational Society led by Harriet Beecher Stowe's father. In 1883, it became the Church of St. John the Evangelist, the mother church for the Cowley fathers of the Society of St. John the Evangelist and the highest Episcopal Church in Boston. The contemporary stained-glass window visible at the entrance was designed by the artist Gyorgy Kepes.

CAMBRIDGE STREET

Cambridge Street forms an abrupt and hard edge separating the historic district of Beacon Hill from the West End. Redeveloped beginning in the 1950s, the West End was the site of some of the first federally funded urban renewal projects in the country. Few remnants survive of the old West End with its teeming street life and intimate streets lined by three- and four-story brick row houses. Many Bostonians have fond memories of growing up there, in a neighborhood that, like the North End, was the first American home for countless families of immigrants. A generation of sociologists studied the impact of the redevelopment on the people who were forced to relocate, and much current social planning theory has its roots here.

As its name tells us, the street leads to Cambridge via the picturesque Longfellow Bridge. Nicknamed the "pepperpot" bridge because of its towers, it was designed in 1907 by Edmund March Wheelwright and was influenced by one he had seen in St. Petersburg, Russia.

Suffolk County Jail Building

Charles Street at Cambridge Street
GRIDLEY J. FOX BRYANT, 1851
National Register of Historic Places

This solid cruciform building was built as a jail in 1851. Made of Quincy granite, it has prominent quoins at the corners and keystones above the windows that add to the dignity and seriousness of purpose communicated by the building. The central hipped-roof octagonal pavilion has four four-story hipped-roof wings. The west wing was originally the sheriff's home and office, hospital, and chapel. In 1901 the north wing was enlarged following Bryant's original design for the earlier building, and in 1920 the west wing was doubled, again following the original design.

George R. White Memorial Building

off Cambridge Street on Fruit Street
COOLIDGE SHEPLEY BULFINCH AND ABBOTT, 1939

The main building of Massachusetts General Hospital, this was designed one year

© Shepley Bulfinch Richardson and Abbott

George R. White Memorial Building

Bulfinch Pavilion and Ether Dome

after the architects' now-classic B. B. Chemical Building in Cambridge (1938, now Polaroid, 784 Memorial Drive). Both buildings were conceived in an Art Deco–International Style vein. The White Building is of light gray brick with stepped massing and faceted projecting bays. Its distinctive form has made it a widely recognized city landmark. Designed to be functional and modern, it avoids historicism, in contrast to much of the firm's work of the period. The firm is noted for its hospitals, including the Boston Hospital for Women, Boston City Hospital, New England Deaconess and Baptist Hospitals, and the Peking Union Medical Center.

🏛 Bulfinch Pavilion and Ether Dome

Massachusetts General Hospital near Cambridge Street and Fruit Street (go to main hospital entrance and ask directions at the information desk)
CHARLES BULFINCH, 1818–1823; ALTERED 1844 AND LATER

National Historic Landmark

In 1816 Bulfinch was sent by the hospital board to examine several hospitals in New York, Philadelphia, and Baltimore. Already $100,000 had been raised for a new hospital, and in 1817 an award of $100 was offered to the designer of the best plan for a hospital to be built specifically of Chelmsford granite cut at the state prison in Charlestown. Bulfinch won the commission, which was his last in Boston. Alexander Parris, who was to become an important Boston architect, prepared the working drawings.

The building, influenced by the work of Robert Adam and John Soane with its central columned portico and wings on a rusticated granite base, was widely admired and employed the most progressive ideas of the time. The operating theater with seating for observers was beneath a skylit dome.

Bulfinch's design for the operating dome was not original, for he had seen similar ones at the Pennsylvania Hospital in Philadelphia and at the Massachusetts Medical College in Boston, completed in 1816.

The first public demonstration of the use of ether as an anesthetic was conducted in the dome in 1846 by Dr. John Collins Warren, one of the founders of the hospital. The patient was Gilbert Abbott, and the ether was administered by William Thomas Green Morton.

On the floors below the dome were administrative offices, the apothecary, and on the lowest floor, the kitchen, bathing room, and laundry. Cantilevered stairways of solid granite were similar to those of University Hall at Harvard and are one of the few interior features that survive intact. Wings contained wards and private rooms for patients totaling one hundred beds. In the basement, furnaces supplied heat to the upper floors through air flues. Water was piped through the building by pump.

Today nineteenth-century medical instruments and documents are exhibited in the building, but most of the space is still used for hospital purposes. The building is substantially altered and has been surrounded by a jumble of unsympathetic structures, making it difficult to find. The south elevation is the least changed, but the wings have been extended and the pediment altered. One of the best views of the dome is from the top of Anderson Street at Pinckney Street on Beacon Hill.

Harvard's Littauer Center, designed by Coolidge Shepley Bulfinch and Abbott in 1938 of Chelmsford granite, was inspired by this building.

🏛 First Harrison Gray Otis House

141 Cambridge Street
CHARLES BULFINCH, 1795–1796;
RESTORATION BEGUN 1916

National Historic Landmark

Open to the Public

This is the first of three grand houses Bulfinch designed in the ten-year period 1795–1805 for Harrison Gray Otis—Mas-sachusetts senator, third mayor of Boston, and flamboyant socialite. The Federal design is based on the William Bingham house Bulfinch saw when he was in Philadelphia in 1789, a house which in turn was derived from one in London.

The elegant facade of brick is symmetrically organized around the central bay containing entrance and stair hall. Above the entrance, which was added after 1801, is a Palladian window with pilasters, and on the third floor a lunette. Each story is defined by a brownstone string course. The floor plan is arranged in the Colonial manner with two rooms on each side of the central stair hall and the kitchen in an ell. Third-floor ceilings are exceedingly low, barely over six feet.

In the 1830s the house was used as a ladies' Turkish bath. Then it became a patent medicine shop, followed by a ladies' boarding-house. By 1916 it was in

First Harrison Gray Otis house

a terrible state when restoration work was begun. In 1926 Cambridge Street was widened, forcing the house to be moved back forty feet. The original expansive front terrace and carriage approach were reduced to barely enough room for the front steps. The house is now owned by the Society for the Preservation of New England Antiquities.

🏛 Old West Church
Cambridge Street
ASHER BENJAMIN, 1806
National Historic Landmark

In 1737 a wood frame church was built on this site. During the British occupation the church became a barracks until 1775 when it was razed by the troops who suspected that the steeple was being used by revolutionary sympathizers to signal the Continental troops in Cambridge. Not until three decades after the Revolution was this handsome red brick Federal church built on the site of the pre-Revolutionary church.

As in Asher Benjamin's earlier Charles Street Meeting House, the entrances and cupola are placed on a three and one half-story projecting block. Four two-story brick pilasters, highlighted with white wood trim, define three entry doors. The third level of the tower is ornamented with pairs of Doric pilasters that support a triglyph frieze. Beneath the square wood cupola are swag-ornamented clocks on both the short and the long sides of the tower. The church has a fine Fisk tracker-action pipe organ.

2–6 Derne Street
c. 1846

On this very short street in the shadow of the State House, the Greek Revival houses at 2–6 form a boundary for residential Beacon Hill in contrast to the massive scale of the State House and Government Center adjoining it. Originally three narrow brick four-story-plus-attic houses, they now have apartments and offices in them. The flat facades are ornamented by cast-iron balconies added later at the second story and by the granite lintels and sills of the windows.

EMBANKMENT ROAD

With the completion of the Charles River Dam in 1910 this street was laid out on filled land and changed the character of the area. Charles River Square and West Hill Place were built where a coal yard had previously been.

Annie Fields (wife of James T. Fields, who was proprietor of the famous Old Corner Bookstore) entertained Charles Dickens during his Boston visit in the lovely garden behind her house at 148 Charles Street (demolished). The garden contained shrubs planted by Henry Wadsworth Longfellow. In *Not Under Forty* Willa Cather told of Annie Fields, the great hostess who was especially fond of artists, writers, and actors. Annie's garden remains in a much altered form and, although private, is visible from Embankment Road adjacent to West Hill Place. The two squares of brick Federal Revival houses relate harmoniously to historic Beacon Hill architecture. Each group focuses on its own inner space rather than on the large-scale river and Esplanade.

Old West Church

HANCOCK STREET

Hancock Street is unique in having large and significant buildings by Charles Bulfinch framing both ends of its two-block length. Walking up Hancock Street one sees the State House, while walking down the street the first Harrison Gray Otis house is the focus. Perhaps inspired by its fine architectural examples at each end, the street has many worthy houses in the Federal, Greek Revival, and even Egyptian Revival styles. The row of seven narrow Federal houses at numbers 11–23 were built about 1808. On the upper block of the street between Myrtle and Mount Vernon streets, several of the mid-nineteenth-century houses have attractive cast-iron balconies based on the anthemion motif.

Home of Charles Sumner

20 Hancock Street

1805

National Historic Landmark

22 Hancock Street

1805

This pair of three-bay brick Federal houses features Greek Revival porticoes. Number 20 was the home of Senator Charles Sumner from 1830 until 1867.

31–37 Hancock Street

ATTRIBUTED TO JONATHAN PRESTON, 1859

The marble facades of these houses set back from the property lines are a great surprise on Beacon Hill. The four houses share a continuous mansard roof with a handsome pedimented dormer in the

20–22 Hancock Street

attic of each house. A projecting string
course separates the third story from the
second story with its oriel windows.
Leading to the raised entry level is a stair
with ornamental cast-iron rail.

Ironwork, Hancock Street

31–37 Hancock Street

apartments. The newer building employs
traditional Beacon Hill brick, but an
angular bay projection and large
unpaned windows declare its modernity.

32–34 Hancock Street
JAMES MCNEELY, 1974

The first contemporary facade within the
Beacon Hill Historic District, 34 Hancock
Street replaces a house destroyed by fire
in 1967 and is connected with the renovated house at 32 Hancock. Because of
its lower ceilings, the recent building is
able to squeeze five floors into the same
height occupied by four of the older
one. A single elevator, stairway, and fire
escape serve both buildings, which
together house twelve two-bedroom,
two one-bedroom, and three studio

57 Hancock Street
C. 1875

This curious French Second Empire
house has a very lively facade of three
five-story bays and a Classical Revival
entrance portico. Each story is identified
by a string course and the most prominent windows on the second and third
stories are pedimented. The entire composition may be flamboyant, but the corner of the left bay reveals attention to
detail in the elegant chamfered corner.
The mansard roof with dormers capping

the bays uses the Egyptian pylon form. This unusual design feature leads to the designation of the house as one of the few Egyptian Revival houses in the country. The house grandly announces the entry to Myrtle Street.

Old Joy Street horse stables

Egyptian Revival dormers

Old Joy Street Horse Stables
40–42 Joy Street
1830–1840

Two brothers built this pair of identical brick stables to avoid disputes. After the end of the horse-and-buggy era the stables served as the Brick Oven Tavern, then as a theatrical playhouse, and finally as art studios. Until the recent renovation, the original horse stalls, horse feeders, and trough remained on the first floor, as well as a huge winch for raising carriages to the second floor.

🏛 Smith Court
off Joy Street

Smith Court became a center of the black population in Boston in the early nineteenth century, when the African Society encouraged blacks to leave the North End for better residences. In 1829 the city directory of employment listed 224 black citizens in a wide variety of jobs, including many sailors and barbers. In the mid-nineteenth century Walt Whitman was impressed by the very different status "black persons" had in Boston than in New York. Commenting especially on their employment in important office positions, he cited an official in the State House and a black lawyer named Anderson who lived in Chelsea and had one of the biggest practices in Boston. Whitman also wrote about the very natural way in which blacks went to any public place such as a restaurant and were served with politeness and with no indication it was out of the ordinary.

Abiel Smith School
46 Joy Street
1830s

The first black school in Boston was built here to serve the blacks who settled on the north slope, beginning in the Smith Court area, in the early nineteenth century. After ten years of operation, the school closed because the black residents demanded integrated schools; their demand was upheld by the state. In the twentieth century the building became the James E. Welch Post 55 American Legion and Ladies Auxiliary.

William C. Nell house

Abiel Smith School

William C. Nell House
off Joy Street at 3 Smith Court
1800
National Historic Landmark

When the blacks moved to the north slope this was a farmhouse, and much of the land on the north slope was part of its acreage. For many years the house served as a black rooming house, and under the ownership of James Scott fugitive slaves were taken in. The three-story clapboard Federal structure was built by William Lancaster and Banajah Brigham in 1800. The center entrance and small square upper windows are typical of the period, but the house is obviously unusual in the Beacon Hill context.

African Meeting House
off Joy Street on Smith Court
1806
National Historic Landmark

The African Meeting House was built by blacks to use as a church. There has been some conjecture that Asher Benjamin participated in the design of the building, both because he often employed blacks and because the brick structure makes use of the inset relieving arches familiar on his Charles Street Meeting House. In 1808 a school for black children was founded here and remained until the city built the first black school in Boston next door at 46 Joy Street in the 1830s. William Lloyd Garrison founded the New England Anti-Slavery Society here on January 6, 1832. Meanwhile the congregation adopted different names; first they became the

African Baptist Church and then in the 1850s the Independent Baptist Church. As the black population increased and moved onto Phillips Street, the Charles Street Meeting House became the African Methodist Episcopal Church.

In the late nineteenth century, blacks were attracted by the availability of better housing in the South End and Roxbury and began leaving first Smith Court, then Phillips Street. By 1925 a new influx of Irish and Jews found shelter in the areas vacated by blacks. The African Meeting House was sold to the orthodox Jewish Congregation Anshe Lebawitz, which followed its congregation to Beacon Hill from its previous location at 188 Hanover in the North End. In the 1970s the building was purchased by the Afro-American Museum.

Holmes Alley
between Joy and South Russell streets
at the end of Smith Court

Holmes Alley is entered through a passage off South Russell Street and then runs through the middle of the block until it connects with Smith Court. Scarcely wider than two feet, it was recorded as one of the hiding places for fugitive slaves during the abolitionist era.

Beacon Hill Civic Association
74 Joy Street
1862
National Historic Landmark

For many years this French Second Empire Victorian building was Police Sta-

African Meeting House

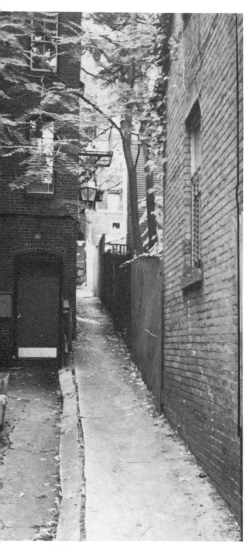

Holmes Alley, site of the Underground Railroad

Beacon Hill Civic Association

tion Number 3. The third-story mansard attic, quoins, and overhanging cornice with wooden supporting brackets are its most prominent features.

MYRTLE STREET

One of Beacon Hill's narrower streets, Myrtle Street rides the crown of the hill like a spine between the north and south slopes. At its west end are a number of Greek.Revival row houses, while the center of Myrtle is mainly back entrances to Revere Street tenements. Thus the street has a mixture of north- and south-slope architecture. From their top floors, many of its houses and tenements have long views over the Charles River, Government Center, and the south slope because of the street's high elevation.

Until 1803 three ropewalks extended along Myrtle Street from Hancock Street past Grove Street, making it impossible to cross Beacon Hill at any point between. Because of this barrier, while mansions and fine homes were being built on the south slope overlooking the Common and the Charles River, the north side had an entirely different development that was rich in social history and ethnic diversity. When the Myrtle Street rope-walks were dismantled in 1803, Belknap's Lane on the north slope was joined to George Street on the south slope, forming a single street that was renamed Joy Street decades later. The north and south slopes were joined at Anderson Street, as well, and the development of the north slope became more intense as

its accessibility increased. The land which had held the ropewalks was converted to house lots. The space between Myrtle and Revere streets is approximately the width of the old ropewalks.

The way the west end of Myrtle Street turns to the north to Revere Street rather than joining West Cedar expresses the historic insularity of the two sides of Beacon Hill. The north and south slopes remain very different, with low-income elderly, young professionals, students, and artists on the north slope. Convenient corner markets and services are prevalent on the north side but are shunned on the south side. Yet condominiums and renovation have come to both areas, and the hill becomes more socially homogeneous with each decade.

PHILLIPS STREET

During its significant abolitionist history, Phillips Street was named Southac Street. For much of the nineteenth century it had many lodging houses. Here fugitive slaves were housed and fed, their bills paid by the Committee of Vigilance, founded by Dr. Samuel Gridley Howe of the south slope. But the street was most closely identified with Lewis Hayden, who lived at number 66.

Old Historic Vilna Synagogue
16 Phillips Street
MAX KALMAN, 1919

This former synagogue was originally built with a narrow Gothic Revival entrance of twin spires framing a crenellated cornice over a drop arch, but was rebuilt in 1919. Founded in 1814, it is one of the oldest Jewish congregations in Boston, having reached its peak with the move to Beacon Hill of many Jews from the North End.

Lewis Hayden House
66 Phillips Street
1814

Lewis Hayden, himself a fugitive slave, became one of the most famous abolitionists. His home served as both a meeting place for abolitionists and a station on the Underground Railroad. Perhaps the reason his house was never searched is that he kept two kegs of gunpowder in his basement and threatened to blow the house up if anyone attempted to search for fugitive slaves. This house, Hayden's home from 1811 to 1889, is

Old Historic Vilna Synagogue

Lewis Hayden house

considered to be the most important existing abolitionist site in Boston. It is a three-story red brick Federal row house. The mansard roof is a later addition.

Primus Avenue and "Flower Lane"
off 82 Phillips Street
PRIMUS AVENUE; CLARENCE H. BLACKALL, 1920s

Primus Avenue was called Wilberforce Place in 1843. Clarence Blackall designed the charming terraced lane of duplex apartments in the 1920s. Opposite Primus Avenue is "Flower Lane," a narrow and dark mid-block passageway made appealing by plantings and a gas lantern.

Primus Avenue

REVERE STREET

In its early history the south side of Revere from Irving to beyond Grove Street was occupied by the sheds of the Myrtle Street ropewalks. The north side of the street thus developed quiet cul-de-sacs perpendicular to the street, where Greek Revival houses were built.

🏛 Rollins Place and Goodwin Place
27 and 73 Revere Street

"Flower Lane"

Rollins Place at 27 Revere Street is one of four charming cul-de-sacs that stem from Revere Street. Two-story red brick Greek Revival row houses built by John Rollins in 1843 line this place, but the focus of attention is the two-story wooden Ionic portico which concludes the vista at the

end of the place. What a charming white house, what a surprise on Beacon Hill! What family lives behind those shuttered windows so genteel, so withdrawn from the public way? In fact, the white portico is nothing but a false facade, an extravagant architectural trompe l'oeil in the

Rollins Place

Sentry Hill Place
79 Revere Street

This little lane was named May Street Place in 1844. An iron gate and gas lamp announce the entrance to the cul-de-sac. The last two narrow brick three-story Greek Revival houses both have two-story frame ells that conclude the vista of the lane in a successful way.

manner of Italian Baroque but in the style of Charleston, South Carolina, rather than Vicenza, Italy. This architectural fantasy creates diversion for passersby—a surprising bit of artifice in the bastion of Boston propriety.

The view of Goodwin Place at 73 Revere Street suffers from the parking lot that is its focus. Three-story brick Greek Revival row houses line the lane, which was given this name in 1859.

Sentry Hill Place

Bellingham Place

85 Revere Street

Bellingham Place was named for Governor Bellingham in 1847. Its east side is lined with narrow three-story brick Greek Revival row houses. On the west side is a two-story-plus-mansard-roof house that has another full story at the level of West Cedar Street below. This clapboard house is another reminder of the early frame houses that previously fronted on these lanes. The garden glimpsed at the end of the lane and the ivy-clad walls add greatly to its attraction.

Bellingham Place

Joseph Ditson House

43 South Russell Street

c. 1797

One of the oldest houses still standing on Beacon Hill, this Federal three-story brick house was freestanding when it was built about 1797. Joseph Ditson was father of the music publisher Oliver Ditson. On the upper part of the street there are two groups of mid-1840s Greek Revival row houses; 42–58 and the charming small houses at 21–35 South Russell Street.

TEMPLE WALK

Converted to a pedestrian street in 1977, Temple Street is the convenient path between the State House, the State Service Center, and North Station beyond. Added to this foot traffic are the students coming and going from Suffolk University, which dominates the upper portion of the west side of the street. Federal and Greek Revival row houses line both sides of the street. Most of these have now been renovated or restored. Until 1952 a pair of wooden houses built c. 1787 stood at 44 and 46 Temple Street, where a parking lot now opens up a view of the fine masonry wall of the Mission Church of St. John the Evangelist (see Bowdoin Street, p. 192).

Temple Walk

TEN

Back Bay

Back Bay

National Historic District

The Back Bay is the largest and most significant surviving example of Victorian architecture and planning in the country. Despite the richness of architectural styles and elements, there is harmony and continuity. In contrast to the South End, which was based on English models and lacks large-scale structure, the Back Bay was conceived on a French model. The highly structured street pattern features Commonwealth Avenue, a central boulevard 200 feet wide that links the open space foci of the Public Garden and the Fens. The cultural focus was Copley Square, with two of the most important buildings of the nineteenth century, the Public Library and Trinity Church.

Land use controls stringently excluded industrial activity and restricted commercial uses. The architecture, too, was subject to rigid controls in height, setbacks, and materials in order to obtain unity of streetscape. Nevertheless, the scheme allowed considerable variety, for the streets are varied in length and width and houses vary in size and style. As part of the progressive plan, alleys were provided for service, and despite changes in life style and technology they still function well today. The eight cross streets were arranged alphabetically to aid in orientation—Arlington, Berkeley, Clarendon . . . to Hereford. Since the Back Bay was filled from east to west, with new development close behind, the parade of architectural styles and changing tastes can be read in the architecture, as one begins at the Public Garden and walks toward Massachusetts Avenue and the Fens.

The filling of the Back Bay, which had been entirely tidal flats, began in 1814 with the construction of the fifty-foot-wide Mill Dam along Beacon Street from the foot of Beacon Hill to Sewell's Point in Brookline. A toll road ran the mile length of the dam, which was dotted with mills. Another dam, the Cross Dam, ran approximately along what is now Massachusetts Avenue. The dams failed to bring the anticipated financial benefits from mills but did create an odorous nuisance by restricting circulation of water. A legislative commission decided to remedy the problem by filling in the 450 acres of tidal flats. Railroads and steam shovels were essential to the gigantic filling operation. Trains of thirty-five cars each ran every forty-five minutes from West Needham with gravel, filling 2,500 cubic yards—the equivalent of two house lots—a day. This thirty-year project began in 1857 and brought about the biggest change Boston had yet experienced. By 1870 land had been filled west to Dartmouth Street, and by the late 1880s it had reached the Fens.

Back Bay in progress in 1872

Many plans had been put forth for the Back Bay, some of them quite fantastic. The final plan of 1856 is credited to Arthur Gilman, an architect who had special interest in French architecture and planning and who had traveled in Europe. George Snell, another architect, and Copeland and Cleveland, landscape gardeners, also made suggestions on the design of Commonwealth Avenue.

Back Bay immediately became the fashionable place to live, but some locations were more desirable than others. It was said that on Beacon Street were the old rich, while Marlborough had the old poor; the new rich resided on Commonwealth Avenue, and the new poor on Newbury Street! Special status was given to the water side of Beacon Street and the sunny (north) side of Commonwealth Avenue.

George Santayana, philosopher, novelist, and poet, lived at 302 Beacon Street (now demolished) as a boy and gave a good impression of what it was like living in the Back Bay in the 1870s:

"Our house was, at that time, one of the last on the waterside of Beacon Street, and there was still many a vacant lot east of it, where on passing in sharp wintry weather it was prudent to turn up one's coat collar against the icy blast from the river. . . . On the opposite side there were straggling groups of houses running further west along the Mill Dam, under which, at some points, the tide flowed in and out from the Back Bay, the shallow lagoon that originally extended to Boston Neck, turning the town almost into an island. The water in 1872 still came up to Dartmouth Street and to what is now Copley Square. Among the provisional features of this quarter were the frequent empty lots, ten or fifteen feet below the level of the street. These lots were usually enclosed by rough open fences, often broken down at the corners, from which a short cut could be made diagonally to the next street; and by this we schoolboys were quick to profit, for a free run on rough ground amid weeds and heaps of rubbish. . . . Our twin houses had been designed to attract the buyer, who might sell his bargain again at a profit if he didn't find it satisfactory; and this was precisely the ground on which my mother was persuaded to buy her house, not expecting a financial crisis and a sudden but prolonged disinclination on the part of the consumer to buy anything that he didn't need. The advantages in our house were in the first place social or snobbish, that it was in Beacon Street and on the better or fashionable waterside of that street; which also rendered every room initially attractive, since it had either the sun if in the front, or the view if in the rear. . . . The grand attraction of the water view was marred by two counter-effects discovered eventually by enthusiastic purchasers. . . . Under your nose was a mean backyard, unpaved, with clothes or at least clotheslines stretched across it. . . . Under your nose too—and this was the second counter-effect—rose now and then the stench from mudflats and sewage that the sluggish current of the Charles and the sluggish tides that penetrated to the Basin did not avail to drain properly." (George Santayana, *Persons and Places*.)

While some areas of the city were developed in a fever of speculation focused on putting up the greatest number of buildings at the least possible cost with little concern for amenities, the Back Bay is remarkable precisely because it was built with quality in mind. Many outstanding architects of the late nineteenth century designed Back Bay houses that spared no effort and no expense to provide the most comfortable and elegant living conditions. They became models for home design across the country.

Most Back Bay houses are twenty-five or twenty-six feet wide, although some are narrower and a few are wider. In height most are four or five stories plus basement. The typical floor plan has a side entrance and a stair hall that leads into the first-floor front drawing room and rear dining room and pantry. On the higher-ceilinged second floor, the *piano nobile,* were the formal drawing room and library, and on the upper floors were family bedrooms. Servants' quarters were on the top floor under the mansard roof, in the French manner. Kitchen and laundry facilities were in the basement. Even in the beginning most houses had furnaces, but these were quite inefficient and heated only the first two floors, the upper floors relying on fireplaces with coal grates. By the mid 1870s many houses had gravity hot-water heating systems throughout the entire house.

While some neighborhoods have become gentrified, the Back Bay has experienced de-gentrification since the Depression. Many families were forced to sell their homes, which were too grand and too expensive for a single family to maintain. Developers purchased houses and converted them into apartments. Others became schools or dormitories for the city's numerous colleges. Often this process was very destructive. Kitchens, bedrooms, and bathrooms were sometimes added to each floor by chopping up the grand old rooms and tearing out plaster and wood ornamentation. Palatial staircases were sometimes boxed in or totally eliminated. Valuable wood paneling was painted or ripped out to expose brick walls, thus reducing acoustical privacy between buildings. Other houses became lodging houses, with the new owners occupying several of the original formal rooms and renting out the rest of the house to elderly or working people. Happily, most of these retained their original architectural character, although often in a somewhat shabby state.

With the condominium craze of the 1970s, developers once again hit the neighborhood. Some were sensitive to the historic character of the houses, but most simply found it a nuisance to deal with. They gutted the buildings of their elaborate French moldings, walnut and mahogany doors, plaster ceiling and wall ornament, and period hardware. Wood-framed windows were replaced with inappropriate aluminum windows. Suburban-style roof decks, wedged into every possible corner of the roofs, increased the sale value of units—but destroyed the French mansard roofscape. Former furnace rooms were turned into new saleable living quarters, with heating systems pushed outdoors in the form of throbbing heat pumps that added noise pollution to the neighborhood. Developers made huge profits while violating the architectural heritage. There seems to be no effective means of preventing the destruction of Back Bay's treasure of superb interior architecture. Yet despite a few wayward high-rise buildings on Beacon Street, the large-scale design of the district is strong and has survived as one of the loveliest neighborhoods in the country.

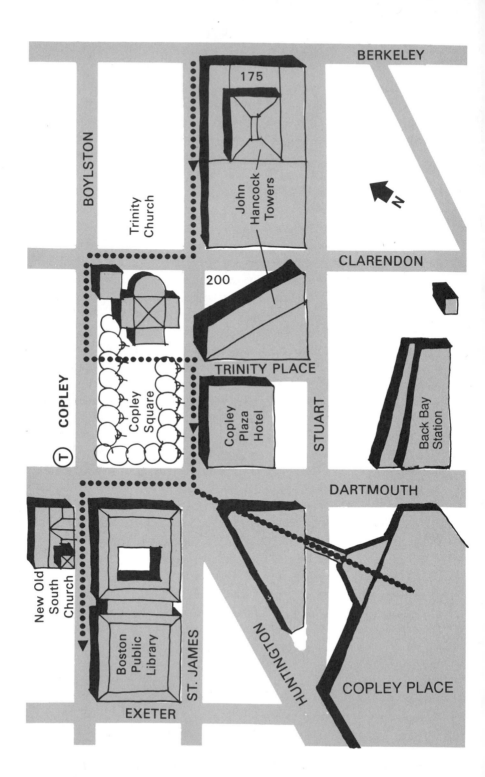

Copley Square

Copley Square Tour

This area is very compact, so you may see all the sites in any order you wish. If you start at Berkeley Street on St. James Avenue (having come from Arlington station or from the Bay Village tour), you will pass the **old John Hancock Tower** and will then see the **new John Hancock Tower** (**224**), which has a visitor observation level and exhibit on Boston's development narrated by Walter Muir Whitehill. Walk around **Trinity Church** (**219**) looking at the cloister and the parish hall staircase as well as the church, which is usually open. Walk through **Copley Square** noting the **Copley Plaza Hotel** (**225**)—you may want to see its grand interiors, too. Then proceed to **Copley Place** (**226**) and the **Boston Public Library.** The library is worth a visit. Note **New Old South Church** enroute to the library entrance (**230**). You may end your tour here or proceed on Exeter Street to the West or East Back Bay tours.

Copley Square Plaza

CLARKE & RAPUANO; DEAN ABBOTT,
DESIGNER, 1984–1990

The great Boston painter John Singleton Copley, who was born here in 1737, is honored by a square that has been the setting for architectural treasures since the nineteenth century, among them the New Old South Church and the trend-setting Trinity Church and Boston Public Library. Several of Copley Square's important buildings have been demolished, including the Museum of Fine Arts, a Ruskin Gothic structure that stood on the site of the Copley Plaza Hotel; the S. S. Pierce building across from it; and Hotel Westminster, which was replaced by the John Hancock tower.

In 1869 Copley Square was the site of the National Peace Jubilee, an extrava-ganza housed in a temporary Coliseum built for the occasion. The highlight was a performance of the Anvil Chorus from *Il Trovatore* with an orchestra of one thousand players and a chorus of ten thousand, along with organ, drum corps, ringing church bells, cannons, and one hundred firemen striking anvils with sledge hammers.

Ever since the square was filled in the 1870s, it had been an awkward piece of leftover land, never given any serious design attention until Sasaki Dawson and DeMay's scheme, which won a national competition, was executed in 1969. Conceived in a 1960s formalist manner, the scheme's elegantly articulated elements related to Trinity Church. The diagonal entrance from Clarendon Street through the precise rows of trees was a particularly successful approach to the complex

Copley Square and Trinity Church

geometry of the site. The plaza was criticized, however, for being too hard-surfaced and unsympathetic to human activity. While the sunken plaza was a popular place for concerts and folk dancing, it also became a haven for less desirable activity, and the fountain suffered maintenance problems.

Thus, in 1983 several symposiums in the Boston Public Library focused on the form and use of the space and laid the groundwork for a competition for its redesign in 1984. A demanding program was specified, including that the space be flat, that it accommodate vendors and market stalls, and that it increase the amount of planting. The winning entry, which responded to all of the program requirements, has been built and emphasizes easy pedestrian access from the surrounding streets, as well as a softening of the space with grass and trees more in the manner of a New England village green. Human presence is encouraged with seating areas, vendors, and a periodic farmers' market.

Alas, this new scheme, too, has been beset with problems. Will it have to be redesigned again in the next decade? In attempting to please every competing desire, the designers created a rather bland, uninspired, and incoherent space. Problem details have plagued the space from the beginning: The sugar maples died and were replaced with red maples, the plane trees also died and had to be replaced; the grass flooded; and the fountain is so complicated it has been an ongoing maintenance headache. The farmers' market area that was a central aspect of the scheme turned out to be too delicate to accommodate the farmers'

trucks. It is not at all clear why Copley Square has been so problematic, especially given the amount of design attention the square has received. Some of the blame may fall to the jury that selected this plan, but the city also failed to provide appropriate urban design guidance.

🏛 Trinity Church

Copley Square
HENRY HOBSON RICHARDSON, 1872–1877;
PORTICO AND FRONT TOWER PEAKS, 1890S
National Historic Landmark

With Trinity Church, H. H. Richardson reached the peak of his career and created one of the great monuments of American architecture (although Richardson himself considered the Allegheny County Courthouse and Jail in Pittsburgh and the Marshall Field Wholesale Store in Chicago to be his finest buildings). The Trinity Church parish, founded in 1734, decided in the 1860s to move from its second church on Summer Street and Bishop's Alley near the present Filene's store. In March 1872 six firms were invited to submit designs for a new church on the triangular Copley Square site, $300 to be paid to each of the designers. Richardson was one of the invited competitors, partly because of the impressive tower of his First Baptist Church (then Brattle Church), nearly completed on Clarendon Street (see Commonwealth Avenue at Clarendon Street, p. 255). Richardson was only thirty-four years old and living in New York City at the time, but he knew several members of the building committee who had been Harvard classmates or

Trinity Church

clubmates at the Porcellian, a definite
asset to him. The other competitors were
Sturgis and Brigham, Richard Morris
Hunt, Ware and Van Brunt, and Peabody
and Stearns, all of Boston, and William
A. Potter of New York City. Richardson
was awarded the commission in June
1872 for a Romanesque design that was
a sharp contrast to the prevailing Victorian Gothic style favored by other competitors. Upon receiving this commission,
Richardson moved his practice to Brookline. There he surrounded himself with
his work, his library, his family, and
many apprentices to whom he was a
great teacher and friend, treating them
almost as members of his own family.

Richardson's design for Trinity
Church solved many problems of a site
that was small, triangular, isolated by
streets, and a visual focus for the surrounding area. Instead of a long Gothic

nave with front or side tower, Richardson
felt a more compact Greek cross plan
with a large central tower was better
suited to the site and would give the
tower prominence from any one of the
surrounding streets. In his words: "The
struggle for precedence, which often
takes place between a church and its
spire, was disposed of, by at once and
completely subordinating nave, transepts,
and apse, and grouping them about the
tower as the central mass." The "lowness"
of the Trinity service gave him design
freedom he would not have had with a
"higher" church. The rector, Phillips
Brooks, preferred the Romanesque style
to the Gothic, because the Gothic was
associated with late medieval Catholi-
cism. It is important to note, however,
that Richardson was not a true revivalist
but had his own style freely drawn and
adapted from many periods, from early

H. H. Richardson, from the portrait by Hubert Herkomer

Syrian Christian to American Colonial.

Bids for the church ranged from $355,000 to $640,000 and far exceeded the $200,000 limit established by the stunned building committee. A contract was finally signed for $290,000 with a contractor from Worcester, but by the time the church was completed several years later, the cost had risen to nearly $750,000, including land, interior finishing and decorations, and site work. Of this, Richardson was paid only $7,218.90 to cover his architectural fee and expenses.

In the course of construction, Richardson greatly improved and simplified his original design by replacing the tall, octagonal, rather slender lantern with a massive square tower inspired by that of the Cathedral of Salamanca. Richardson had the rare ability to see faults in his own work and to improve it, as illustrated by his final design for Trin-

ity, which far surpasses his original winning conception. Richardson himself said, "I really don't see why the Trinity people liked them, or, if they liked them, why they let me do what I afterwards did." Stanford White, later of McKim, Mead, and White, apprenticed under Richardson for several years (1872–1878) and worked on the tower. The more detailed, intricate design of the tower is thought to be the influence of White, for the lower part of the church is more simple and massive in the Richardson tradition. Richardson had been under pressure from the engineer and building committee to reduce the weight of the tower as originally planned, since the church was to be built on the wet filled land of Back Bay. The final tower weighs ninety million pounds and rests on two thousand wooden piles arranged in a ninety-foot square. On top of the piles stand four granite pyramids thirty-five feet square and seventeen feet high; they support the corner piers of the tower. Because the pilings are of wood, they must be kept submerged in water. The level of the water table beneath the church is constantly monitored.

The auditorium is actually three squares in plan, one square being the apse, one the crossing, and one the nave. The total length from the apse to the facade is 160 feet, the width of the transepts, 121 feet. The ceilings are 63 feet at the highest point and the tower ceiling is 103 feet. The tower roof rises 211 feet from the ground to the top of the finial.

Richardson's conceptual sketch for Trinity Church

Granite was chosen for the major building material because of its strength, and was quarried in Dedham, Quincy, Westerly, Rhode Island, and the Maine Coast. Color was an important part of Richardson's concept for the building, both inside and outside. He chose red

Longmeadow sandstone for the trim. For the roof and louver boards he used semiglazed red tiles made in Akron, Ohio, while the rolls and crockets—the knobby projections on the tower ridges—were made in Chicago. The influence of the Romanesque of the Auvergne region of southern France is evident in the marquetry. Several years ago when the exterior was cleaned Bostonians were shocked to see its original lively colors.

Richardson persuaded the painter John La Farge, assisted by the young Augustus Saint-Gaudens, to execute the rich and colorful interiors he envisioned. He had thought carefully about how to treat the interior and considered the possible compromise to structural integrity that would result from plastering over the granite rather than exposing it. But the color of the granite was too cold and harsh for Richardson's concept and painted plaster was the best way to introduce color. The granite piers were encased with furring and plaster to appear like a cluster of columns. The plastered walls were painted and stenciled in dull terra-cotta, gold, and blue-green. Black walnut woodwork was used in the church and chapel, ash and oak in the vestibule. The wooden truss-like members at the arches of the crossing are actually decorative casings for iron tie rods that were installed as a precaution, not a necessity. None of the stonework in the building requires any metal reinforcement. The present chancel was designed by Charles D. Maginnis in 1938. The nave interior was restored in 1957, and the Parish House interior was rebuilt in 1959–1960.

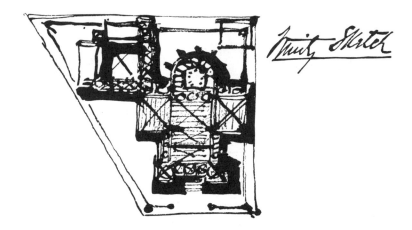

Richardson's early sketch for the plan of Trinity Church

The central scaffolding built inside the tower was in place for two and one-half years and was used not only for the masonry work but also for constructing the roof and plastering and painting the interiors. It was finally taken down in the first three days of February 1877, and by February 8 the floors, pews, and other interior furnishings had been installed. The building was ready for consecration the following day.

When the church was finished, the facade did not appear as it does today, with its projecting sculpted portico, but had an imposing tall flat facade, rather abrupt in its effect. The two front towers were also much simpler—and much disliked by Richardson, who urged the church to have them rebuilt. In 1882 Richardson visited St. Trophime in Arles, France, and sketched a design for a portico addition to Trinity based on it. The porch and front towers were finished after Richardson's death by his successor,

Cloister, Trinity Church

© Trinity Church

Sanctuary, Trinity Church

church. The two dormers relate to the four tower dormers.

A statue of Phillips Brooks, first rector of the Copley Square church, Episcopal Bishop of Massachusetts, and author of "O, Little Town of Bethlehem," was finished by Augustus Saint-Gaudens in 1910 and stands on the north side of the church.

🏛 John Hancock Towers
Copley Square at
200 Clarendon Street
I. M. PEI, 1972–1975

175 Berkeley Street
Cram and Ferguson, 1947
(Clarendon Street Building)

Hugh Shepley, between 1894 and 1897 and are probably more elaborate and Romanesque than Richardson actually intended.

The Parish House, begun March 1874, was in use that November. The parish, desperate for a meeting place after the great Boston fire of November 1872 destroyed its Summer Street building, had been meeting in temporary quarters in the MIT lecture hall across the street from the new church site for two years. The design of the Parish House roof resembles in some ways the Sherman house in Newport, designed by Richardson in 1874. The pyramidal roof forms build up to the larger mass of the church. The cascading cloistered exterior staircase, which leads to the chapel on the second floor, relates to the main facade and links the cloister and the

The old John Hancock tower, unlike many new towers, makes a uniquely identifiable form on the skyline, with its truncated stepped pyramid and weather beacon:

> Clear blue, clear view;
> Flashing blue, clouds due;
> Steady red, rain ahead;
> Flashing red, snow ahead.

The stylized, rather heavy decoration visible at the ground-floor entrance to the auditorium on Berkeley Street is not unlike some postmodernist work done in the 1980s.

In contrast to the mass and solidity of the old tower, the new tower pretends not to be there at all. Its finely detailed reflective skin makes it more sky and light than building. In fact, there was considerable debate as to whether a

Copley Square and the John Hancock Towers

© Gurchev and Gurchev

Even more remarkable than its visual form is its engineering—or should one call it after-the-fact engineering—which required complete replacement of its large plate-glass curtain-wall panels, reinforcement of the steel frame of the structure, installation of a complex monitoring system to detect deflections in the glass to warn of possible breakage, and a "tuned mass damper," a rolling weight on a film of oil on the fifty-eighth floor to counter high wind stresses.

Both towers have observation decks; the old tower has exhibits of old Boston, while the new tower has an observation deck with an exhibit on Boston's development narrated by historian Walter Muir Whitehill.

Back Bay Station
between Clarendon and Dartmouth streets near Stuart Street
KALLMANN, MCKINNELL, AND WOOD, 1987

tower should be placed on this important and difficult site, with two nineteenth-century monuments—Trinity Church and the Public Library—so near. The way the narrow slab is twisted with its knife edge thrusting into Copley Square makes it appear ever so slender from some vantage points, from all angles the reflections of clouds and Trinity's tower are striking. Some have called it a good solution to an impossible design problem.

One of a series of stunning new transit stations built as part of the Southwest Corridor Transportation Project, this wonderful light and airy space invites transit users. Giant arches of laminated wood span the great concourse space of glass block and concrete. The Clarendon Street entrance is reminiscent of an Italian piazza, with a pair of elegant campanilelike ventilation towers. The piazza is defined by an elaborate brick and concrete wall with arched relief motifs related to the barrel vault of the main hall. The station serves Amtrak, the MBTA Orange Line, and commuter lines.

Back Bay Station

Copley Plaza Hotel
Copley Square
BLACKALL AND HARDENBERG, 1910–1912

Henry Hardenberg, architect of the Plaza Hotel and the Dakota apartment building in New York City, designed the hotel in association with Clarence Blackall, a local architect. The Italian Renaissance Revival facade is of rusticated limestone, with a large central bow front flanked by two entry porticoes. The lavish theatrical interiors of its ballroom, restaurants, bar, function rooms, and lobby are well preserved and deserve a look. John Singer Sargent had a suite of rooms in the hotel from 1919 until his death in 1925.

Copley Place
Copley Square
THE ARCHITECTS COLLABORATIVE, MASTER PLAN ARCHITECT FOR ENTIRE DEVELOPMENT, PLANNER FOR MARRIOTT HOTEL, AND DESIGN ARCHITECT FOR WESTIN HOTEL, AND RETAIL, OFFICE, AND MAJOR PUBLIC SPACES; HUGH STUBBINS AND ASSOCIATES, MARRIOTT HOTEL; ZALDASTANI ASSOCIATES, HOUSING; 1980–1984

Designers have long felt the need to fill the open corner of Copley Square that was once effectively anchored by the neo-Romanesque S. S. Pierce building. This has now come about with the Cop-

Copley Plaza Hotel

ley Place development, which in many ways recalls the development of Prudential Center more than twenty years earlier over former rail yards (see Prudential Center, p. 292). The gigantic and controversial Copley Place project, the largest mixed-use single-phase development in the country at that time, was built on a complicated site amidst conflicting community, real-estate, and government interests. Located at the edge of Copley Square and next door to some of Boston's most cherished landmarks, the nine and one-half–acre site is at the intersection of several major streets and over the Massachusetts Turnpike and railroad tracks. Besides solving the complex circulation system, the form had to relate to the surrounding areas, particularly the monuments of Copley Square and the small-scale residential South End. How would pedestrians be drawn to this remote corner from Back Bay shopping streets across several streets and the turnpike entrance? How would the densely developed site provide attractive circulation and gathering spaces for its users? How could the exterior treatment of the mammoth complex relate to its more intimate, varied historic surroundings to avoid becoming a huge anonymous development? How would the program for use of the space benefit the surrounding neighborhoods?

Such problems were addressed in the long and intensive design process, which involved representatives of the neighborhoods, the city, and the developers. However successful the development may be in real-estate terms, it does not live up to its eloquent surroundings, though it does them no great harm either. As one plan-

Copley Place

ner intimately involved with the project noted, "It may not be great, but it could have been a lot worse." The precast-concrete facades were worked out in terms of scale, color, and joint treatment to relate to the older neighbors, an effort that was only partially successful, since the facades have none of the engaging sculptural qualities of the neighbors. Pedestrian access is tenuous, depending too much on upper-level bridges, and the entire project is too introverted and claustrophobic. It is unfortunate the project does not have a stronger sense of place—it might be equally at home in Atlanta, Houston, or Los Angeles and does little to recognize its unique Boston surroundings.

Wrought-iron lanterns, Boston Public Library

Built at a cost of over $500 million, the 3.25 million square-foot development includes two major hotels, four office buildings, a shopping center with several restaurants and a nine-cinema complex, one hundred apartments, and parking for 1,400 cars. A skylighted and landscaped retail gallery links the various buildings, as well as parking and transportation services.

🏛 Boston Public Library
Copley Square
McKim, Mead, and White, 1887–1895;
Addition: Philip Johnson, 1971
(Boylston Street)

National Register of Historic Places

The Boston Public Library was founded in 1848 by an act of the Massachusetts Legislature. Opened in 1854, it was the first large city library for the general public in the United States.

Charles Follen McKim had attended Harvard and apprenticed under H. H. Richardson in Boston. Later he married into the Boston Appleton family. These Boston connections certainly helped him secure the commission, but the crucial factor was that a library trustee much admired the Villard houses he had designed in New York. His Renaissance Revival design for the library was a sharp change of direction for American architecture, and remained influential for the next forty years. It stirred considerable comment, not all of it positive. The *Boston Globe* compared it to the city morgue, while another critic termed it a warehouse.

In fact, it is more an Italian Renaissance palazzo, influenced strongly by both Alberti's San Francesco at Rimini and Labrouste's Bibliotheque Saint Genevieve (1843–1850) in Paris. A row of equally-spaced arched windows rise above the rusticated ground floor with three entry arches graced by fine iron gates and lanterns that swoop down. The handsome bronze doors are by sculptor Daniel Chester French and represent Music and Poetry, Knowledge and Wisdom, and Truth and Romance. The building effectively integrates sculpture, painting, architecture, and engineering.

Interior space is organized about the grand staircase and entrance hall of beautiful "Monte Riete" or "Convent Siena" marble, a marble difficult to obtain. Murals around the staircase and the second-floor corridor are by Puvis de Chavannes of Paris. The tile vaults on the ground floor, the first extensive use of tile vaulting in the country, are by the Guas-

Bates Hall, Boston Public Library

tavino firm of New York and Boston.

Bates Hall, the grand reading room, 217 feet long, 42 feet wide, and 50 feet high, runs along the entire front of the second floor and has a barrel-vaulted ceiling terminating in coffered apses. The hall is named after Joshua Bates, the library's first great benefactor. In the delivery room, Pre-Raphaelite murals depicting "The Quest of the Holy Grail" can be seen. At the opposite end of the corridor is the Elliott Room, with ceiling painting "The Triumph of Time" by Boston artist John Elliott, husband of Maud Howe Elliott, daughter of Julia Ward Howe. At each end of the Chavannes Gallery are the Venetian and Pompeian lobbies, which lead to the delivery room and Elliott Room.

Ascending the staircase to the third floor one reaches the Sargent Gallery, named for John Singer Sargent, who decorated it with his murals "Judaism and Christianity." One of the great surprises of the library is the inner Italian courtyard, always a place of repose, based on the Cancelleria Palace in Rome.

Making an addition to such an extraordinary piece of architecture was a challenge of the highest order. Philip Johnson matched the dignity and monumentality of the original building, but introduced a different scale with the three large bays and slanting arches, composing a striking but unrelated facade. The interior connection between the two buildings is tenuous and circuitous and involves inept routing past service doors and back stairs. The rarebook room on the third floor is dignified and elegantly detailed.

🏛 New Old South Church

Copley Square at 645 Boylston Street
CUMMINGS AND SEARS, 1874–1875;
TOWER REBUILT 1941; INTERIOR RESTORATION:
SHEPLEY BULFINCH RICHARDSON AND
ABBOTT, 1985
National Historic Landmark

The Old South Church moved to Copley Square from its eighteenth-century meeting house, which still stands today on Washington Street (see Washington Street, p. 16). The northern Italian Gothic design creates wonderful skyline views from many directions with its tall campanile and Venetian lantern. It is the perfect focus for the pivotal corner of Copley Square, counterpoint to the hori-

New Old South Church

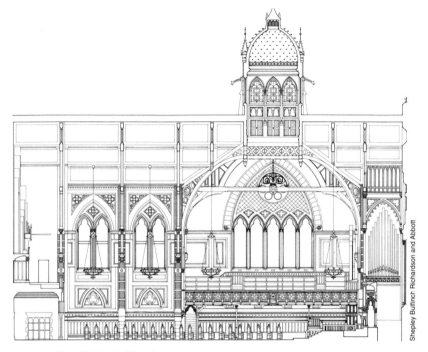

Shepley Bulfinch, Richardson and Abbott

Interior, New Old South Church

zontal mass of the Public Library and the monolithic Trinity Church. Exterior ornament is abundant and well executed, including multicolored stone inlays, zebra-striped arches, tracery, and iron work. A stone set into the portico wall records the death of one of the original members of Old South Church, John Alden, eldest son of John and Priscilla Alden of Plymouth Colony. A Paul Revere chalice is in the silver collection of the church. After the original 246-foot tower was built it began to lean until it was thirty-six inches out of plumb. It was finally taken down in 1931 and rebuilt lower in 1940.

Back Bay

The historic Back Bay is so large and has so many fascinating sites that it has been divided into two tours, the East and West loops.

Back Bay East Loop Tour

The Back Bay East tour begins at the corner of Arlington and Boylston streets in front of **Arlington Street Church** (**238**), opposite the corner of the **Public Garden** (**451**). Walk north on Arlington Street for one block to the **Ritz-Carlton Hotel** (**238**), then turn left and walk down one block of Newbury Street, passing **Emmanuel Church** and **37 Newbury Street** (**279–80**). Turn right on Berkeley Street and go to the Commonwealth Avenue Mall (**454**). As you walk up the mall toward the Public Garden, note the **Victorian mansions** on the left and unified **row houses** on the right (**253**).

At **Harbridge House** (**236**) turn left on Arlington Street and left again onto Marlborough Street at **8–11 Arlington Street** (**236**). After passing several sites in the first block of Marlborough Street (**272**), turn right onto Berkeley Street, passing two churches and the **French Library** (**272**). If you want to see the **Gibson House Museum** of the Victorian era (**239**) turn right to 137 Beacon Street. Otherwise, turn left onto Beacon Street, passing several significant sites including the **Fuller mansion** and the **Goethe Institute** (**240–41**). After seeing the sculpture court of **180 Beacon Street** (**242**), turn left onto Clarendon Street and walk to the Commonwealth Avenue Mall, passing **271–279 Clarendon** (**273**).

Turn right onto the mall in front of the **"Church of the Holy Bean Blowers"** (**255**). Notice the Ruskin Gothic facade of **121 Commonwealth Avenue** and the Beaux Arts facades of **128–130 Commonwealth Avenue** as you approach the **Chilton Club** and the **Hotel Vendome** (**256–60**). Turn right onto the wide brick sidewalk past the Dartmouth Street facade of the **Ames-Webster mansion** (**257**) and the **Crowninshield house** (**274**). Across Dartmouth Street is the **Hollis Hunnewell mansion** (**275**). Cross Marlborough Street to the **Cushing-Endicott** house (276) and turn left, passing 165 and 191 **Marlborough Street** (277).

Turn left on Exeter Street and return to Commonwealth Avenue, where you may either begin the Back Bay West loop—if you are energetic—or continue on the East loop, glancing at 191 and 195 **Commonwealth Avenue** (261) before proceeding to the **Prince School** and **Exeter Street Theatre** building (285–86). Turn left onto Newbury Street in front of **Exeter Towers** (285). Enjoy the colorful displays of the shops and galleries in the next two blocks as well as the **Boston Art Club, Hotel Victoria,** and 277 **Dartmouth Street** (283–84). At 109 **Newbury Street** (282), turn right onto Clarendon, passing **The New England building** (252). Turn left on Boylston Street and proceed to the end of the tour past **Louis,** the **Berkeley Building, Warren Chambers,** and **Shreve, Crump, and Low** (248–50), arriving back at the starting point.

Back Bay West Loop Tour

Back Bay West begins at the corner of Commonwealth Avenue and Exeter Street opposite 191 and 195 **Commonwealth Avenue** (261). Follow the many sites on Commonwealth Avenue (262–71) as you walk three blocks to the large **John Andrew** and lavish **Burrage mansions** (268, 270) at the corner of Hereford Street opposite the former **Miss Farmer's School of Cookery** (269).

Proceed left on Hereford for one block and turn right onto Newbury Street at the **Boston Architectural Center (BAC)** (286). Continue down Newbury Street (288) for one block to Massachusetts Avenue and turn right for several blocks of busy traffic on what was once peaceful West Chester Street. En route to Beacon Street, see the **Ames mansion** (271), the **Marlborough** (279), and the **Hotel Cambridge** (245). If you would like to see another elaborate turn-of-the-century apartment hotel, turn left on to Beacon for one block to find the **Charlesgate** (246).

Otherwise turn right onto Beacon Street in front of **Church Court** (244) and notice 448 **Beacon Street** and the **New England College of Optometry** buildings (243–44). Turn right onto the quiet residential Hereford Street, noticing many fine oriel windows (244) before turning left onto Marlborough Street. You will pass several harmonious groupings of **row houses** (277). At the corner of Fairfield Street pause to admire 8–12 and 18–20 **Fairfield Street.** Continuing on Marlborough Street, pass the attractive row of small houses at 225–239 **Marlborough Street** (277), where this tour ends.

You may begin the Prudential Center–St. Botolph Street tour (291) by going to Gloucester Street at Boylston Street.

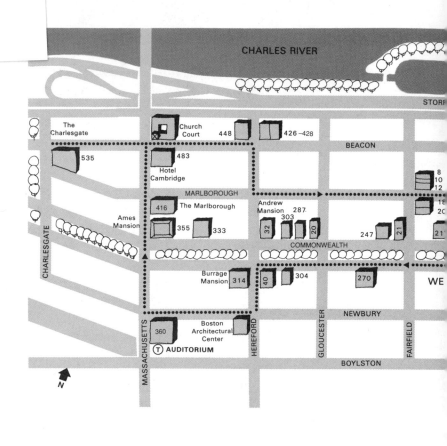

CHARLES RIVER

STORR

The Charlesgate

Church Court

448

426–428

BEACON

535

483

Hotel Cambridge

MARLBOROUGH

416 The Marlborough

Andrew Mansion 287

8
10
12

18
2C

Ames Mansion

355 333

32

303
20

247 21

21

CHARLESGATE

COMMONWEALTH

Burrage Mansion 314

40 304

270

WE

NEWBURY

360 Boston Architectural Center

(T) AUDITORIUM

HEREFORD

GLOUCESTER

FAIRFIELD

BOYLSTON

MASSACHUSETTS

N

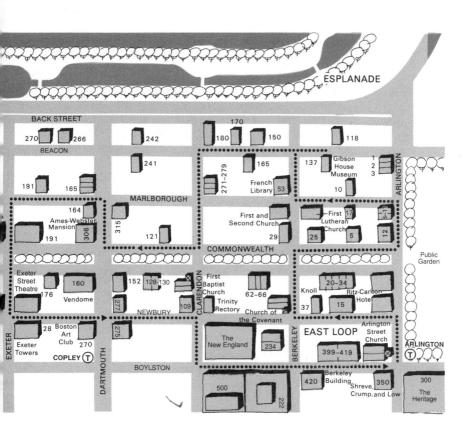

ESPLANADE

BACK STREET

270 266

BEACON

270 266 242 180 170 150 118

241 271-279 165 137 Gibson House Museum 1 2 3

191 165 French Library 53 10

164 First and Second Church First Lutheran Church 17

Ames-Webster Mansion 315 121 COMMONWEALTH 29 25 5 12

191 306

Public Garden

Exeter Street Theatre 152 128-130 First Baptist Church 62-66 Knoll 20-34 Ritz-Carlton Hotel

176 160 Vendome 277 NEWBURY 109 Trinity Rectory Church of the Covenant 37 15

28 Boston Art Club 270 275 BERKELEY EAST LOOP Arlington Street Church

Exeter Towers COPLEY (T) DARTMOUTH The New England 234 399-419 ARLINGTON (T)

BOYLSTON 500 222 420 Berkeley Building Shreve, Crump, and Low 350 300 The Heritage

EXETER CLARENDON

1, 2, and 3 Arlington Street
ATTRIBUTED TO GRIDLEY J. FOX BRYANT,
1861

Arlington Street originally presented a
handsome continuous mass of five-story
brownstone houses with mansard roofs
from Beacon Street to Boylston Street.
Built in the French academic manner
then current in Paris, these three houses
are massed together to give the impression of a single monumental edifice. The
center house is slightly set back and the
two end houses frame it with their projecting mansard roofs. Each story has a
different window treatment expressing
the relative importance of each floor,
with tall, heavily pedimented windows
on the second-floor drawing rooms and
small arched dormers on the top-floor
servants' quarters. The stone of the
ground floor is rusticated in contrast to
the smooth finish of the upper floors.

8–11 Arlington Street
NO. 8, 1870; NOS. 9, 10, AND 11,
1861; RENOVATION, 11 ARLINGTON STREET:
PERRY, DEAN, ROGERS, AND PARTNERS, 1982

Although somewhat altered on the exterior and greatly altered inside, the group
of four houses at 8–11 Arlington still provide the kind of architectural continuity
the developers of the Back Bay had in
mind. Like 1, 2, and 3 Arlington Street,
these four separate houses are treated as
one mass.

The Atlantic, first published in 1859
by William D. Ticknor and James
Thomas Fields and originally located
above the Old Corner Book Store on
Washington Street, was at 8 Arlington

8–11 Arlington Street

from 1920 until the 1980s. Among its
notable founders were James Russell
Lowell, Ralph Waldo Emerson, Henry
Wadsworth Longfellow, and Oliver Wendell Holmes.

Harbridge House
12 Arlington Street
ARTHUR GILMAN, 1859–1860

The grandest of the surviving houses on
Arlington Street, this five-story mansion
in the French-Italian academic style is
faced in smooth Nova Scotia sandstone.
The projecting central entrance bay con-

Harbridge House

tains the entrance portico with oriel window above. Its architect, Arthur Gilman, also designed the Arlington Street Church. In 1893 Mrs. J. Montgomery Sears, patron of the arts and social figure, joined this house to the immediately adjacent 1 Commonwealth Avenue in order to accommodate her growing art collection and to make a palatial music room on the second floor. The entrance of the Commonwealth Avenue house was removed. Mrs. Sears's notable visitors included pianist Ignace Paderewski and violinist Fritz Kreisler, as well as Prince Henry of Prussia and painter John Singer Sargent, who did a portrait of Mrs. Sears and her daughter in the house.

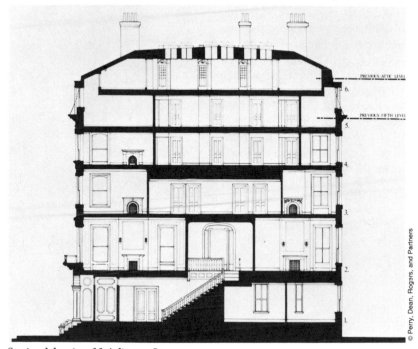

Sectional drawing, 11 Arlington Street

© Perry, Dean, Rogers, and Partners

Ritz-Carlton Hotel

15 Arlington Street
STRICKLAND, BLODGET, AND LAW, 1927;
ADDITION: SKIDMORE, OWINGS & MERRILL,
1981

A perfect match of a building and its users, the Ritz expresses the reserved sense of elegance and impeccable service that have become its trademark. A quintessential Boston institution, it is neither glamorous nor imposing. The building makes its quiet impact through its detailing, a blend of Regency and Art Deco, found in the low-relief fans over the second-story windows and the plasterwork on the low ceilings of the lobby. Art Deco murals and other details in the Cafe were removed during the 1985 redecoration.

Although the Art Deco style was never strong in Boston, it is evident in several other buildings by this firm, including the Katharine Gibbs School at 0 Marlborough Street (originally the Junior League Building, 1929) and two storefronts at 69 and 83 Newbury Street.

The new addition to the Ritz demonstrates an effort to maintain the general massing, proportions, and facade organization of its older neighbor.

🏛 Arlington Street Church

Arlington Street at Boylston Street
ARTHUR GILMAN, 1859–1861
Boston Landmark
National Register of Historic Places

Arlington Street Church is considered the "mother church" of Unitarianism in America and was the first building in the Back Bay. William Ellery Channing, noted Unitarian minister and abolitionist, served here for many years, and his statue now stands at the corner of the Public Garden facing the church. The church became famous and controversial again in the 1960s with the Vietnam protests.

Influenced by the work of English architects James Gibbs and Christopher Wren, the building is topped by an elaborate tower of many levels. The simple

Arlington Street Church

brownstone exterior is organized by two-story pilasters capped by a deep entablature. The pedimented front portico contains a tall round-arched entrance flanked by single unfluted Corinthian columns. Inside, the interiors recall the light, airy white spaces of many New England churches. Some of Solomon Willard's interior carvings for Bulfinch's Federal Street church (demolished) are preserved here and display a rudimentary knowledge of the Gothic style. Willard was the multitalented designer of the Bunker Hill Monument.

118 Beacon Street

LITTLE AND BROWNE, 1907

Reminiscent of McKim, Mead, and White's Pickman house at 303 Commonwealth Avenue, built twelve years earlier,

this grand Classical Revival bowfront house of granite is now occupied by Fisher Junior College. The single broad bow and center entrance are unusual for Back Bay architecture.

🏛 Gibson House Museum and Victorian Society, New England Chapter

137 Beacon Street

EDWARD CABOT, 1860

Open to the Public

Here the visitor has the rare opportunity to see the interior of a Back Bay row house just as it was left by its last occupant, Charles Hammond Gibson, who established it as a museum. The nineteenth-century interiors are intact and reflect the

118 Beacon Street

Gibson House Museum

typical middle-class Back Bay house of the period. This and the house next door at 135 Beacon were built together by related families, the Russells and the Gibsons. Although the exteriors are nearly identical, the interiors are quite different.

Fuller Mansion
now Emerson College Abbott Library
150 Beacon Street
ALEXANDER WADSWORTH LONGFELLOW, 1904
Open to the Public

Isabella Stewart ("Mrs. Jack") Gardner's father built her a house here in 1861. In 1880 the Gardners bought the adjacent house at 150 Beacon and connected it with their own house to make space for a music room. It was here that she had her portrait painted by John Singer Sar-

Fuller mansion

148 Beacon Street

gent and assembled the greatest private art collection in Boston. In 1902 she moved to her newly completed "palace" in the Fenway. E. S. Draper demolished both houses in 1904 to build the light stone mansion that now stands here.

Alvan T. Fuller, governor of the Commonwealth, member of Congress, founder of Fuller Cadillac Company, and important art collector, was the mansion's most famous owner. The double-width house is Italian Renaissance Revival with a rusticated ground floor and two-story fluted Ionic pilasters embracing the second and third floors. A handsome high wrought-iron fence with stone gateposts adds to the monumental effect.

154 Beacon Street

Brownstone Gothic House
165 Beacon Street
1869

The Victorian Gothic never took hold in Boston as it had in England. This house is one of three examples in the Back Bay, the others being at 76 and 80 Commonwealth Avenue and 117 Marlborough Street. Only the first- and fifth-floor windows are actually pointed; the rest have flat tops with pointed arches and tracery infill panels above. The top-floor gingerbread gable is reminiscent of many Victorian "cottages" in wood.

Goethe Institute, German Cultural Center
170 Beacon Street
OGDEN CODMAN, 1900
Open to the Public

Built of light sandstone in the Italian Renaissance Revival manner for E. H. Gay, this house somewhat resembles the Fuller mansion at 150 Beacon Street. Arched windows appear both on the rusticated first floor and on the second floor with its window balustrades. The heavily

Goethe Institute

ornamented interiors are still visible in the foyer and first-floor rooms. The house was designed as a setting for Mr. Gay's extensive collection of Chippendale furniture, the story of which is told in Gay's book *Chippendale Romance.*

The first floor was executed in the English style of the early eighteenth century and features elaborate plasterwork done by Italian workmen over a two-year period. The fine doors are of flame mahogany and have brass hardware from France. A music room was in the front and joined the library in the middle of the floor. The dining room was in the rear.

The second floor was in the Adam style of the late eighteenth century and had a handsome game room overlooking the river with billiard table and exceptional English doors dating from 1785. A bedroom was in the front. The upper floors are substantially altered. The building now serves as the German Cultural Center for New England, a branch of the Goethe Institute in Munich.

180 Beacon Street

S. J. KESSLER, 1965

All of the design standards established by the Back Bay's fine Victorian architecture were violated with this building's height, bulk, and extensive use of metal and glass. Ornament is studiously avoided, and the elegant, cool entry court is uncharacteristically walled off from the street. Although successful on its own terms, it is one of the buildings that sounded the alarm and helped reinforce the preservation of historic Back Bay architecture.

241 Beacon Street

1868

242 Beacon Street

STURGIS AND BRIGHAM

1881

Julia Ward Howe lived at 241 Beacon Street after the death of her husband, Dr. Samuel G. Howe. Godfrey Lowell Cabot and his wife Maria lived at 242 Beacon Street. Mr. Cabot was the foremost member of the Watch and Ward Society, that bastion of Bostonian virtue, which battled sin and corruption. It was about him that the now famous jingle was composed:

And this is good old Boston
The home of the
        bean and the cod
Where the Lowells talk only to
        Cabots
And the Cabots talk
        only to God.

266 Beacon Street

SHAW AND HUNNEWELL, 1886

An early example of the Italian Renaissance in the Back Bay, this forty-foot-wide house built for Elizabeth Skinner organizes the upper facade with two-story fluted pilasters and a strong cornice topped by a balustrade with urns that conceals the set-back top floor. The foundation stones have a vermiculated surface. The same firm designed a similar but less interesting house a year later at 412 Beacon Street.

270 Beacon Street

RICHARD TUCKER, 1956

A house by McKim, Mead, and White
originally occupied this site, while next
door at 274 Beacon was a large house
by H. H. Richardson. The current apartment complex has considerable design
interest and, despite its innovations, fits
well into its context.

Perhaps the most original and essential feature is the open piazza that passes
through the entry level, terminating with
a view to the Charles River, unifying the
entire design. The projecting bow fronts
are in the Back Bay vernacular but are
executed in a simple manner with large
expanses of glass. Ornament is found in
the stepped corners, the bas-relief panels
above the entrance, and the bold entry
pylons and ironwork. The rear elevation
is different but equally appealing—a rar-
ity in the Back Bay, which usually

270 Beacon Street

ignored the rear facades. A small parking
garage with turntable was ingeniously
worked into the rather small site.

New England College of Optometry

426–428 Beacon Street

JULIUS H. SCHWEINFURTH,
1904

Julius Schweinfurth, architect of two other
Back Bay houses (43 and 304 Commonwealth Avenue), won a Rotch Fellowship
that allowed him to study European architecture firsthand. Some of his European
architectural sketches are in the collection
of the Boston Athenaeum. His knowledge
of French styles is evident in the rich

New England College of Optometry

facades of these paired houses with their
handsome balustraded mansards, high-
relief stonework, and second-floor balcony with ornamental iron railing. The
added fire-escape balconies are a serious

blemish. Number 426 is twenty-nine feet wide, while 428 is twenty-two feet. The houses are unified in their ground-floor treatment, balcony, balustrade, mansard, and fourth-floor windows, but the windows of the second, third, and fifth floors differ. Number 426 retains its magnificent four-story gallery with circular oak stairway and large round leaded glass skylight. Unfortunately, 428 was gutted. Compare these houses with the French pair at 128 and 130 Commonwealth, which were remodeled in the French style one year later.

Entrance and oriel window, 12 Hereford Street at Beacon Street

448 Beacon Street
ANDREWS AND JACQUES, 1889

A handsome sandstone cornice carved with the shell motif adorns this chateau-inspired mansion. Besides the cornice, its main attractions are its round corner tower and its materials—yellow brick and red stone—which are unusual for the Back Bay.

Shell cornice, 448 Beacon Street

Church Court
Beacon Street at Massachusetts Avenue
GRAHAM GUND ASSOCIATES, 1983;
LANDSCAPE DESIGN: CAROL R. JOHNSON AND ASSOCIATES, INC.

A spectacular fire in mid-1978 ravaged the Mount Vernon Church designed by Walker and Kimball in 1891. In this

Church Court

© Steve Rosenthal

development, portions of the ruins are melded into a new L-shaped building to make forty-two condominium units. Most of the apartments overlook the Charles River, but several are oriented to the courtyard located where the sanctuary had been. Townhouses are built into the tower, entrance portico, and side wall of the ruin. In contrast to the mellow textured and ornamented stone of the original church, the new addition is outfitted in gay pastels and assorted ornamentation in parody of traditional Back Bay architecture. Through this complex mixture of formal languages,

the architects hope to provoke "reflection, imagination, and a mystique about the past and the passage of time."

Hotel Cambridge
483 Beacon Street
WILLARD T. SEARS, 1898

Architecturally this is one of the most successful of the large Back Bay apartment hotels. The bulk of Hotel Cambridge is organized by means of a two-story rusticated base and by a mansard roof that unites the top two floors. Most of the win-

Hotel Cambridge

dows of the top floors are grouped in two
tiers of dormers topped on each side by a
pediment bearing the "H-C" monogram of
the building. Compare this with another
but less successful apartment hotel by the
same architect, The Marlborough, one
block away (see 416 Marlborough Street,
p. 279).

The Charlesgate Hotel

The Charlesgate Hotel
535 Beacon Street
J. PICKERING PUTNAM, 1901

J. Pickering Putnam, also architect of
Haddon Hall (see 29 Commonwealth
Avenue, p. 254), studied architecture at
the Ecole des Beaux Arts as well as at
the Royal Academy of Architecture in
Berlin. Here his imagination reveled in
assorted bays, oriel windows, bartizans,
and towers. A finely carved Romanesque
entrance arch is reminiscent of Louis Sul-

Entrance archway, Charlesgate Hotel

livan, its intricate plant forms intertwined with the name of the building. Even into the 1920s, when many Back Bay apartment buildings had begun to decline in social status, this one was still desirable. Today it is a dormitory.

Ancient Fish Weir
Boylston Street

During the excavations for the old Boylston subway station (now called Arlington station) in 1913 and for the New England Mutual Life Insurance building in 1939, 65,000 sharpened wooden stakes were found at a level thirty-one feet below the current street level. Archeologists concluded that they formed a part of an ancient fish weir, possibly used between 2,000 and 3,600 years ago by the aborigines of New England. One section of the excavated weir is located in the northeastern part of a

block bounded by Stuart Street and St. James Avenue on Berkeley Street, and another is under Boylston Street between Berkeley and Clarendon streets. A diorama model showing a reconstruction of the fish weir may be seen in the lobby of the New England Mutual Life building (see 501 Boylston Street, p. 252). The Peabody Museum at Harvard also has an exhibit devoted to the use and construction of fish weirs.

The Heritage on the Garden
300 Boylston Street at Arlington Street
THE ARCHITECTS COLLABORATIVE, 1989

This large mixed-use development combines retail and office space with luxury residential condominiums. Originally, the site was part of the notoriously controversial Park Plaza project of the early 1970s. Because of intense public outcry, however, the project was scaled down and

The Heritage on the Garden

guidelines were established for relating the new development to the Public Garden and its surroundings. While the small-scale massing of the building tries to relate to its context, the large-scale form is much less convincing, consisting essentially of three large repeated units.

Louis

Boylston Street at 234 Berkeley Street
WILLIAM G. PRESTON, 1862

The predecessor of the Museum of Science, the Museum of Natural History, founded in 1830, was the original occupant of this building in the French Academic style. Two-story brick pilasters with Corinthian capitals encase the building and rest on a high rusticated sandstone ground floor. Animal heads were carved in the keystones on the ground-floor arches, but these have been removed.

The first MIT building, also designed

by Preston, was located next door where the New England Mutual Life Insurance building now stands and bore a strong resemblance to this building. It is hard to imagine that even in 1872 nothing had been built west of the MIT building on Boylston Street.

Shreve, Crump, and Low

330 Boylston Street
RENOVATION OF STORE: WILLIAM T. ALDRICH, 1930

One of Boston's Art Deco shops is preserved at Shreve, Crump, and Low. Stylized pilasters, column capitals, and grillework below the windows combine the zigzag with plant motifs. These are temporarily obscured by gaudy awnings. Inside there are decorated columns and a silvered ceiling. Down the street at 384 Boylston, another prominent Boston jeweler, Bigelow Kennard, also had an Art

Louis, former Museum of Natural History

Deco facade, parts of which remain. Note particularly the "entablature" and the cut stonework over the window at number 384. The original projecting sign of Bigelow Kennard is now in the Museum of Fine Arts.

399 Boylston Street and the Warren Chambers Building
399–419 Boylston Street

419 BOYLSTON STREET: BALL AND DABNEY, 1896; RENOVATION AND 399 BOYLSTON STREET: CHILDS, BERTMAN, TSECKARES, AND CASENDINO, 1982–1984

The Warren Chambers building was built in 1896 as Boston's premier doctors' building and featured luxury materials and the latest concepts in office layout and services for the period. The imposing Renaissance Revival facade of brick and marble features a coffered triumphal arch entrance with bronze gates that leads to a fine lobby of golden and dark green marble. While the building served its original purpose for many decades, it had become very outdated by the 1950s. This project restores the original facade and creates new interior spaces.

The large adjacent office building attempts to relate to the nineteenth-century scale and character of Boylston Street while maximizing floor area. To accomplish this, a front facade of brick and limestone with bay windows and "punched" windows relates to the older buildings, while a setback glass facade rises considerably higher to the height limit of 155 feet. Its reflective glass is intended to mirror the sky and contrast with the masonry below. A similar approach was used in Exeter Towers (see Newbury Street at 28 Exeter Street, p. 285).

Art Deco details, Shreve, Crump, and Low

Warren Chambers Building, 419 Boylston Street

Berkeley Building

420 Boylston Street
CODMAN AND DESPRADELLE, 1905;
RENOVATION: NOTTER, FINEGOLD &
ALEXANDER, 1988
Boston Landmark

The advantages of steel-frame construction are explored in this early twentieth-century Beaux Arts–influenced office building. Its walls are mainly glass and metal curtain wall organized into flat and bay windows, which are unified vertically over the five upper floors by slender arches of white-glazed terra-cotta. The cornice rises a full story to demarcate the entrance bay; the steel supports for this bit of stage scenery can be seen from farther down Boylston Street. The original ground-floor treatment has been largely obliterated by unsympathetic alterations.

Berkeley Building

222 Berkeley Street

Berkeley Street at Boylston Street
ROBERT A. M. STERN, 1991

500 Boylston Street

JOHN BURGEE ARCHITECTS WITH PHILIP
JOHNSON, 1988

This pair of buildings evolved from one of Boston's famous urban design battles of the 1980s. Originally the entire block was to have been occupied by twin towers, each with a forecourt, like the one eventually built at 500 Boylston by Johnson and Burgee. Community opposition was so intense, however, that the developer agreed to hire another architect to design the other half of the site. Robert A. M. Stern, known for his eclectic house designs, was selected through a design competition.

The result, unhappily, is a pair of almost completely unrelated buildings that side-by-side produce architectural indigestion. They are both heavy-handed and intrusive at the street level; yet when viewed on the skyline, they are of quite modest size compared with the old John Hancock tower, which avoids intruding on the neighborhood, and are far smaller than the elegantly chiseled John Hancock tower by I. M. Pei. The new pair are too pompous in their architectural expression, and neither is fully effective at creating a warm, inviting, and active street edge, although the Stern building is somewhat better in this respect, particularly the concave corner with convex oriel window at the Boylston/Berkeley corner (much like that of Jordan Marsh; see p. 19).

The Johnson/Burgee building at 500 Boylston Street is a staid neo Neoclassical Revival style and has been compared to a 1930s Philco radio in its overall form. The hulking mass has ruined the view of Trinity Church as seen from Copley Square. It is surprisingly successful on St. James

222 Berkeley Street and 500 Boylston Street

Street, however; in fact it brings a real improvement to that edge. The large forecourt on Boylston Street is far too grand for this location and for this type of private office use, but even worse is the way in which it ignores the microclimate. The space is almost always in shadow and is a trap for the high winds the tower draws into the space.

The Stern building of red brick and limestone is highly mannered and eclectic, drawing on motifs and materials found in many Boston buildings—acanthus leaves, monstrous urns, and gold capitals (inside); a tiny gold State House dome can even be found over the Boylston Street entry portico. The only alterations to the design submitted to the competition are oriel windows sprinkled here and there that dimly recall the wonderful rippling glass bays of the demolished Coulton Building that previously stood here. Inside there is a vaulted and skylit "Winter Garden" framed by shops and four levels of offices.

The pair of buildings painfully illustrates the lack of appropriate urban design guidelines for the site. Yet the clients were trying to produce well-designed buildings, as indicated by the fact that they hired architects with large reputations.

The New England
501 Boylston Street
CRAM AND FERGUSON, 1939–1942

Of this building, designed for the New England Mutual Life Insurance Company, poet David McCord quipped:

Ralph Adams Cram
One morning said damn,
And designed the Urn Burial
For a concern actuarial.

The design was actually done by Cram's partners and is said to have displeased Cram greatly. The large granite mass with its small cupola contains highly stylized references to Colonial architecture and perhaps is at its best inside the auditorium, bank lobby, and main entrance hall. However conservative its appearance, the structure was innovative in its engineering and rests on a floating foundation. Dioramas of the Indian fish weir that was discovered during excavations for the building may be seen in the lobby.

🏛 Boston Center for Adult Education
5 Commonwealth Avenue
THOMAS AND RICE, 1912
Open to the Public (by appointment)

For the Back Bay, this is a very recent house, built in 1912 by Walter C. Baylies, a Boston textile industrialist. It replaces an earlier house dating from 1861 which was identical to the house next door at number 3. Designed in an Italianate Style, the 1912 house has two symmetrical bows flanking a center entrance and rising three stories, while the top floor with its small square windows and swag panels sits back behind the third-floor cornice.

One of the Back Bay's most glamorous ballrooms, reminiscent of the Petit Trianon at Versailles, was added about 1913 and has a separate entrance through the tall wrought-iron gate. A stable was located behind this facade before it was rebuilt as a ballroom. The first floor of the house contained the library, parlor, dining room, pantry, and ballroom. Bedrooms were on the upper

Ballroom entrance, Boston Center for Adult Education

floors and the kitchen and laundry were in the basement. Much of the ornament and interior finishes are intact, marred only by the addition of classroom lighting and furnishings.

20–34 Commonwealth Avenue

BRYANT AND GILMAN, 1861

Each of the houses is only nineteen feet wide, but a very strong and harmonious effect is created by the repetition of oriel windows against the plain brick facade and a continuous mansard roof with deep cornice. There is some variation in treatment of doors and windows without ill effect on the whole composition.

25–27 Commonwealth Avenue

1861

Samuel Hooper, congressman and merchant, built 25 and 27 Commonwealth Avenue as one house, but they were divided in 1883. The only house in the Back Bay with a large corner yard, it is also unusual for its set-back side entrance and its height of only three stories.

Hooper mansion, 25–27 Commonwealth Avenue

Entrance, 25 Commonwealth Avenue

Haddon Hall

29 Commonwealth Avenue
J. Pickering Putnam, 1894

Haddon Hall caused quite a stir when it was built because of its eleven-story height, which eventually led to height restrictions on the rest of Back Bay, restrictions that obviously have been violated a few times since. The building was designed as luxury apartments. Yet as an oddity it has interest. Unlike most buildings in the Back Bay, it is of yellow-tan brick and brownstone. Each floor is demarcated with brown string courses, which are appealing in the way they ripple over the bays on the Commonwealth Avenue end. The triangular bay is a delight.

62–66 Commonwealth Avenue

1872

Three separate houses were conceived together to form a grand composition. The center house rises a full story higher with its tall mansard roof ornamented with iron cresting. The oriel window also rises an extra story. The flanking houses are mirror images of each other. Horizontal string courses of stone unify the facade.

62–66 Commonwealth Avenue

Haddon Hall

**Art Deco entrance,
56 Commonwealth Avenue**

Animated Georgian Revival bow fronts, 58–60 Commonwealth Avenue

🏛 First Baptist Church, "Church of the Holy Bean Blowers"

Commonwealth Avenue at
Clarendon Street

H. H. RICHARDSON, 1870–1872

National Register of Historic Places

Originally built for the Brattle Square Unitarian congregation, which had decided to sell its 1772 Colonial meeting house, this was Henry Hobson Richardson's earliest use of Romanesque forms.

Although he was to become one of Boston's most famous architects, Richardson was born far from Boston on Priestley Plantation in St. James, Louisiana, in 1838. His original intention was to enter military service, but because of his stutter, his wealthy parents encouraged him to pursue another career—for-

tunately for American architecture. After graduating from Harvard, where he was a member of the Porcellian, an exclusive club, Richardson headed for Paris. He was admitted to the Ecole des Beaux Arts in 1860 and remained there for seven years, studying European architecture and developing his skills as a designer. While he was in Paris the American Civil War cut off his funds from home, forcing him to work as a draftsman by day and study at night.

The new church for the Brattle Square congregation was Richardson's first important commission. Like many Boston churches of the period, it is built of Roxbury puddingstone laid in random ashlar. Its plan is basically cruciform. The monumental tower, almost freestanding like an Italian campanile, is (as Richardson himself felt) the most innovative and successful part of the building. The square tower, topped by a decorative

"Church of the Holy Bean Blowers"

frieze and corbeled arches that are in turn surmounted by a low-peaked overhanging roof, is one of the majestic forms on the Boston skyline. It is best viewed from Commonwealth Avenue Mall.

The frieze is notable, for it was modeled by Bartholdi (sculptor of the Statue of Liberty) in Paris. Italian workmen carved the frieze after the stones were set in place. It depicts the sacraments, and the faces are said to be likenesses of noted Bostonians of the time such as Longfellow, Emerson, Hawthorne, and Sumner. The trumpeting angels on the corners who look down over Back Bay have earned the building its nickname, "Church of the Holy Bean Blowers." The trumpets were originally gilded.

The Romanesque feeling of the church is conveyed by many round corbels, windows, and arches in the tower and by the portico arches. The theme is further developed in the beautiful windows based on a circle motif. It is interesting to note that Charles F. McKim, who was nine years younger than Richardson and later to become renowned as designer of the Boston Public Library and numerous other public edifices, worked on this project as a draftsman.

Four years after the new church was completed, the Brattle Square congregation dissolved, unable to bear the heavy costs of the new building. For several years it stood empty and there was even thought given to tearing it down, perhaps leaving the tower standing alone. But in 1881 the First Baptist Church, fleeing its former quarters in the declining South End, came to the building's rescue. They solved the acoustical problems of the sanctuary by adding galleries in 1884 to reduce echoes.

121 Commonwealth Avenue
CUMMINGS AND SEARS, 1872

The Ruskin Gothic style was characterized by abundant decorative and colorful elements which together make a picturesque ensemble. Two colors of brick, two of slate, stone, wood, wrought iron, and polychrome tile are used. The bay window is treated almost like a tower,

Ruskin Gothic house, 121 Commonwealth Avenue

with an ornamented peak that projects out from and above the mansard roof. Two years later the same architects designed New Old South Church on Boylston Street, which also explores a variety of surface decoration.

128–130 Commonwealth Avenue

S. D. KELLEY, 1882;

RENOVATION: ARTHUR BOWDITCH, 1905

Elaborate stone facades in the Baroque style of the Ecole des Beaux Arts of Paris were added to these houses twenty-three years after they were built. The style was more popular in New York than in more conservative Boston, which has only a handful of examples. The wrought-iron fence, gate, and balconies of number 130 are particularly fine. Bowditch also designed the Stoneholm at 1514 Beacon Street in Brookline, one of the most elaborate apartment buildings in the Boston area.

Chilton Club

152 Commonwealth Avenue

PEABODY AND STEARNS, 1870

The Chilton Club, founded in 1910, is of greater significance socially than architecturally. It is named in honor of Mary Chilton, the only Mayflower passenger to leave Plymouth and live in Boston with her husband John Winslow. They built a house in Spring Lane, where she died in 1679.

Like the fabled Boston hat handed down for generations, the building is serviceable, sturdy, unpretentious, and rather plain. The club was for many years the female counterpart of the exclusive men's club, the Somerset. It has three entrances originally intended for different social levels: The Commonwealth Avenue entrance was for members only, the Dartmouth Street entrance was for members with guests, and the alley was for servants and deliveries. Life for many women of Boston society was structured around their clubs, of which several still exist. Traditionally, sewing circles were the core of clubdom, a new one formed from each year's flock of debutantes.

🏛 Ames-Webster Mansion

Commonwealth Avenue at
306 Dartmouth Street

PEABODY AND STEARNS, 1872;

ENLARGED: JOHN H. STURGIS, 1882;

RESTORATION: CHILDS, BERTMAN, TSECKARES, CASENDINO, 1969

Built for Congressman Frederick Ames and enlarged ten years later for Oakes

Wrought-iron gate, Ames-Webster mansion

Beaux Arts facades, 128–130 Commonwealth Avenue

Ames, the house has some of the most elaborately ornamented interiors in the Back Bay. Sturgis enlarged the house in 1882 by adding a four-story monumental tower with a commanding mansard roof and a chimney ornamented with pediments and bas-reliefs. Next to this he created a new entrance and porte cochère with fine wrought-iron gates.

Inside, a grand hall was created, sixty-three by eighteen feet with an eighteen-foot ceiling, paneled in richly carved oak woodwork. At the end of the hall a grand staircase rises beneath a skylit dome of stained glass by John La Farge, surrounded by the murals of the French painter Benjamin Constant. Guests arriving for parties drove into the porte cochère, took the elevator to the second floor, where they removed their coats,

Ames-Webster mansion

Hall, Ames-Webster mansion

© Robert Perron

then made a grand entrance descending the broad staircase into the glittering hall. The Commonwealth Avenue side features an elaborately worked wrought-iron fence of spiral posts and intertwined floral vines and a two-story projecting plant conservatory.

The most recent occupant was Mrs. Edwin Webster, whose husband founded Stone and Webster Engineering in 1889. The house is now used as offices.

Hotel Vendome

160 Commonwealth Avenue

WILLIAM G. PRESTON, 1871 (CORNER BUILDING); J. F. OBER AND R. RAND, 1881 (MAIN BUILDING); RENOVATION: STAHL BENNETT, 1971–1975

The former Hotel Vendome is one of the finest buildings in the French Second Empire style in Boston and was built at the then exorbitant cost of one million dollars. The French Renaissance style is evident in the elegant facade of white Italian and Tuckahoe marble, ornamented with pediments, bays, and balustrades and topped by a mansard roof with an elaborate three-story peak over the main entrance. The roof was greatly altered and simplified by the renovation of the 1970s. The building is now condominiums and virtually none of its interior decor survives.

When built, the hotel boasted of its many luxuries, including private bathrooms, fireplaces, and steam heat in each room. In 1882 it was the first public building in the city to have electric lights. During its many glorious years as Boston's premier hotel, dozens of notables stayed here, including General Ulysses S. Grant, President Grover Cleveland, P. T. Bar-

Hotel Vendome

num, Mark Twain, Oscar Wilde, Sarah
Bernhardt, and John Singer Sargent.

176–178 Commonwealth Avenue
CHARLES ATWOOD, 1883

What a strange and provocative assemblage! A rusticated stone porch with three
entrance arches (serving two houses)
joins the buildings, and out of it rise
both a bay window and a bowfront
tower with conical roof. Rusticated
quoins and window trim are set into the
brick facade. By the time we reach the
top floor the style has changed from
Romanesque to Flemish in the dormer
pediments.

176–178 Commonwealth Avenue

191 Commonwealth Avenue
WESTON AND RAND, 1872

Henry Lee Higginson, a Boston stockbro-
ker and philanthropist best remembered
for founding the Boston Symphony
Orchestra, built and lived in this building. He called it Hotel Agassiz after his
wife, Ida Agassiz, daughter of famed
Harvard zoologist, Louis Agassiz. Originally there was only one vast apartment
of several thousand square feet on each
floor, but these have now been divided
up. A rather simple building in the
"panel brick" style identified by architectural historian Bainbridge Bunting, it
makes its major statement through a
series of alternating towerlike bays and
gabled projections. String courses demarcate each floor. Ornament is concentrated around the windows and at the
top of the fourth and fifth floors.

Higginson detested motor cars and
walked from his apartment to his State
Street office each day. He had served in
the Civil War and made his fortune in
the post-war boom. As his motto he took
the epitaph of the Duke of Devonshire:
"What I gave, I have; What I spent, I
had; What I kept, I lost."

195 Commonwealth Avenue
J. PICKERING PUTNAM, 1881

Elaborate brick and terra-cotta ornament
adorn this house, notable both for its
octagonal corner tower and its strong and
varied pattern of windows defined by
stone. A recessed balcony has been
tucked in under the roof next to the
chimney.

195 Commonwealth Avenue

St. Botolph Club
199 Commonwealth Avenue
McKim, Mead, and White, 1890

The Federal Revival flourished in Boston in the late nineteenth century and early twentieth century. According to Bainbridge Bunting, forty-nine houses in the Back Bay had been done in the style by 1917. This house, the largest in the style, has a symmetrical facade with two bows flanking a central Ionic portico entrance. Small-paned windows would have been more appropriate to the style. The fourth-floor servants' quarters are set back behind a balustrade. The building now houses the St. Botolph Club, established in 1881 at 85 Boylston Street for artists, writers, and professional men. The club sponsored the first exhibit of John Singer Sargent paintings in America in January 1888.

Mason House
211 Commonwealth Avenue
Rotch and Tilden, 1883
music room added c. 1897

Surprisingly, behind the simple facade are some of the most elaborate Queen Anne interiors in Boston. The only clue is the entrance set within a curved paneled niche with leaded glass, said by architect Ogden Codman to have been inspired by two doorways of Asher Benjamin. The arch has a decorative band of large and small voussoirs. Inside the house each room is treated differently. The library has a cove ceiling with woodwork of quartered oak and a tapestry wall covering, the stair hall is dark mahogany, and the oval dining room has an ornate coffered plaster ceiling and silver chandelier. Arthur Rotch designed the woodwork and much of the furniture for the house, which was built for William Powell Mason and later occupied by his daughter, Miss Fanny Mason.

About 1897 a large thirty- by forty-five-foot music room in the Italian Renais-

Mason house

sance Revival style was added at the rear of the house. It may be the finest music room in a Boston house. It has a coffered ceiling with shallow recessed dome, illuminated by indirect electric lighting, probably the first architectural element designed expressly for electric light in the Back Bay. Coffered round arches surround three sides of the room, while the fourth side at the entrance to the room is a coffered apselike space. Much of the furniture for the room was purchased in Venice by Miss Mason, who traveled there with her friend Mrs. Jack Gardner. The extensive use of Carrara marble in the room created a very bright sound.

Miss Mason was noted for her musical interests and knowledge. She had frequent concerts, not only in her Boston home, but also at her estate in Walpole, New Hampshire and her homes in Beverly Cove and Paris. The list of interna-

tionally renowned musicians who performed in her music room would be the envy of any concert hall. Ferruccio Busoni played the inaugural concert and was followed over the decades by many other eminent pianists, including Ignace Paderewski, Alfred Cortot, Arthur Rubinstein, Alexander Brailowsky, Egon Petri, George Copeland, Paul Doguereau, and Earl Wild. Vocal recitals were given by Mary Garden, Maggie Teyte, Emma Calvé, and tenor René Clément; and Nadia Boulanger performed with her choral group. Cellist Pablo Casals and violinist Jacques Thibaud also played here in individual recitals and performed as a trio with pianist Alfred Cortot in Miss Mason's Paris apartment. Her musical interests brought her the acquaintance of composers as well. She commissioned a quintet by Bohuslav Martinu (1890–1959) that had its premiere in her music room. The

Courtesy Paul Doguereau

Music room, Mason house

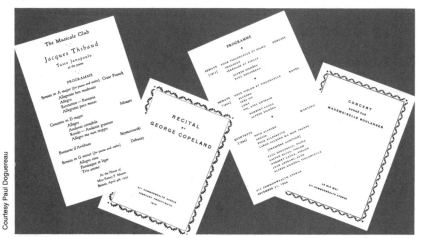

Programs for concerts held in Miss Fanny Mason's music room

musical traditions begun by Miss Mason were carried on by the Peabody Mason Music Foundation established by Paul Doguereau in her memory.

Algonquin Club

217 Commonwealth Avenue

MCKIM, MEAD, AND WHITE, 1887

Like the Public Library begun the same year, Back Bay's most palatial club has a limestone facade in the Italian Renaissance Revival style favored by Stanford White, the architect. Projecting bays anchor each end of the facade, which is framed by a heavy cornice and over-scaled frieze on top and a rusticated ground floor. A two-level Ionic porch rises above the center entrance and is further elaborated by the Palladian window above it on the fourth floor. The ground floor originally projected beyond the face of the building for the entire length, form-

ing a terrace for the second floor. In 1889, however, the club was ordered by the Commonwealth to alter the building to conform with the Back Bay's precise setback requirements.

Algonquin Club

Queen Anne oriel window detail, 239 Commonwealth Avenue

Commonwealth Avenue at 21 Fairfield Street

W. WHITNEY LEWIS, 1881

W. Whitney Lewis was much influenced by Richardson's Rectory for Trinity Church (see Newbury at 233 Clarendon Street, p. 281) in this house with a projecting chimney–bay window combination on the end, arched side entrance, and gabled peak. The fenestration is disorderly, however, and the ornamentation has gotten out of hand. The recently painted sandstone trim gives the building a Flemish feeling and is out of character with the original intent.

21 Fairfield Street

247 Commonwealth Avenue

WILLIAM RANTOUL, 1905

Almost Georgian in feeling, this granite bow front is reminiscent of McKim, Mead, and White's 303 Commonwealth (1895) and Little and Browne's 118 Beacon Street (1907). This house, however, is less monumental, more domestic, with its small-scaled entry portico, second-floor balconies, center windows with slender sidelights, and stepped-back fourth floor with dormers.

247 Commonwealth Avenue

270 Commonwealth Avenue
DUNHAM AND McKAY, 1896

Built as the Hotel Tuileries, a residential hotel, this is now a dormitory. The Classical vocabulary popularized by McKim, Mead, and White was put to good use here. This time, the rusticated base rises two stories, as does the triumphal arch entry portico with two levels of columns. Windows above are spaced rhythmically—three-two-three—and surmounted by three orders of lintels: flat, segmental, and triangular pediments. A cornice with frieze based on the Greek anthemion rises almost a full floor above the top windows.

Hotel Tuileries, 270 Commonwealth Avenue

Charles Francis Adams House
Commonwealth Avenue at
20 Gloucester Street
PEABODY AND STEARNS, 1886

Peabody and Stearns were content to leave the strong forms of two gables and a round corner tower with conical slate roof quite unadorned and straightforward in their design for the home of Charles Francis Adams. What ornament there is counts. The handsome chimney stack has a single spine running from a carved bracket on the third floor all the way to the top, which has simple bands of moldings. The date "1886" is mounted on the chimney in large numerals. Around the entrance is a somewhat Richardsonian broad border of carved filigree.

Charles Francis Adams house

International Institute

International Institute
287 Commonwealth Avenue
ROTCH AND TILDEN, 1892

Greek decorative motifs abound in this basically simple extra-wide Classical Revival house of limestone built for Herbert M. Sears. Anthemion cresting tops the Corinthian entry portico and another anthemion border runs along the top of the cornice. An egg-and-dart molding follows under the string course at the top of the first floor. First-floor windows are framed with lintels resting upon brackets and a rosette border.

Pickman House
303 Commonwealth Avenue
MCKIM, MEAD, AND WHITE, 1895

The most monumental and austere residence in the Back Bay is perhaps the Pickman house—McKim, Mead, and White's last Back Bay residence. The simple thirty-three-foot-wide bowed facade has a mausoleumlike center entrance. Ornament is confined to the cornice, a garland string course above the third floor, a Greek-key course above the first floor, roundels between the fourth-floor windows, and a relief panel above the center window of the second floor. Inside, a grand staircase with bronze balustrade rises gently to the second floor behind a row of Ionic columns. Mrs. Pickman held coming-out balls for

Pickman house

her two daughters here, transforming the house into a Paris street scene for Nancy and into a garden scene for Lucy.

🏛 John F. Andrew Mansion
Commonwealth Avenue
at 32 Hereford Street
McKim, Mead, and White, 1884–1888

McKim, Mead, and White introduced the Italian Renaissance Revival style to the Back Bay in their mansion for John F. Andrew, one year before their noted Villard mansions were built in New York City. The elliptical projecting corner mass adds much to the interest of the building and to the street intersection. A simple round tower such as the one two blocks away at 448 Beacon Street is static by comparison. The visual interest of the mass is further enhanced by the

304 Commonwealth Avenue (Julius Schweinfurth, 1895)

continuous balustrade and cornice wrapping around the hip roof and by the string courses beneath the windows of the third and fourth floors. The low-ceilinged ground floor contains a billiard

John F. Andrew mansion

room and other minor rooms and is faced in stone in contrast to the brick above. Heavy wrought-iron grilles project from the windows. The tall windows above are given lacy iron balconies. The wrought-iron balcony on the third floor above the Palladian window is from the Tuileries Palace in Paris, which was burned in the revolt of 1874. Windows are trimmed in limestone and reduce in size above the second floor. The house has the first street-level entrance in the Back Bay, which because of the area's high water table resulted in a basement barely six feet high. Many of the interiors have been preserved (except for furnishings) and are proudly maintained by the MIT fraternity that occupies the house.

Miss Farmer's School of Cookery

now condominiums
Commonwealth Avenue at
40 Hereford Street
SHAW AND HUNNEWELL, 1886

Fannie Merrit Farmer founded her school of cookery in 1902, and it was located at this address for many years until the building was converted to condominiums. The house is interesting to compare with the Andrew house across the avenue, built about the same time. Both are topped by balustrades that conceal top-floor servants' quarters, and both have stone-faced ground floors with entrances in the center of the long facade. Instead of the elliptical bay and tower of 32 Hereford, here we see two square projecting bays. Curved elements are restricted to the odd entry portico and a bow front on Commonwealth Avenue. The stone window trim is evocative of the Georgian style rather than the Renaissance style of the Andrew house.

🏛 Burrage Mansion
314 Commonwealth Avenue
CHARLES BRIGHAM, 1889

Here is one exception to Boston's avoidance of flamboyant New York–type buildings. Reminiscent of the earlier Vanderbilt mansion by Richard Morris Hunt in New York, this limestone chateau was inspired by the French chateau Chenonceaux. Both inside and outside the lush French Gothic and Early Renaissance ornament are quite overwhelming. The roofline along Hereford Street is particularly evocative, with two turret towers, several decorated chimneys, and dorm-

Burrage mansion

ers. A charming greenhouse with curved glass roof and dome is attached to the back of the house.

Burrage mansion, Hereford Street

The Lafayette

333 Commonwealth Avenue
DUNHAM AND MCKAY, 1895

Built as the Hotel Lafayette, this is by the
same architect-contractors who designed
and built the former Hotel Tuileries (see
270 Commonwealth Avenue, p. 266) in
the same neoclassic vein. Window spacing and treatment are identical except for
the two bay windows here. Also, the
entrance is less monumental.

Ames Mansion

355 Commonwealth Avenue
CARL FEHMER, 1882

Chimney, Ames mansion

H. H. Richardson prepared a sketch
design for the Oliver Ames mansion, but
for some reason Carl Fehmer became the
architect. Ames made a fortune in manufacturing and railroads and was governor
from 1887 until 1890. The mansion is the
largest in Back Bay and has some of the
most opulent interiors. It was the first
Back Bay house to draw on the style of
the French chateaus of the Loire Valley.
A solid brownstone block without the
three-dimensional modeling of the Burrage chateau one block away (see 314
Commonwealth, p. 270), it has a deep
mansard roof penetrated by dormers and
chimneys. The end bays of the Massachusetts Avenue facade project slightly
and are expressed in the roof. Running
around the house between the first- and
second-floor windows is a frieze of putti
and floral ornament depicting household
activities such as dining, reading, and
music. For many years headquarters of
the National Casket Company, the mansion is now an office building.

Wrought-iron window guard, Ames
mansion

10 Marlborough Street

LITTLE AND BROWNE, 1905

This early twentieth-century Georgian Revival house was once the home of Edwin O'Connor. O'Connor wrote *The Last Hurrah,* a story of Boston politics and of the conflicts between Boston Brahmins and the Irish during the years of James Michael Curley.

17 Marlborough Street

1863

An unusual solution to the challenge posed by the narrow bayfronted house, the entrance is placed in the center of the bay, rather than to one side. An entry portico with columns projects beyond the bay, flanked by narrow arched windows. Henry Lee Higginson conceived the founding of the Boston Symphony Orchestra here in the home of his friend, George Howe.

First Lutheran Church

Marlborough Street at 299 Berkeley Street

PIETRO BELLUSCHI, 1959

An intimate and inviting landscaped courtyard provides access to the simple and tranquil church interior, illuminated by a narrow band of clerestory windows beneath the shallow vaulted ceiling. Natural wood and tan brick are the primary materials. The exterior form largely ignores its Victorian neighbors.

Harvard Club (Parker, Thomas, and Rice, 1912), 374 Commonwealth Avenue

French Library in Boston

53 Marlborough Street

1867

The house now used as the French Library was built for Edward and Charles Codman and given to the Library by a later Francophile owner, Katherine Lane Weems. The large house has a symmetrical facade with mansard roof, three-story bays on each side of the center entrance, and a rusticated ground floor. A library extension was added to the side. The salon is said to be based on the Empress Josephine's private parlor at Malmaison. A fine tall iron fence surrounds the property.

🏛 First and Second Church

Marlborough Street at Berkeley Street
WARE AND VAN BRUNT, 1867;
PAUL RUDOLPH, 1971

William Robert Ware and Henry Van Brunt, both Harvard graduates in the early 1850s, studied architecture in the New York atelier of Richard Morris Hunt. In 1863 they formed their Boston partnership where, like Hunt, they also taught students. Ware established the School of Architecture at MIT in 1865, based on the Ecole des Beaux Arts in Paris.

For First and Second Church, founded in 1630 and one of the nation's oldest congregations, the architects looked to the English country churches of the middle ages for inspiration. The square stone tower is particularly appealing. Its slender octagonal stone spire, a broach spire, becomes four-sided at its base, the juncture pointed up by four small Gothic windows called lucarnes. The base of the tower widens as it approaches the ground and has diagonal buttresses at the corners.

Most of the church burned in 1968. Paul Rudolph's replacement preserves the tower, porch, and end wall—except for the unfortunate removal of the peak—and creates an inviting amphitheaterlike entry on Marlborough Street that is sympathetic both to the fragments of the old church and to the street scene. A small parking garage has been worked in underneath, unique for a Boston church. The odd-angled geometry is

First and Second Church

reminiscent of Frank Lloyd Wright, but some of the conjunctions do not seem to be fully resolved. The main structural material inside and out is rough striated concrete, which Rudolph has explored in several buildings, including his State Service Center (see Cambridge Street at New Chardon, p. 32) and his School of Arts and Architecture at Yale.

Marlborough Street at 271-279 Clarendon Street

1869

Five houses are grouped together in a single mass with an apparently common mansard roof, and enormous gains are made esthetically. Imagine the jumble if each house had tried to differ from its neighbor! The projecting oriel windows provide three-dimensional interest, as do the two bows on the corner house. The entrance of the corner house was originally located on Marlborough Street where there is now a bay window, but was moved to Clarendon Street when the house was joined to its neighbor at 273.

Entrance, 81 Marlborough Street

Douglas A. Thom Clinic
Marlborough Street at
315 Dartmouth Street
1870

Mansard-roofed towers are the theme of several buildings in this immediate area. In this mansion built for Hollis Hunnewell, square towers of different heights flank the entrance. Similar towers appeared six years later in the adjacent house at 151 Commonwealth Avenue, then in 1881 in the Vendome addition and in 1882 in the addition to the Ames-Webster mansion across the street.

Crowninshield House
164 Marlborough Street
H. H. RICHARDSON, 1870
National Register of Historic Places

One of the least interesting of Richardson's works, this early house built for Katherine Crowninshield does exhibit some imaginative decorative work including a wrought-iron entry canopy and ornamental tiles set into the brick, as well

Chimney detail, Crowninshield house

Hollis Hunnewell mansion, now Douglas A. Thom clinic

271–279 Clarendon Street

as decorative brickwork and odd hooded dormers. The wrought-iron fence by an unknown designer is seen at several locations in Back Bay and features balls atop all the verticals and hearts penetrated by forged diamond pendants.

🏛 Cushing-Endicott House
165 Marlborough Street
SNELL AND GREGERSON, 1871

326–328 Dartmouth Street
SNELL AND GREGERSON, 1872

This house and the two next door on Dartmouth Street were designed as an ensemble. The two taller matched end houses balanced the lower but wider and symmetrical facade of the center house with its two projecting bays flanking the entrance. Unfortunately, the three houses have not been maintained as a group and no longer match.

Although the center house looks wide on the facade, its plan is T-shaped and reduces to a fifteen-foot width in the rear, while the end house becomes wider at the back. The facade of number 165, executed in the French Academic style, is particularly handsome. Symmetrical bays with double dormers balance the center entrance portico of four columns topped by an ornamental iron railing. Windows are outlined in inventive stone trim, not strictly in the classical tradition. The main rooms of the house are on the second floor, which has fourteen-foot ceilings. The kitchen was placed on the entry level, unusual for a Back Bay house of the period.

Cushing-Endicott house

Until 1958, the house had many of its fine original furnishings and decor and had been continuously occupied by only two families, the Cushings and the Endicotts. In 1903 Mrs. Endicott lent John Singer Sargent one of the bedrooms to use as a studio.

191 Marlborough Street

CARL FEHMER, 1881

The thirty-two-foot wide site made possible a generous Romanesque recessed portico with columns and wrought-iron infill in the arch and broad porch, both of Nova Scotia sandstone. The house is considered to be one of the best examples of Ruskin Gothic in the area.

191 Marlborough Street

225–239 Marlborough Street

225–231, LOUIS WEISSBEIN, 1873;
233–239, 1874

An exceptionally pleasing and harmonious row of narrow houses, mainly four stories, has been created within a limited vocabulary. Each has a mansard roof with pedimented dormers and an oriel

window on the second floor. Small front gardens are defined by wrought-iron fences. On the first floor there are two arched openings, one the door, the other a window in a small reception room.

Marlborough Street

at 12 Fairfield Street

CABOT AND CHANDLER, 1879

8, 10 Fairfield Street

STURGIS AND BRIGHAM, 1879

Often in the Back Bay a particular style took root on one street and spread to neighboring houses. On Fairfield Street the Queen Anne style, with its picturesque massing and variety of surface ornament, is seen at numbers 8, 10, and 12. A variety of brick types—Bainbridge Bunting counted twenty at 12 Fairfield—creates wonderful decoration, from rolled window jambs or cornices, to a fantastic base for the oriel window. A delightful wrought-iron fence of S scrolls and tridents defines the side yard.

Wrought-iron fence, 12 Fairfield Street

Oriel windows, 286–290 Marlborough

Marlborough Street
at 18 Fairfield Street
PEABODY AND STEARNS, 1878

20 Fairfield Street
W. WHITNEY LEWIS, 1875

Here are two more charming Fairfield Street houses, one almost miniaturized by its larger, more aggressive neighbor. W. Whitney Lewis, architect of number 20, was born in England and in 1871 came to Boston, where he designed a number of houses in the Ruskin Gothic style. Lewis also designed the house across the street at 21 Fairfield (see Commonwealth Avenue at 21 Fairfield Street, p. 265).

18–20 Fairfield Street

The Marlborough
416 Marlborough Street
WILLARD T. SEARS, 1895

Apartment hotels were said to shelter, "the newly wed and the nearly dead." Many had restaurants as well as maid service. Elevators, private bathrooms, and central heating were, by the late nineteenth century, standard luxuries in such buildings. While this building has some interesting brownstone trim and ironwork and an appealing round corner, its overall massing and facade organization lack the imagination of Sears's later Hotel Cambridge (see 483 Beacon Street, p. 245).

Stonework, The Marlborough

Emmanuel Church
15 Newbury Street
ALEXANDER R. ESTEY, 1862;
ENLARGEMENT; FREDERICK R. ALLEN, 1899;
LESLIE LINDSEY MEMORIAL CHAPEL: ALLEN
AND COLLENS, 1920–1924

This towerless church was actually built in three parts designed by three different architects. The original church was a small Gothic country church by Alexander R. Estey, who also designed the fine and well-preserved Church of Our Saviour at 23 Monmouth Street, Brookline (see Longwood and Cottage Farm, Brookline, p. 466). Emanuel Church was the first church in the Gothic Revival style in the Back Bay and also one of the first to

Door hardware, Leslie Lindsey Memorial Chapel

use Roxbury puddingstone. In 1899 the church was enlarged by the addition of a new east-west nave, which filled in the former church lawn. The original nave then became a transept. The Leslie Lindsey Memorial Chapel, the westernmost part of the complex, was designed in the 1920s by the nationally recognized Gothic architects of New York's Riverside Church, Allen and Collens. The chapel was built by Mr. and Mrs. William Lindsey in memory of their daughter, Leslie, who had drowned in the sinking of the *Lusitania*. The ornamental work here is of high quality, with ironwork by F. Koralewski and the high altar and stained glass by Sir Ninian Comper.

37 Newbury Street
GWATHMEY, SIEGEL, 1980

Built as the showroom and office building of Knoll International, manufacturers of contemporary designer furniture and textiles, this building proclaims its modernism in concrete, glass block, and plate glass. Replacing a brownstone gutted by fire, it pays little attention to the forms, materials, or general character of its surroundings and might be more at home in Los Angeles or New York. A glass-block stairwell, reminiscent of Le Corbusier's Carpenter Center (see Harvard University, p. 402), rises the full height of the building. A glass entrance is tucked in between this and a projecting curved plate-glass show window. The first three floors of showrooms are expressed on the exterior, being transparent and set back, while the offices above have window bands divided into squares.

Church of the Covenant
67 Newbury Street
R. M. UPJOHN, 1865–1867

R. M. Upjohn was the son of Richard Upjohn, a leader in the English Gothic Revival and architect of Trinity Church in New York City. Upjohn senior had moved to Boston in 1834 and worked for Alexander Parris for several years. Young Upjohn followed his father's lead in this Gothic Revival structure of Roxbury puddingstone with its impressive 236-foot spire, accentuated with two levels of pinnacles and lucarnes. Three-stepped setback buttresses give the tower its solid monumental feeling of growing from the ground to lofty heights. The Gothic forms

37 Newbury Street (formerly Knoll International)

© Steve Rosenthal

of the church's nave, transept, and buttresses are further heightened by their pinnacles and pointed gablets at the rooflines. Its main entrance is through a tripartite porch of Gothic trefoil arches with gablets. Interior decoration includes a Favrile glass lantern by one of Tiffany's designers, from the Tiffany Chapel at the 1893 Chicago World's Fair. The church was originally the Central Congregational Church, formed in 1835 on Winter Street.

Trinity Church Rectory
Newbury Street at 233 Clarendon Street
H. H. RICHARDSON, 1879;
THIRD STORY ADDED 1893
National Register of Historic Places

Richardson designed the Rectory for his friend Phillips Brooks, rector of Trinity Church. The entrance facade, balanced but asymmetrical, is organized in thirds. A large Romanesque arch with light and

Church of the Covenant

brick panels, and marquetry. The brick for both buildings came from the North Cambridge brickworks of M. W. Sands.

A floor was added to the house in 1893 to accommodate the new rector and his family (Brooks was a bachelor). The original roof design with dormers was retained and the new floor was in effect slipped between the second floor and the roof, with remarkably little esthetic damage.

Trinity Church Rectory

dark stone voussoirs and recessed entrance dominates the center third, and the end thirds are defined by the pointed gables. On the end wall on Newbury Street the chimney is imaginatively combined with projecting windows, making a sort of bay.

The house was designed about the same time as Sever Hall at Harvard (see Harvard University, p. 400) and exhibits some of the same features, among them the rhythmic placement of window openings and the fine brickwork including edge roll moldings of brick around windows, ornamental carved

109 Newbury Street

CHARLES A. CUMMINGS, 1871

This and the house down the block at 277 Dartmouth Street were designed by architects as their own houses, and both express a penchant for the medieval. Two donjon towers with conical slate roofs flank the center entrance bay. A variety of decorative brickwork is used. The architect, Charles Cummings, was selected to design New Old South Church shortly after the completion of his house.

109 Newbury Street

Hotel Victoria

now condominiums
Newbury Street at 275 Dartmouth Street
J. L. FAXON, 1886

Faxon indulged in a variety of fantasies in his design for the Hotel Victoria. Its castellated form with crenellated parapet and corner battlement ripples with bays of every type. Window treatments vary from floor to floor, with emphasis on the Moorish in the lower levels.

277 Dartmouth Street
Newbury Street at 277 Dartmouth Street
J. PICKERING PUTNAM, 1878

J. Pickering Putnam, architect, built this as his own house. Like the earlier house at the other end of the block (see 109 Newbury, p. 282), it draws its inspiration from the medieval period. This is most evident in the complex, picturesque roof with its projecting gabled bay, two bay towers, and a charming bartizan visually supported on a column in the rear corner. For many years the building was a restaurant founded by Josef, society restaurateur, who served for over twenty years in the Ritz and the Copley Plaza before starting his own restaurant.

277 Dartmouth Street

🏛 Boston Art Club

now Copley Square High School
Newbury Street at 270 Dartmouth Street
WILLIAM RALPH EMERSON, 1881

What a fanciful building! At first glance the Boston Art Club may appear awkward, even ugly in its odd assemblage of dissimilar forms. An example of the Queen Anne style, it was inspired by a variety of picturesque medieval elements.

On the corner, a hexagonal tower with an odd double curved roof emerges from the square foundation, the transition effected by means of another peculiar detail, a stone balcony visually supported on a single Byzantine column. Related to the tower roof is the charming small dormer on the Dartmouth Street facade over the handsome carved archway. Enormous carved terra-cotta scroll brackets visually reinforce the gable-roofed portions of

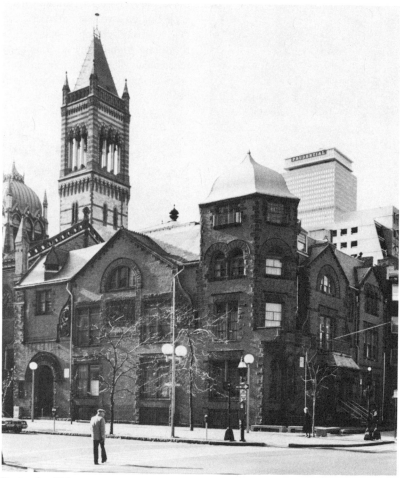

Boston Art Club

both facades. Rusticated quoins, voussoirs, and lintels dramatize the form.

William Emerson was the nephew of Ralph Waldo Emerson and was also the designer of "the house of odd windows" on Beacon Hill (see 24 Pinckney Street, p. 186), the Massachusetts Homeopathic Hospital on East Concord Street between Harrison and Albany, and the peculiar One Winthrop Square. Emerson always toyed with the traditional architectural vocabulary, testing its limits. Even today, more than a century after its construction, this building is a surprise and an enigma.

Exeter Towers
Newbury Street at 28 Exeter Street
STEFFIAN BRADLEY ASSOCIATES, 1979

In designing this nine-story commercial and residential structure, the architects had to relate to the character and scale of

Newbury Street, part of the Back Bay historic district. The red brick and the projecting bay window forms echo the surroundings. The architects made the building's height seem less intrusive on Newbury Street by stepping the brick facade up from the level of the neighboring four- to five-story buildings to a ninety-foot tower at the corner. The upper floors pretend to be invisible or part of another building, being set back somewhat and finished in a light color.

🏛 Exeter Street Theatre Building
Newbury Street at Exeter Street
HARTWELL AND RICHARDSON, 1884;
RESTAURANT RENOVATION: CHILDS, BERTMAN,
TSECKARES, CASENDINO 1974–1975

If the Exeter Street Theatre reminds the reader of a church, that is because it was built for the Working Union of Progressive

© Peter Vanderwerker

Exeter Towers

Exeter Street Theater Building

Spiritualists. The First Spiritualist Temple later moved downstairs, and in 1914 the upper auditorium became the theater. Until 1984 it was preserved intact as the oldest continuously operating movie theater in Boston. For many years it was the only movie theater a proper Boston woman would enter, probably because of its spiritual overtones. Richardsonian Romanesque, the facade employs two col-

ors of stone. The entry arch is marred by the theater marquee and signs, but these in themselves are now landmarks. In 1985, despite intense neighborhood opposition, the significant theater interior was demolished to accommodate a home furnishings shop. Upper floors are offices, and the ground floor has been renovated as a restaurant with a greenhouse extension.

Prince School
Newbury Street at Exeter Street
GEORGE A. CLOUGH, 1875
RENOVATION: GRASSI SHARKEY DESIGN GROUP, 1985–1987

This school has been recycled as a residential/commercial complex. The original building was far more attractive. Its tall French mansard and hipped roofs topped by iron cresting and cupolas organized the mass into a center pavilion and two end pavilions. When the third floor was added, however, the roof was removed.

Prince School in the late 1800s

© George Zimberg

Boston Architectural Center

🏛 Boston Architectural Center

320 Newbury Street

ASHLEY, MYER AND ASSOCIATES 1963–1966

Besides being an admirable piece of contemporary architecture, the Boston Architectural Center surprisingly fits quite happily into its nineteenth-century context, partly because of the way in which the mass is broken down, but primarily because of the open, inviting nature of its ground floor.

The design was the winner of a competition to design a building devoted to architecture where students and practitioners could meet to learn and teach. The jury praised the design for the economy of its prefabricated components and for its simple form, which is suited to the site and which clearly communicates its functions from both inside and out. The long-span concrete frame permits maximum flexibility in interior arrangements and a variety of facade treatments, from the open ground floor to partially screened studios to the almost completely enclosed meeting room and library. The ground-floor exhibition hall features frequently changing public exhibits on architecture, urban design, and related arts. The stark concrete rear elevation has been decorated with a trompe l'oeil Renaissance sectional view by Richard Haas (1977), visible from Boylston and Newbury streets.

The Boston Architecture Center (BAC) provides students with the opportunity to study architecture while maintaining full-time jobs. Its faculty is made up largely of volunteer practicing architects in the Boston area.

Newbury Street Stables

Newbury Street between Hereford Street and Massachusetts Avenue
1875 AND LATER

Back Bay residents who did not have their own stables kept their horses and carriages in the stables in this block or in the area of Beacon Hill between Charles Street and the river. Stables still survive in both areas, converted to commercial and residential space, while large automobile garages have been built to store vehicles. An area of unique charm for the Back Bay, the low carriage houses retain their individualistic character and now house many businesses related to photography, paints, and the arts. Two contemporary outdoor murals are to be seen in the block. Besides the Boston Architectural Center mural (see 320 Newbury Street, p. 286), *Tramount Mural,* a provocative surrealist painting by Morgan Bulkeley (1981), appears on the MBTA building next to Auditorium station.

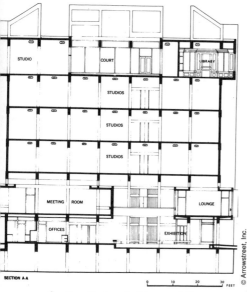

Section, Boston Architectural Center

Richard Haas mural and converted Newbury Street stables

360 Newbury Street

Tramount Mural (Morgan Bulkeley, 1981) Newbury Street near Massachusetts Avenue

360 Newbury Street

ARTHUR BOWDITCH, 1918; RENOVATION: FRANK O. GEHRY AND SCHWARTZ/SILVER ARCHITECTS, 1989

This is an example of importing architectural talent to Boston and obtaining a result that is worth talking about. The collaboration between Schwartz/Silver, the Boston firm known for its refined and respectful renovations, and Frank Gehry, the Los Angeles architect most famous for his use of chain-link fence as a decorative element, produced a design more elegant and subtle than Gehry's characteristic design expression. Designed as a warehouse, the building has always towered over Newbury Street, a sore thumb when viewed from Back Bay streets. The blank back wall of the building is newly clad in sheets of slate-colored lead-coated copper to protect the deteriorating concrete. Slate-gray metal-sheathed struts define the new projecting penthouse on the top two floors and also climb the facade on several lower floors over the main entrance on Newbury Street, creating an aggressive profile that is visible far down the street. The lobby is an elegant lair of backlit yellow onyx and dark birch wood panels framed in brass. At the base of the office building are three floors of retail space.

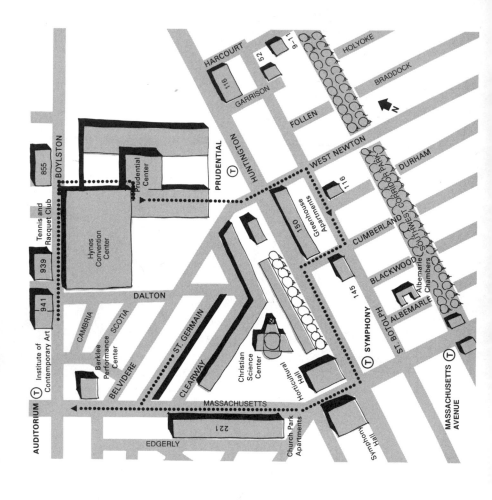

Prudential Center Area

Prudential Center/St. Botolph Street Tour

Start at the **Institute of Contemporary Art (294)** and **Engine and Hose House Number 33 (294)** on Boylston at Hereford Street. The **Tennis and Racquet Club (293)** is across the street. At the corner of Gloucester Street turn right and ascend the escalator into the **Prudential Center** complex (**292**). Proceed all the way through the concourse past shops and banks and exit on Huntington Avenue between the Colonnade Hotel and **Greenhouse Apartments (295)**.

If you want to see the interesting and very different character of St. Botolph Street, which was cut off from the Back Bay by railroad tracks for most of its history, walk down West Newton Street and turn right onto **St. Botolph Street (300)**. Turn right on Cumberland Street at the **School-House (302)** and return to Huntington Avenue and the **Christian Science World Headquarters (296)**. You will have a good view of the reflecting pool and the long facade of the publishing headquarters. Cross Huntington Avenue and turn left, walking through the trees next to the pool in the direction of **Horticultural Hall** and **Symphony Hall (298)**.

Then turn right onto Massachusetts Avenue and pass the entrance plaza of the **Christian Science Church** and the walled garden. On the opposite side of the street is the **Church Park** apartment building (**297**). As you pass **St. Germain Street** on your right, notice the cast-iron street lamps, brick sidewalks, and renovated bowfront apartments of this short street. At the end of the tour is the **Berklee Performance Center (296)** and Auditorium Station.

Prudential Center Complex

800 Boylston Street

PUBLIC OBSERVATION DECK: CHARLES LUCK-
MAN AND ASSOCIATES AND HOYLE, DORAN,
AND BERRY BEGUN 1959; HYNES CONVEN-
TION CENTER EXPANSION AND RENOVATION:
KALLMANN, McKINNELL, AND WOOD,
1985–1988

A new scale was introduced into the Back
Bay with the construction of Prudential
Center, built over the expansive old railroad yards as one of Boston's early and
controversial urban renewal projects. It
was one of the first expressions of urban
designer David Crane's later "capital web"
concept, which focused new high-density
development along a spine while retaining the historic infill. The scheme has
now filled out, with a spine of high-rise
construction stretching from Prudential
Center to Government Center.

In Prudential Center large freestanding masses—offices, hotel, and apartments—hover over vast open plazas that
conceal underground parking garages and
attempt to address needs of twentieth-
century Boston. The tower, whether
loved or despised, has become a regional
as well as a local landmark. It can be
seen popping up at the most surprising
places, whether from Cambridge, from
Brookline, or from the north side of Beacon Hill, where its massive top awkwardly rises behind the mound of tiny
brick houses. Spectacular views of the
region may be had from the viewing deck
and restaurant.

Design of the plazas and the uses to
which they might be put were never well
considered, and they still present an
oddly sinister and surrealist landscape.
The shopping mall, too, has had to strug-

Hynes Convention Center

gle for survival because of basic flaws in its conception. Raising it one level above the street, where it could be neither seen nor easily reached, was the first mistake. The apparent attempt to minimize pedestrian traffic past shops by placing commercial space on only one side of each wide walkway and separating the four already weak sections by more open space and revolving doors has presented a challenge to the most magnetic merchandising. Heavy winds still funnel through the shopping arcades despite the addition of protective walls.

The major expansion and renovation of the ungainly Hynes Convention Center in the late 1980s created a completely new image by bringing the facade out to define Boylston Street with a colonnade. At the same time it slices off the right side of the vast empty Prudential forecourt. It attempts to relate in scale and materials to its Back Bay neighbors with granite and a setback from the curb like that of the Boston Public Library a few blocks away. Unlike the Boylston Street facade, the facade adjacent to the Sheraton Hotel is multicolor tan brick with Richardsonian rose granite bands and a light gray granite top. The long articulated mass along Boylston Street helps define the street space and expresses the public hallways inside, which offer relief from the convention halls with places for relaxation and views of Back Bay. The severe gray interior is reminiscent of an early twentieth-century German railroad station, as is the striking entrance canopy not quite on axis with Gloucester Street.

855 Boylston Street
THE ARCHITECTS COLLABORATIVE, 1986

The construction of this office and retail building brought about a major improvement in this section of Boylston Street. The brick bowfront facade with granite and cast-stone details fits into its context yet is not an imitation. The apparent size has been somewhat reduced by recessing the upper floors behind the street facade.

Tennis and Racquet Club
939 Boylston Street
PARKER, THOMAS AND RICE, 1904

The handsome Tennis and Racquet Club started out as one of the Back Bay's exclusive social clubs for men, and still provides rare facilities for court tennis and rackets (not racketball), early forms of the modern game of tennis. Courts are housed behind the solid upper walls of patterned brick, circled by a clerestory of squarish windows just beneath the gener-

Tennis and Racquet Club

ous eaves of the hip roof. A monumental entrance with overscaled brackets, voussoirs, and laurel garland is set into the ground-floor brickwork, which has been treated like rusticated stone.

round-arched windows and doorways with wide trim in both rough and smooth stone. The picturesque turret tower served as a hose drying tower. Renovation of the fire station replaced the windows with

Engine and Hose House Number 33
941 Boylston Street
ARTHUR H. VINAL, 1885;
RENOVATION: ARROWSTREET, 1971

Institute of Contemporary Art
955 Boylston Street
ARTHUR H. VINAL, 1886; RENOVATION: GRAHAM GUND ASSOCIATES, 1975
Open to the Public

These buildings were originally designed to serve as fire station, police station, and stable. Romanesque inspired, they feature

Institute of Contemporary Art

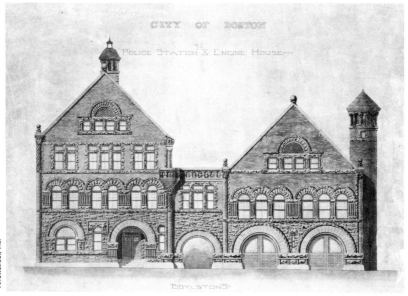

Arrowstreet, Inc.

Engine and Hose House Number 33 and Institute of Contemporary Art

large clear sheets of glass, providing full view to gaily painted interiors.

The Institute of Contemporary Art was established in 1936 with the purpose of bringing contemporary art to the Boston cultural scene. After numerous temporary locations, the Institute moved to this building in 1976. It has no permanent collection but has frequently changing exhibits. The renovation created contemporary exhibit spaces on several levels.

116 Huntington Avenue

CHILDS, BERTMAN, TSECKARES, 1990

This round-cornered building helps define the street space of Huntington Avenue, which still has many holes. Conceived to fit into its Prudential Center context, 116 Huntington is built of brick and limestone-colored precast concrete. The restrained and subtle design makes intriguing use of flat decoration and recalls buildings of the 1920s and '30s, especially in the facade organization; yet it is quite original in its execution. One example of the effects of the overbuilding encouraged in the late 1980s, this building stood locked and empty soon after construction was completed.

Greenhouse Apartments

150 Huntington Avenue

COSSUTTA AND ASSOCIATES, 1980–1982

The faceted concrete bays of the Greenhouse Apartments recall the geometry of the Christian Science Church Center across Huntington Avenue, in which architect

116 Huntington Avenue

Araldo Cossutta was associated with I. M. Pei. Precast-concrete panels and flush bands of windows have the flatness of folded cardboard, in contrast to the deeply sculpted buildings of the Christian Science complex. Angled bay projections create varied apartment interiors with considerably more interest than the standard boxy rooms. The apartments consist of two twelve-story buildings connected by a four-story atrium or greenhouse. The complex contains 322 apartments and underground parking for 214 cars.

Berklee Performance Center (Kubitz and Pepi), 136 Massachusetts Avenue

🏛 **Christian Science World Headquarters**

Massachusetts Avenue at Huntington Avenue

CHAPEL: FRANKLIN J. WELCH, 1893–1894
CHURCH: CHARLES E. BRIGHAM AND SOLON S. BEMAN; BRIGHAM, COVENEY AND BISBEE, 1903–1906 ADMINISTRATION BUILDING, COLONNADE BUILDING, SUNDAY SCHOOL: I. M. PEI AND PARTNERS AND COSSUTA AND PONTE, 1968–1973
LANDSCAPING: SASAKI, DAWSON, DEMAY

The most monumental public space in Boston has been created in the Christian Science complex. The development began modestly, with the small square-towered Romanesque church by Welch, which now seems to be tacked onto the back. The mammoth "addition" by Brigham and Beman, basically a Classical Revival basilica, is designed to seat five thousand people and has the largest pipe

© Christian Science Publishing Society

Christian Science World Headquarters

organ in the western hemisphere, an Aeolian Skinner manufactured in Boston.

It was not until the Pei-Cossuta involvement, however, that the complex assumed its truly monumental scale. Until the late 1960s a row of residential and commercial buildings along Massachusetts and Huntington avenues obscured all but the dome of the church. Their plan demolished these obstacles and made geometric sense of what had been built, much in the way of Bernini's piazza for St. Peter's in Rome monumentalized an already existing building. A large semicir-

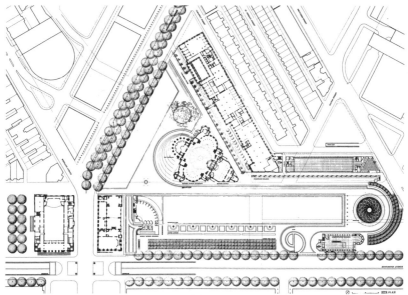

Site plan, Christian Science World Headquarters

© Llona Rider

cular portico was constructed of limestone to form the new main entrance on the Massachusetts Avenue facade.

The Colonnade Building, seemingly inspired by Le Corbusier's highly sculptural Chandigarh with its deep recesses and trough roof, screens the chaotic urban fill behind it. It also creates a backdrop for the plaza and its nearly seven-hundred-foot-long reflecting pool. The tower is a vertical focus balancing the dome and terminating the plaza. Access to the underground parking garage is nicely worked into the plaza with minimal visual and functional interference. At the southwest corner of the plaza the quarter-circle Sunday School both screens Horticultural Hall and connects the Huntington and Massachusetts Avenue faces.

Throughout, the concerns have been

largely with form and space, in the Renaissance and Baroque traditions, not with the human use of the space. It is instructive to compare this important piece of urban design with the Public Garden, the Charles River Embankment, Harvard Yard, or Quincy Marketplace, all soft people places that also have strong formal qualities.

Church Park Apartments and Garage
221 Massachusetts Avenue
THE ARCHITECTS COLLABORATIVE, 1973

The long repetitive concrete grid of the Church Park facade was designed to serve as a low-profile background for the foreground architecture of the Chris-

Church Park Apartments

Horticultural Hall

tian Science complex and Symphony and Horticultural halls. Ten floors of spacious and varied apartments, several with exterior balconies and floor-through layouts, rise above the ground-level shopping arcade. Laundry facilities and outdoor space for tenants are on the roof. The 508-unit building is divided into three sections, each with its own entrance. Parking space is below grade and in the circular garage behind the building, which also contains a supermarket.

🏛 Horticultural Hall

300 Massachusetts Avenue
WHEELWRIGHT AND HAVEN, 1901
National Register of Historic Places

The Massachusetts Horticultural Society was founded in 1829 to advance the knowledge and practice of horticulture. Besides having one of the finest horticultural libraries in the country, it conducts many activities, including workshops, information services, and an annual spring garden and flower show. Their

grandiose English Baroque building is an appropriate partner to the more sedate Symphony Hall across the street but is far less restrained, with overscaled pilasters, garlands, and wreaths. The large exhibition hall is expressed on the exterior by the tall archway beneath a pediment. The brick of the giant corner pilasters has been set in the manner of large rusticated stones. Edmund March Wheelwright was the city architect of Boston and designed a number of buildings, including the New England Conservatory and the Massachusetts Historical Society.

🏛 Symphony Hall

Massachusetts Avenue at Huntington Avenue
McKIM, MEAD, AND WHITE, 1900
National Register of Historic Places

Symphony Hall, along with Horticultural Hall, Jordan Hall, the Boston Opera House (now demolished), and the Museum of Fine Arts, made up Boston's new Fenway cultural center at the turn

Symphony Hall

of the century. Henry Lee Higginson, founder of the Boston Symphony Orchestra in 1881 and its major benefactor, wanted the new Hall to be one of the finest in the world. He insisted that a young assistant professor of physics at Harvard, Wallace Clement Sabine, be consulted on the acoustics.

Sabine was one of the first to study acoustics in a quantitative way and was so sure of his scientific basis that he guaranteed the hall would be acoustically perfect. Fortunately, he was correct, and the result is a Stradivarius among concert halls. Modeled after the Leipzig Gewandhaus, the interior concert hall space is basically a double cube. Plentiful high-relief ceiling ornament, wall niches with statuary, and 2,631 hard seats resting on

resilient wood flooring provide the resonance and reflectivity needed for a rich, sonorous hall. The shallow balconies prevent any acoustically dead spots. McKim, Mead, and White's design in the Italian Renaissance style is serviceable and properly focuses on the concert hall.

Bostonians cherish their Symphony, support it generously, and treat it much like an heirloom. The best opportunity for visitors to see the legendary old Boston families is at the Friday afternoon Symphony concert, which is as much a social as a musical event. The Friday afternoon subscription seats are jealously guarded and handed down from generation to generation, so many of the best seats have been in the same families for fifty years or more.

Massachusetts Avenue MBTA Station

Massachusetts Avenue MBTA Station

Massachusetts Avenue near
St. Botolph Street

ELLENZWEIG ASSOCIATES, INC., 1986

This elegantly streamlined transit station of aluminum and glass is one in a series built as part of the Southwest Corridor Transportation Project. It is inviting, transparent, and clearly visible along Massachusetts Avenue, a major arterial street. The station serves the Orange Line, which was relocated here when the elevated line on Washington Street was torn down.

ST. BOTOLPH STREET AREA

Boston Architectural Conservation District

St. Botolph Street was named for the sainted monk for whom Boston, England (a contraction of "St. Botolph's town) was named. During the filling of the

Back Bay from 1857 until 1882, the triangular area surrounded by the Boston-Albany railroad tracks on the north, the Boston-Providence on the south, and Massachusetts Avenue on the west remained unfilled. In 1871 the land was sold to the Huntington Avenue Land Trustees, who subdivided it into lots and sold them at auction. Speculative builders began building houses there in the 1880s, near the Massachusetts Avenue end of the triangle. The early brick row houses were single-family dwellings, but by the 1890s they were mainly four-family flats.

From the beginning the area has had a somewhat Bohemian atmosphere because of the artists, writers, and musicians who were attracted there. Among the artists and writers who have lived or worked in the area were sculptor Bela L. Pratt, poet Edwin Arlington Robinson, and writer Philip Henry Savage. A painting of the street, *Noontime, St. Botolph*, by the New York painter George Benjamin Luks (known as "Lusty Luks" for his earthy subjects) hangs in the Museum of Fine Arts. As described in the Museum's slide catalogue, "Ochre-brown and red-brick houses with their purple and white striped blinds are streaked with purple shadows. An ice man, in yellow, walks in the pink and yellow street beside green grass."

Harcourt Street was the original location of the Harcourt Bindery, now located on Melcher Street in the leather district (see page 114), which practices the art of hand binding of books. Also on Harcourt Street is the stained-glass studio of master craftsman Charles Connick, now operated by his successors. Since its founding in 1912 the studio has made about 40,000 stained-glass windows, mainly religious, including those for St. Patrick's and St. John the Devine in New York. Connick's book *Adventures in Light* was praised by architects and critics both in Europe and America. Following Connick's lead, another stained-glass shop, the John Terrance O'Duggan Studio, opened in 1935 in a house at 116 St. Botolph Street and

continues today.

Throughout its history and up to the present time the area has had an interesting mixed-use character combining residences, businesses, a series of schools, and light industry. The railroad-track barriers kept it separated from the Back Bay until the development of the Prudential Center. Thus its orientation was toward Massachusetts Avenue and, over several bridges, to the South End. The redeveloped Southwest Corridor has reduced the barriers between the South End and the St. Botolph Street neighborhoods.

Musicians' Mutual Relief Society Building
52–56 St. Botolph Street
CABOT AND CHANDLER, 1886; RENOVATIONS: MAHER AND WINCHESTER, 1913
EISENBERG HAVEN ASSOCIATES, 1982

This Neoclassical brick hall resembles a simpler version of Horticultural Hall (see 300 Massachusetts Avenue, p. 298). Above the large arched windows with

Musicians' Mutual Relief Society Building

keystones, the names of composers are carved in stone beneath the cornice. Separating each pair of composers is a decorative stone lyre at the top of a pilaster. The building was originally the Allen Gymnasium Company, but was converted and newly ornamented for use by the Musicians' Mutual Relief Society in 1913. It housed a large meeting hall, offices, and later a restaurant, barber shop, and billiard alcoves.

The School-House Condominiums
145 St. Botolph Street
EDMUND MARCH WHEELWRIGHT, 1891;
REUSE: GRAHAM GUND ASSOCIATES, 1980

Originally the Charles E. Perkins Elementary School, designed by City Architect Edmund March Wheelwright in 1891, the building was recycled in 1980 as twenty-one condominiums, ranging from one to three bedrooms. Each of the original ten classrooms became a one- or two-bedroom unit, with living rooms located at the corners to obtain a double exposure through the large windows. Six units—three flats and three duplexes—are located in the trussed flat hip roof where recessed outdoor decks and windows have been added. The entrance lobby has been treated as a work of art one walks through, rather than as a conventional lobby to be decorated with art. The building was the first in the area to use buff-colored brick.

Albemarle Chambers
off St. Botolph Street on Albemarle Street
ISRAEL NESSON, 1899

Although this group of twelve "three-decker" apartments was designed as modest tenements, the bowfront facade about a courtyard provides unexpected amenity. A purely ornamental Dutch gable projects above the central section while swags, wreaths, and pilasters in a Classical vein ornament the simple facade.

Lobby, The School-House

Albermarle Chambers

Southwest Corridor Park

MASTER PLAN AND COORDINATING LANDSCAPE
ARCHITECT: ROY MANN ASSOCIATES; LAND-
SCAPE ARCHITECTS: MOREICE AND GARY
(BACK BAY), CAROL R. JOHNSON ASSOCIATES
(RUGGLES STREET STATION), MASON AND
FREY (FOREST HILLS), HUYGENS AND
DIMELLA, INC. (JACKSON SQUARE STATION);
COMMUNITY COORDINATION CONSULTANT:
HARRY ELLENZWEIG ASSOCIATES, INC.; PARK
MANAGEMENT CONSULTANT: CHILDS BERTMAN
TSECKARES AND CASENDINO, INC., 1989

From the nineteenth century until the late 1980s, Roxbury was separated from Jamaica Plain and the Fenway, and the Back Bay from the South End, by a railroad corridor. Now this gap has been bridged by the Southwest Corridor Park, part of a massive $780 million rail, transit, and park project developed by the Massachusetts Bay Transit Authority. Boston has never been timid about large-scale projects, but this nearly five-mile, fifty-five-acre linear park is the largest of its type since Frederick Law Olmsted conceived the Emerald Necklace. The Orange Line elevated transit line was rerouted from Washington Street in the South End and Roxbury to run alongside the existing depressed commuter and intercity railroad tracks. The entire South End section beginning at Back Bay Station was then decked over to create space for a new park. The park, which varies in width from sixty feet to one-quarter mile, continues into Roxbury and Jamaica Plain on a swath of land cleared for the notorious and unbuilt Inner Belt highway. Since the Southwest Corridor cuts through several neighborhoods that are diverse socially, economically, and physically, the design varies from traditional park settings with bicycle and walking paths in the St. Botolph Street neighborhood and South End to basketball courts and land for urban gardeners in Roxbury. Each part appears quite utilitarian, with no sense

Southwest Corridor Park

of an overall design concept. Fifteen community groups participated in programming the facilities for their segments of the park, and the Southwest Corridor Farm, a community group, is under contract to care for a portion of the park and provide management and training for urban gardeners. The South End segment provides views of side streets and the interesting lower-level alleys. Near Dartmouth Street is a literary sculpture with quotations from contemporary Boston writers incised on granite stelae.

ELEVEN

South End

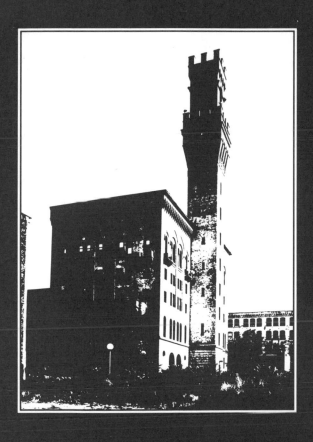

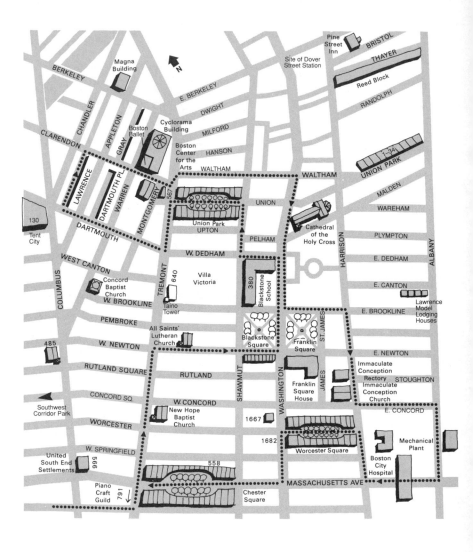

South End

Boston Landmark District

National Historic District

In the eighteenth century the South End was largely marshland, except for a narrow natural causeway along Washington Street. The Neck, as it was called, was a desolate and windy place where one was likely to be drenched in sea spray, but it was the only approach by land to Boston. The grim aspect of the place was heightened by the fortified gate and gallows where Washington and Dover streets now intersect.

The first plan for filling in the tidal flats of the South End was made in 1801, but extensive land making did not begin until 1834. Most of the present layout dates from 1848, and by the 1870s the area was fully developed more or less in a grid pattern with blocks of uniform row houses. A number of attractive oblong parks surrounded by brick or brownstone row houses reflect English influence on Charles Bulfinch, whose Tontine Crescent, built on Franklin Street, may have served as the model for the South End squares.

Unlike the Back Bay, which was organized around large boulevards and green spaces in the French manner, the South End has no large-scale focus or axis to structure its repetitive blocks. No doubt this is one reason the Back Bay was a more successful development favored by people of means and social prominence. The South End experienced a brief period of social prestige, but when its wealthier residents left for the newer Back Bay after only a decade or less, the neighborhood welcomed the working-class and immigrant residents who were to live there for the rest of the nineteenth century. Lithuanian Bernard Berenson and Lebanese Kahlil Gibran arrived here with their immigrant parents as the neighborhood was becoming more pluralistic.

The Panic of 1873 was hard on the South End, putting many speculatively built houses into possession of the banks, who then sold them for whatever they would bring, further depressing real-estate values. At the same time there were thousands of new Irish immigrants in need of housing. By the turn of the century there were not only Irish, but also Jewish, Italian, Chinese, Greek, Syrian, and Lebanese residents in the South End. Thus many fine South End houses became lodging houses and remained so well into the 1950s and 1960s. Today the neighborhood continues to be a socially diverse area of great interest to the Victorian enthusiast with many of its old row houses restored or renovated.

South End Tour

The South End tour is best taken by car to get a quick overview of the large area. Begin at the **Harriet Tubman House (313)** on Massachusetts Avenue, then turn left on Tremont Street and pass the **New Hope Baptist Church (323)** on your right. Turn right on West Newton Street to see the **All Saints' Lutheran Church** where Albert Schweitzer played the organ **(332)**. Continue past **Blackstone Square (329)** and some once fine brownstone row houses on your right **(329)**. Turn left on Washington Street **(326)** and turn left again at West Dedham Street in the center of **Villa Victoria (322)** and right onto Shawmut Avenue, then turn left into **Union Park (325)**.

As you leave the square, turn left onto Tremont Street and immediately right onto Dartmouth Street. Look to your right as you pass the pleasant Dartmouth Place and turn right onto Lawrence Street **(311)** for one block, then right again onto Clarendon Street. This section of the South End is known as **Clarendon Park (311)**. Look quickly to your left as you pass Gray Street and then the **Boston Center for the Arts (320)** before jogging slightly to your left to enter Waltham Street opposite the Center. Turn right onto Washington Street and drive past the **Cathedral of the Holy Cross (327)** on your left and the **Blackstone School (320)** on your right.

Once again back at the pair of parks, turn left on East Brookline Street and view **Franklin Square House (329)**. Then turn right on Harrison Avenue, passing the **Immaculate Conception Rectory** and **Church (316–17)** on your right. Turn left onto East Concord Street, and then make three right turns to circle **Boston City Hospital (317)**, driving beneath the air-rights addition. If you are very observant you can catch several short glimpses of what remains of the early nineteenth-century hospital buildings. Turn left into **Worcester Square (332)** and pass the **Allen house (330)**, an amusing oddity, as you turn left onto Washington Street. Then turn right onto Massachusetts Avenue to complete your tour in the once serene English-style **Chester Park (318)**.

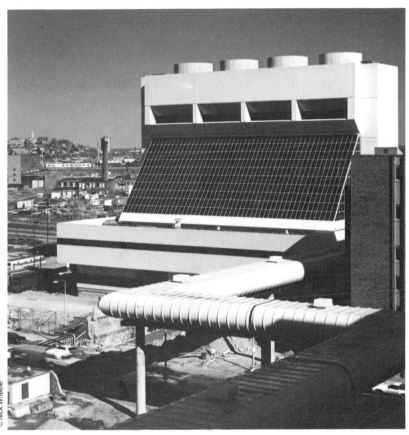

© Nick Wheeler

Mechanical plant, Boston City Hospital

Mechanical Plant
Boston City Hospital
Albany Street
HUGH STUBBINS/REX ALLEN PARTNERSHIP,
1976

The mechanical plant is the first phase of a comprehensive plan for the hospital service center and is designed to serve existing as well as future buildings. An aboveground "service tube" is totally accessible for any future modifications to the mechanical system without disruption of ongoing services. Future additions are to include areas for receiving and storage of all hospital supplies and materials, which will then be distributed via automated materials handling systems installed within the tube.

Magna Building

originally Theodore Parker
Memorial Hall
49 Berkeley Street
1872–1873; RENOVATION: BOSTON ARCHI-
TECTURAL TEAM, 1974–1975

This building was built for the twenty-
eighth Congregational Society of Boston, a
Unitarian Church founded by Theodore
Parker in 1845. Since then it has had many
uses including schools, a Jewish community center, and the Magna film company.
Today it contains thirty-three apartments
and ground-floor commercial space.

The large auditorium on the second
and third floors of the original building is
expressed on the facade by the tall side
windows and a center window with the
Star of David. The imposing French Second Empire facade has a pronounced
center pavilion rising above the mansard
roof, which is penetrated by two dormers.
The second story is notable for the shoul-
dered architraves above the windows,
while the third story features groupings of
round-arched windows.

Magna Building

Site of Dover Street Station

Berkeley at Washington Street
1899–1901; DEMOLISHED

The elaborate copper-and-wood elevated
station that stood here exemplified Victorian industrial architecture. It served the
first mass-transit line across the neck of
the Shawmut peninsula. Nearby, the old

Dover Street bridge had a floating bathhouse, the first public bathhouse in the
country. There one could have a towel,
soap, and a shower for two cents.

The old town gate and gallows were
located here, the first view presented to
anyone approaching Boston on foot or
on horseback. Fortifications were built in
1710 of stone and brick with a parapet of
earth. Guns included two twenty-four-
pounders and eight nine-pounders. An
earlier barrier had stood between what
are now Dedham and Canton streets,
where seven men protected the settlement from Indians in the early 1630s.

🏛 Fire Department Headquarters

now Pine Street Inn
60 Bristol Street
EDMUND MARCH WHEELWRIGHT, 1894;
RENOVATION: CHILDS, BERTMAN, TSECKARES,
AND CASENDINO, 1980

Wheelwright was Boston city architect for a time and worked successfully in several styles. His other Boston work includes Horticultural Hall (see 300 Massachusetts Avenue, p. 298) and the Longfellow Bridge (see Cambridge Street, p. 193). This former fire station was based on the Palazzo Vecchio in Florence, Italy. The medieval Italian fortress–style design features a fine tower of yellow brick with crenellated turret supported on machicolated projections. The tower was used for drying hoses. A smaller-scale, denser machicolation forms the cornice of the five-story brick building. The structure has been renovated to house Pine Street Inn, which provides food, shelter, and social services to homeless men and women.

CLARENDON PARK

Clarendon Park is an area of the South End comprising Appleton, Warren, Chandler, Lawrence, and Gray streets. It has been suggested that these attractive small-scale versions of Beacon Hill houses were built to house servants of the prominent Beacon Hill families for whom the streets are named. The predominant style is two- or three-story brick with stone lintels, recessed side entrances, and occasional oriel windows and dormers. They make delightful single-family homes today.

Lawrence Street

Pine Street Inn

Dartmouth Square condominiums, the former Rice School renovated by Arrowstreet, 1985

Boston Ballet

Clarendon Street at Warren Street
GRAHAM GUND ASSOCIATES, 1991

The postmodern brick box boasts bold window shapes characteristic of Gund scattered playfully on the facade with cookie-cutter scallops and a half-moon balcony on top. Four cast-stone roundels at the entrance level illustrate the history of the Boston Ballet, whose studios and practice rooms are housed here.

No. 2 Clarendon Square

2 Clarendon Street
1868; RENOVATION: NOTTER FINEGOLD + ALEXANDER, INC., 1988

The former Clarendon Street Baptist Church is one of a number of South End churches that have become condomini-

Boston Ballet

No. 2 Clarendon Square

dingstone is a landmark for Columbus Avenue and Rutland Street. The prominent architectural features include the angle buttresses and the fine broach spire of stone, similar to that of another Estey design, Church of Our Saviour (see Longwood and Cottage Farm, Brookline, p. 466). Estey was also architect of the original Emmanuel Church (see 15 Newbury Street, p. 279).

Union United Methodist Church

ums or apartments after being victimized by arsonists or abandoned by their shrinking congregations. It was here the Blind Asylum movement originated and the Chinese Sunday School was founded in 1887. A new cast-iron fence was added as part of the renovation.

Union United Methodist Church

485 Columbus Avenue

ALEXANDER R. ESTEY, 1872

The congregation of the Universalist Church was organized in 1817 in a church on School Street. Like many other churches, it followed its congregation to the South End, constructing this building in 1872. Now home to the Union United Methodist congregation, the Gothic Revival country church of Roxbury pud-

🏛 Harriet Tubman House, United South End Settlements

566 Columbus Avenue
at Massachusetts Avenue

STULL ASSOCIATES, 1974

The headquarters for the United South End Settlements, a social service organization, is a strong architectural statement

© Stull Associates

**Harriet Tubman House, United South
End Settlements**

at a corner that was much in need of an
activity and visual anchor. The many programs and services are well served in this
building, which is both open to the street
and passersby and reasonably protected.
The building is named after Harriet Tubman, "Moses of the South," who was a
runaway slave and an organizer of the
Underground Railroad.

CONCORD SQUARE

Brick bowfront houses, some with three
stories and some with four stories plus
dormered top floor, line a narrow oval
park. The high front stairs all originally
had elaborate cast-iron balustrades. These
squares demonstrate the influence of

English urban planning in Boston before
the French style became more popular
with the laying out of the Back Bay.

Tent City
130 Dartmouth Street
GOODY, CLANCY & ASSOCIATES, 1988

Tent City's name commemorates a week-
end demonstration by a group of South
End residents who camped out here in
1968 to protest the lack of affordable
housing in the South End as it became
gentrified. In conjunction with the Copley
Place project, the site was donated for
affordable housing. It was a precedent for
the city's later "linkage" projects, in which
funds were siphoned off "high end"
development to serve neighborhood
needs—until the development bubble
burst and developers had to be enticed
with guarantees. After years of struggle,
the 269-unit mixed-income Tent City
complex was built with 25 percent of the
units reserved for low income and 50 percent for moderate income; the balance
are market rate units.

The development attempts to relate
to both the scale of Copley Place and the
South End neighborhood by stepping
down from twelve stories to four-story
townhouses. Varying shades of red and
tan brick face the structures, with highlights of brightly colored glazed brick and
precast-concrete lintels. One of the more
successful aspects of the project is its
four-story section. On Columbus Avenue
its facade blends in with the South End
vocabulary, and near Yarmouth Place it
attempts to relate to adjacent residential
streets with the suggestion of mansard
roof segments and iron-railed porches.

Tent City

DARTMOUTH PLACE

Off Dartmouth Street is this quiet cul-de-sac of brick row houses with second-story oriel windows and recessed entries a few steps above the street. The houses face the rear gardens of the Appleton Street houses.

Lawrence Model Lodging Houses

79, 89, 99, 109 East Canton Street

CHARLES K. KIRBY (79, 89, 99), 1874–1875;
WILLIAM F. GOODWIN (109), 1892

National Register of Historic Places

These four buildings are the oldest remaining examples of philanthropic housing in Boston, built in accordance

with the will of Abbott Lawrence to provide "Model Lodging Houses . . . to be let to poor, temperate and industrious families . . . at reasonable rents." Lawrence, who died in 1855, was a leading Boston philanthropist and industrialist and founded the textile city of Lawrence, Massachusetts. As Ambassador to the Court of St. James in 1849–1852, Lawrence may well have seen the first model dwellings for the poor built by the Birkenhead Dock Company in 1847. Such housing was later built for the prince consort by the Society for Improving the Condition of the Labouring Classes and displayed at the Great Exhibition in London in 1851; Abbott Lawrence participated in planning the American section of the Great Exhibi-

Lawrence Model Lodging Houses

tion. Each of the buildings has a name: Lawrence, Abbott, Bigelow, and Groton. The five-story structures are built of brick in a simplified French mansard style and contain twenty apartments each. The interior stairways are entirely of cast iron with lattice-patterned risers. The quartet offers an instructive contrast with the nearby twentieth-century public housing.

Immaculate Conception Rectory
761 Harrison Avenue
LOUIS WEISSBEIN, 1858–1860

Immaculate Conception Rectory

Boston College was founded in this imposing brick building with Classical ornamentation. The windows on the first story are set within recessed arches and have prominent keystones. On the second and third stories the windows are capped with pedi-

ments of contrasting styles. Only the fourth-story windows are plain. The center of the facade is adorned with a gabled pavilion the full height of the facade, with a projecting Corinthian portico over the entrance. Both the college building and the church next door have a bold cast-iron fence with arch-and-circle motif capped with an inverted-arch cresting.

Immaculate Conception Church/ Jesuit Urban Center

Harrison Avenue at East Concord Street
PATRICK C. KEELEY, 1858–1861

The Irish immigration into Boston and the South End brought with it the need for new Catholic churches. Patrick C. Keeley designed many of these for the diocese, including the gigantic Cathedral of the Holy Cross (see Washington Street at Union Park Street, p. 327). Here he has freely combined Classical, Renaissance, and Georgian themes. Ionic pilasters ornament the corners and frame each of the three entrance portals of the granite church. The central Palladian window

Immaculate Conception Church

and all the tall arched windows feature the Gibbs surround of blocks of stone punctuating the jambs. The side facade is particularly animated, with Ionic pilasters and seven tall windows with the Gibbs surround. The central pavilion projecting from the facade is unusual in placing a broken pediment in front of a larger pediment. In 1987 Boston preservationists were outraged when the church leaders suddenly ripped out much of the historic interior to accommodate offices. The Boston Preservation Alliance prepared petitions to the Vatican and to the Boston Landmarks Commission to preserve the interior, and a group of preservation leaders worked with the church over several months to develop a compromise solution. As a result the church interior has been renovated; the renovation restores the most important features while creating new administrative spaces and a contemporary glass-walled entry hall.

Boston City Hospital

818 Harrison Avenue
GRIDLEY J. F. BRYANT, 1862–1864

After more than a decade of need for a city hospital, land was appropriated and construction begun on a fine symmetrical group of buildings in brick with dormered mansard roofs. At the center was an administration building with Ionic pilasters, a raised formal stair of white marble, and two domes as the focus for the handsome grounds. Curving arcades connected the central building with medical and surgical pavilions, boiler house, laundry, isolating wards, outpatient clinic, morgue, and kitchen. Some sections of

King's Handbook

Boston City Hospital, original building

the original hospital still stand here and there amidst the hodgepodge of later buildings, but the elegant and reposeful architectural composition has been destroyed.

Outpatient Department, Boston City Hospital

818 Harrison Avenue

HUGH STUBBINS/REX ALLEN PARTNERSHIP AND SAMUEL GLASER PARTNERS, 1977

A major entrance to central Boston from the south is defined by this dramatic air-rights structure, which crosses Massachusetts Avenue to link nurses' and interns' housing with a new fifteen-story inpatient building. Large round ventilation grilles are used decoratively and look like pairs of eyes at the top of the building. At ground level the brick plaza swoops up around them. Through the windows passersby see colorful murals of the heart, lungs, and other body parts relating to the

various departments. Waiting rooms of the twenty-two outpatient departments are treated like those of an airlines terminal and are aligned along the perimeter corridor with views outdoors. The facility, the first patient-care construction at the hospital in thirty years, is designed to improve the delivery of health care to outpatients and to treat the patients with the same dignity they would receive from a private physician.

Chester Square

Massachusetts Avenue

1850–1851

Chester Square was planned in 1850 as a fine oval park. Where today there are six lanes of traffic, in the nineteenth century there was a fountain at the center of a spacious park. Children were tended by nursemaids. The square has lost not only its fountain and white-aproned nursery-maids but much of its beauty and seren-

© Edward Jacoby/APG

Outpatient Department, Boston City Hospital

ity as well. This, the grandest of the South End residential squares, is surrounded by seventy of the most opulent houses built in the neighborhood. Flat-fronted houses with lanterns in the center are flanked by bow-fronted houses that step out to enclose the oval ends of the large park. When it was built, the street was not a thoroughfare, for Massachusetts Avenue did not yet cross the Charles River into Cambridge.

John Farwell House
now League of Women for
Community Service
558 Massachusetts Avenue,
Chester Square
1860

John Farwell, a sea captain and abolitionist, hid fugitive slaves in his house, which has a hidden staircase and tunnel

for that purpose. On the first floor is a large double salon with dining room behind. Adjacent to the dining room and above the street-level kitchen is the butler's pantry. Above the main floor are a sitting room at the rear and a library at the front of the house. The top two floors were bedrooms. The house has been maintained and some of the original furniture remains. Today the house is headquarters of the League of Women for Community Services, an organization of black women who have maintained the house since 1920. The original manuscripts of Frederick Douglass's abolitionist speeches are here.

RUTLAND SQUARE
1860s

Rutland Square is a narrow park, just a slice down the center of the street with

© Stull Associates

Blackstone Square Elementary School

trees and grass enclosed by an iron fence. The Italianate bowfront houses do not step back to enclose the square, yet the slender park creates an important focus and identity for the block, accomplishing far more as green space than its meager size would add to the roadway. The houses and park are more modest versions of those in the large South End squares.

Blackstone Square Elementary School
380 Shawmut Avenue
STULL ASSOCIATES, 1976

An upper-level "street" connects the five autonomous and ungraded houses of the Blackstone School, which are expressed in the building's form. It also provides access to central facilities, including a media center, science center, cafeteria, community clinic, auditorium, music and seminar rooms, and gymnasium. In addition to the regular curriculum, the school offers neighborhood programs for all ages. Except for the screen wall of square

brick, the style and materials are those of an industrial building built to withstand considerable abuse.

Reed Block
Thayer Street off Harrison Avenue

This handsome brick industrial block has granite lintels and sills on the upper-level windows. The large window and door openings of the first floor are framed in rockfaced granite posts and beams. Two cast-iron posts are placed between every pair of granite posts. The six-over-six-paned windows of wood contribute to the dignity of fine nineteenth-century industrial buildings such as these.

Cyclorama Building, Boston Center for the Arts
539 Tremont Street
CUMMINGS AND SEARS, 1884
National Register of Historic Places

The large steel-trussed dome of the central building in this complex originally

The present facade is a twentieth-century alteration that gives no indication of the domed space within. The small exterior turrets surrounding the dome are best seen from Warren Avenue behind the building. The highly decorative kiosk on the plaza was designed as a cupola for a now demolished building in Roxbury.

Reed Block

St. Cloud Hotel
567 Tremont Street
NATHANIEL J. BRADLEE, 1870;
RENOVATION: ARROWSTREET, INC., 1987

This French Academic–style building stood vacant for several years before the Boston Center for the Arts renovated it, along with the adjacent 1879 Mystic River Bridge Building, as retail space and condominiums. A new penthouse was

Cyclorama Building

St. Cloud Hotel, Tremont Street

housed the enormous 400-by-50-foot cyclorama painting of the Battle of Gettysburg, which attracted throngs of people. It is now exhibited in Gettysburg. Boston's famous prizefighter John L. Sullivan also fought here. From 1923 to 1968 the structure served as the flower market.

added to the St. Cloud Hotel, and three stories were added to its neighbor. The tall, elegant first-floor retail areas with black cast-iron columns serve a vibrant local neighborhood.

Typical entrances, 690–692 Tremont Street

Villa Victoria

Tremont Street between Shawmut Avenue, West Dedham, and West Newton streets

JOHN SHARRATT ASSOCIATES, 1972–1982

Villa Victoria is the result of collaboration between a far-sighted architect and a Puerto Rican neighborhood that fought demolition and displacement by urban renewal. After many years' work and the total involvement of the community in the planning and development process, over six hundred new and renovated units of affordable housing have been created,

along with shops, recreation space, a plaza, and social services. The street grid of the South End has been replaced with two loop streets that allow a pedestrian spine to extend from the community plaza to the main playground while still providing street access to the front door of every housing unit. The project was designed to be barrier-free for the handicapped and elderly. The community also demanded housing it could be proud of, that in no way resembled public housing. Town houses together with mid-rise and high-rise structures offer varied housing choices. The cultural background of the residents is expressed in the emphasis on outdoor social spaces, as well as in the bright colors, brick and stucco, pitched roofs, private gardens, and private entrances.

Taino Tower

640 Tremont Street

1872; RECONSTRUCTION: COMMUNITAS, INC., 1991

The congregation that built the church here in 1872 began on Shawmut Avenue in 1845 as the Suffolk Street Union Church, reorganized in 1849 as the Shawmut Congregational Church, and built a new meetinghouse in 1852. The 1852 building was soon inadequate, however, so the congregation bought this site and built a brick Romanesque Revival church. At about the same time, H. H. Richardson designed his Romanesque Brattle Square Church (now First Baptist Church), also with a square campanilelike tower. The tower here had a short spire with pinnacles when it was built. The strong form of the tower is now capped by machicola-

Tremont Street

Taino Tower

tion with loop windows punctuating its faces. A blind arcade runs above the three round entry arches.

The church was hit by arsonists and stood vacant for several years. Now it has been reconstructed as affordable housing, and the old tower and part of the entrance facade have been incorporated into the new structure.

New Hope Baptist Church
740 Tremont Street
HAMMAT BILLINGS, 1862

Roxbury puddingstone was used in this unusual Gothic Revival church with two towers, each with a spire, lancet windows, and buttresses. To add to the architectural ambiguity two entrances and two nave forms are melded together.

New Hope Baptist Church

Piano Craft Guild

Piano Craft Guild, Chickering Piano Factory

791 Tremont Street

C. 1853; RENOVATION: GELARDIN, BRUNER, AND COTT, 1974

The expansive Chickering Piano Factory was built in the 1850s of massive timber posts and beams and a skin of brick punctured with hundreds of windows. The focus of the composition is an octagonal entrance tower with lantern. The 1974 recycling of the building as artists' housing was one of the earliest and largest mill conversions in Massachusetts. One hundred seventy-four residential units for both living and working were created. Emphasis was on open, rough spaces with low rents suited to artists' needs. Public areas including a gallery, mail room, laundry, and commercial spaces are clustered around the entrance.

🏛 Union Park

1857–1859

Union Park is one of the loveliest green spaces in the South End and was the first square in the neighborhood to be completed. Two fountains, flowers, mature trees, and an iron fence make a lush foreground for the large Victorian brick row houses. The sense of a special place is heightened by the facades that step forward to enclose the park. The ornamental ironwork is noteworthy, especially the simple modern pattern at 23–25 Union Park and the Victorian cast-iron fence, balcony, and stair rail at 43 Union Park, which are found in many nineteenth-century ironwork catalogues.

Courtesy Bostonian Society

Chickering Piano Factory

Union Park

Union Park

Row Houses
1–34 Union Park Street

Just beyond an attractive triangular park with Victorian cast-iron fence is a long and striking row of brick flats. Upper-level windows have stone lintels composed of prominent stepped voussoirs. Entries are recessed with large semicircular stilted arches with large keystones. Separate doors to each building's basement, first floor, and upper floors are contained within its archway.

1–34 Union Park Street

Route of Washington Street El
Demolished

The Washington Street El, built in 1899–1901, was one of the first elevated train lines in the country. Noisy, dirty, and a blight to the area through which it clattered, it nevertheless provided a scenic ride with views above street level. It was demolished when the Orange Line was rerouted along the Southwest Corridor.

In the seventeenth and eighteenth centuries the only road through the neck

Washington Street El (demolished)

was where Washington Street is now located. Originally it was called Orange Street and was surrounded mainly by pastureland and salt works, the only structures between Dover Street and Roxbury being the George Tavern, the Enoch Brown house, a windmill, and the gallows. In the eighteenth century wharves were built along the eastern shore approximately along today's Harrison Avenue near Dover Street. In front of these, facing on Washington Street, dwellings and stores were erected.

The demolition of the El resulted in an overly wide, empty-looking street. The street cries out for a wide green boulevard down the center with a double row of trees, as on Commonwealth Avenue,

and consistent lighting appropriate to the architectural character and safety needs of the neighborhood.

Cathedral of the Holy Cross
Washington Street at Union Park Street
PATRICK C. KEELEY, 1867–1875

As the diocese grew rapidly in the mid-nineteenth century, the Cathedral of the Holy Cross on Franklin Street became inadequate. The archbishop then built this cathedral, the largest Catholic church in the country at the time. In fact, it is as large as Westminster Abbey. Situated in the South End, where large numbers of Irish Catholic immigrants had settled, it is

Cathedral of the Holy Cross

on the site of the old town gallows. It is 364 feet long and 120 feet high and accommodates 3,500 people seated or 7,000 standing. The Gothic Revival complex of Roxbury puddingstone consists of the sanctuary and its chapels, the vestry, and the chantry with its own small organ. The mansion of the archbishop was also here at one time. The two towers were intended to have spires, but these were never built.

Blackstone and Franklin Squares

Washington Street at West Newton Street

BASED ON 1801 PLAN OF CHARLES BULFINCH

Although constructed in the 1860s, Blackstone and Franklin Square were actually planned in 1801 by Charles Bulfinch acting as chairman of the Board of Selectmen. Six decades later his plan was followed in the layout of these two large squares with Washington Street between them. They have formal geometry of diagonal paths crossing in the center, where each square has a fountain. The grandeur and formality of the parks are marred by inappropriate lighting.

Blackstone Square

Row Houses

Washington Street at West Newton Street, on Blackstone Square

The former elegance of Blackstone Square is reflected in this row of brownstone houses with unusually fine facades

of pedimented formal windows. The doors are framed by pilasters and the cornices are heavily bracketed.

Franklin Square House

Washington Street at 11 East Newton Street

MATURIN M. BALLOU, 1868;

RENOVATION: BOSTON ARCHITECTURAL TEAM AND ARCHPLAN, 1976

When built as the St. James Hotel, this was one of the most luxurious hotels in Boston. It had reading and smoking rooms, club rooms, ladies' and gentlemen's parlors, a telegraph office, billiard rooms, and two steam-powered elevators. Since the social position of the South End neighborhood never reached expectations, however, the hotel suffered. In 1882 the four hundred–room hotel was taken over by the New England Conservatory of Music. Today it is called Franklin Square House and has been converted into apartments for the elderly.

The large brick building is in the

Franklin Square House

French Second Empire style with central and corner pavilions, mansard roof, and quoins defining each of the pavilions. Behind the Franklin Square House is one of the oldest cemeteries in Boston, Old South Cemetery. Across Washington Street from the cemetery was O'Donnell's Gymnasium, where John L. Sullivan trained to become a prizefighter.

Remains of Deacon House

1667 Washington Street
CHARLES LEMOULNIER, 1848

Fragments of the most elegant house ever built in the South End still stand behind a commercial building at 1679 Washington Street. Mr. Peter Parker built the house for his daughter and son-in-law, Mr. and Mrs. Deacon. It was decorated in the greatest elegance he could import from France. Among the fine furnishings were the eighteenth-century carved and gilded panels from the Hotel de Montmorency in Paris that are now exhibited in the Museum of Fine Arts. The original entrance to the house was on Concord Street through double gates guarded by a porter's house, which gave access to the courtyard and porte cochère. Within the house was an imposing entrance hall with a gallery at the upper level, drawing room, ballroom, dining room, and boudoir.

While the couple were visiting Europe, Mr. Deacon died, and although Mrs. Deacon returned to Boston to live in her grand house, it never again possessed the gay and glamorous atmosphere of earlier years. After the death of her father, the house and its contents were sold at auction in 1871. In the 1880s it became an art school and later a dance hall. Today the ballroom with its columns, gallery, and frescoed ceiling is used for paint storage.

Allen House

1682 Washington Street
1859

This brownstone house is an incongruous mixture of elements, from lion's paws on the porch columns and windows to oriels popping out unexpectedly under elaborate mansard central gables with pear-shaped windows, corner quoins, and a rusticated basement level. Only a domed lantern is missing—and indeed one existed when the house was built as a freestanding mansion for Aaron Allen, a furniture dealer. It has been suggested, in fact, that the odd ornamentation is derived from furniture of the period. When Allen moved to the Back Bay in 1871, the house became the Central Club. Ten years later the Central Club, too, moved to the Back Bay, and the house was leased to various organizations. In 1894 it was sold to the Catholic Union of Boston, which added a bowling alley in the basement and an auditorium in the rear. Its diverse ownership patterns continued into the twentieth century, but today it stands boarded up.

WEST BROOKLINE STREET

West Brookline Street has a strong and harmonious pattern of brick bowfront row houses with paired entrances and front steps. Several of the small front gardens have attractive Victorian iron fences.

Concord Baptist Church

West Brookline Street at
190 Warren Avenue
1869

In the 1870s many Baptist congregations moved to the South End. Several new Baptist societies also originated here, including the Ebenezer and Day Star, which formed on West Concord and Appleton streets. This brick church features a portico of three pointed arches and pointed arch windows. A large octagonal clerestory is centered above the auditorium.

WEST CANTON STREET

Well-maintained and renovated brick bow fronts with projecting cornices of wood line West Canton Street. At number 197 a contemporary ornamental iron fence uses a design developed by the authors for Victorian Boston houses, with simple curves and alternating spacing of verticals that can be executed economically with materials and technology of today.

West Canton Street

All Saints' Lutheran Church

85 West Newton Street near
Tremont Street
1899

This rather austere German Gothic–style church of buff-colored brick features a square tower with angle buttresses and a

Concord Baptist Church

shingled spire above a belfry with plate tracery. A small octagonal tower at the right side of the entrance has a smaller spire. Albert Schweitzer came to play the organ in this church.

WORCESTER SQUARE

Worcester Square has a quiet architectural consistency that lends dignity and grandeur to its composition. All the houses surrounding the park are bow-fronted raised-entrance houses. At each house the high front stairs rise a full story to the second floor while a door beneath the stairway enters directly to the low first floor, called an English basement. This arrangement made later conversion into multifamily homes quite easy. There have been some alterations to doorways, entries, and mansard rooflines that are generally destructive to the architectural quality, but the square remains impressive.

All Saints' Lutheran Church

Worcester Square

TWELVE

Fenway

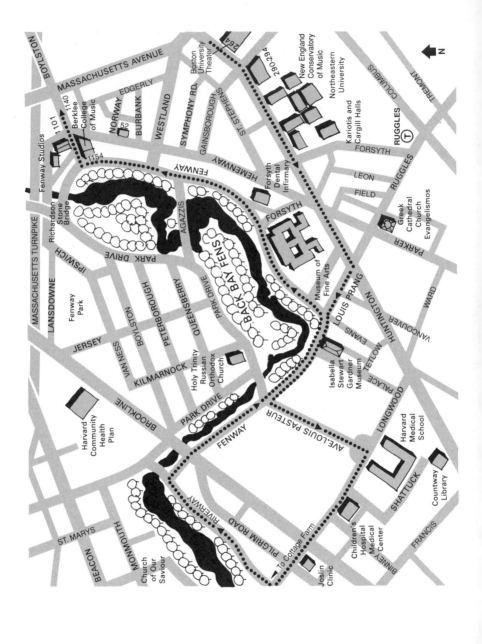

Fenway

The development of the Fenway area began in the 1890s amidst great enthusiasm, an enthusiasm that was certainly justified by the attractive park at the center of the new district and by the nearby cultural institutions such as the Isabella Stewart Gardner Museum, the Museum of Fine Arts, the Massachusetts Historical Society, the Boston Medical Library, the Boston Opera House, and Symphony Hall, among others. While several fine homes were constructed in the area, the development soon took on the aspect of respectable facades behind which the new apartments were little more than tenements. Light and views were inadequately considered, as were connections to the prime resources of the area. Street patterns, site plans, and building-height requirements all take poor advantage of the enormous potential the area offers. Properly developed, it could have been as successful as either Beacon Hill or the Back Bay.

Fenway Tour

The easiest way to see the Fenway is by car, but the athletic and adventurous might want to walk instead. Start at **Symphony Hall** and drive down Huntington Avenue past the **Boston University Theater** and **New England Conservatory** on your left and the **Northeastern University** campus on both sides of the street (**344**). After passing the **Museum of Fine Arts** (**345**) turn right onto Louis Prang Avenue and turn left after the **Isabella Stewart Gardner Museum** (**340**). Proceed toward the **Harvard Medical School** (**350**) on Avenue Louis Pasteur, turning right onto Longwood Avenue. Pass the **Children's Hospital Medical Center** (**349**) and turn right onto the Riverway (**456**) at Temple Israel, noting the sculpture by Louise Nevelson, **Sky Covenant.** At this point you may prefer to continue on Longwood Avenue for a side trip to see the **Longwood** and **Cottage Farm** areas of Brookline just beyond the Tudor-style **Longwood Towers** visible through the trees (**467**). Otherwise follow the Riverway as it curves into the Fenway and circle the **Back Bay Fens** (**455**) seeing the rear side of the Museum of Fine Arts and the West Wing, the **Forsyth Dental Infirmary for Children** (**340**), and the **stone bridge** designed by H. H. Richardson (**455**). Turn right onto Boylston Street at the **Massachusetts Historical Society** (**337**). Before the tour ends pass the **Berklee College of Music** and **St. Clement's Archdiocesan Eucharistic Shrine** (**337**).

St. Clement's Archdiocesan Eucharistic Shrine
1101 Boylston Street
ALLEN AND COLLENS, C. 1920

The fine Gothic Revival interior of St. Clement's is a wonderful retreat from the noisy street scene. Although its tower has been demolished, the strong form of its nave with set-back stepped buttresses can be admired. The architects, who specialized in the Gothic style, also were responsible for Lindsey Chapel (see Emmanuel Church, 15 Newbury Street, p. 279) and the Riverside Church and the high altar of St. Patrick's Cathedral in New York City.

Berklee College of Music
1140 Boylston Street
ARTHUR BOWDITCH, 1901

The animated facade of the Berklee College of Music might be termed "cartoon Georgian." Gibbs surrounds run wild, and on the second-story windows they are extended to form three stone string courses. Several of the windows have elaborately carved brackets added to their keystones. The third-story windows have heavy bracketed projecting lintels and delicate cast-iron balconies, while the small windows have the Gibbs surround. All the fourth-floor windows are ornamented with Gibbs surrounds and each large window has a carved swag beneath the sill. The fantasy continues in the entrance portico of banded Ionic columns with alternating stripes of fluting and vermiculated stone.

Berklee College of Music

Massachusetts Historical Society
1154 Boylston Street
EDMUND MARCH WHEELWRIGHT, 1899
National Historic Landmark

The new park called the Back Bay Fens encouraged the development of Boylston Street beyond Massachusetts Avenue to the Fenway—and then farther west. The Massachusetts Historical Society, founded in 1791 and America's oldest historical

Massachusetts Historical Society

society, had been located in the arch over Bulfinch's Tontine Crescent until 1833, when it moved to 30 Tremont Street, next to the King's Chapel Burying Ground. After it relocated into its new building at this address, the Boston Medical Library

Glazed terra-cotta facade, Fenway

decided to build on the lots next door, dedicating its building in 1901. Its architect, Robert S. Peabody, built his large house beside it. Both of these buildings still stand, but have been put to new uses.

The dignified Georgian Revival brick and stone double bowfront Historical Society building employs many classical motifs. Doric columns support a narrow architrave and frieze ornamented with triglyphs to form the entrance portico in the chamfered rusticated stone of the street-level facade. On the upper levels Ionic pilasters frame the central windows, which have partial Gibbs surrounds and a fanlight over the third-story center window. Windows of the bows are simpler, with keystoned lintels and no surrounds. Four bas-relief swags complete the ornamentation beneath the cornice and balustrade.

Harvard Community Health Plan

Brookline Avenue at 2 Fenway Plaza
ORIGINAL BUILDINGS, 1925–1939;
RENOVATION: STEFFIAN BRADLEY ASSOCIATES,
1979

These buildings, built as warehouses and offices for the S. S. Pierce and Firestone Tire and Rubber Companies, have been recycled as a new ambulatory health-care center and management offices for the

Harvard Community Health Plan

Harvard Community Health Plan (HCHP). The top three floors of the six-story building are devoted to various medical departments, while the lower floors contain parking space. The glass-enclosed

atrium with elevator core and the automobile ramp are additions to the original structures. Each medical department has been treated as a separate unit to reinforce the sense of individualized medical care for both staff and patients. On the ground floor a three hundred–foot pedestrian arcade connects the health center with the management offices. The same firm designed the original HCHP building, completed in 1972, at nearby Kenmore Square.

Fenway Park

Brookline Avenue at Jersey Street
1912; 1934

Red Sox fans regard Fenway Park as a sacred place. The audience is mainly at field level and feels intimately involved in the game. In an era when vast sports facilities are the norm, with synthetic turf and seating capacities so large they keep fans far from the action, Fenway Park is that rare breed with a real grass field and the smallest dimensions of any facility in major-league baseball. The "Green Monster," the 37-foot-tall green left-field wall, compensates for the short 315-foot depth of left field. The stadium's peculiar size and shape were determined by the surrounding city streets, which predated its construction. Bostonians have always walked to their ball park; it is tucked tightly into an urban corner of Kenmore Square, and before and after ball games the surrounding streets are a sea of pedestrians sharing their postgame euphoria or disappointment. Constructed for the 1912 season and rebuilt in 1934, with numerous additions and alterations since, Fenway Park has a "depression-

The Boston Globe (Bill Brett, photographer)

Fenway Park

style" brick facade with raised panel patterns and stucco triangles that is hard to work up any enthusiasm over and lacks any architectural presence. Long overdue is a facelift with a designed facade that would make clear the entries, ticket windows, and offices. Inside, where the legendary intimacy keeps the audience in the center of the action, is another matter.

Forsyth Dental Infirmary for Children
140 Fenway
EDWARD T. P. GRAHAM, 1915

The classical style was considered to be appropriate to any institution of this period, from post office or police station to school or morgue. Early nineteenth-century Boston architects such as Alexan-

der Parris also turned to Classical sources for a variety of public buildings (including Faneuil Hall Marketplace, U.S. Custom House, and St. Paul's Cathedral). Here an arcade of engaged Doric columns with Ionic capitals wraps around the building, resting on a first story of chamfered rustication.

🏛 Isabella Stewart Gardner Museum
280 Fenway
WILLARD T. SEARS, 1902
National Register of Historic Places
Open to the Public

Here is the personal "palace" of Mrs. John Lowell Gardner, Jr. It was built to house an extraordinary Boston woman and her unique collection of art and furnishings, much of it acquired with the advice and assistance of Bernard Berenson, the noted art historian. Fabulous stories circulated about "Mrs. Jack" walking down Tremont Street with a lion on a leash, taking up Buddhism, spending lavish sums on her wardrobe and jewels when neither was an appropriate concern for a proper Boston lady (which she was not), but the force of her personality and her extravagance are undeniable in the museum she built and the art she collected. The stories may seem suspect until one considers the tangible evidence that survives. This museum was indeed her personal home, and that is the most outlandish story of all. Everything is still in exactly the place where she left it and can never be relocated, according to the strict terms of her will.

The plain matter-of-fact exterior

Isabella Stewart Gardner Museum

encloses a fantastic Venetian villa interior with a four-story central courtyard as its focus. An arcade of colonnettes supporting semicircular arches surrounds the garden level of the landscaped courtyard. At the upper level the pink-and-white mottled walls are punctuated with tripartite windows with balustrades or balconies. The courtyard is a pleasant space to see by day, but by night it becomes magical, with candelabras and sconces glowing in the richly decorated rooms overlooking the courtyard.

New Riding Club

52 Hemenway Street
WILLARD T. SEARS, 1892
National Register of Historic Places

The New Riding Club was organized in 1891 as a private club for prominent Bostonians, with stables convenient to the new bridle paths through the Fenway. The riding instructor, Henri de Bussigny, was as famous and socially indispensable as the dance master Papanti. The former French cavalry officer was a rigid product of St. Cyr and a first-rate horseman of the French classical style. Despite too many materials and motifs, this very long stable in the Tudor Revival/Queen Anne style resonates with appealing bits and pieces. Stucco with faux half-timbering and asphalt shingles dominate the upper floors, while tan brick with red brick round arches on the first floor produce a bizarre juxtaposition of northern European and Mediterranean styles. The building contained clubhouse facilities, a stable, a riding room, and space for grooming, shoeing, feeding, exercising, and veterinary care of members' horses.

New Riding Club

Today the riding ring holds tennis courts, and other parts of the building have been converted to residences.

Boston University Theater

264 Huntington Avenue
J. WILLIAMS BEAL'S SONS, 1925

A charming small theater is behind this Georgian Revival facade of brick and stone. Originally called the Repertory Theater, it is reminiscent of the Wilbur Theater (see 246 Tremont Street, p. 125), built eleven years earlier. Ornamentation is concentrated at the two ends of the facade, where symmetrical porticoes on slender columns are at the entry level and matched pairs of fluted Corinthian pilasters frame pedimented windows and festooned oculi above.

New England Conservatory of Music and Jordan Hall

290–294 Huntington Avenue
WHEELWRIGHT AND HAVEN, 1901, 1904
National Register of Historic Places

The New England Conservatory, the first music college in the country, was established in 1867 after many years of effort by Dr. Eben Tourjee. Its early classes were held in rooms of the old Music Hall building, now the Orpheum Theater (see Tremont Street at Hamilton Place, p. 11), until in 1882 it took over the former St. James Hotel on Franklin Square in the South End (see Washington Street at 11 East Newton Street, p. 329). Twenty years later the Conservatory moved into a new structure built specifically for it in the new Boston cultural center developing on Huntington Avenue.

New England Conservatory of Music and YMCA

The conservative Classical Revival facade offers no surprises or innovations. The brickwork is modeled to suggest coursed rustication on the ground floor, and quoins define corner pavilions and the entrance bay on the upper floors.

The most interesting part of the complex is the interior of Jordan Hall, an auditorium built in 1904 by Eben Jordan. The founder of the Jordan Marsh department store had also provided funds for two other Boston theaters: The Majestic, later the Saxon (see 219 Tremont Street, p. 124), and the old Huntington Avenue Opera House that was demolished in 1958. This fine concert hall has a peculiar seating and floor design that gives patrons the tipsy feeling of being on a boat. Presumably to provide good sight lines, all the rows of the balcony slant downhill, while on the main floor odd sections of seats create aisles that dead-end in the middle of the auditorium.

Boston University Theater

Northeastern University

360 Huntington Avenue

SHEPLEY BULFINCH RICHARDSON AND
ABBOTT, 1934 AND LATER

In their original master plan and architectural designs for Northeastern University in 1934, the architects Shepley, Bulfinch, Richardson, and Abbott sought a completely different image from that of their many Harvard buildings which were rooted in American and English traditions. Stripped of all specific historical refer-

ences, the austere light gray brick buildings nevertheless have a Neoclassical feeling in their symmetry and proportions.

The more recent Carl S. Ell Student Center (1965) offers spatial drama in the sixty-foot-high Great Hall, the focus for student extracurricular activities. The modular structure of sandblasted concrete columns, beams, and exposed coffered ceilings accommodates a variety of spaces including a cafeteria, ballroom, experimental theater, banquet hall, meeting rooms, practice rooms, and offices.

© Shepley Bulfinch Richardson and Abbott

Carl S. Ell Student Center

Kariotis and Cargill Halls
Northeastern University
Huntington Avenue
HERBERT S. NEWMAN, 1982

The architect of these recent buildings has had some fun breaking out of the rigid context established in previous decades while still retaining visual connections. Elements of neighboring buildings are drawn in, such as the quoins and the combination of brick with light concrete trim in Kariotis Hall, but the Baroque curves and bulges seem to come only from the architect's imagination. The end result is positive and improves the older buildings by juxtaposition. The interiors are far less interesting than the exterior form and are simply adequate. In some areas, the project is purely formalist, with little concern for expressing or enhancing the actual activity patterns of the spaces. For example, the attention-getting form of Cargill Hall on Huntington Avenue might be a chapel, a subway station, or a heating plant, but actually is a lecture hall. The

raised plaza connecting the new buildings with the older Gryzmish Hall, although filled with formal planting and seating areas, does not seem to attract users.

Museum of Fine Arts
465 Huntington Avenue
GUY LOWELL 1907–1909;
ADDITIONS: HUGH STUBBINS AND ASSOCIATES, 1966–1970; THE ARCHITECTS COLLABORATIVE, 1976; AND I. M. PEI, 1981

Tenshin-En, Japanese Garden
Fenway side of Museum of Fine Arts
KINSAKU NAKANE, 1988

The Museum of Fine Arts, incorporated in 1870, was first located in the top floor of the Boston Athenaeum. In 1876 it moved into a new and larger building on Copley Square at Dartmouth and St. James streets, an ornate Victorian Gothic building which it also outgrew. The current massive granite building in the Classical Revival style was located in the newly developing

Kariotis Hall, Northeastern University

West Wing, Museum of Fine Arts

Interior, West Wing

Huntington Avenue cultural center on a large twelve-acre site and opened its doors in 1909.

Its two original facades, one on Huntington Avenue and the other on the Fenway, are quite different. An Ionic temple portico announces the Huntington en-

Museum of Fine Arts

trance (now closed), and the two flanking wings, each with smaller temple porches, embrace the entrance courtyard and its incongruous equestrian statue of the American Indian. On the Fenway side the scale is much more monumental, with a long Ionic colonnade rising two stories is across the flat facade. The exterior form may convey a sense of simplicity and organization, but complexity and confusion are the rule in the layout of circulation and galleries.

I. M. Pei's West Wing addition is refreshingly clear and straightforward in its interior organization and is an ideal reception area for visitors. The understated facade of gray granite matches the granite of the original building and leads into a 200-foot-long, 53-foot-high light-filled galleria covered with a glass barrel vault faced with a sun screen of aluminum tubing. The space is surrounded with galleries, a cafe and restaurant, an auditorium, and a gift shop and is connected with one of the main circulation axes of the museum. As part of this addition, a new climate-control system for the

entire museum was installed with water, steam, air, and electrical systems to control pollution, humidity, and temperature.

Tenshin-En, The Garden of the Heart of Heaven, is a walled Japanese garden designed by landscape architect Kinsaku Nakane of Kyoto to suggest mountains, ocean, and islands in the New England landscape. As one enters the gate and walks along the accessible side the hard-surfaced, rigid garden is immediately revealed. The perspective does not change.

Fenway Studios
30 Ipswich Street
PARKER, THOMAS, AND RICE, 1905
National Register of Historic Places

Happily, the Fenway Studios building is still populated by artists, and hopefully, it always will be. The cleverly organized two-story units have abundant light from the large windows. A skip-floor corridor system allows cross ventilation, as well. The interiors are redolent of the turn-of-the-century artistic life usually found only in novels.

Fenway Studios

Joslin Diabetes Center

near Longwood Avenue at 1 Joslin Place
PAYETTE ASSOCIATES, 1974–1976

This project accommodates a complex
and innovative program for the study and
training of ambulatory diabetic patients, a
field pioneered by Dr. Eliot P. Joslin.
Facilities were required for a group prac-

tice of twenty physicians specializing in
diabetes, a treatment unit with living
accommodations (including recreational
facilities) for seventy patients, and a
research laboratory. All construction work
took place in the context of an existing
functioning nursing unit that could not be
disrupted.

© Nick Wheeler

Joslin Diabetes Center

Children's Hospital Medical Center

300 Longwood Avenue
THE ARCHITECTS COLLABORATIVE,
1962–1971

TAC prepared the long-range master plan for the Children's Hospital as well as a number of its component buildings, including a diagnostic and outpatient treatment center, a radiology and surgery building, a parking garage, an intensive care unit, a research laboratory, and the Children's Inn and Residence Group. Since the components were to be built over an extended period, the plan had to allow construction activities without disruption of service. The multiuse buildings

© Phokion Karas

Children's Hospital Medical Center

are zoned horizontally rather than vertically. Architectural harmony has been maintained among structures built at different times by use of poured-in-place concrete as the main material and by adherence to similar scale and style throughout. The resulting complex is a complete therapeutic and research community.

Harvard Medical School

Harvard Medical School

Longwood Avenue
SHEPLEY, RUTAN, AND COOLIDGE, 1907

A grand composition in white marble on axis with Avenue Louis Pasteur, the Harvard Medical School is one of the high points of Boston's turn-of-the-century Classical Revival style.

Francis A. Countway Library of Medicine

Harvard Medical Center
off Longwood Avenue at
10 Shattuck Street
HUGH STUBBINS AND ASSOCIATES, 1965

One of the largest medical libraries in the country is housed in the Countway Library. The open stacks overlook the seven-story court. Reading alcoves ring the perimeter and are articulated on the exterior as projections on the upper lev-

Francis A. Countway Library of Medicine

els, while individual study carrels project over the central space. The square and symmetrically organized mass is topped by a projecting floor decorated with light-catching fins.

PARK DRIVE

Park Drive and Boylston Street enclose a small neighborhood that should have been one of the most desirable locations in Boston, sited as it is among some of the outstanding institutions of the city and convenient to the Back Bay and the downtown. The developers of the Fenway in the early twentieth century had expected this area to become one of the most fashionable and sought-after in the city, but as it turned out the streetcar suburbs of Newton and Brookline took precedence. Although much of the architecture was purely speculative development and with little individual merit, there is some outstanding terra-cotta ornament. Along the west side of the Back Bay Fens the curving roadway is lined with harmonious facades. The simple blocks of apartments enjoy an enviable view of Frederick Law Olmsted's landscape design for the Fens.

Holy Trinity Russian Orthodox Church
165 Park Drive
CONSTANTINE PERTZOFF, 1960

This Russian Orthodox church might be described as modern Russian Revival in style. Intersecting elliptical barrel vaults are decorated with traditional Russian motifs. The annual festival is an opportunity to enjoy Russian food and music.

Greek Cathedral Church Evangelismos
514 Parker Street

Classical pedimented pavilions project from the central-domed church. The real attraction, architecturally, is inside. The richly decorated interiors are executed in the Byzantine manner with gold mosaics and a profusion of color.

QUEENSBERRY STREET

Red brick four-story apartment buildings line the street in a harmonious row that could be elegant. Each building has a columned portico center entrance with bay windows at each end. White-glazed terra-cotta tile provides ornamentation for windows, string courses, and entrances, although much of this has been removed. Balconies project from occasional second- and third-floor windows.

Charlestown

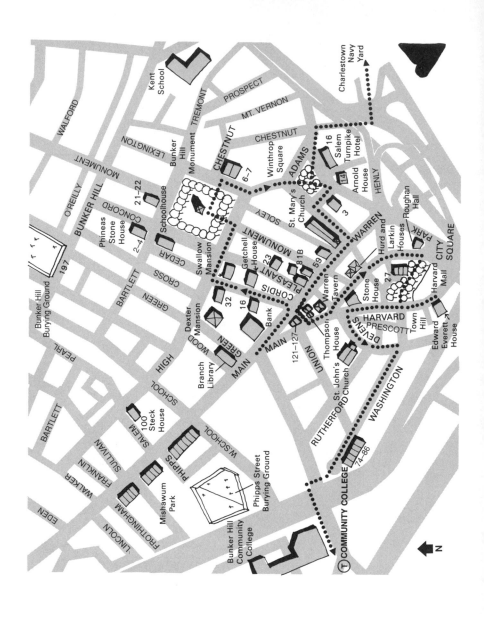

Charlestown

The Colonial town of Charlestown was founded in 1629, one year before Boston, as the first settlement of the Massachusetts Company. It was centered on City Square, which is today the heavily trafficked rotary at the far end of the bridge from Boston. But in the early seventeenth century Charlestown was a wooded peninsula of roughly triangular shape. It has been noted for political leadership since its beginning and had a particularly large role in the Revolutionary War. Most of the town was burned by the British in 1775, a loss of more than five hundred pre-Revolutionary houses, barns, mills, and shops. Its citizens returned and began rebuilding their town in the late eighteenth century. As a result of its long and glorious history, Charlestown is interesting to American history buffs and an essential part of any architectural tour of today's Boston.

Charlestown–Bunker Hill and Town Hill Tour

Start at the **Savings Bank Building** on Main Street (**369**) and turn left onto **Cordis Street,** passing several interesting Charlestown houses (**359**). Turn right at the top of the hill and enter Monument Square, circling the **Bunker Hill Monument (372)**. Walk past **6–7 Monument Square (374)** and turn left onto the short street leading to **Winthrop Square (379)**. Here you will see the **Old Training Field School,** the **Arnold house,** and the **Salem Turnpike Hotel (379–80)**. At this point you can take a side trip to the **Charlestown Navy Yard** by leaving the Square and weaving your way under the expressway (**381**).

Returning to the Square, continue down Winthrop Street past **St. Mary's Church (377)**. Turn right onto Warren Street and pass **59, 81, 81B, 81½,** and **83 Warren Street (377–78)**. Turn left onto Thompson Street, passing the **Thompson houses (367–68)**. At the **Warren Tavern (367)** turn left onto Main Street in front of **General Austin's stone house (366)**. Continue on Main Street as it curves around the base of **Town Hill (360)**. Walk through the Mall to the center of Town Hill, viewing the small houses on **Harvard Square (362)**. When you reach Harvard Street, the central spine of Town Hill, turn left to see the **Edward Everett house (363)**. Retrace your steps and return to Austin's stone house and turn left onto Devens Street to see **St. John's Church (360)**. From here you may either return to your starting point or walk down Washington Street past the early nineteenth-century row houses and then on to **Bunker Hill Community College (375)** and the MBTA station.

William Kent Elementary School

50 Bunker Hill Street

EARL R. FLANSBURGH AND ASSOCIATES, 1970–1972

Located on a steeply sloping site in a neighborhood of nineteenth-century row houses, the school uses the classroom module to reflect the scale of the neighboring architecture. The large masses of the auditorium and gymnasium are tucked into the hill, serving as a backdrop for the tiered classrooms. The main stair-

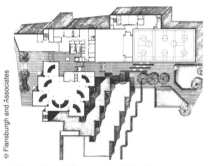

Plan, Kent Elementary School

way connecting all levels of the school is covered by a stepped skylight, giving constant visual connection to the site. The classrooms have windows and skylights that provide a repetitive rhythm reminiscent of the adjacent row houses. The school has a number of facilities for community use during and after school hours.

Bunker Hill Burying Ground

197A Bunker Hill Street

FOUNDED 1801

As morning dawned on June 17, 1775, the circumstances of the defense of the Revolutionary forces against the British revealed a need for protection from the north. There was an old rail fence offering none, but they quickly covered that with hay so at least there would be visual screening of their movements. Beyond the end of the fence a stone wall was reinforced down to the river edge. The shots fired from behind this wall foiled

Kent Elementary School

the British attack from along the beach. Within the Bunker Hill Burying Ground is a granite marker showing the location of the old rail fence from the Battle of Bunker Hill. Also on the grounds are two old street signs relating to Charlestown's early nineteenth-century past.

308 Bunker Hill Street

LATE NINETEENTH CENTURY

This large, handsome Victorian house has a mansard roof and projecting central pavilion above the entrance. The two brick stories are capped by a cornice at the base of the mansard-roofed third story. Stone window lintels are connected by a horizontal string course.

St. Francis de Sales Church

Bunker Hill Street

PATRICK C. KEELEY, 1859

While English descendants had dominated Charlestown in the first century of the town's history, by 1860 forty percent of the population was Irish. Thus there was a sudden surge in the building of Roman Catholic churches in the second half of the nineteenth century. St. Francis de Sales was an important parish church constructed in 1859 in the Romanesque-Celtic Revival style of the Victorian period. The stone exterior is decorated freely with quoins and has both Romanesque and Gothic windows. The stubby spire is ornamented with diagonal ribs.

St. Francis de Sales Church

Charlestown Bridge

1899

The Charlestown Bridge was built in 1899 to replace a much lower bridge built in 1786 and demolished after the new bridge was completed. Before 1786, traffic between Boston and Charlestown was by ferry on the Great Ferry established by Edward Converse in 1601. In the mid-eighteenth century the profits from the ferry were donated to Harvard College until it went out of business after completion of the first bridge.

CORDIS STREET

Cordis Street was named for Captain Joseph Cordis, who lived nearby on Main Street and laid this street out in 1799. It is a short street with many early houses, including the 1802 Getchell and Hyde houses at 21 and 32 Cordis. The Swallow mansion at 33 is a large white Greek Revival house with four Ionic columns across the Greek temple facade.

DEVENS STREET

Once named Bow Street, it was in 1640 called Crooked Lane and was the site of the first huts and tents of early settlers Ralph, Richard, and William Sprague about 1630. At the point where the street met the waterline on Tyler's Wharf, there was an establishment in the nineteenth

Swallow mansion, 33 Cordis Street

Getchell house, 21 Cordis Street

century with "bathing machines" where ladies and gentlemen could enjoy private saltwater bathing in the summer.

St. John's Episcopal Church and Parish House
Devens Street
RICHARD BOND, 1841

At the corner of Devens Street and old Rutherford Avenue, this Gothic Revival church was built in 1841. Its heavy granite facade features a square tower with quatrefoil windows below the crenellated roofline. The wooden building standing next to it was built three decades later. Compare this church with the 1831 Mission Church of St. John the Evangelist by Solomon Willard on Beacon Hill (see 35 Bowdoin Street, p. 192).

Dexter Mansion
now VFW Memorial Hall
14 Green Street
1791

The Dexter mansion was one of the most significant buildings in the Boston area when it was built in 1791 for Samuel Dexter. It is difficult to imagine its eighteenth-century grandeur today. Samuel Dexter was a congressman, senator, and secretary of the treasury and of war under President John Adams. The two-story wooden house still has its original cupola, although the roof was raised to accommodate a third floor and a wing was added.

St. John's Episcopal Church

🏛 Harvard Mall and Town Hill
National Register of Historic Places

Town Hill was the first community settlement in Charlestown and was laid out by an engineer, Thomas Graves, who assigned each settler a plot of two acres. The first settlers came from Salem in 1629, and by 1630 they had built a small palisaded fort atop the hill (then much higher than now) as protection against the Indians. The name Town Hill has been used since 1629, except for the decade 1635–1645, when it seems to have been referred to as Windmill Hill, after the windmill Robert Hawkins built there in the early seventeenth century to grind the settlers' corn. Harvard Place is a serene corner of Town Hill with fine old cobblestone paving. The narrow street is nicely framed by dormered brick row houses from the mid-nineteenth century.

The John Harvard Mall is the site of the hill fort built by the settlers. The young John Harvard was the son of a wealthy tradesman in England and the first member of his family to go to college. He graduated from Emmanuel College of Cambridge University at the age of twenty-five and three years later received a Master's degree. Ordained as a minister, he inherited the remainder of the family fortune, married, and sailed to America with cattle he planned to raise. On the ship with the newlyweds was another recent graduate of Cambridge University, Nathaniel Eaton, and his wife. Both cou-

ples settled in Charlestown, where John Harvard began performing the service in the First Parish on a temporary basis.

Less than fourteen months after his arrival in Massachusetts, on September 24, 1638, Harvard died of consumption. Only thirty-one years old, he left half the family fortune he had inherited and his entire library to a college that was to be founded. Nathaniel Eaton was appointed to establish and administer it. The General Court of Massachusetts had voted 400 pounds to start the new institution, which was originally to be called Emmanuel College, but after receiving the library and an 800-pound bequest from John Harvard the General Court voted in 1639 that the name should be Harvard College. In 1943 a Harvard alumnus donated the Mall to Charlestown in memory of John Harvard. The plaques lining the brick mall describe the history of Town Hill.

Harvard Mall

Harvard Square

EARLY NINETEENTH CENTURY

At the edge of Harvard Mall is a charming place named Harvard Square with a small row of dwellings typical of the early nineteenth century in Charlestown. Each two-storied house with dormered attic has one fireplace on each of the two main floors—the only heat source for much of the nineteenth century. The attics, although inhabited, often had no heat, or just a small coal stove.

27 Harvard Square

c. 1800

This house is one of the few stone buildings ever built in Charlestown. For many years it was the Charlestown Free Dispensary, established in 1814, a combination clinic and pharmacy where drugs and bandages were made and administered. The house was built by General Nathaniel Austin of split stone quarried on Outer Brewster Island, which Austin owned.

Harvard Square

HARVARD STREET

Harvard Street is the unifying element of Town Hill and is thought to be the site of the first schoolhouse in America. A dignified and lovely curving street today, it has long been the residence of New England notables. On the corner of Harvard Street fronting on City Square stood Robbins Tavern until 1818 when it was

Harvard Street

replaced by the old Town Hall, torn down in 1868. The fine row houses now lining the street were primarily built in the 1850s and 1860s on land then owned by Moses Dow, publisher and educator, who built his own house at number 28. While the brick row houses provide continuity of enclosure for the street, there is a surprising variety of mid-nineteenth-century styles. Numbers 7–23 are fine flat-facade houses with only the most restrained decoration, an intentional emphasis on simplicity. Opposite them are richly ornamented larger houses at numbers 22 and 24 and the Dow house at 28, with brownstone arched entrances, oriel windows projecting from the second floors, and elaborate lintels, cornices, and

French-inspired mansard roofs. Farther up the hill are bowfront houses, making almost a survey of mid-nineteenth-century row house styles between City Square and Washington Street.

Edward Everett House
16 Harvard Street
1812

This fine Federal house was built in 1812 by Matthew Bridge, a shipping merchant and state legislator, for his daughter. Edward Everett purchased it in 1830 but lived there only six years, moving when he was elected governor of Massachusetts. Later he was to serve as secretary of state, U.S. senator, and president of Harvard College. When he left Charlestown in 1836, Everett sold the house to William Carleton, who lived there for almost three decades before founding Carleton College in Northfield, Minnesota. The large but unostentatious freestanding house of three stories has a hip roof and central entrance door highlighted by a portico with Ionic columns and pilasters. Square granite posts and curb support a fine old cast-iron fence.

29–41 High Street
MID-NINETEENTH CENTURY

This distinguished row of Victorian houses has flat facades, mansard roofs, and handsome granite front steps leading to the raised entrances. Each of the row houses has an arched window pair on the front parlor overlooking High Street.

Edward Everett house

Steck House

100 High Street

c. 1790

Originally built as a double house in 1790, 100 High Street now stands as a fine single house facing its yard rather

Steck house

than the street. It has double chimneys and a basement kitchen opening onto the garden, and the third story has the small square windows typical of its period.

MAIN STREET

Main Street is the long spine running from City Square to the ancient town limits. Since 1640 it has had many names, beginning with the descriptive Country Road, which it truly was when Town Hill was the center of settlement. After 1670 the town developed further and it became Town Street. It was paved in 1730 and became Broad Street, where one often heard the horns of fox hunters in October. As more stores were built near the Charlestown Bridge to sell the many leather products of the morocco factories on Cook's and Henley's lanes, the name became Market Street. When growth

Main Street

spread farther west it became Main Street, which it has been for more than one hundred years.

It is rich in old buildings. Many of the brick structures built adjacent to Town Hill along Main Street originally had a combination of uses, with shops on the first floor and residences above as seen today at 18–34. Across Main Street, taller wood and brick commercial buildings such as number 51 were built in the late nineteenth century.

Roughan Hall

Main Street at 15–18 City Square
ARTHUR H. VINAL, 1892; ADDITION, 1896
National Register of Historic Places

From the seventeenth century until well into the twentieth century the City Square area was the center of Charlestown commerce and government. None of the early structures survive on City Square, but remains of what may have been the foundation of the Great House, built about 1630 as the governor's residence and public meeting house, were discovered during excavations for the new harbor tunnel in 1991. The only reminder of the activities once centered on the square is the awkward late nineteenth-century Roughan Hall. Standing across the street from the Town Hill Historic District, it is very dominant and particularly disruptive to the townscape and unrelated to the materials and scale of historic Charlestown. The tan brick facade folds back away from the square toward Main Street. The skin is punctuated with oversize win-

Roughan Hall

dows and decorated with basket-weave panels. A large hall is located in the double-height fourth floor spanned by Howe trusses. The elaborately decorated hall was first used for dances and lectures and in later years for movies and roller skating. The building also held offices and shops, and in the basement were three bowling alleys along with billiard and pool tables.

John Larkin House
55–61 Main Street
c. 1795

Deacon John Larkin is best remembered as the man who lent Paul Revere a horse for his midnight ride. His horse, incidentally, was never returned. Larkin built this house to replace his City Square house, which was burned down by the British during the Battle of Bunker Hill. The three-story square wooden house with hip roof, small third-story windows, quoins, and capped and pegged window frames

was a prominent Main Street residence.

John Hurd House
65–71 Main Street
c. 17951

Next door to Deacon Larkin's house is another late eighteenth-century mansion, this one built for John Hurd, a wealthy Charlestown citizen of the time. Like the Larkin house it has three stories and a hip roof. Decorative quoins of wood at the corners mimic the shapes of stone blocks used in earlier European architecture.

General Austin's Stone House
92 Main Street
1822
Boston Landmark

In 1822 General Nathaniel Austin, Middlesex County sheriff and major general of the Massachusetts militia, built this house with commercial space. It was here that

John Hurd and John Larkin houses

General Austin's stone house

Warren Tavern

the first successful Charlestown newspaper, *The Bunker Hill Aurora and Farmers and Mechanics Journal,* was published from 1827 to 1871. Like the small house Austin built at 27 Harvard Square, this building is faced with split stone quarried on the Outer Brewster Island, then owned by Austin.

Warren Tavern
105 Main Street at 2 Pleasant Street
C. 1780; RENOVATED 1972

This tavern was one of the first buildings erected after the burning of Charlestown by the British. It was named in honor of the General Joseph Warren, who had died in the Battle of Bunker Hill. General Warren was a member of the Committee of Safety and president of the Provincial Congress in 1774. He arrived on Breed's Hill (known and memorialized erroneously as Bunker Hill) and refused

Colonel Prescott's offer to relinquish command, Warren being a higher-ranking officer. Instead the thirty-four-year-old fought as an ordinary soldier under Prescott and was promptly killed.

The original tavern sign carried a painting of his head as its decoration over the door. The first Masonic lodge in the area, King Solomon's Lodge, was founded here in 1784. It was this lodge that first commemorated the Battle of Bunker Hill with a wooden column in what is now Monument Square. This three-story wooden building and the hall added by the Masonic Lodge in 1786 are typical of the utilitarian structures built following the Revolution. It is now restored and occupied by a restaurant.

Timothy Thompson, Sr. House
119 Main Street
C. 1794; RESTORED 1970s

Timothy Thompson and his wife, Mary Frothingham, lost their earlier Charlestown house when it was burned by the British in 1775. Like many other inhabi-

Timothy Thompson, Sr. house

tants, they returned and ultimately built a new home. After the death of Mr. Thompson, the first floor was converted to a store and an additional one-story store was attached to the Main Street side of the house. It has not been restored to its eighteenth-century appearance.

Thompson-Sawyer House
Main Street at 9 Thompson Street
1805

Timothy Thompson, Sr., who built 119 Main Street, also lived in this house, and it became his daughter's home when she married a Sawyer. Their son, Timothy Thompson Sawyer, was the author of *Old Charlestown* and served as mayor of Charlestown. He was born and raised in this house, which at that time was attached to another house. A two-story addition elongates the front facade of the house, creating a very imposing presence. The main house is actually one room deep, part of a double house divided by a brick party wall.

Thompson-Sawyer house

Round-Corner House
121–123 Main Street
c. 1814

The dwelling of Captain Joseph Cordis, who laid out Cordis Street, was on the upper two floors of this brick building. Commercial space was on the first floor. The shop windows are framed by long granite lintels and posts. The most distinctive feature of the building is its inset round corner on Main Street.

Round-corner house and Edmands Hall

Armstrong Press and Edmands Hall
125–127 Main Street
1808

The mixed-use building was built by John T. Edmands but acquired the name of the publisher and printer whose business was located on the first floor. Samuel T. Armstrong was a prominent politician, serving as mayor of Boston and lieutenant governor of the state. The very controversial First Universalist Society had its first meetings in the hall upstairs before their church was built. There was stern disapproval at the time of anyone who would attend such meetings.

Savings Bank Building
Main Street at 1 Thompson Square
MOFFETTE AND TOLMAN, 1876
Boston Landmark

Built in the Victorian Gothic style of Pugin, the building has a tall mansard

Savings Bank Building

roof penetrated with ornamented peaked dormers. The center bay projects slightly and contains two Gothic arch entrances. Windows of the second floor are topped with pointed arches, while those of the next floor are round. Several string-course bands wrap around the facade, connecting the window arches and sills.

Charlestown Branch Library
Boston Public Library
169–179 Main Street
EDUARDO CATALANO
1970

The old Indian Chief Hotel built in the eighteenth century occupied this site until about 1820, when the Second Congregational Unitarian Church built their brick church on the site. The original Charles-

town Public Library first opened in the Bunker Hill Bank building (Main Street at Henley Street) in 1862 with a collection that included a number of subscriptions to foreign newspapers, since educated Americans at that time read several languages and expected to keep abreast of international affairs. A catalogue of the collection was printed and sold to card holders, who numbered over three thousand by the end of the first year.

This new library building on Main Street was built to serve neighborhood rather than research purposes. The inverted U-form of poured concrete is dramatically cantilevered from two points, one on each side of the entrance. The floating effect of the massive concrete form is dramatized by its juxtaposition with glass. But why was such a tour de force necessary in a branch library?

© George Zimberg

Charlestown Branch Library

Mishawum Park Housing

Main Street

FREEMAN AND HARDENBURGH

1974

The clapboard style of much of Charlestown's old architecture is used in this contemporary housing development. The pedestrian walkways on the third

Mishawum Park housing

floor and other provisions for outdoor space are an imaginative approach to adapting the living patterns found in Charlestown to a higher-density configuration of housing.

Phipps Street Burying Ground

off Main Street

1630

National Register of Historic Places

One of the oldest burial grounds in the country, "Burying Hill," as it was first called, has Revolutionary heroes among its one thousand pre-1800 burials, and early Charlestown citizens among its three hundred pre-1700 burials. It escaped the British fire in 1775 because it was not associated with any church. Many fascinating examples of early American tombstones can be seen. Originally its setting was prettier, with water on three sides, before extensive filling was undertaken. In 1828 a monument to John Harvard was erected here by Harvard graduates in memory of the young Charlestown resident whose contribution made possible Harvard College. He is not buried here, however; his grave site is presumed lost in the fire of 1775.

Phipps Street Burying Ground

Monument Avenue

🏛 MONUMENT AVENUE

This attractive avenue leading uphill to
Monument Square is formally completed
by the obelisk-shaped monument at the
end of the vista. Bordering the avenue are
a diverse but harmonious mixture of brick
row houses. Some feature bow fronts,
some flat facades with oriel windows projecting from the second floors, some elaborate cornices edging flat roofs, or
mansard roofs with dormers. There are
even clapboard and shingle row houses
with bow or stepped facades. There is
much lovely detailing in granite, wood, or
cast iron.

🏛 **Bunker Hill Monument**

Monument Square
SOLOMON WILLARD, 1825–1843
National Historic Landmark

The hill on which Bunker Hill Monument
stands is commonly, and mistakenly,
referred to as Bunker Hill. This error
began about midnight on June 16, 1775,
when one thousand revolutionary troops
under Colonel Prescott's command arrived
at what they thought to be Bunker Hill
and began digging fortifications. Not until
dawn could they see their position clearly.
Thus the Battle of Bunker Hill was actually fought on Breed's Hill, named for the
homestead of Ebenezer Breed, who kept
a pair of antelope in his yard.

　　The initial monument was erected by
the King Solomon's Lodge of Charlestown
in 1794 in the form of a Tuscan pillar in
James Russell's pasture. A desire to pro-

tect and memorialize the site further led to the formation in 1823 of the Bunker Hill Monument Association, which raised money and purchased the land for the monument. The Marquis de Lafayette journeyed from France to lay the corner-stone in 1825, and in 1843 the dedication ceremony took place with Daniel Webster as orator. A model of the original 1794 monument is displayed inside the obelisk.

Solomon Willard, the monument's designer, was a diversely talented man highly regarded by his contemporaries. He began as a carpenter, then carved fig-ureheads for ships. From there he went into sculpture, then architecture, followed by work as a scientist, quarry master, and scientific agriculturist. In Washington,

Cast-iron fence, Bunker Hill Monument

D.C. he assisted Bulfinch in his work on the Capitol. Besides designing the Bunker Hill Monument, Willard bought a quarry in Quincy to supply the granite. A special tramway was built to move the slabs from Quincy to Charlestown, a significant engi-neering achievement for the time. The monument was built by Gridley Bryant, father of architect Gridley J. Fox Bryant.

Today the 220-foot obelisk and the nearby 1881 statue of Colonel William

Prescott by William Story are the central focus of a handsome formal square laid out in 1839. Beginning in the 1840s, fine brick row houses for prominent Charlestown citizens were constructed on the four sides of the square park. With bow fronts, projecting oriel windows, and dormers or cupolas, the inhabitants took advantage of the long views over Boston Harbor, the Mystic River, or the Charles River from their favorable location.

Phineas Stone House
2–4 Monument Square at Concord Street
c. 1860

This pair of houses opposite the northeast corner of Monument Square was once the handsome Greek Revival Phineas Stone house, which explains the central place-ment of the cupola. The entrance was originally on the uphill end facing the square and had a handsome large white wooden two-story porch with pediment supported by four tall Ionic columns. In front of the porch was a garden enclosed by an ornamental iron fence.

Phineas Stone house

Phineas Jones Stone came to Charlestown as a boy when his father opened a grocery store in 1824. He was for many years a retailer of West Indian goods, selectman of Charlestown, representative to the State Legislature, the first president of the Five Cents Savings Bank in Charlestown, and mayor of the town in 1862–1864.

6–7 Monument Square

c. 1858

This pair of Greek Revival brick bowfront houses is distinctive in having three bows for the two houses. Building the pair in this way, rather than giving one bow to each house in the conventional manner, created a handsome balanced and symmetrical facade with the front entrances equally spaced between the bows for individual identity. The unusual facade produces an even more unusual interior, with the location of the cupola and the chimneys revealing the double-width house on the left. The cast-iron porches are late nineteenth-century additions.

6–7 Monument Square

21–22 Monument Square

MID-NINETEENTH CENTURY

Two sisters, Helen Sherkanowski Rush and Mary Sherkanowski, operated rooming houses here for years, describing their adventures and their fascinating guests in a book, *Rooms to Let*. Both houses are of French-inspired design with mansard roofs, but the one on the left is more elaborately decorated, with both front and side oriels, string courses between floors, and prominent quoins on the corners.

21–22 Monument Square

The Schoolhouse on Monument Square Residences

1907; RENOVATION: GRAHAM GUND ARCHITECTS, 1987

The former Charlestown High School has been recycled into forty-four apartments, each with a different floor plan. The major interior space is a two-story skylit circulation core with a screen wall with "windows" separating the corridors from the atrium.

23 Pleasant Street

The Schoolhouse on Monument Square

c Steve Rosenthal

23 Pleasant Street

LATE EIGHTEENTH CENTURY

One of the fascinations of Charlestown is its rich treasure of history. On any street one may encounter architectural remnants of America's earlier years. This simple wooden house is typical of the late eighteenth-century gambrel-roofed houses of the area.

Bunker Hill Community College
Rutherford Avenue
SHEPLEY BULFINCH RICHARDSON AND
ABBOTT, 1973 TO 1980

The Bunker Hill Community College is composed of linked buildings around an open space and is raised one level above the street. A pedestrian plaza and bridge connect the thirty-five-acre site with transit service. Since the site is surrounded by roads, most people see the campus from the car. To counter this automobile dominance, the designers felt that the bold planes and mass of striated concrete block were needed. The campus is planned to accommodate five thousand day students and eight thousand night students. The first phase, including classrooms, laboratories, offices, and student lounges, was completed in 1973. The second phase includes a cafeteria, library, bookstore,

Bunker Hill Community College

© Nick Wheeler

Restored house, Monument Square at Pleasant Street

conference rooms, and audiovisual department. These are connected by a monumental stairway which leads to the rooftop dining area. The combined library and cafeteria functions afford a meeting place for the students, who are a mixture of ages and social groups.

The site of the Community College was formerly known as Lynde's Point and later as Prison Point, site of the old prison designed by Charles Bulfinch. Nearby, ropewalks were built at the corner of Lynde and Arrow streets in 1794. Workers made rope of every type here, walking back and forth along the walk, twisting and pulling the fibers to form the rope.

St. Mary's Church

55 Warren Street

WARREN, WINTHROP, AND SOLEY, 1892

This was the site of the thatched house of Thomas Walford, first settler of Charles-

town in 1625. Walford left in 1631 because of disagreements with the groups of settlers from Salem on Town Hill. Since 1892 the site has been occupied by an imposing stone Gothic Revival church of granite with brick trim. It has set-back buttresses and a massive tower with lancet windows set in pointed arches on the upper stories. Above each door is an ornamental patera rendered in low relief within the equilateral archway. This structure replaces the small church dedicated in 1829 for the first Roman Catholic congregation in Charlestown.

Victorian House

59 Warren Street

This picturesque bowfront house features a charming bartizan projecting from one second-story corner. A corbeled chimney and second-floor oriel window adorn the side. The mansard roof has pointed-arch dormers with iron cresting above the cornice line.

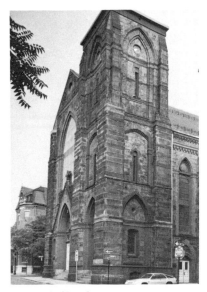

St. Mary's Church

59 Warren Street

81 Warren Street
1790–1800

This large three-story wood frame house stands perpendicular to the sidewalk and has the small square third-story windows and corner boards typical of the Federal style. The handsome front door has sidelights of glass. A two-story ell is attached to the far side of the house. This house forms the entrance to Donnell Court, where 81B and 81½ Warren Street are located.

81B Warren Street
c. 1800

Behind the Federal houses on Warren Street is a small late-Georgian wood frame house with gambrel roof. Two and a half stories high and only one small

81, 81B, and 81½ Warren Street

room deep, the house is a charming example of eighteenth-century Charlestown. It is most easily viewed from Pleasant Street.

81½ Warren Street
1875

Within the group of houses in this picturesque court, 81½ is the newest, being a Victorian clapboard house of three stories built in 1875. Note how successfully the various houses cluster together to form a setting in which they will enhance each other with very efficient use of a limited land area.

83 Warren Street
c. 1800

This large three-story clapboard house with hip roof is typical of the early nineteenth century. It was restored in 1969 with the corner boards and small square third-story windows retained. Even the corner store was happily integrated into the Federal facade. Its location at the corner of Warren and Pleasant streets makes it doubly important as a visual anchor for the other early houses clustered about it.

Row Houses
74–86 Washington Street

This fine row of brick houses has foundations as well as door and window lintels of granite. The gable roofs of the two and one-half–story houses are topped with peaked dormers and chimneys. The row is typical of the workers' housing that was often built in nineteenth century New England industrial towns. It might even have been associated with one of the shipyards, such as Josiah Barker's, not far from here on Washington Street between 1804 and 1835.

🏛 Winthrop Square
Winthrop Street at Adams Street

Training Field was the name given to this area after it was set aside in 1632 for the use of the militia. For two and one-half centuries men trained here and in 1775, 1812, and 1860 departed for battle from this field. It was built up in the late eighteenth and early nineteenth centuries, and today is a fine urban space, very different from the open meadow surrounded by settlers' farmlands where local men trained to defend their town and country.

Old Training Field School

Old Training Field School
Winthrop Square at 3 Common Street
1828

For 140 years this building served as a public grammar school, first in the middle of the training field and, after 1847, in its present position at the side of the square. It then became a private secondary school and later was acquired by the Catholic church, which used it for St. Mary's School. It is now a private residence. The old school building has the simplest of lines. It is embellished only with a roundel centered in the pediment and a semicircular relieving arch in low relief on the front facade.

Arnold House
Winthrop Square at 14 Common Street
c. 1805

This very large and handsome early nineteenth-century clapboard house with corner boards, hip roof, and small square third-story windows forms an attractive edge for the ancient training field. The large two-story ell on its right is now a separate residence.

Arnold house

Salem Turnpike Hotel

Salem Turnpike Hotel
Winthrop Square at 16 Common Street
1810

The old Salem Turnpike ran close to the edge of the ropewalk building of the Charlestown Navy Yard and behind this house. The two and one-half–story hip-roofed building was originally the Salem Turnpike Hotel. Today the original window pattern has been altered on one end. Two small square dormers light the attic at the top of the old hotel.

Charlestown Navy Yard

National Historic Landmark

OPEN TO THE PUBLIC

The Naval Shipyard in Charlestown was founded in 1800 on forty-three acres at Moulton's Point, where the British landed for the Battle of Bunker Hill. Among the famous ships constructed here were the *Boston* (1799–1800), the *Independence* (1814), and the *Merrimac* (1854–1855), the ship captured by the Confederate forces who ironclad it before its defeat by the Union ironclad *Monitor.* It was here, beginning in 1813, that ships were first built indoors to speed up construction and protect the partially constructed vessels from the weather. At its peak the Navy Yard employed almost 50,000 workers, and in 1943 a record of forty-six destroyer escorts were built. In 1956 the USS *Suffolk County* was the last ship built at the Navy Yard, and in 1971 rope production ceased. In 1974 President Nixon decommissioned the Navy Yard when it was established as part of the Boston National Historic Park.

Today the Navy Yard has become the largest and one of the most remarkable preservation and reuse projects in the country, with nineteen buildings renovated and over two million square feet of new construction. This water-oriented mixed-use community combines housing for all income groups with recreation opportunities, office and research facilities, and educational and museum sites, all in a setting of unique historic and scenic appeal. The streetscape is tree-lined, with paving of brick and granite and historic-style lighting fixtures. Second Avenue, the focus for retail activity in the Navy Yard, has been made into a pedestrian mall. A central feature of the urban design is the Harborpark, a continuous open and accessible waterfront nearly three miles long and part of the forty-three-mile long Harborwalk that will eventually encompass the entire Boston waterfront down to the Neponset River in Dorchester. A water shuttle provides convenient access between Dry Dock Number 2 and Long Wharf on the Boston waterfront. The two-time America's Cup winner *Courageous* is now based at the Courageous Sailing Center situated at Pier 4.

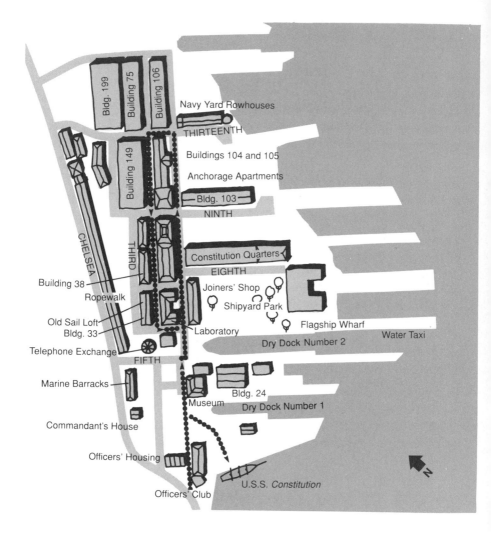

Bldg. 199

Building 75

Building 106

Navy Yard Rowhouses

THIRTEENTH

Building 149

Buildings 104 and 105

Anchorage Apartments

Bldg. 103

NINTH

CHELSEA

THIRD

Constitution Quarters

EIGHTH

Building 38

Joiners' Shop

Ropewalk

Shipyard Park

Old Sail Loft

Bldg. 33

Flagship Wharf

Laboratory

Water Taxi

Telephone Exchange

Dry Dock Number 2

FIFTH

Marine Barracks

Bldg. 24

Museum

Dry Dock Number 1

Commandant's House

Officers' Housing

N

Officers' Club

U.S.S. Constitution

Charlestown Navy Yard Tour

Enter the gate and turn right, passing the **Officers' Club.** The **USS** *Constitution* and **Dry Dock Number 1** will be in front of you. Proceed to the **USS** *Constitution* **Museum (384),** and from there you may walk through the inner gate to the area being developed by the Boston Redevelopment Authority. On your left are the **Telephone Exchange** and the **Ropewalk (387, 388).** In front of you are the large granite **Sail Loft, Laboratory,** and **Joiners' Shop.** To your right are **Shipyard Park,** the redeveloped **Constitution Quarters** in the old foundry, **Flagship Wharf (386), Dry Dock Number 2 (387),** and the water taxi to Long Wharf. At this point you may want to walk down First Avenue, passing **Building 103** (the Anchorage), **Buildings 104** and **105,** the **Navy Yard Row houses (386),** and **Building 106** (The Basilica). Return on the Second Avenue pedestrian mall, where you will see **Buildings 75, 149** (Constitution Park), **38** (The Cooper Building), and **33** (The Billings Building). Returning to the part of the Navy Yard operated by the National Park Service, you will pass the **Marine Barracks,** the **Commandant's House,** and the **Officers' Housing** on your right as you leave (**389–90**).

🏛 USS *Constitution*, "Old Ironsides"

Constitution Wharf,
JOSHUA HUMPHREY, DESIGNER, 1797
NATIONAL HISTORIC LANDMARK
Open to the Public

The USS *Constitution*, built in Boston in 1797 at Hartt's Shipyard, is the oldest commissioned vessel in the U.S. navy. It fought the Barbary pirates and then was victorious in forty-two battles during the War of 1812. It was planned to carry more guns than the typical frigate, but also had more sail area on its thirty-six sails so it could use its speed to sail away from any battle in which it found itself outgunned. It never lost a battle. After the war it served as a training vessel until this century. The frigate's permanent location is now the Charlestown Navy Yard, but each year it makes a tour of the harbor.

Dry Dock Number 1

LAOMMI BALDWIN, JR., ENGINEER,
1827–1833

This and the dry dock built in Norfolk, Virginia, in 1833 are the first dry docks built in the United States. Both were engineered by Colonel Baldwin. Because the USS *Constitution* was the first ship docked here, it is called the Constitution dock and was in continuous use from that time until 1974. It remained the only dry

Dry Dock Number 1

Old Ironsides and Officers' Club

dock at the shipyard until 1905, when the second one was built on the other side of the Shop and Docking Office.

Wood and Metal Shop

Building 22

now Constitution Museum

ALEXANDER PARRIS, 1832

Open to the Public

In 1828 the Naval Architectural Office developed a master plan for the shipyard that affected the siting and configuration of all subsequent buildings. The Wood and Metal Shop was the first building planned after the rectilinear grid for the site was laid out. It is located adjacent to the previously constructed Dry Dock Number 1. The straightforward three-story building is constructed of ashlar granite and features twelve-over-twelve paned window sash. The woodworking shop

was responsible for all the carpentry involved in the fittings for the ships. The metal shop forged wrought-iron chains and other metal items for the ships.

Shipyard Park

CHILDS, BERTMAN, TSECKARES, AND CASENDINO, 1980

Design of the four and one-half–acre park provides access to the waterfront for the surrounding community, offers a variety of recreational outlets for people of all ages, and complements the future development of the surrounding historic sites of the Navy Yard. Features include a fountain plaza, pavilion, and children's play area. Nautical artifacts reminiscent of the former shipbuilding industry of the Navy Yard are incorporated into the park to reinforce the unique character of the site.

Shipyard Park

Flagship Wharf

Building 197
adjacent to Shipyard Park
ORIGINAL BUILDING, 1941; RENOVATION AND
ADDITION: THE ARCHITECTS COLLABORATIVE,
1990

The original brick building was enlarged with two new eleven-story wings and accommodates 200 luxury condominiums as well as retail and commercial space. All units have water views or Boston skyline views.

Anchorage Apartments

Building 103
First Avenue at Ninth Street
1901; RENOVATION: BRUNER/COTT
& ASSOCIATES, 1985

This handsome brick building was built in a restrained Greek Revival style. It has been recycled to provide 112 units of subsidized housing for the elderly.

Charlestown Navy Yard Rowhouses

First Avenue at Thirteenth Street
WILLIAM RAWN ASSOCIATES, 1988

Design quality and affordability rarely coexist in housing today. Here they do. Fifty units of affordable housing, most with water views, were developed by the Bricklayers Union. The larger units are floor-through to provide cross ventilation by ocean breezes. Upper units have private terraces, while lower units have pri-

vate yards. The building forms are designed to relate to the simple industrial forms of the Navy Yard yet have a pleasing domestic scale and detailing. The complex is announced on First Avenue by its large gabled mass with two tiers of brick arches and striped brick facing. A perpendicular arm of brick row houses reaches down to the water and is terminated by a round tower with copper roof. The result is so contextually convincing one feels parts were preexisting buildings. Two other housing developments by the same architect, the Back of the Hill Rowhouses in Mission Hill and Battle Road Farm in Lincoln, are outstanding examples of mixed-income housing design.

One Forty Nine at the Navy Yard

Buildings 149 (built 1917) and 199 (built 1945)
Second Avenue between Ninth and Sixteenth streets
RENOVATION: HUYGENS DIMELLA SHAFFER, 1986

These structures were originally used by the navy to provide warehouse space for the shipbuilding operations and stood vacant after the shipyard was closed in 1974. This adaptive reuse project created 1.3 million square feet of office and retail space. The industrial character of the exterior was retained, but two atriums were cut into the center of Building 149 to bring in natural light. A major portion of the building is used for biomedical research by the Medical Research Division of Massachusetts General Hospital.

Charlestown Navy Yard Rowhouses

Other Navy Buildings

Shop and Docking Office (Building 24, 1847). Originally this two-story ashlar granite structure had a cupola and a bell that was used to summon men to the carpenters' shop and rigging loft located here. Sited between Dry Docks 1 and 2, it is one of the few structures built after the 1828 master plan that violates the grid pattern established.

The hexagonal three-story **Telephone Exchange** (Building 21, 1852) is unusually small and ornate in the con-text of the naval shipyard architecture. Ornamentation includes the projecting string courses between each floor and the elaborate modillion block cornice edging the hip roof. A wooden cupola is atop the roof.

Near the telephone exchange is the **Bank** (Building 31, 1857). This small one-story building was originally built as an ordnance shell house with no windows. Later it became the commandant's office and portions of the walls were torn out to make windows; some were bricked up again when it finally became a bank.

Telephone Exchange

The **Ropewalk** was designed by Alexander Parris in 1834–1836. Nearly a quarter of a mile long, this is the only remaining ropewalk in the United States. For 135 years all the rope for the U.S. navy was made here, from jute to hemp ropes to modern nylon ropes. Ropemakers wrapped the fibers around their waists and fed the fibers into the rope being spun as they moved down the walk on foot. The structure's load-bearing walls are handsome ashlar granite with restrained use of decoration at the corners and entrance. Adjacent to the old Salem Turnpike, it has provided an effective boundary along much of the northwest side of the shipyard property.

The **Tarring House** (Building 60, 1830s), also by Parris, was the long narrow building parallel to the entrance end of the ropewalks. Here all the tar was made and applied to waterproof the rope.

Ropewalk

Old Sail Loft (Building 33, 1850). Sails for the ships were cut and assembled in this building from 1850 until sailing ships were no longer made or repaired here. All the work on the sails was done on the floor, which had to be kept absolutely clean, smooth, and free of

Old Sail Loft

debris that could damage the cloth. After extensive use the sails would stretch so far out of shape that they no longer provided the original speed and would be returned to the sail loft for recutting and repairs. Behind the Old Sail Loft is a long, narrow granite storehouse built in 1854. It was here that the canvas and materials for the sails were kept and the completed sails stored until needed.

The earlier of the two **Laboratory Buildings** (Buildings 34 and 62) was originally designed as a storehouse by Alexander Parris in 1837. This three-story building of ashlar granite later became a laboratory where new techniques and products could be tested. The primary ornamental element of the building is the central pavilion with a pedimented gable. Located near one end of the ropewalk is the second laboratory building, also designed by Parris and built in 1842. It was originally used to store hemp for making the ropes.

Old Joiners' Shop (Building 36, c. 1850). The woodworking that required detailed fitting for cabinetry and combinations of different woods and forms was

carried out here beginning in the 1850s, when the combination wood and metal shop built in 1832 was no longer large enough for the scale of production. This long structure of granite ashlar is ornamented with smooth granite window lintels and door frames, corner quoins, cornices edging the ridge roof, and the string course of projecting stones running in a horizontal band. The building is sited in accordance with the horizontal grid established by the 1828 master plan for the shipyard.

The **Marine Barracks** were constructed to the right of the Commandant's House in 1823. Used throughout its history as barracks, the original building did not include the porches now attached to the exterior. The parade grounds were directly in front of the barracks.

Old Joiners' Shop

The **Commandant's House** (Naval Architectural Office, 1809) is a square brick Georgian-style mansion that was continuously occupied by the shipyard's commanding officer following its construction in 1809. It stands on a small hill with a fine view over Boston Harbor. The house is distinguished by two bows on the front corners that create oval rooms

inside, and by its decorative wooden
balustrade and porches. The kitchen and
formal rooms are all located on the second floor of the mansion, with bedrooms
on the third and fourth floors and service
functions on the ground floor.

Begun in 1833, the **Officers' Housing** was located in five brick row houses.
The row is located between the gate, the
Officers' Club and the Commandant's
House and faces the grass lawn that
served as the approach to the Commandant's House. The houses are dignified
examples of the prevailing residential
architectural style of the period in
Charlestown and Beacon Hill.

The **Officers' Club** (Building 5,
1799–1803) was the first building constructed at the Navy Yard. It is a simple

Commandant's House

three-story hip-roof brick building twenty
bays long. With this structure a collection
of significant architecture built over three
centuries began.

Constitution Quarters (Anderson, Notter, Finegold, 1978–1981) and Shipyard Park

FOURTEEN

Cambridge

Cambridge

Cambridge presented a challenge to the authors of this guide. To cover Cambridge as well as Boston thoroughly would change the book significantly and might make the volume too unwieldy for a guide. Yet several Cambridge buildings are too significant to omit. Therefore we have included two distinct zones of interest as outlying sites for the Boston architecture enthusiast—Harvard and MIT. The other Cambridge sites discussed had to be limited to the most-visited and best-known works.

Harvard University and Brattle Street

Harvard University and Brattle Street Tour

Start in Harvard Square in front of the old **Benjamin Wadsworth House (395)** and enter Harvard Yard through the gate on your left. Continue past several buildings until you reach **Massachusetts Hall, Harvard Hall, Hollis Hall, Holden Chapel,** and **Stoughton Hall** on your left and **University Hall** on your right (**398**). Enter Tercentenary Quadrangle with **Memorial Church** on your left and the huge **Widener Library** on your right (**399–400**). Walk past **Sever Hall (400)** and the underground **Pusey Library** to Quincy Street. After exploring the several levels of Le Corbusier's **Carpenter Center for the Visual Arts,** proceed on Quincy Street past the **Fogg Art Museum** and the **Sackler Museum** on your right (**403**). Crossing Cambridge Street, **Gund Hall** is on your right and **Memorial Hall** is on your left (**404–5**). Continue to the **Center for European Studies.** Here you may take a side trip to the **Fairchild Biochemistry Laboratory, Biology Laboratory, Divinity Hall,** and **Rockefeller Hall (406–8).** Or you may continue past the **Science Center** and **Austin Hall (409).** You may take a side trip to the **Harkness Commons** and **Graduate Center (411)** or continue on to the Cambridge Common, returning to Harvard Square or turning right at **Christ Church (412)** and left at Appian Way to Brattle Street.

Turn right on Brattle Street, passing **Loeb Drama Center, Gutman Library,** the **Burleigh, Stoughton,** and **Vassall-Craigie-Longfellow houses (416–18).** Off Brattle Street at **9 Ash Street** you may see Philip Johnson's small courtyard house. Returning on Brattle Street to Harvard Square you will pass **"architects' corner,"** the home of Longfellow's **village blacksmith,** and the **William Brattle House (412–13).** Don't miss the courtyard at 44 Brattle Street.

Since there are no street addresses for many of the buildings in the Harvard University area, the sites are organized topographically, following the suggested tour.

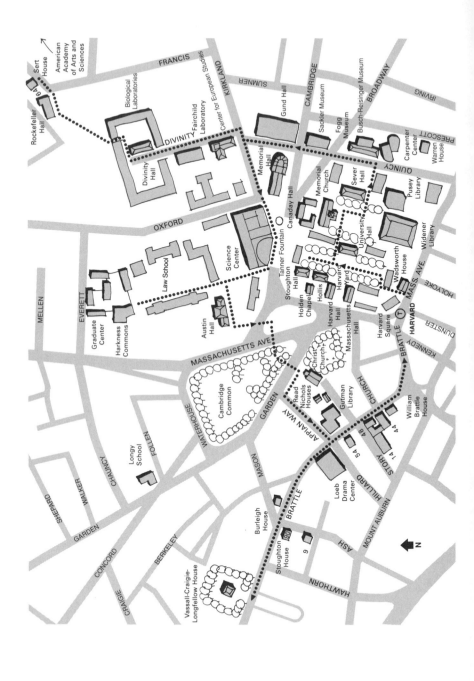

🏛 Harvard Yard

National Register of Historic Places
(Old Harvard Yard)

For most visitors Harvard Yard is the essence of Harvard. Today it remains the center of Harvard life, as it has since the beginning of the development of the Harvard campus in the 1630s. Its early planning was inspired by Cambridge University, where the first leaders of the college had been educated. In turn, it influenced the form of countless colleges across the United States. Despite its English roots, it is expressive of New England tradition, with its solid and separate buildings placed around fields of green. The oldest Harvard buildings are clustered in and around the Yard and include Wadsworth House, Harvard Hall, Massachusetts Hall, University Hall, Holden Chapel, Hollis Hall, and Stough-ton Hall. The great Victorian landmark, Sever Hall, designed by H. H. Richardson, is also in the Yard.

Although the campus includes a number of outstanding architectural achievements, the siting and relationships between buildings are often disappointing because of insufficient concern with planning the form of the campus. Several campus plans were prepared over the years, including one by Bulfinch and another by Cass Gilbert, but these were ignored. Instead the university has chosen to scatter buildings, suggesting that architecture is of some importance but site planning of no importance at all. For example, Carpenter Center for the Visual Arts, the only North American building by Le Corbusier, could not be more inappro-priately located and landscaped. Other architectural treasures pop up here and there about the Harvard campus, tolerated perhaps, but never given much consideration. Yet a conscious effort seems to have been made to collect at least one building by many of the major architects of this century. One area planned by Harvard, Tercentenary Quadrangle, is heavy-handed, with the overscaled Widener Library and the overcute Memorial Church playing off each other to achieve a very effective high kitsch.

Benjamin Wadsworth House

1341 Massachusetts Avenue
1726

The Wadsworth house was built as the residence for the college's fourth president on the site of the earliest Harvard building, the Peyntree House, used by Harvard College in the mid-seventeenth century. It was the residence of nine Harvard presidents. When Massachusetts Avenue was widened the house lost its front yard.

Benjamin Wadsworth house

🏛 Massachusetts Hall

1718

National Historic Landmark

Three halls—Massachusetts, Hollis, and Stoughton—surround two early quadrangles of the Yard. All were built as dormitories. The stacked suites are organized around entries with individual stairways that minimize corridors. The social orientation is thus vertical rather than horizontal, and the basic social unit is limited to the number of suites that can have direct access to a stair. Most of the later Harvard dormitories, called houses, followed this layout. While the suite concept was retained, their composition was altered to include a shared sitting room and separate bedroom-studies. The interiors of Massachusetts Hall have been extensively altered.

Massachusetts Hall

🏛 Harvard Hall

Harvard Yard

THOMAS DAWES, 1764–1766;
ALTERATIONS: RICHARD BOND, 1842;
WARE AND VAN BRUNT, 1870;
ASHLEY, MYER, 1968

The present Harvard Hall is the third building of the same name and the second to occupy this site. The 1642 hall collapsed. Since its condition was considered too poor to repair, the second Harvard Hall was constructed between 1672 and 1682. But the second hall burned and the present structure was its replacement.

Harvard Hall was the center of the early college, with the library and rooms for tutors and students on the upper floors. Like their English university models, the accommodations were organized as suites with a bedroom for two students attached to a tiny study for each. The ground floor was dominated by the great hall that served as chapel, lecture hall, dining hall, and ceremonial center for the college. Built perpendicular to the street, the third Harvard Hall began the definition of two quadrangles. Major alterations since its construction include the 1842 central pavilion and the wings of 1870.

Harvard Hall

🏛 Stoughton Hall
Harvard Yard
CHARLES BULFINCH, 1804–1805

Hollis Hall
THOMAS DAWES, 1762–1763

The first Stoughton Hall, built in 1763, was demolished. Bulfinch, a Harvard graduate, was asked by the college to replace it with a design based on Hollis Hall, where he had resided during his last year of college. The brick mass is the essence of the "Harvard look," standing solidly and simply on its low granite foundation and penetrated by dozens of twelve-over-twelve paned windows. The hip roof is pierced by massive chimneys. The central pediment contains a single window with bull's-eye windows on each side. The building cost $29,048.31,

Stoughton Hall

of which $18,400 was raised by lottery; Bulfinch was paid only $300 for his drawings and supervision of construction.

Holden Chapel

1742

National Register of Historic Places

This tiny Georgian chapel has had numerous minor alterations throughout its history. The doors, windows, entablature, and pediment have all been changed and the original west entrance was abandoned and a new entrance installed on the rear east facade. While technically an eighteenth-century building, it really is more of a severely wounded refugee after generations of mistreatment.

Holden Chapel

🏛 University Hall

Harvard Yard

CHARLES BULFINCH, 1813–1814;
ALTERED 1842

National Register of Historic Places

Bulfinch prepared three alternative designs for University Hall, of which the two rejected designs were the most mon-

umental, having pediments, columns, and domes. This building is a straight-forward hip-roofed mass of Chelmsford granite ashlar with a rusticated basement. The two entrances are defined by a favorite Bulfinch device of paired two-story Ionic pilasters, joined by a central entablature topped by a balustrade. A portico was added during construction and then removed in 1842, to the benefit of the building.

The first floor was organized into four dining halls, one for each class, separated to minimize friction between classes. The walls separating the rooms contained large round openings high on the walls, however, through which food and harsh words were tossed! Kitchens were in the basement, and the second floor had a chapel in the center and recitation rooms in the wings. The third floor held more recitation rooms and the galleries for the chapel. The chapel is expressed on the exterior by the tall arched windows. The interiors have been altered.

University Hall

Memorial Church

Harvard Yard

COOLIDGE SHEPLEY BULFINCH AND ABBOTT,
1931

Under President Lowell, Widener Library and Memorial Church were built to define an entirely new kind of space in the Yard, Tercentenary Quadrangle. Designing a church to face the enormous, static colonnade of Doric columns on Widener's facade was not easy. Yet Memorial Church, small as it is in comparison to its gigantic neighbor, manages to be equally emphatic in its Georgian Revival style. The small and precise Doric colonnade exaggerates the apparent size of the spire above. A significant landmark on the Harvard skyline, Memorial Church seems older and more significant than it actually is, but fulfills its function as a visual focus for the University.

© William M. Rittase

Memorial Church

Widener Library

Harvard Yard

HORACE TRUMBAUER, 1913

The Harvard Library outgrew several buildings before Widener Library was built to remedy the problem. Today it has over three million volumes in addition to the more than eighty department libraries scattered about the campus. Widener was designed by a Philadelphia architect selected by the family of Harry Elkins Widener, whose memory they wished to honor with the library. Widener had died on the *Titanic*. Much of Trumbauer's work was designed by Julian Francis Abele (1881–1950), a black architect who was Trumbauer's chief designer from 1908 to 1938, when Trumbauer died. Abele studied architecture at the University of Pennsylvania and at the Ecole des Beaux Arts in Paris, where he was the first black graduate. Among Abele's many notable designs are Widener Library, the Duke University campus, the Philadelphia Museum of Art, and numerous grand homes; he designed Newport mansions such as the Elms and Miramar, the summer home of the Wideners.

Widener Library

Canaday Hall

Harvard Yard

THE EHRENKRANTZ GROUP, 1974

The architects wished to relate to the older buildings of Harvard Yard. The Canaday Hall eave line matches that of adjacent buildings and brick is the major material, but it deviates from its context in its windows, scoop roof skylights, and detailing. The dormitory provides housing for 210 students and seven proctors, organized into seven "houses." Each floor of a house contains two suites of four bedrooms and a living room that share a stairway and bathroom.

🏛 Sever Hall

Harvard Yard

H. H. RICHARDSON, 1878–1880

National Historic Landmark

One of Richardson's finest works, Sever Hall succeeds on several levels. It relates well to the eighteenth-century buildings of the Yard by adopting similar massing, proportions, and materials, and a feeling of symmetry. The large pediment on the front entrance and the small one on the rear relate to the Colonial era of the neighboring buildings. As in the Trinity Church Rectory in the Back Bay (Newbury Street at 233 Clarendon Street, p. 281), built about the same time, the brickwork is extraordinary, with roll moldings around doors and windows and fluted brick chimneys. For every six courses of stretchers, there is one of headers. Red mortar was used in the original building, but this has not been maintained. In addition to the red brick, the facade has

Sever Hall

© Steve Rosenthal

Canaday Hall

Longmeadow sandstone. The roof is of red tile. Note the bowed section of the rear facade, an original Richardson device for animating the solid flat plane. The size and rhythmic spacing of the many window openings are a key part of the design, and rather than being regular and static, are richly varied. The ideal time to appreciate this is at night with the building lit from within. Children will enjoy the "whispering gallery" effect of the arch at the main entrance; speak quietly toward one side of the arch and the sound will be reflected around to someone listening at the other side.

Warren House
12 Quincy Street
EARLY NINETEENTH CENTURY

This wood frame house has been the location of the English Department since it was donated to Harvard in 1899 by Henry Clarke Warren, who suffered severe spinal pain all his life as the result of a childhood injury. It has a trapdoor leading to a secret room on the second floor that was built by Latin Professor Charles Beck, a former owner, to shelter slaves escaping on the Underground Railroad.

🏛 Carpenter Center for the Visual Arts

Quincy Street
LE CORBUSIER WITH SERT, JACKSON, AND GOURLEY, 1961–1963
National Register of Historic Places

Nathan Marsh Pusey Library

The only building in North America by the French architect Le Corbusier, the Carpenter Center for the Visual Arts is a piece of sculpture designed for human use. The form expresses the architect's desire to expose students to the arts. A diagonal ramp gradually ascends from Quincy Street to the second level, a glass-enclosed exhibition hall, and then passes through to the other side and down to street level, offering views into varied exhibition and studio spaces along the way. Another pathway cuts through underneath the ramp to the lower lobby and lecture hall. The spatial drama is stunning, as are the bold concrete forms with some of the architect's trademarks: round concrete columns, sun screens, and glass block. The building has rarely been used in the way Le Corbusier envi-

Carpenter Center for the Visual Arts

sioned it and sits rather crowded and uncomfortable amidst its tradition-bound neighbors. It is the work of a master and deserves better treatment in its use and site development.

Fogg Art Museum

Quincy Street
COOLIDGE SHEPLEY BULFINCH AND ABBOTT,
1925–1927

Behind the dignified neo-Georgian facade of the Fogg Museum is a replica of the San Gallo loggia at Montepulciano, Italy, the most striking aspect of the building.

Fogg Art Museum

Werner Otto Hall

Prescott Street, behind Fogg Art Museum
GWATHMEY SIEGEL AND ASSOCIATES, 1991

The Busch-Reisinger collection moved here from the picturesque German Romantic Revival building at the head of Quincy Street. This structure was added to the back of the Fogg Museum next to Carpenter Center and provides a destination for Le Corbusier's ramp. The former Busch-Reisinger Museum building is now Adolphus Busch Hall, home of the Center for European Studies.

Sackler Museum

Quincy Street at Broadway
JAMES STIRLING, MICHAEL WILFORD AND ASSOCIATES; PERRY, DEAN, ROGERS AND PARTNERS, 1984

Across Broadway the Sackler Museum occupies a difficult and important site and must be viewed in the context of its

Courtyard, Fogg Art Museum

Sackler Museum

neighbors: Gund Hall by John Andrew, the Victorian fantasy of Memorial Hall, the Germanic nostalgia of Adolphus Busch Hall, and Le Corbusier's Carpenter Center. Except for the Fogg Museum of Coolidge et al., none of these relate to each other or to the Harvard campus in an obvious way. In presenting his design, British architect James Stirling described the surrounding Harvard campus as an "architectural zoo." The Sackler Museum adds another strange beast to the lineup.

Working in the postmodernist idiom, Stirling seems to have borrowed one theme from each of the neighbors. The building is faced in polychrome brick in response to the colorful Memorial Hall. At the narrow end facing the Fogg Museum is a monumental entrance flanked by pylons reminiscent of the Gund Hall

columns and framed by a herculean Gibbs surround, mimicking Harvard's Georgian pretensions. The 38,000-square-foot building houses the permanent collection of ancient, Oriental, and Near Eastern art and includes space for special exhibitions, classrooms, offices, curatorial and service departments, library collections, and a large lecture hall.

🏛 Gund Hall
Quincy Street
JOHN ANDREWS, ANDERSON AND BALDWIN, 1969

Gund Hall, the Graduate School of Design, is like a giant stairway with the design studios on the steps and the entry area, library, and lecture hall sheltered beneath the steps. Having all the design studios in one vast stepped space is an appealing notion and promotes communication between students and classes in a curriculum in which so much is learned from one's peers.

Gund Hall

Adolphus Busch Hall

Kirkland Street at Divinity Avenue
GERMAN BESTELMEYER, 1916–1917;
RENOVATION: GOODY, CLANCY &
ASSOCIATES, 1989

Designed by Dresden architect German Bestelmeyer to house a Germanic museum, this building was a gift to Harvard from beer magnate Adolphus Busch and his wife, Lilly Anheuser Busch. Their son-in-law, Hugo Reisinger, and his wife continued to contribute to the museum, and thus the name was later changed to the Busch-Reisinger Museum.

Although the structure was completed in 1917, the museum did not open until 1921 because of anti-German sentiments after World War I. Before its opening, twelve stained-glass windows were destroyed by vandals. During World War II German art banned by the Nazis was exhibited here and much of the building was used by the U.S. Army.

In 1989 the interiors were totally renovated with a new stairway constructed in the main hall. The original porphyry marble columns, quarry tile floor, wooden ceiling, chandelier with Hapsburg double-headed eagle, and the courtyard suggest the extravagance of the original building. The Germanic Romantic Revival exterior retains its decorative urns, balustrades, and the figures of Wotan, Brunnhilde, Siegfried, and Alberich from Wagner's *Ring* cycle. Today much of the building is devoted to the Minda de Gunzberg Center for European Studies.

🏛 Memorial Hall

just north of Harvard Yard
WARE AND VAN BRUNT, 1870–1874
National Historic Landmark

"Mem" Hall is a sentimental favorite and a wonderful Victorian medieval pile in the colorful Ruskin Gothic style. Two Harvard graduates won the architectural competition to design a memorial to the students and graduates who had served on the Union side in the Civil War. William

Memorial Hall

© Paul Ferrino

Sherman Fairchild Biochemistry Laboratory

Robert Ware, class of 1852, and Henry Van Brunt, class of 1854, had been students of Richard Morris Hunt in New York and set up a practice in Boston in 1863. Their solution was a building on an entirely different scale from the established seventeenth- and eighteenth-century campus. In plan it is a Gothic cathedral with the transept serving as entrance. The apse is Sanders Theater and the nave is a large hall, originally a dining hall. Sanders Theater is said to be modeled on London's Fortune Theater. The interiors feature fine trusses, woodwork, and decorated walls. The hall has not only housed large lecture classes, registration, and ceremonial functions, but has been the location of many important lectures and concerts since its dedication.

Sherman Fairchild Biochemistry Laboratory
9 Divinity Avenue
PAYETTE ASSOCIATES, 1979–1981

This DNA research facility houses laboratories, offices, and classrooms. Since the research requires sophisticated technology and is potentially hazardous, it was necessary for the architects to meet unusually rigid requirements to protect the researchers and the surrounding community. The design, through proper air movement, can control the flow of organisms riding on small particles in the air. Barriers prevent researchers from inadvertently contaminating themselves or the environs. Other safety features include break-out panels between adjoining labs and balconies outside each module for refuge. Despite all of the safeguards, the brick building has a sense of openness both outside and inside, with large recessed windows, glass-enclosed stairway, and a welcoming two-story recessed entrance.

Divinity Hall
Divinity Avenue
SOLOMON WILLARD AND THOMAS W. SUMNER, 1825

One of the early and most important buildings constructed outside the Yard is still a prominent Harvard landmark. The chapel was extensively modified in 1904 by A. W. Longfellow.

Divinity Hall

Harvard Biological Laboratories
off Divinity Avenue
COOLIDGE SHEPLEY BULFINCH AND ABBOTT, 1930

This was the first "modern" building at Harvard and possibly the first significant "modern" one in Boston. The simple masses punctured with factory sash windows are humanized with delightful and well-integrated ornamentation based on biological themes. A pair of large but friendly rhinos stand guard outside the entrance while above them a herd of elephants cavort in the carved brick frieze executed by Katherine Ward Lane. Each of the three pairs of doors has different grillwork; one is based on shellfish, the second on insects, and the third on plants.

© Shepley Bulfinch Richardson and Abbott

Carved brick bas-relief, Biological Laboratories

Rockefeller Hall
Francis Avenue
EDWARD LARRABEE BARNES, 1971

The irregular form of this small dormitory for the Divinity School confronts varied boundary conditions, including a Gothic classroom building, an older residential neighborhood, a parking lot, and a large cyclotron. The building is intimate yet quite elegant, with its stepped-back massing and butt-joint corner windows. The ground floor and basement contain teaching and community spaces, while the upper floors provide housing for thirty-nine students. Each floor has thirteen rooms, organized into clusters around three bathrooms, as well as a shared kitchen and dining room.

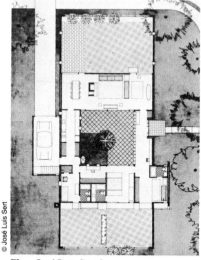

Plan, José Luis Sert house

Rockefeller Hall

José Luis Sert House
64 Francis Street
JOSÉ LUIS SERT, 1958

Behind the one-story natural brick perimeter wall is a very successful house organized around three courtyards, Sert's experiment with a Mediterranean-style house in a northern climate. All rooms are oriented to the courts, each of which has a subtly different and restrained paving and landscape plan. The house combines unusual privacy and a spacious sense of openness, with wall and floor planes carried outdoors along the white-painted brick walls of the courtyards.

Tanner Fountain
in front of Science Center
JOAN BRIGHAM, PETER WALKER AND THE
SWA GROUP, 1984

This unusual fountain is made of a casual circular grouping of 159 New England field boulders set in grass and asphalt. It is intended to evoke the mystery of primeval places and to express the rocky landscape of New England. The fountain is designed for all seasons and all times of day and night; in summer dozens of nozzles emit a fine mist, and in winter the rocks are shrouded in clouds of steam.

Tanner Fountain

People are attracted to the rocks as sitting places; when the fountain begins spraying it does so slowly so that people sitting on the rocks have time to escape without getting very wet.

Science Center
north of Cambridge Street Underpass
SERT, JACKSON AND ASSOCIATES,
1970–1973

The Science Center, the largest building on the Harvard Campus, is best experienced from the sunny glass-roofed arcade that provides access to the major public spaces of the building. The complex exterior form expresses the five components of the center: the long laboratory mass paralleling the arcade, the terraced classroom wing for the mathematics department, the low science library and

administrative wings, and the spider-roofed building containing four demonstration theaters. Use of precast-concrete components—"ladder" columns and girders—allowed rapid construction.

Austin Hall
Harvard Law School
near Massachusetts Avenue
across from the Common
H. H. RICHARDSON, 1881–1883
National Register of Historic Places

Richardson's concern with color in architecture is evident here, as it is in his earlier Trinity Church and Sever Hall. The dark Longmeadow sandstone ashlar is trimmed with pale yellow Ohio stone and decorated with bluestone marquetry inspired by southern Romanesque decoration that Richardson had studied in the

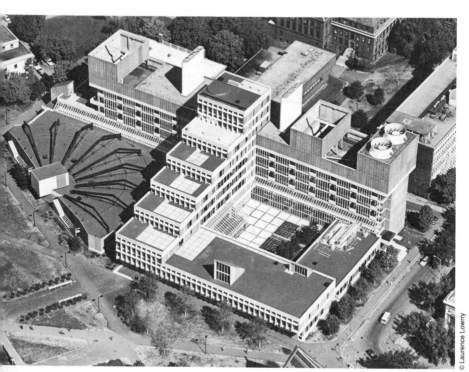

© Laurence Lowry

Science Center

Auvergne region of France. The stone arches and columns are decorated with delightful carving, including Richardson's monogram interwoven with tools of the architect. Originally the exterior appeared gaudy to many observers, but with the passage of time, either it has mellowed or we have become accustomed to it. Inside, the fireplace in the James Barr Ames Courtroom (originally the library) is a Registered National Historic Landmark in itself, an outstanding example of Richardson's ornament with rich stone corbels supporting the mantle.

Austin Hall

The interior spatial organization is communicated on the exterior both by the massing and by the window treatment. The large central mass is flanked by lower wings. Three massive Romanesque arches with a deeply recessed porch define the entrance, while the off-center stair tower provides counterpoint in the generally balanced design. The building was constructed for the now unbelievably small sum of $145,000.

🏛 Harkness Commons and the Graduate Center

near Oxford and Everett streets
WALTER GROPIUS AND THE ARCHITECTS COLLABORATIVE, 1950

The first Harvard building in the International Style was the work of Walter Gropius, founder in 1919 of the influential Bauhaus, a school of architecture and design in Dessau, Germany. After the Bauhaus was closed by the Nazis, Gropius was invited to head the Harvard Graduate School of Design, a position that he held for many years. A number of his students and associates followed him to America, including Marcel Breuer, Gyorgy Kepes, Laszlo Moholy-Nagy, and Mies van der Rohe. In 1945 he founded The Architects Collaborative, which continues to practice today in its Cambridge offices and elsewhere.

Gropius's principles of functional design, using technology to serve social needs and making a sharp break with sentimental tradition, are evident in this austere factorylike complex. Seven buff-colored brick dormitories are linked by covered walkways, forming several courtyards. The focus of the group is Harkness Commons, which contains recreational areas and a second-floor dining hall reached by a long ramp. Gropius felt that art and architecture should be integrated, and this building incorporates several works of art: a brick design by Joseph Albers, a tile wall by Herbert Bayer, a ceramic mural by Joan Miró, a wood bas-relief by Jean Arp, and a metal sculpture by Richard Lippold.

© Robert Damora

Harkness Commons and the Graduate Center

🏛 Christ Church

0 Garden Street
PETER HARRISON, 1760
ALTERED 1790 AND 1825–1826
National Historical Landmark

The oldest church building in Cambridge, Christ Church was designed by the Newport architect Peter Harrison. It is similar to King's Chapel, also by Harrison (see 58 Tremont Street, p. 9) with its square tower, but it has no gallery and is constructed of wood. Since it was a Tory church it suffered bad treatment during the Revolution, and not until the nineteenth century was well under way did it have a rector again.

Christ Church

🏛 BRATTLE STREET

Until 1638 Cambridge was called Newtowne, a grid-pattern fortified settlement surrounded by stockades. The primary motivation for the planning of Cambridge had been defensive. The area was closely gathered south of the present Brattle Square, and Brattle Street connected it with the Watertown settlement. Wealthy British sympathizers lived along Brattle Street and thus it gained the popular name, Tory Row. A common conception of the street is one of a continuous string of pre-Revolutionary mansions, but in fact it is not nearly as uniform as imagined. In reality Brattle Street has a number of late-nineteenth-century houses, including the 1882 Stoughton house by H. H. Richardson, and one-third of the houses between Brattle Square and Elmwood Avenue are twentieth century. The section of the street immediately adjacent to the Brattle Square commercial area was part of the twenty-two-acre Thomas Brattle estate, which ran from Story Street to James Street and to the river. Houses were not built here until the early nineteenth century, when the estate was broken up after Brattle's death.

William Brattle House

42 Brattle Street
c. 1727
National Register of Historic Places

The Brattle house begins the series of eighteenth- and nineteenth-century clapboard houses along Brattle Street. It is followed by the 1808 Hancock-Dexter-Pratt house at number 54 (the home of Longfellow's village blacksmith), the 1772

William Brattle house

Read house, the 1827 Nichols house, and the seventeenth- and eighteenth-century Henry Vassall house at 94 Brattle.

"Architects' Corner"

Brattle at Story Street

44 Brattle Street Office Building

SERT, JACKSON AND ASSOCIATES, 1970–1971

The Architects Collaborative

TAC, 1967, 1970

14 Story Street Office Building

EARL R. FLANSBURGH AND ASSOCIATES 1970–1971

Benjamin Thompson's Design Research building (now Crate and Barrel) is the focus of "Architects' Corner." Three architects built quarters for their own offices, along with rental space, in the same block. The three buildings relate in general scale, window treatment, and materials, but allow the DR building to remain

Design Research Building

14 Story Street

© Steve Rosenthal

the star. The Sert building at 44 Brattle is most visibly related, but has more complicated massing and detailing. The skylit top story is the architects' office. One of

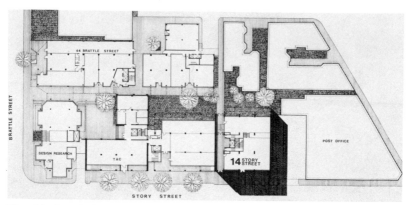

Plan, "Architect's Corner"

© Steve Rosenthal

Courtyard, 44 Brattle Street Office Building and The Architects Collaborative

the best things about the entire complex is the interior pedestrian walkway through the center of the block, a quiet, tree-shaded brick alley connecting the four buildings. The floor-to-ceiling heights of the 14 Story Street building and the adjacent TAC building are different, but the architects, Earl R. Flansburgh and Associates, minimized the discrepancy by slightly recessing the six-story tower and by matching the first-floor heights and carrying the roofline of the TAC building through the parapet of 14 Story Street.

🏛 Design Research Building
now Crate and Barrel
48 Brattle Street
BENJAMIN THOMPSON AND ASSOCIATES,
1969

The home furnishings and design firm called Design Research or DR started a national love affair with modern design products for the home and body, a trend that is still building on Thompson's concept, but that no longer has the creativity and variety of the original Design Research. Benjamin Thompson, founder of DR, imagined that Americans could be convinced to buy the best new industrial design from Scandinavia and Italy and showed everyone else how to do it, choosing the products himself and designing all display fixtures and fittings for the shops. This building is essentially a large glass display case, totally exposed to the street. Its six levels openly connect in a way that draws customers through all departments. The concrete slab construction uses continuous unframed glass sheets sealed with transparent silicone as walls.

Longfellow Chestnut Tree Memorial
54 Brattle Street
DIMITRI GERAKARIS, 1989

A chestnut tree of forged steel by artist-blacksmith Dimitri Gerakaris commemorates that of the village blacksmith in Longfellow's poem. It also marks the fiftieth anniversary of the nearby Cambridge

© 1989 Dimitri Gerakaris

Longfellow chestnut tree memorial

Center for Adult Education. The anvil and tools were made by the artist to fabricate much of this piece and were then incorporated into the sculpture.

Gutman Library
Brattle Street and Appian Way
BENJAMIN THOMPSON AND ASSOCIATES, 1972; LANDSCAPE: CAROL R. JOHNSON AND ASSOCIATES, INC.

To preserve the openness of Brattle Street and the side streets, the building mass is set back from the corners, creating small landscaped areas. It is symmetrically formed about a diagonal axis running through the corner entrance. By placing one floor below grade with depressed landscaped areas to bring in light and view, the architects reduced the building's apparent height and mass. The disciplined structure of sandblasted concrete exposes its lively interior color and activity to the street, relating to Thompson's Design Research Building (now Crate and Barrel) across the street and to the general Brattle Street ambience. Two historic buildings, the Read house (1772) and the Nichols house (1827), were preserved by being moved from the site and are now adjacent at Farwell Place.

Loeb Drama Center
64 Brattle Street
HUGH STUBBINS AND ASSOCIATES, 1959

The planning and site design for the Loeb Drama Center are noteworthy. When it was built in 1959, it was the first fully flexible theater in the country. It can be quickly and automatically converted

Read and Nichols houses

Gothic Revival Burleigh house (1847), 85 Brattle Street

Terrace, Loeb Drama Center

from a proscenium stage to Elizabethan thrust or to theater-in-the-round. Sight lines and acoustics are excellent and the ceiling grid allows great flexibility in lighting arrangements. Entrance and lobby areas are inviting and comfortable. Particularly attractive is the side terrace with serpentine wall for the audience to enjoy during intermissions. Although the theater was built for Harvard and Radcliffe undergraduates, it now is the home of the American Repertory Theater as well.

Stoughton house

🏛 Stoughton House

90 Brattle Street

H. H. RICHARDSON, 1882; RENOVATION: ARCHITECTURAL RESOURCES CAMBRIDGE, INC., 1990

Mrs. M. F. Stoughton commissioned Richardson to design her house in 1882, only a year after he started to work on Sever Hall. Termed by Henry-Russell Hitchcock "perhaps, the best suburban wooden house in America," it is a horizontal L-shaped mass. As in Sever Hall, the stairway is expressed in a towerlike projection with conical roof on the inside corner. Next to the stair is the front entrance in a recessed two-story porch. Windows are composed of many small panes with heavy muntins. Originally the roof had wood shingles and the wall shingles were smaller, but these have been replaced. Additions and interior alterations have been made to Richardson's design.

Philip Johnson Courtyard House

off Brattle Street at 9 Ash Street

PHILIP JOHNSON, 1941

After beginning a career in art history, Philip Johnson returned to Harvard to study architecture. For his student thesis, he built himself this house. Behind the high wall surrounding the property is a comfortable small house oriented inward to the courtyard.

Philip Johnson's courtyard house

Vassall-Craigie-Longfellow house

🏛 Vassall-Craigie-Longfellow House
105 Brattle Street
1759
National Historic Landmark
Open to the Public

The most famous Brattle Street house was the residence of Henry Wadsworth Longfellow for most of his life. It is sometimes attributed to Peter Harrison, the admirable architect of King's Chapel (see 58 Tremont Street, p. 9), Christ Church (see 0 Garden Street, p. 412), and other New England landmarks. The house is an elaborate and elegant Georgian mansion with two-story pilasters and center pediment on its facade, the whole set on a terrace surrounded by a balustrade.

Concert Hall, Longy School of Music

Longy School of Music Concert Hall

1 Follen Street

HUYGENS AND TAPPÉ, 1973

The outstanding music school in Cambridge, the Longy School of Music is located in the 1889 Edwin H. Abbot house, a Richardsonian Romanesque structure of brownstone and brick. The concert-hall addition very successfully combines library and concert functions in one space, since schedules of the two groups of users do not overlap. Warmtoned oak and brick are the featured materials, and several details of the old house are repeated in the concert hall. The fine acoustics of the intimate hall have made it a popular performance hall for many Boston musicians.

© Phokion Karas

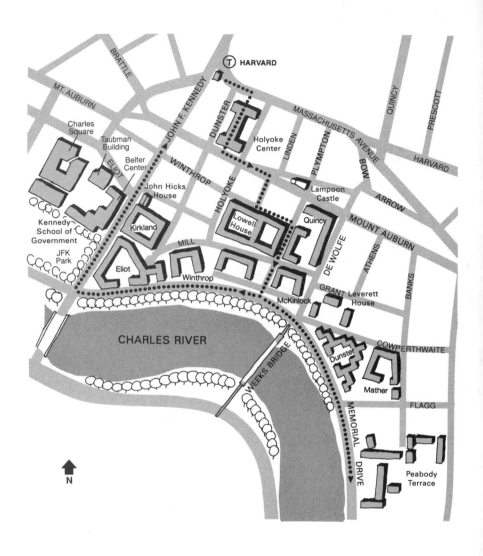

T HARVARD

BRATTLE

MT. AUBURN

JOHN F. KENNEDY

DUNSTER

MASSACHUSETTS AVENUE

QUINCY

PRESCOTT

HARVARD

Charles Square

Taubman Building

Belfer Center

ELIOT

WINTHROP

Holyoke Center

LINDEN

PLYMPTON

BOW

John Hicks House

Kennedy School of Government

Kirkland

HOLYOKE

MILL

Eliot

Winthrop

Lowell House

Quincy

Lampoon Castle

ARROW

MOUNT AUBURN

DE WOLFE

ATHENS

BANKS

JFK Park

McKinlock

GRANT

Leverett House

CHARLES RIVER

WEEKS BRIDGE

Dunster

COWPERTHWAITE

Mather

FLAGG

N

MEMORIAL DRIVE

Peabody Terrace

Harvard Square South

Harvard Square South Tour

Start at Harvard Square in the active plaza in front of **Holyoke Center** (422). Walk through the central walkway of shops, coming out on Mount Auburn Street. Walk left toward the building with a face, **Lampoon Castle** (423), then turn right and walk around **Lowell House.** Walk to Memorial Drive and the river, passing several other houses. Sert's **Peabody Terrace** (424) is a side trip in the opposite direction along the river. At the Weld Boat House, turn right onto John F. Kennedy Street, passing the **Kennedy School of Government** (426) on your left and the **John Hicks house** (424) on your right and complete the tour in Harvard Square.

Since there are no street addresses for many of the buildings in this area, the sites are arranged topographically, following the suggested tour.

Harvard Square Station

SKIDMORE, OWINGS & MERRILL,
1981–1985

Harvard Station was rebuilt as part of the subway extension north to Porter Square. The two station levels are visually connected to make users aware of the movement of the trains. Design features include a deep coffered concrete ceiling, gracefully curved walls, and a stained-glass mural by artist Gyorgy Kepes. On the crowded street level, roads and plazas were redesigned with an emphasis on pedestrian needs. Excavations for the new line kept Harvard archeologists busy retrieving and classifying 150,000 fascinating artifacts, including stone tools from a prehistoric hunting camp dating from 1500 B.C.

Holyoke Center

1350 Massachusetts Avenue

SERT, JACKSON AND GOURLEY, 1961,
1965; LANDSCAPE: SASAKI, DAWSON, DEMAY

Despite its size, the Holyoke Center mixed-use complex of shops, offices, health center, and parking manages to have a human scale. The H-shaped high-rise structure is set back from Mount Auburn Street and Massachusetts Avenue to form small, pleasant pedestrian plazas that connect with the two-story pedestrian way passing through the site and linking the two streets. The facades are organized around a human-scaled module of clear and translucent panels placed according to the needs of individual office occupants. Sun screens, fins, and varied concrete finishes are used to enrich the form.

© William Tobey

Holyoke Center

The interiors, also by the architects, emphasize the architecture, with ample exposed concrete structural elements juxtaposed with brightly colored fabrics and specially designed furnishings.

Lampoon Castle
Mt. Auburn Street at Bow Street
WHEELWRIGHT AND HAVEN, 1909
National Register of Historic Places

The home of Harvard's undergraduate humor magazine, the *Lampoon,* is a whimsically delightful example of the triumph of sentiment over sense. The entrance tower at the point of the tiny triangular site has eyes (round windows), nose (center window), mouth (the door), and a hat.

🏛 HARVARD'S HOUSES

Harvard's environmental planning and design has been somewhat haphazard since the beginning, yet its site is so fine that parts of it are unavoidably impressive. The splendid houses lining the Charles River are more skillfully blended than any other part of the expansive campus. Perhaps this is because they were all designed by the firm of Shepley Bulfinch Richardson and Abbott, which was also

Harvard's houses

Lampoon Castle

Lowell House

© Paul J. Weber

Library, Leverett House

responsible for the planning and design of the Stanford campus in Palo Alto. Except for the recent houses—Leverett, Quincy, and Mather—these were carried out with great continuity of scale, materials, and design. The view of Harvard's houses along the Charles River is one of the most impressive faces of Cambridge.

(vertical credit) © Shepley Bulfinch Richardson and Abbott

🏛 Peabody Terrace

900 Memorial Drive
SERT, JACKSON AND GOURLEY, 1964

The innovative design for Peabody Terrace married student housing contains five hundred varied units, from efficiencies to three-bedrooms. Low-rise structures of three, five, and seven stories relate to the scale of the neighborhood and form courtyards, recalling the designs of other Harvard housing along the river. The three twenty-two-story towers employ an ingenious skip-floor system in which elevators stop every third floor, allowing several floor-through apartments. A three-dimensional grid of balconies, sun screens, and privacy baffles humanizes the scale and enlivens the architecture.

John Hicks House

64 John F. Kennedy Street
1762

A pre-Revolutionary house, it is now the library of Kirkland House and was moved to this site from Dunster and Winthrop streets.

John Hicks house

Peabody Terrace

Belfer Center for Public Management

John F. Kennedy Street at Eliot Street

ARCHITECTURAL RESOURCES CAMBRIDGE, INC., 1984, 1986

Adjacent to this firm's Littauer Center, the second phase of construction at the John F. Kennedy School of Government offers an engaging and amusing twist on the red brick campus traditions with a vocabulary of exaggerated gables, chimney forms, and pitched slate roofs. The designers took their cues from the animated rooflines of the nearby Harvard houses. The building defines a private grassy retreat.

Belfer Center for Public Management

John Fitzgerald Kennedy Park

John F. Kennedy Street at
Memorial Drive

CAROL R. JOHNSON AND ASSOCIATES, INC.,
1987

This new park interrupts the Georgian line of Harvard houses that complements and defines the greensward along the banks of the Charles River. The site cries for small greens and interlocking courtyards enclosed by distinguished low red brick buildings. This was an opportunity to provide an interesting pedestrian sequence entirely lacking in Harvard building of the past several decades.

A. Alfred Taubman Building

John F. Kennedy School of Government
Eliot Street at Bennett Street
THE ARCHITECTS COLLABORATIVE, 1990

Charles Square

CAMBRIDGE SEVEN, 1985

The stepped red brick mass with limestone banding of the A. Alfred Taubman Building invites entry at its concave corner. The adjacent central landscaped pedestrian spine leads to the Charles Hotel, John F. Kennedy Park, and to the Charles River. A view easement to the Charles Hotel was one of the program requirements. Adjacent to the spine is

the Charles Square complex with its large, formless interior square courtyard. The Taubman Center for State and Local Government and the Joan Shorenstein Barone Center on the Press, Politics and Public Policy are located in this third phase of the John F. Kennedy complex.

A. Alfred Taubman Building

Kennedy School of Government

Massachusetts Institute of Technology

F ounded in 1861 by William Barton Rogers, MIT was first located in the Mercantile Building in downtown Boston. In 1863 it moved to a new building in the Back Bay next door to its near twin, the Museum of Natural History, now Louis (see Boylston Street at Berkeley, p. 248). By 1902 the school had outgrown this building with no possibility of expanding in the built-up Copley Square district. An extensive search was conducted, and the present site on marsh lands that had been filled for real-estate development in the 1880s was chosen in 1909.

MIT Tour

Begin on Massachusetts Avenue across from the main entrance to the domed **Rogers Building (429)**. Walk past the **Stratton Student Center (430)** and to the right of **Kresge Auditorium** to see the **Athletics Center (431)**. Return past Saarinen's Kresge Auditorium and visit his small **Kresge Chapel (433)**. Turn left onto Danforth Street and walk past Alvar Aalto's **Baker House (433)**. Then return on Memorial Drive, passing the **Maclaurin Building** and Killian Court with its Henry Moore and other sculptures **(435)**. Turn left onto McDermott Court toward the Calder sculpture and the **Green, Dreyfus,** and **Landau** buildings of I. M. Pei beyond it. You may take a side trip into Compton Court and the **Compton Laboratories (437)** or continue to the **Wiesner Building (437), Whitaker Building (438)**, and down Amherst Street to see the Picasso sculpture and Eduardo Catalano's **Hermann Building** and **Eastgate (439)**. If you wish to end your tour and see MIT life from the inside, enter Building 8 off McDermott Court and walk down the long corridor that will take you back to the starting point of the tour.

Since there are no street addresses for most of the buildings at MIT, the sites are arranged topographically, following the suggested tour.

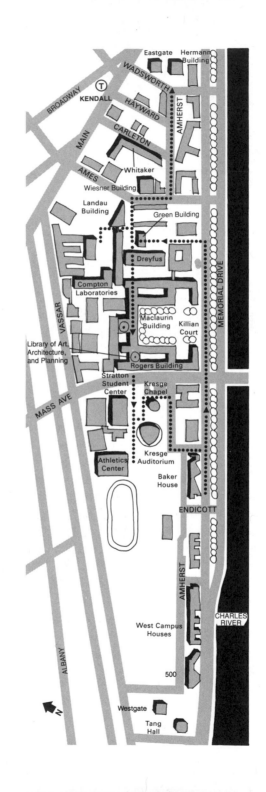

Massachusetts Institute of Technology

🏛 Maclaurin and Rogers Buildings

WILLIAM WELLES BOSWORTH, 1913–1916;
BOSWORTH AND HARRY J. CARLSON, 1937

MIT selected William Welles Bosworth as architect, after having considered Désiré Despradelle, a French-born member of the architecture faculty, and Cass Gilbert, MIT graduate (1879) and designer of the University of Minnesota campus. Besides being an MIT graduate (1889), Bosworth had worked for H. H. Richardson and Frederick Law Olmsted and had studied at L'Ecole des Beaux Arts in Paris. In contrast to Harvard's individual brick buildings set in open green space, Bosworth's design is conceived as a single Neoclassic limestone building that reaches out to define space in the manner of Versailles. Bosworth's expertise in French style was later reaffirmed by his work in the 1920s as director of the reconstruction of Versailles, Fontainebleau, and Rheims Cathedral.

Two Pantheon-inspired domes identify the foci of the grand composition. The largest dome on the axis of the Great Court (now Killian Court) rises behind the imposing Ionic portico, while the other dome defines the main entrance portico and four-story hall on Massachusetts Avenue. Ironically, the big coffered dome with oculus can only be experienced from the upper level of Baker Engineering Library. Another mismatch between form and function is found in the Great Court, which wants to be the major entrance and activity space but in fact is largely symbolic and little used. The real hub of activity is the Massachusetts Avenue entrance and the spine that links the campus from east to west.

Except for the Pantheon entrance hall on Massachusetts Avenue, the sev-

© Eduardo Catalano

Stratton Student Center

eral miles of monotonous interior corridors have no Classical pretensions. They are more like a factory and in fact are built for industrial live loads. Despite the building's lack of interior charm, it has proved to be remarkably rugged and adaptable to changing needs. Through its interconnected corridors the life of the Institute moves at a brisk pace, but it is not picturesque, quiet, or sentimental. Thus MIT achieved for itself a fitting contrast to Harvard, representative of the differences in the education offered. The traditional quadrangle organization of Harvard is nowhere echoed at MIT, whose several formal courts are dramatically highlighted by powerful sculptures by Calder, Lipschitz, Moore, Nevelson, Picasso, and others.

Julius Adams Stratton Building, Student Center

Building W 20
west of Massachusetts Avenue
EDUARDO CATALANO, 1964; RENOVATION: BRUNER/COTT & ASSOCIATES, INC., 1988

The bold horizontal forms of the Student Center relate well to the MIT campus and dramatically exhibit the structural possibilities of reinforced concrete. The building steps to the side of the main MIT axis, allowing the Pantheon dome entrance of the Rogers Building across Massachusetts Avenue to command the space. The precisely detailed concrete recalls the limestone of the main buildings. A major renovation was undertaken to accommodate a variety of fast-food kiosks and to create more informal dining spaces. A new two-level lounge, multipurpose spaces, and three-story atrium were also

© Chuck Choi

Library of Art, Architecture, and Planning

provided. A massive window opening onto the Kresge Oval brings light into the new lounge.

Library of Art, Architecture, and Planning

RENOVATION AND ADDITION: SCHWARTZ & SILVER, 1990

Elegantly and precisely slipped into a nonsite above a truck turnaround on the cramped back side of 77 Massachusetts Avenue is a new six-story library stack. This crisp design creates form with an assurance rarely seen since the demise of modernism. The steel-framed, clear anodized aluminum–clad thirty-by-one-hundred-foot sliver nestles against the

retained exterior of the original building, grazing rather than joining it. The books are protected from ultraviolet radiation by heat mirror glass, a glass and plastic sandwich developed at MIT in the 1970s. Since the best view is from outside, it is essential to take the considerable trouble to find the truck loading zone it faces.

Athletics Center

Building W 34 near Kresge Auditorium
DAVIS AND BRODY, 1980

The Athletics Center is sited on the main east-west axis of the campus amidst the other athletic buildings. Except for this building and the fanciful J. B. Carr indoor tennis bubble, these are all the work of Anderson, Beckwith, and Haible and include Briggs Field House (1939), Rockwell Cage (1948), and the Dupont Athletic Center (1959).

The best view of the Athletics Center is from the playing fields. This elevation is treated sculpturally, with zigzag stairs relating to the back of Alvar Aalto's Baker House to the south. The fifty-thousand-square-foot field house is raised to the second-story level, forming a protective entrance area.

Athletics Center

🏛 Kresge Auditorium
Building W 16
west of Massachusetts Avenue
EERO SAARINEN, 1954–1955

Saarinen quite properly argued against the river site that had been chosen for Kresge Auditorium. Fortunately, he was successful in convincing the Institute that his building would be much more effective as a focus on the main axis of the campus. Saarinen prepared the site plan as well as the architectural designs for the auditorium and chapel. While Harvard seems almost the unwilling possessor of a Le Corbusier building, MIT proudly displays these two Saarinen gems. Kresge auditorium is an elegant shallow dome, recalling the domes of the MIT main buildings, balanced on three corners with glass-walled public gathering spaces around the periphery. The wood-paneled hall is arguably the finest twentieth-century auditorium space in the Boston region in terms of design.

Kresge Auditorium

Interior, Kresge Auditorium

🏛 Kresge Chapel

Building W 15
west of Massachusetts Avenue
EERO SAARINEN, 1955

The MIT Chapel is as exquisite and understated as it is small. The brick cylinder with small moat is handsomely paired with the Kresge Auditorium and relates to the domes of the main MIT buildings and to the brick curves of Baker House. Low arches at the bottom allow the light reflected from the water to cast fascinating shifting patterns on the undulating interior brick shell. A luminous Bertoia altarpiece screen shimmers with light from the skylight above.

Interior, Kresge Chapel

🏛 Baker House

Building W 7, Memorial Drive
ALVAR AALTO WITH PERRY, SHAW AND HEPBURN, 1947–1949

Baker House reflects the scale and linear orientation to the river established in the Maclaurin and Rogers buildings. It is a successful continuation of the tradition of formalism. The interior entirely lacks the flexibility of the early buildings and is instead a fascinating arrangement of rooms which maximizes river views. Where the main MIT buildings turn square corners, Baker House undulates along the river bank. From the entrance pavilion there is a view through the building to the playing fields beyond. In contrast to the river facade, the rear side has a strong angular expression of the staircases. The building is best viewed from an angle while one walks along the sidewalk so the rippling facade can be enjoyed. The building appears to be squeezed between its neighbors, too big for its site, much like Le Corbusier's Carpenter Center (see Harvard at Quincy Street, p. 402).

Baker House

West Campus Houses

Building W 70
adjacent to 500 Memorial Drive
SERT, JACKSON AND ASSOCIATES, 1975

This dormitory is organized into six linked
but separate houses, each with a river
view. Each house has its own dining and
social areas and a prominent staircase.
The stepped roofs of the south-facing
houses form roof decks. The same architects are responsible for the adjacent dormitory, 500 Memorial Drive (1980–1982).

West Campus houses

Tang Hall

Building W 84
far west end near Audrey Street
HUGH STUBBINS AND ASSOCIATES, 1972

High-rise development on the MIT campus has been carefully controlled to protect the scale and dominance of the
original horizontal buildings. A few towers
do appear, however, on the west and east
ends, including Westgate and the twenty-
four-story Tang Hall, both by Stubbins.
The chamfered-corner layout provides
eight corner living rooms on each floor.
Each apartment has a view of the Charles
River. Precast fifty-nine-foot facade components are structural and consist of a
spandrel and two columns. The designers
significantly reduced building costs by
combining structure and cladding.

Tang Hall

Green Building,
Center for Earth Sciences

Building 54, east of main building
I. M. PEI AND PARTNERS, 1962–1964;
LANDSCAPE: SASAKI, DAWSON, DEMAY

Pei, who helped prepare the master plan

for this section of the campus, also
designed three buildings in the quadrant.
The most prominent of these is the
Green Building, a highly sculptural tower
of twenty-one stories that dominates

Henry Moore's *Three-Piece Reclining Figure*, Draped (1976) in Killian Court

the disparate surroundings. Constructed of cast-in-place sandblasted architectural concrete, its color is similar to that of the limestone of its neighbors. The load-bearing exterior walls allow column-free floors forty-eight by ninety-three feet. Alexander Calder's monumental black steel sculpture, *The Big Sail* (1965), is effectively sited in front of the building at the entrance to the courtyard from Memorial Drive.

views of MIT from Boston. It is interesting how frequently Pei has chosen to introduce vertical elements into essentially horizontal contexts, for example his Christian Science tower and the Harbor Towers (see Massachusetts Avenue at Huntington, p. 296, and Atlantic Avenue at East India Row, p. 66). In the case of MIT, he felt the tower would provide a vertical focus and would help organize

Dreyfus Building

Building 18
next to Green Building
I. M. PEI AND PARTNERS, 1967–1970;
LANDSCAPE: SASAKI, DAWSON, DEMAY

The design of the Dreyfus Building incorporates existing pathways by cantilevering the end of the structure on two diagonal columns. The window grid is formed of

Alexander Calder's *The Big Sail*, (1965) and Dreyfus Building

Green, Dreyfus, and Landau buildings

diagonal columns and spandrels, which frame deeply recessed windows. An elegant three-level bridge of glass and concrete connects the building with Anderson, Beckwith, and Haible's precisely detailed Dorrance and Whitaker Buildings (1952, 1963).

Landau Chemical Engineering Building

Building 66, Ames Street
I. M. PEI AND PARTNERS, 1973–1976

With the Landau Building, Pei completed his group of related spaces and buildings for MIT. The thirty-degree angle of Main Street to Memorial Drive is reflected in the form with its chisel-pointed end that threatens to slice Ames Street. A two-story portico forms a doorway to the

Landau Chemical Engineering Building

campus. Louise Nevelson's dramatic black steel sculpture, *Transparent Hori-*

Beverly Pepper's *Dunes 1* (1971) and Compton Laboratory (Skidmore, Owings & Merrill, 1957)

zon (1975), stands outside the building between Bosworth's East Campus Alumni Houses (1924).

Louise Nevelson's *Transparent Horizon* (1975)

Wiesner Building

20 Ames Street

I. M. PEI & PARTNERS, 1985

While I. M. Pei did not regard the Wiesner building as a major architectural statement, it is an example of a major collaboration between an architect and three artists. The artists took responsibility for aspects of the building that would normally be in the domain of the architect alone. This was inspired by the very purpose of the building, which is to link technology and the arts. The Wiesner Building houses the Arts and Media Center, including three art galleries, workshops and laboratories, auditorium, and the Experimental Media Theater, a four-story windowless cube for exploring nontraditional performance media. The building accepts the surrounding diversity of architectural styles and is intentionally unrelated to any of them. The white aluminum–sheathed box is rather antiseptic both outside and inside; the shiny panels suggest a laboratory, an impression that is reinforced by the clinical detailing. The multistory atrium space is dominated by Kenneth Noland's relief mural. Scott Burton, a sculptor who specializes in seating, designed the stairwell and balustrades and related seating in the atrium. Richard Fleischner, an environmental artist, designed the plantings and geometrically paved courtyards surrounding the building, as well as the new lattice benches in a Wiener Werkestatte or MacIntosh revival style. A sculptural arch of concrete forms a gateway to the East Campus.

Bench, Wiesner Building

Wiesner Building

Whitaker College of Health Sciences, Technology and Management and Health Services Buildings
Buildings E 23 and E 25
Carleton Street
GRUZEN PARTNERS AND MITCHELL, GIURGOLA,
1979–1981

The form of this building clearly notes its two components in the two legs of the L, which are joined by a luminous atrium. The geometry of this space is governed both by the skewed grid of the east-campus streets and by the main MIT axis, which penetrates the atrium at an odd angle. The architects prepared the master plan for this sector with the aim of integrating the Sloan School with the main campus.

Eastgate Married Student Housing

Building E 55
Kendall Square at Wadsworth Street
EDUARDO CATALANO, 1967

The thirty-story Eastgate tower marks the east end of the MIT campus and balances the Tang tower on the west end. Constructed of cast-in-place concrete, the carefully formed building houses 208 apartments and two floors of recreational facilities. Adjacent is another Catalano design, the Hermann Building (1965), a social-sciences and management building. Picasso's concrete sculpture, *Figure découpée* (Cut-Out Figure, 1963), is the perfect foil for the monumental Hermann Building. The sculpture was originally done in oil paint on wood and was enlarged and cast by Carl Nesjar, a Norwegian artist who developed the technique called *betongravure* used in this work.

Eastgate married student housing, and above, Picasso's *Figure découpée* (1958, 1963)

Other Cambridge Sites

🏛 American Academy of Arts and Sciences

136 Irving Street

KALLMANN, MCKINNELL, AND WOOD, 1979–1981; LANDSCAPE: CAROL R. JOHNSON AND ASSOCIATES, INC.

For this fine award-winning building the architects developed a completely new esthetic far removed from the monolithic concrete of their Boston City Hall (see Government Center, p. 27). The highly specific program, developed by architect Lawrence B. Anderson, called for intimate, comfortable spaces suited to conversation and reflection. Edwin Land, one of the influential members, insisted that emphasis should be on the individual rather than on groups. Exposed concrete was specifically forbidden.

The deep-eaved hip roofs, set on substantial brick piers, are immediately welcoming and unintimidating in the five and one-half–acre wooded setting. The entrance focuses on a skylit staircase and hearth area and leads through tall Hon-

© Steve Rosenthal

American Academy of Arts and Sciences

© Steve Rosenthal

Sonic sculpture in Kendall Square MBTA Station

duras mahogany doors into a labyrinth of rooms of varied sizes, some with provocative mantels, others with bookcases, seating nooks, or French doors opening onto the garden. Materials and detailing are impeccable, and the furnishings of varied styles and eras are unremarkable but comfortable in their settings. It is a building of great integrity that does not shriek "new and different" but speaks with quiet authority. In the landscaping, railroad ties, earthmounds, wood chips, and highly hybridized plants should have been avoided in keeping with the character of the building and its users.

Kendall Square MBTA Station

SCULPTOR: PAUL MATISSE; RENOVATION: ELLENZWEIG ASSOCIATES, INC., 1987

Not found in any other city are these delightful sonic sculptures that curious subway users can operate by levers on the walls of the platform. Suspended between the tracks, the sculptures are named *Galileo, Pythagoras,* and *Kepler.* Graphic panels along the platforms depict the history of Cambridge on one side and a timeline of major technological achievements at MIT on the other side.

Cambridgeside Galleria

Cambridgeside Galleria
160 Cambridgeside Place
ARROWSTREET, INC., 1990

Thomas Graves Landing
Edwin H. Land Boulevard at
Monsignor O'Brien Highway
UNIHAB, 1989

Lechmere Canal Park
CAROL R. JOHNSON AND ASSOCIATES, INC.,
1988

The Cambridgeside Galleria urban mall rejected several mall myths to create one million square feet of new retail space in a lively and intimate style near the old discount shopping area of Lechmere. It is an inviting setting that avoids the vast wastelands that have plagued the country since Victor Gruen's 1950s-model shopping centers. Can it succeed with a wide economic range of retailers, which had been thought to be anathema to mall developments? Many extra amenities are provided, including boat and bus shuttles to major public transit stations and free personal services. The animated facade curves around a lagoon with cafe space and paddleboat rentals. No fence or wall is needed to keep people out of the lagoon, despite its continuous pedestrian edge; a minimal six-inch granite curb and nautical bollards are sufficient definition. Inside, the Tinker Toy brutalism is warmed up with hanging plants and Hyatt Hotel–style glass elevators outlined by lights. Huge skylights bring natural light into the narrow linear space, which is somewhat like nineteenth-century French and English shop-lined arcades.

Old Lechmere Canal has become an attractive lagoon between Cambridgeside Galleria and Thomas Graves Landing and inspired a nautical theme on the west facade of the eight-story condominium building with its repeated pipe balconies. The roofline is punctuated with sheet metal mansards alternating with pronounced red brick gables. Thomas Graves, the first settler in Cambridge in 1628, lived on this site.

Bulfinch Square

47 Thorndike Street between Second and Third streets

MIDDLESEX COUNTY COURTHOUSE ATTRIBUTED TO CHARLES BULFINCH, 1814, WITH ADDITIONS BY AMMI YOUNG, 1848; RENOVATION: GRAHAM GUND ARCHITECTS, 1984

National Register of Historic Places

A group of six Middlesex County buildings threatened with demolition has been restored and renovated for public and private offices. These include the 1814 Middlesex County Courthouse (attributed to Charles Bulfinch), the Old Superior Courthouse (now Clerk of Courts Building), the Registry of Deeds, and a group of 1830s merchants' row houses of brick. An old courtroom has been restored for use as a theater, and a former parking lot has been transformed into a landscaped courtyard and public park.

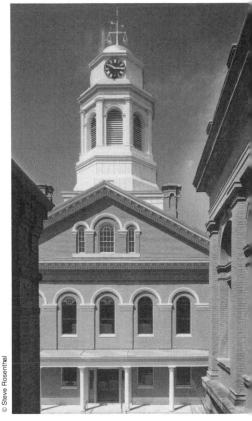

© Steve Rosenthal

Bulfinch Square

FIFTEEN

The Emerald Necklace

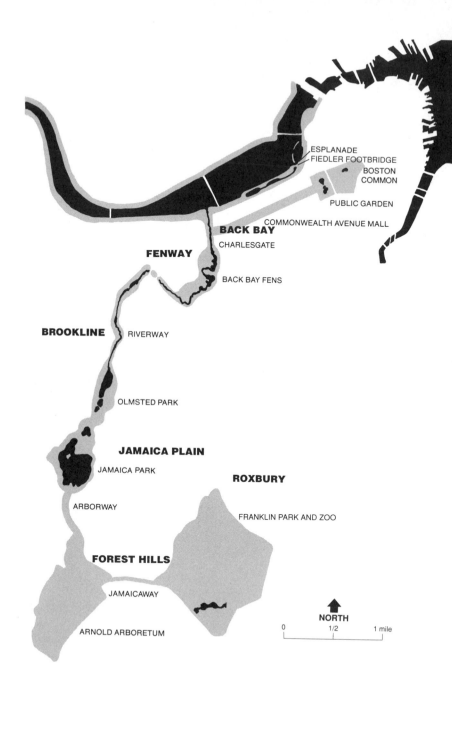

ESPLANADE
FIEDLER FOOTBRIDGE
BOSTON
COMMON

PUBLIC GARDEN

COMMONWEALTH AVENUE MALL

BACK BAY

CHARLESGATE

FENWAY

BACK BAY FENS

BROOKLINE

RIVERWAY

OLMSTED PARK

JAMAICA PLAIN

JAMAICA PARK

ROXBURY

ARBORWAY

FRANKLIN PARK AND ZOO

FOREST HILLS

JAMAICAWAY

NORTH

0   1/2   1 mile

ARNOLD ARBORETUM

The Emerald Necklace
National Historic Landmark

T he network of parks beginning with the Boston Common and extending out to Franklin Park is the largest continuous green space through an urban center in the United States and the finest achievement of landscape architect Frederick Law Olmsted.

From its beginning the nineteenth century saw numerous movements that idealized nature. The Romanticists communed with nature to experience God, and the New England Transcendentalists went even farther in venerating nature. In an era when nature was valued in an almost religious sense, public parks multiplied.

Frederick Law Olmsted was a landscape design genius eager to carry out these popular ideals on the grandest possible scale. His vision of environmental design was too far reaching for New York, however, and after designing Central Park he was frustrated in his desire to carry out a full scheme of continuous green open space throughout the city. It was in Boston that he was able to realize this noble concept.

His association with Boston began in 1869, when he was consulted about general park planning for the city. He next advised on the planning of the Arnold Arboretum and proposed improvements for the Back Bay Charlesgate and the Fens in the late 1870s. In 1887 he made his plan of an interconnected park system for Boston that would stretch from the Common to Franklin Park, passing through many Boston neighborhoods. Beyond this, he designed a number of other parks and initiated a metropolitan open space plan.

Albert Fein observed, "Olmsted's record of achievement in Boston after his defeat in New York City was owing to the social and political support he found there. Boston, unlike New York, still retained an effective intellectual and social elite committed to large-scale environmental planning."

The Emerald Necklace Tour

If you visit Boston, you will sooner or later find yourself walking in the **Boston Common, Public Garden, Commonwealth Avenue Mall,** and perhaps even the **Esplanade (453).** You will find your own pleasant way to explore these. With the usual alertness and caution, you can feel quite safe in these areas, especially during the day. The other parks are fascinating, but some of them have acquired less reliable reputations for safety and are best visited in groups or in a car. A bicycle is a pleasant way to tour the **Riverway (456),** and a car may be the best way to visit the largest parks, the **Arnold Arboretum** and **Franklin Park (456–57).**

Since there are no street addresses for the sections of the Emerald Necklace, sites are arranged topographically, beginning at the center and moving outward.

🏛 The Boston Common

1634

Boston Landmark

National Historic Landmark

It is appropriate that the Boston Common is the beginning of the park system, since it was the earliest public green in seventeenth-century Boston and was mentioned in town records as early as 1634.

In shape the Common is five-sided, but with three long sides making it more of a triangle. It served many purposes in its early history—military, recreational, and practical, including the grazing of cattle. In 1823 no person was allowed to graze more than one cow, and finally in 1830 cows were forbidden.

Throughout Boston's history the Common has been the site of recruitments, troop encampments, landings, and protests. The paved mall paralleling Charles Street, MacArthur Mall, fulfills the requirement that there be a walk the width of a regiment. The first section of iron fence around the Common was erected in 1735 and the Park Street side was fenced in 1737–1739. Much of the fencing was taken down for scrap metal during World War II, but it was never used because it was of cast rather than wrought iron. The beautiful old fence, nevertheless, disappeared and was said to have been thrown into Boston Harbor.

Public amusement was a primary attraction of the Common. When the British troops camped on the Common just prior to the Revolution and destroyed the snow slides of Beacon Hill boys, the boys complained directly to General Gage, who ordered his troops not to disturb their sledding in the future. But Bostonians did insist upon limits to the enjoyment of pleasures on the Common, and early in the nineteenth century prohibited both bathing on the Sabbath on the Charles River edge (where Charles

The Public Garden and Boston Common

Street now runs) and the sale of liquor. This ordinance was first put to the test when constables had to drive liquor and gambling stands off the Common on July 4, 1827. But many amusements did remain. It was a favorite launching site for balloon flights. Oyster stands were popular, as were "India crackers," which were sold at the fireworks stands. There were traveling entertainments, puppet shows, telescopes, scales, blowing machines, and booths selling gingerbread, sugar plums, confectionery, spruce beer, and lemonade.

In the mid-nineteenth century even smoking became legal on the Common and a Smoker's Circle was established that became the haunt of fashionable young dandies from Beacon Hill. Palm-leaf hats were first worn on the Common on August 11, 1827, and immediately became a raging Boston fad. Throughout the eighteenth and nineteenth century a most curious custom was the semiannual Feast of Squantum, for which upper-class Bostonians performed Indian rites while mounted cavaliers rode back and forth dressed in white boots and spurs. Above the 1895 subway line, the old American tradition of soapbox oratory is still practiced at the corner of Park and Tremont streets, known as "Brimstone corner."

All was not frivolity on the Common, for there were many hangings and whippings until the gallows were removed in 1817. One of the most infamous injustices was the hanging of Rachell Whall in the late 1700s for the crime of highway robbery—she had stolen a bonnet worth seventy-five cents. Blacks were not allowed free access to

Parkman Bandstand, Boston Common

Fountain, Shaw Monument

the Common until July 4, 1836.

The Frog Pond may seem to be an imposition on the Common, but there was a marshy pool in this location in the seventeenth century. The pond was curbed in 1826 and has remained a popular feature of the Common, though inappropriately edged and lighted today. The Parkman Bandstand, built with funds from the Parkman bequest, is a handsome Neoclassical bandstand with lovely symmetrical walkways, trees, and benches. It is no longer used as a bandstand, however, and has attracted an undesirable element in recent years.

Over the centuries, many structures and areas for activities have been added to the Common, encroaching on the open green. Parking-garage entrances, subway stations, and the information building are not consistent with the New England green that the Common is. Landscape architect Arthur Shurtleff quite properly called for the removal of the large structures housing the subway stairs, pointing out that they ruined the vistas of the Common. He also objected to the vast paved areas along Tremont Street and advocated returning that area to green with a fence along Tremont Street, opening broadly at each street intersection.

The Boston Common ought to look like what it is, a traditional New England green. Within it one should feel surrounded by this style of bucolic landscape without the intrusion of structures. The temptation to fill every square foot of open space with plaques or planters, fountains, statues, buildings, paved areas, playing fields, or play equipment must be resisted because any of these compromises and restricts the widest use of the green and eliminates its role as a passive green space in contrast to its urban surroundings.

🏛 Public Garden

founded 1839

DESIGNED BY GEORGE V. MEACHUM, 1859

Boston Landmark
National Historic Landmark

The informality of the Boston Common contrasts with the formality of the Public Garden, which is reminiscent of a French park of the Second Empire. Until the early nineteenth century, the land now occupied by the Public Garden was salt marshes like the rest of the Back Bay. In the winter of 1775 British troops skated on the ice there, and as a boy, Benjamin Franklin fished on the bank along Charles Street at the foot of the Common.

A botanical garden was begun on the newly filled site in 1839 by Horace Gray and Charles Francis Barnard, a Unitarian minister. In 1859 flower beds and paths were laid out in the French manner, and in 1861 an idyllic English pond was added with a delightful suspension bridge crossing in the center. In the same year a municipal competition was held for the design of the iron fence around the garden. Sixteen years later the famous Swan Boats began plying the waters and have become a Boston tradition, operated by the Paget family since 1877.

Weeping willows edge the pond while many fine trees grace the twenty-four-acre garden, including large dark beeches, pagoda trees, dawn redwood, American elms, and other interesting and ornamental species. As a Victorian flower garden, it is filled with several ornamental elements including five granite fountains, numerous statues and memorials, a Victorian-style

Public Garden and Swan Boats

Cast-iron fence and Edward Everett Hale monument, Public Garden

martin house, a wooden pagoda, and a cast-iron Japanese lantern. Near the Charles and Beacon Street entrance, see the *Make Way for Ducklings* sculpture by Nancy Schon, installed in 1987 as a tribute to Robert McCloskey for the book that "made the Public Garden familiar to children throughout the world."

Make Way for Ducklings sculpture

Detail, Ether Monument

© George M. Cushing, Jr.

Fiedler Footbridge and Esplanade

The Public Garden has survived and much more successfully avoided the predations that have beset its more ancient neighbor, the Boston Common. Perhaps its rigid and highly structured form has helped protect it. The Garden accommodates large crowds of people, but their activities are far more restricted than in the Common. One walks or sits and admires the formal beauty, certainly an important function of a garden, and to judge from the huge numbers of promenading visitors, a function successfully fulfilled.

Fiedler Footbridge

near Arlington Street at Beacon Street
SHEPLEY BULFINCH RICHARDSON AND
ABBOTT, 1954

One of several footbridges connecting the Esplanade with the Back Bay and Beacon Hill, this is the most elegant, with its simple continuous curves of poured concrete.

It is named after Arthur Fiedler, founder of the Esplanade Concerts, who conducted several concerts each summer in the Hatch Memorial Shell near the bridge.

The Esplanade
1931
National Register of Historic Places

It is curious to many visitors that the backs, rather than the fronts, of Back Bay houses face onto the Charles River and Esplanade. In fact, the houses were built before the Charles River was dammed. At that time the area was smelly mudflats—an area to be avoided; thus, the houses faced Beacon Street instead. The mudflats were eliminated by the 1910 dam, creating a very pleasing fresh-water recreational basin. The Alster Basin in Hamburg was the prototype for the improvement.

The Esplanade began as a simple

walk along the water, but in 1931 Mr. James J. Storrow provided the funds to landscape a spacious park with areas for outdoor music and a basin for more protected water activities. The Esplanade provides a pleasant setting for picnicking, strolling, sailing, sitting, and bicycling. During the summer, outdoor concerts and ballet attract thousands to the Hatch Shell. It was certainly an insult to name Storrow Drive—the 1951 highway that usurped much of the park—for the benefactors who made such an effort to create a quiet place of natural beauty.

🏛 Commonwealth Avenue Mall

BEGUN 1858

Boston Landmark

Commonwealth Avenue forms the spine of the Back Bay and is Boston's version of a Parisian boulevard. Large American and English elms contribute to the stateliness of the mall, but only with great effort have they been protected from Dutch elm disease. A hardier, smaller variety of elm has been planted to replace diseased elms. Originally the mall was separated from the street by an iron fence, but this was taken for scrap iron during one of the wars. The mall is ornamented by statues of personages including Alexander Hamilton, John Glover, Patrick Andrew Collins, William Lloyd Garrison, Samuel Eliot Morison, and Dominic Sarmiento. The procession concludes with Leif Eriksson gazing over Charlesgate toward Kenmore Square.

Monument to historian Samuel Eliot Morison
> To my readers young and old
> "A flowne sheate
> A faire winde
> A boune voyage"

Charlesgate

The original connection between the Commonwealth Mall and the Back Bay Fens was the Charlesgate, now almost entirely destroyed by the elevated access road built over it. Through the Charlesgate parkway flowed Stony Brook, its steep banks heavily covered with overhanging trees. Pedestrian pathways lined the Charles River Esplanade, Commonwealth Mall, and the Back Bay Fens. It is no longer possible to follow this route, since the few traces of the former park are now uninviting and lead nowhere.

Leif Eriksson at the Charlesgate

🏛 Back Bay Fens

FREDERICK LAW OLMSTED, 1879

Boston Landmark
National Historic Landmark

The Back Bay Fens and their adjoining parks formed the first linear park system

in the country. It is a good example of the nineteenth-century English landscape movement. The idyllic views, romantic bridges, floating mists, and tall reeds also make it one of the most attractive parks in Boston. It is all the more impressive when one considers that the area was once reeking salt marshes but was transformed into a freshwater parkway through artful damming and landscape design.

The wild English garden quality that is part of the attraction of the park is an example of the beneficial results neglect can have. As Olmsted, its designer, said, one of the nicest things an insensitive parks commission can do for its properties is simply to neglect them, since landscaping is rarely damaged and often enhanced by neglect, whereas the construction of facilities within park properties can cause damage that requires generations to correct.

Norman Thomas Newton wrote in *Design on the Land* that "The `blooming islets' that Olmsted planned are gone. What were once quiet marsh-meadows

H.H. Richardson's puddingstone bridge, Back Bay Fens

are now occupied by an athletic field of indifferent quality, a geometric rose garden, and a war memorial. East of Agassiz Road the former marsh-meadow has been given over for many years to 'victory gardens,' flower and vegetable plots planted and maintained by individual citizens on application and permit. All of these varied elements are of course laudable in themselves, but they hardly represent appropriate uses for the Fens, if only because they are wholly disruptive of what would otherwise be a placid scene. Moreover, for their own good these activities deserve locations better adapted to their several purposes."

Recent improvements to the park bridges and pathways have not been in the picturesque tradition, but their utilitarian character has not severely compromised the park style. All of Olmsted's original swamp plantings should be restored for the park to realize its full glory. Happily, H. H. Richardson's fine puddingstone bridge of 1880 survives as he designed it. In cities throughout the country, green parks are often seen as an opportunity for development. Olmsted's work has suffered most in New York, where a series of administrations throughout much of the twentieth century has run amuck in Central Park with projects from megalomaniacal museums to brash theme restaurants. By comparison, the Fens seems relatively unspoiled. It is truly an outdoor room for the city. Here people can lean on the railing of a bridge overlooking sleepy water, follow meandering paths, or lie in the grass with a good book and listen to the birds.

🏛 Riverway and Olmsted (Leverett) Park

FREDERICK LAW OLMSTED, 1881

Boston Landmark
National Historic Landmark

The Riverway links the Back Bay Fens with Olmsted Park and Jamaica Pond. This winding linear park follows the route of the Muddy River it contains. Paths designed for pedestrians, bicyclists, and even horseback riders follow the bank of the river. The most serious interruption of the park's continuity occurs shortly after it leaves the Fens, where the Park Drive section has lost its original landscape character completely. An entire block-long segment was sold to Sears for use as a parking lot, a serious relinquishing of the public trust by city officials. The opportunity to restore it occurred when Sears abandoned its building and left it boarded up and empty. Every effort should be made to return this portion of the park to its public use and original design. Most of the Riverway remains close to the original landscape design of Olmsted and is thus a major asset to the city. It includes fine stone bridges—three vehicular and two pedestrian—linking the two banks at several points.

Jamaica Park

FREDERICK LAW OLMSTED, 1892

Boston Landmark
National Historic Landmark (Jamaica Pond Boathouse)

Three adjacent ponds—Jamaica, Ward's, and Leverett—form the focus for Jamaica and Olmsted parks, with Jamaica Pond the largest body of water in the greenspace network. Jamaica Park was designed by Olmsted in 1892 as an active water-oriented park with a passive path area surrounding it. Boating and fishing are still popular here. The boathouse and dock are in a Tudor Revival, half-timbered style. The white pine trees inspired the name Pine Bank for the site of the former Perkins mansion at the northern side of the pond. Opposite Pine Bank was the summer home of Francis Parkman, the historian, where a monument by Daniel Chester French was erected in 1906.

Arnold Arboretum

CHARLES SPRAGUE SARGENT AND FREDERICK LAW OLMSTED, 1872

National Historic Landmark

The Arborway, a vehicular parkway, links Jamaica Park to the Arnold Arboretum and the Arboretum to Franklin Park. When built, it contained a carriage road, a saddle path, and a pedestrian walk down the central green space between two traffic ways. The Arboretum was laid out by Charles Sprague Sargent with the advice of Olmsted in 1872. The intention was to make a living museum of trees for both study and pleasure. The planting areas are arranged in a species-by-species progression that is scientifically formal, but the original design was intended to look like a typical New England rural landscape with no sense of formal landscaping and no open lawns or meadows. At one time more than five thousand species and varieties of trees and shrubs grew in the Arboretum. The city provides policing and road maintenance, but the plants and

park areas are all under the care of Harvard University, which has a 999-year lease on everything but the roads.

Franklin Park

FREDERICK LAW OLMSTED, 1885

Boston Landmark
National Historic Landmark

The largest park in the greenspace system was conceived as a rural park on 520 acres and was Olmsted's masterpiece. Its primary landscape design areas were the Country Park, the Playstead, the Greeting, and Refectory Hill, all beautifully conceived to develop existing natural features into an idyllic setting.

The park is named after one of its important benefactors, Benjamin Franklin. Olmsted's design was influenced by Joseph Paxton's "People's Park" at Birkenhead, England. In the nineteenth century a park carriage service was operated by Bacon and Tarbell, providing up to eleven passengers with the pleasures of a carriage drive through the grounds and allowing them to dismount for a picnic and return in a later carriage, since frequent rounds were made. The park was enormously popular and intensely used into the early twentieth century.

The character of the park has changed greatly since Olmsted's time—the Country Park is now a golf course, the zoo was built in the Greeting, the stadium was built in the Playstead, and the Refectory was demolished. Nevertheless, some elements of the original design may be discovered by the determined visitor.

© Huygens and DiMella

TROPICAL FOREST

Section, Tropical Forest Pavilion

Franklin Park Zoo

HUYGENS AND TAPPÉ, 1972–1979;
WEIDLINGER ASSOCIATES; HUYGENS AND
DIMELLA; ENGINEERING AND ARCHITECTURAL
CONSULTANTS; COMPLETED 1989

The zoo, which occupies the area of the Greeting, has been improved with a radically different group of exhibit pavilions. African wildlife is the theme for the zoo, with four major African ecologies represented: desert, tropical forest, veldt, and

© Tappé and Associates

Tropical Forest Pavilion, Franklin Park Zoo

bush forest. Emphasis is on providing settings as close as possible to the actual African habitats, where the animals can move fairly freely and with the human visitors restricted—quite the opposite of the traditional zoo. In addition to wildlife, the pavilions contain botanical exhibits as part of the settings. The structure of each pavilion consists of long-span steel arches with a translucent teflon-coated, fiberglass-reinforced fabric membrane supported on a cable grid. The rolling landscape of the park flows into earth berms that cover animal holding facilities at the perimeter of each pavilion, creating a smooth transition from the natural setting to the pavilions. A sophisticated mechanical system handles air movement, heat and ventilation, humidity control, and odor evacuation.

Another zoo structure worthy of attention is the 1913 Chinese Pagoda Bird House, renovated by Geometrics in the 1970s. Exhibits present birds in representations of their habitats and minimize the cage feeling.

SIXTEEN

Outlying Sites

Boston University
and Bay State Road

Boston University and Bay State Road Tour

This is an entirely linear tour that can begin at Beacon Street and Massachusetts Avenue. Walk down Beacon Street past the **Charlesgate Hotel** (**246**) and under the expressway where you can see remnants of the old **Charlesgate Park** (**454**). Turn right onto Bay State Road, passing the **Arthur Little house, Dr. Charles Goddard Weld house,** and **William Lindsey house** (**462–63**). Turn left onto Granby Street and right on Commonwealth Avenue to see the **Ralph Adams Cram Chapel** and **Courtyard,** and beyond it the **Law and Education Tower** and other buildings by Sert, Jackson and Associates (**463**). The tour ends here unless you choose to cross Commonwealth Avenue and enter the **Cottage Farm** and **Longwood** (**466**) section of Brookline.

Bay State Road

Boston Architectural Conservation District

Bay State Road, actually an extension of the Back Bay, was laid out in 1889. The filling of this land was made possible by Frederick Law Olmsted's plan for the Fens, which channeled the Muddy River (a sluggish waterway into which the Roxbury sewers emptied) into the Charles River at Charlesgate. The problem of the odorous mudflats of the Charles River Basin was finally solved between 1903 and 1910 when the dam was built to maintain the water level. This, along with extension of the Esplanade to Bay State Road, made the area more attractive.

Arthur Little house, 57 Bay State Road

Many fine houses were built on the street in a variety of turn-of-the-century revival styles. Architect Arthur Little of Little and Browne built his own house at number 57 in the conservative Federal Revival style. The house has a two-story ballroom with large Palladian windows. Dr. Eliot P. Joslin, the noted specialist in the treatment of diabetes for whom the Joslin foundation in the Harvard Medical area is named, lived in the Classical Revival house at number 81.

Dr. Charles Goddard Weld's houses, built in 1900 at 145–149, were designed by W. Y. Peters of Peters and Rice in an exuberant High Georgian Revival style. Heavy-handed quoins, Gibbs surrounds, and a cartouche window ornament the facade of 149. In the Tudor Revival mansion by Chapman and Frazier (1905) at number 225 lived the William Lindseys who built the Lindsey Chapel at Emmanuel Church (see 15 Newbury Street, p. 279).

Entrance, Dr. Charles Goddard Weld house, 149 Bay State Road

The Bay State Road area proved too remote to become as fashionable as the Back Bay—particularly after the building in 1891 of the Harvard Bridge that connected Cambridge's Massachusetts Avenue with the quieter Boston street, West Chester Park (now Massachusetts Avenue). Traffic could now flow from Dorchester to Arlington along what became a heavily trafficked thoroughfare, further isolating Bay State Road from the Back Bay. Most of the Bay State Road houses are now owned by Boston University and serve as offices, clubs, and residence halls.

William Lindsey house, 225 Bay State Road

© Lois M. Bowen

Boston University, Gothic Revival chapel and courtyard with Law and Education Tower (Ralph Adams Cram)

© Steve Rosenthal

Boston University buildings by Sert, Jackson and Gourley

Boston University

GEORGE SHERMAN UNION AND MUGAR
MEMORIAL LIBRARY: SERT, JACKSON AND
GOURLEY; HOYLE, DORAN, AND BERRY;
1963, 1966; MASTER PLAN, PAPPAS LAW
LIBRARY, AND LAW AND EDUCATION SCHOOLS
TOWER: SERT, JACKSON AND ASSOCIATES;
EDWIN T. STEFFIAN, 1964;
LANDSCAPE DESIGN: SASAKI, DAWSON, DEMAY
ASSOCIATES, 1967

In their master plan for the university, the
architects addressed the special problems
of the long narrow urban campus
squeezed between a major artery, Commonwealth Avenue, and the Charles
River. The plan proposed vertical expansion to accommodate new growth and
included four major new buildings, all

designed as an ensemble but built indi-
vidually over a seven-year period. The
new section of the campus has been
reoriented away from Commonwealth
Avenue toward the river. Spaces between
buildings have been carefully designed
for student circulation and enjoyment.
The terracing of the library reduces its
apparent bulk and, together with the central quadrangle, provides a broad, low
setting for the Law and Education Tower.
Fabricated largely of various shades of
concrete, the buildings illustrate many of
Sert's techniques for enriching the form:
sun screens, decorative window divisions,
scoop clerestories, asymmetrical massing,
expressed structure, and projecting bays
or balconies.

Longwood and Cottage Farm

Longwood and Cottage Farm Tour

Longwood and Cottage Farm are quiet old Brookline residential districts separated from central Boston by only a few blocks. So conveniently located between **The Fenway (339)** and **Boston University (464)**, they can be visited as a side trip from either of these tours. Choose your own route, but Chapel, Colchester, Hawes, Monmouth, and Ivy streets are particularly interesting.

⌂ Longwood and Cottage Farm

off Beacon Street near Carlton Street,
Brookline

National Register of Historic Places

David Sears, a wealthy Bostonian whose
home became the Somerset Club (see
42–43 Beacon Street, p. 156), developed
the Longwood area in the 1860s as an
exclusive inner suburb for himself and his
family and friends. For his model he took
the English country village of Colchester,
his family's ancestral home. Streets with
English names—Colchester, Monmouth,
Kent—focus on Longwood Mall. The
name Longwood is from Napoleon's St.
Helena country estate.

Amos Lawrence house (1851), 135 Ivy
Street

Although Sears's own estate is now
gone, several churches and "cottages" of
Roxbury puddingstone in the romantic
English country style remain and give the
area its distinct flavor. Christ Church, built
in 1860–1862 by Sears as his family
chapel, was designed by Arthur Gilman,
also architect of the Arlington Street
Church (see Arlington Street at Boylston
Street, p. 238), and was based on St.
Peter's Church in Colchester. It stands on
a slope next to the Tudor Revival Longwood Towers and overlooks Olmsted's
green Riverway Park. St. Paul's (on St.
Paul Street), built in 1848–1851 and
designed by Richard Upjohn, is another
of the picturesque churches and perhaps
the first to use puddingstone. Unfortunately, it suffered extensive fire damage,
but the shell survived and has been
rebuilt as one of Boston's first solar-
heated churches.

Church of Our Saviour (23 Monmouth Street), with its handsome square
puddingstone tower (the tower was

George Minot Dexter house (1851), 156
Ivy Street

rebuilt in 1932 from plans by Allen and Collens), was designed by Alexander R. Estey, also architect of Emmanuel Church (see 15 Newbury Street, p. 279). Although the work of several architects over many years, the complex skillfully joins church, parish hall (Cabot and Chandler, 1880, and Sturgis and Cabot, 1913 and 1921), and rectory (Arthur Rotch, 1885) by a cloister. The stained-glass windows are by Edward Burne-Jones, Tiffany, Charles Connick, and others. The church was built in 1868 by brothers William and Amos Lawrence for their family and friends who had built homes in the Cottage Farm area across Beacon Street from David Sears's Longwood estates. "It was a sight seen oftener in old England than in this country—the two venerable brothers with their families joining the group of neighbors as they walked to the door of the memorial church, then worshipping together like one large family" (Victorian Society, *Victorian Boston*). Remarkably, this remains even now a picturesque Victorian parish church with English village atmosphere.

Until the turn of the century the area remained rural in feeling, with only a few houses scattered among the fields. Although now surrounded by development, the 1851 stone houses George Minot Dexter designed for himself and Amos Lawrence can be seen at 135 and 156 Ivy Street and still possess their original charm.

Longwood Towers
formerly Alden Park Manor
20 Chapel Street, Brookline
K. M. DE VOS AND COMPANY WITH
GEORGE R. WIREN AND HAROLD FIELD
KELLOGG, 1922–1925

An extraordinary site-planning concept incorporates a vast three-story structure beneath a pastoral green. Garages, meeting rooms, service facilities, and a restaurant are united under one roof with access to all three Tudor-style apartment towers—which appear from outdoors to sit neatly and separately on English lawns. The Tudor-style underground areas are entered at grade level on a lower street. Crenellated brick towers and parapets are details at the service of an ingenious site plan. Compare this

Lawn entrance, Longwood Towers

Motor entrance, Longwood Towers

with the analogous needs of Prudential Center, where the solution was far less successful (see 800 Boylston Street).

Ruggles Street Church
Audubon Circle at 874 Beacon Street
RALPH ADAMS CRAM, 1913–1917

This handsome Georgian Revival church, now sited at the edge of a bleak intersection, was built by the congregation of the Second Unitarian Church of Boston. An elaborate tower stands at the intersection of the low gambrel-roof Colonial wing and the taller Classical gable of the nave, certainly a strange juxtaposition of styles. A Palladian window tops the gambrel end, while the sanctuary entrance is highlighted with banded rustication and quoins.

Ruggles Street Church

Other Sites

Ruggles Street Transit Station
Columbus Avenue at Ruggles Street
STULL AND LEE, INC., 1988

The new Ruggles Street Transit Station is a multimodal transportation node servicing the Orange Line, buses, and commuter rail and Amtrak lines. The station is dramatically marked by a long barrel vault framed within a concrete arch that serves as an entry portal to Northeastern University as well as a pedestrian link to the neighborhood. The station is located near some of Boston's major institutions, including Wentworth Institute, the Museum of Fine Arts, Northeastern University, and Roxbury Community College. The master plan calls for intensive devel-

opment of the land around the station as offices, shops, and a hotel.

Madison Park High School
100 New Dudley Street
MARCEL BREUER AND TICIAN PAPACHRISTOU, 1974–1978

The old Madison Park neighborhood of Roxbury was cleared to provide a ten-acre site for the new Madison Park Campus High School, built as a "magnet school" to attract students from all parts of the city into voluntarily integrated education. The interconnected buildings housed some of the most outstanding facilities of any high school in the country at the

Ruggles Street Transit Station

Madison Park High School

Swimming pool, Madison Park High School

time. The gymnasium building includes three swimming pools and a rowing tank. The performing arts building includes a music department with a fine organ, harpsichord, concert grand piano, numerous harps, and soundproofed practice rooms. The media arts component includes a complete television station with full capabilities to videotape, edit, and broadcast throughout the school.

The architectural solution is a precast-concrete–faced group of tightly linked buildings somewhat fortresslike in appearance. There are six interconnected components: an administration/library building with mechanical services and main kitchen, two classroom buildings, a gymnasium, a science center, and a shop/drama building. One of the best views of the campus is across the athletic fields toward the gymnasium and science center.

Hubert H. Humphrey Occupational Resource Center
55 New Dudley Street
SHEPLEY BULFINCH RICHARDSON AND ABBOTT, 1980

In contrast to the fortresslike Madison Park High School next door, the Occupational Resource Center has an inviting openness. The exterior, faced in exposed-aggregate concrete panels and lively orange window trim, steps back from the

Madison Park town houses (John Sharratt Associates and Glaser, De Castro, Vitols, 1975–1983)

Occupational Resource Center

curved street to accommodate a terraced entry plaza. An interior pedestrian mall connects various parts of the center and allows students and visitors views into each work area through glass partitions. Eight types of work environments for vocational training are provided, including television studios, banks, automotive shops, retail stores, supermarkets, and restaurants.

Roxbury Community College
1234 Columbus Avenue
STULL AND LEE, INC., 1987

This linear arrangement of red brick gable-roofed buildings serves a student body of 1,500. The major buildings are the Student Center, the Academic Core, Media Arts, and Administration.

Boston Design Center
One Design Center Place
RENOVATION: EARL R. FLANSBURGH & ASSOCIATES, INC. AND STUBBINS ASSOCIATES/INTERIOR DESIGN GROUP, 1986

Originally built in 1919 by the U.S. Army Corps of Engineers to warehouse tanks and trucks, this building was engineered for tremendous live loads. The largest military warehouse in the world at that time, it is an impressively long structure with 1.5 million square feet of floor space. The building has been adapted as a show-place for the design and contract furnish-

© Ben E. Watkins

Roxbury Community College

ings industry of New England and contains 550,000 square feet of showroom space, professional offices, and seminar and conference rooms. The narrow west end facing downtown Boston has been dramatically redesigned with an entry plaza and new facade with giant segmental pediment to provide a glamorous new lobby and entrance facade in harmony with long side facades that are largely unchanged. A two-story extension of the lobby serves as a transitional element between the eight-story facade and the public plaza.

🏛 John F. Kennedy Library
Columbia Point
I. M. PEI AND PARTNERS, 1977–1979;
LANDSCAPE DESIGN: KILEY, TYNDALL, WALKER
AND MRS. PAUL MELLON; EXHIBIT DESIGN:
CHERMAYEFF AND GEISMAR ASSOCIATES

Stephen E. Smith Center
PEI COBB FREED & PARTNERS, 1991

After ten years of controversy and consideration of eight different sites, this dramatic site on Columbia Point overlooking open sea was chosen for the Kennedy Library. The simple forms of a nine-story

© Steve Rosenthal

Boston Design Center

© Nathaniel Lieberman

John F. Kennedy Library

white pyramid connected to the two-story cylinder by a parallelogram and the gray glass form of the 110-foot-high Presidential Pavilion make a strong symbolic statement. The visitor is led from the reception lobby overlooking the glass pavilion to an exhibition lobby and two auditoriums seating three hundred people each. Leaving the auditoriums, visitors descend to the lower-level exhibition area and finally enter the large glass space frame with its expansive view of the bay. A 1991 addition provided a large function room, classroom, and archives. Kennedy's sailboat, *Victura,* is displayed on the granite Bay Plaza. The Point is planted with flora associated with Cape Cod: pines, dune grass, bayberry, and rugosa roses.

Harbor Point

1 Harbor Point Boulevard, Dorchester (near Kennedy Library)

RECONSTRUCTION: MINTZ ASSOCIATES ARCHITECTS/PLANNERS, INC.; SITE MASTER PLAN AND NEW CONSTRUCTION: GOODY, CLANCY & ASSOCIATES, 1988

Transformation of failing public housing projects into successful communities has not happened often enough, but several Boston area projects indicate the potential for this kind of recycling. Harbor Point, which transforms one of New England's largest and most troubled housing projects into a new community, was given a new face as well as a new name. The original 1950s scheme consisted of twenty-seven nearly identical oppressive buildings that completely ignored the dramatic setting on the Boston Harbor. By

Harbor Point

Goody, Clancy & Associates

the time a drastic renovation occurred, there were only about 350 families left, but they actively participated in the redesign. A new street grid with a central tree-lined mall has been inserted and brings harbor views into the site. Several new buildings were built, and old build ings were totally renovated or demolished. The community now provides 1,283 units of mixed-income housing; about one-third are low-income subsi-

dized units, and two-thirds are market rate. Building form and details are loosely inspired by a variety of traditional New England features including varied brick colors and stained clapboard. Several of the original flat-topped towers were lowered and given pitched roofs. Units include two- and three-story townhouses as well as apartments in the five-, six-, and seven-story elevator buildings. All units with more than two bedrooms have ground-level access to private gardens. The redevelopment was made possible by an innovative government-assisted partnership that included private companies and Harbor Point residents. Another notorious public housing project, Washington Elms in Cambridge near MIT, was significantly upgraded in the 1980s by Bruner/Cott & Associates.

Northeastern University Henderson Boathouse
1345 Soldiers Field Road, Brighton, near Arsenal Bridge
GRAHAM GUND ARCHITECTS, 1989

For more than a century boathouses have been on the banks of the Charles River to store the dozens of sculls and shells that delight the many fans living on both sides of the river. In the boathouses crews exercise and shower, and their shoes are nailed or screwed into the shells. All boathouses have repair shops for the delicate shells, and handmade oars and the long slender lightweight shells are still turned out in some. The daily drills and races of dozens of rowing crews are some of the most fascinating activities on the river.

The Henderson Boathouse is the newest addition and was spurred on when Northeastern University attracted the late legendary Charlie Smith away from Harvard. "He was the kind of guy who could do anything—weld, patch, make structural repairs, even make his own oars from scratch," according to Dan Boyne, Harvard's recreational sculling director. Northeastern decided it was time to stop renting boathouse space and build its own. The towers, dormers, and porches were chosen to mirror the elements of the nearby nineteenth-century boathouses.

Northeastern University Henderson Boathouse

© Robert Damora

Walter Gropius house

🏛 Walter Gropius Residence
Bridge Road, Lincoln
WALTER GROPIUS AND MARCEL BREUER,
1937

Walter Gropius built this house in the first year after he came to America, and with it proclaimed many of the Bauhaus design principles. Its boxy shape, vertical siding, flat roof, and large windows were a curiosity, and as the first "modern" house within one hundred miles it attracted throngs of sightseers.

SEVENTEEN

Special Interest Tours

Special Interest Tours

Five tours have been designed according to particular themes rather than by the topographic system used elsewhere in this guide. The first special interest tour is for enthusiasts of Charles Bulfinch and includes all of his Boston and Cambridge buildings. Most of these will be found on Beacon Hill and are treated in detail elsewhere in the guide. Similarly, the complete existing work in central Boston and Cambridge of another significant Boston architect, Henry Hobson Richardson, is covered in Tour B.

Tour C treats the work of Ralph Adams Cram, a less well known but very influential Boston architect, writer, and teacher whose work is found throughout the country. Cram was a leader in the Gothic Revival movement and is best known for his religious buildings. Although he was the son of a Unitarian minister, Cram converted to the Anglican church under the influence of the Oxford movement. He never attended college but apprenticed in architecture in the office of Rotch and Tilden, wrote two dozen books and many articles, and was head of the MIT School of Architecture for several years. Examples of his work can be found in Boston and several surrounding communities.

Outstanding works of contemporary architecture in central Boston and Cambridge are offered in Tour D. While the "landmark" status of some of these might be debated, many of the sites are now classics of modern architecture.

The final itinerary, Tour E, deals with design at the large scale—urban and landscape design. Areas of both historic and contemporary development where outstanding quality has been achieved are included. These are excellent study areas for learning about urban design and planning. Each of these districts has a special character and form uniquely expressive of Boston. Although many of the areas have historic roots, through thoughtful and creative urban design they have been adapted to meet the needs of contemporary users without losing important connections with the past. Some areas, however, are being stressed to their limits by development pressures, especially the financial district and Broad Street. For this reason it is important for the public to become better acquainted with these districts and fight for their survival. Another area—the Emerald Necklace—has never achieved its enormous potential, largely through neglect, but also through poor management. Again, public awareness and concern are essential to head one of the country's great open space systems in a new direction.

TOUR A: Charles Bulfinch

Beacon Hill

- Third Harrison Gray Otis house, 45 Beacon Street
- John Phillips house, 1 Walnut Street at Beacon Street (altered)
- Amory-Ticknor house, 9 Park Street at Beacon Street (altered)
- State House, Beacon Street
- Beacon Hill Memorial Column, behind State House
- 49–57 Mount Vernon Street
- Second Harrison Gray Otis house, 85 Mount Vernon Street
- 87 Mount Vernon Street
- 29A Chestnut Street
- Swan houses, 13, 15, 17 Chestnut Street and stables at 50–60 Mount Vernon Street
- Charles Paine houses, 6–8 Chestnut Street
- First Harrison Gray Otis house, 141 Cambridge Street
- Massachusetts General Hospital (Bulfinch Pavilion and Ether Dome), off Cambridge Street

Government Center

- Faneuil Hall (enlargement by Bulfinch)

Custom House District

- Central Wharf, 146–176 Milk Street and several buildings on Broad Street (5, 7–9, 63–65, 64–66, 67–73, 68–70, 72, and 102)

North End

- St. Stephen's Church, Hanover Street

Harvard University
- Stoughton Hall, Harvard Yard
- University Hall, Harvard Yard

TOUR B: Henry Hobson Richardson

Back Bay
- Trinity Church, Copley Square
- Trinity Rectory, Clarendon Street at Newbury Street
- First Baptist Church, Clarendon Street at Commonwealth Avenue
- Crowninshield house, 164 Marlborough Street

Theater District
- Hayden Building, 681 Washington Street

Fenway
- Stone bridge, Boylston Street, Back Bay Fens

Cambridge
- Sever Hall, Harvard Yard
- Austin Hall, north of Harvard Yard
- Stoughton house, 90 Brattle Street

North Easton
- Several buildings

TOUR C: Ralph Adams Cram

Central Boston
- Church of the Advent, Lady Chapel interior, Mount Vernon Street at Brimmer Street, Beacon Hill
- Post Office, Post Office Square, financial district
- Telephone Building, 185 Franklin Street, financial district

- John Hancock Tower, 180 Berkeley Street, Back Bay
- The New England (originally New England Mutual Life Insurance Company), 501 Boylston Street, Back Bay
- Ruggles Street Church, Audubon Circle, Beacon Street at Park Drive
- Boston University Chapel, Commonwealth Avenue

Dorchester
- All Saints' Church, 209 Ashmont Street

Hyde Park
- Christ Church, 1220 River Street

Brookline
- All Saints' Church, 1773 Beacon Street
- Richmond Court Apartments, 1213 Beacon Street

Cambridge
- Conventual Church of Saints Mary and John and Monastery of the Order of St. John the Evangelist, 980 Memorial Drive

Arlington
- St. Anne's Convent Chapel, 14 Claremont Avenue

Somerville
- First Unitarian Church, 125 Highland Avenue

West Newton
- First Unitarian Church, 1326 Washington Street

Milton
- St. Michael's Church, 112 Randolph Avenue

Sudbury
- St. Elizabeth's Church, Concord Road (Cram's own chapel)

TOUR D: Contemporary Landmarks

Central Boston

- State Health, Education, and Welfare Service Center, Cambridge Street, Paul Rudolph et al.
- City Hall, City Hall Plaza, Kallmann, McKinnell, and Knowles et al.
- Boston Five Cents Savings Bank, 10 School Street, Kallmann and McKinnell
- Post Office Square Park, Congress Street, The Halvorson Company
- Back Bay Station, between Clarendon and Dartmouth streets near Stuart Street, Kallmann, McKinnell, and Wood
- John Hancock Tower, 200 Clarendon Street, I. M. Pei and Partners
- Boston Architectural Center, 320 Newbury Street, Ashley, Myer
- Boston University Buildings, off Commonwealth Avenue, Sert, Jackson and Associates et al.
- Museum of Fine Arts, West Wing, 465 Huntington Avenue, I. M. Pei and Partners

Charlestown

- Charlestown Navy Yard Rowhouses, First Avenue at Thirteenth Street, Charlestown Navy Yard, William Rawn Associates

South Boston

- Kennedy Library, Columbia Point, I. M. Pei and Partners

Cambridge

- Carpenter Center for the Visual Arts, Quincy Street, Le Corbusier
- Fogg Museum Addition, Quincy Street, James Stirling, Michael Wilford, and Associates
- Gund Hall, Quincy Street, John Andrews, Anderson and Baldwin
- Tanner Fountain, in front of Science Center, Harvard University, Joan Brigham, Peter Walker and the SWA Group
- Harkness Commons and Graduate Center, north of Harvard Yard, Walter Gropius and The Architects Collaborative
- Design Research Building (now Crate and Barrel), 48 Brattle Street, Benjamin Thompson and Associates
- Peabody Terrace, 900 Memorial Drive, Sert, Jackson and Gourley

- Baker House, Memorial Drive, MIT West Campus, Alvar Aalto
- Kresge Chapel and Auditorium, MIT West Campus, Eero Saarinen
- Library of Art, Architecture, and Planning addition, MIT, Schwartz & Silver
- Green, Dreyfus, Landau, and Wiesner Buildings, MIT East Campus, I. M. Pei and Partners
- Academy of Arts and Sciences, 136 Irving Street, Kallmann, McKinnell, and Wood

Lincoln

- Walter Gropius residence, Bridge Road, Walter Gropius and Marcel Breuer

TOUR E: Boston Urban Landscape and Design

The following areas are particularly recommended for outstanding examples of urban and landscape design in Boston, both historic and contemporary:

- Waterfront, especially the Harborwalk and Rowe's Wharf
- Financial district, focusing on Post Office Square, Liberty Square, Winthrop Square, and Church Green
- Faneuil Hall Marketplace
- Government Center and Blackstone Block
- Bay village
- Beacon Hill, especially Beacon, Chestnut, Mount Vernon, and Pinckney streets
- Back Bay, especially Commonwealth Avenue, Newbury Street, and the Esplanade
- Charlestown Navy Yard
- Emerald Necklace, from the Boston Common to Franklin Park
- New and renovated MBTA stations, especially on the Orange and Red lines.

Glossary

acanthus An ornamental form derived from the broad, curling leaf of the acanthus plant. It is always found on Corinthian and composite column capitals.

acroterion A small pedestal, often of stone, located at the three corners of a pediment to support a figure or ornament.

anthemion A Classical decorative pattern based on alternating lotus and palmette with scrolls, creating a continuous design. It is a favorite decorative device in Greek Revival architecture.

apse The semicircular or multifaceted conclusion of the chancel (the altar area) in a church.

arcade A row of arches supported by posts and columns.

arch A curved opening created by wedge-shaped blocks of brick or stone. The curve may assume a variety of shapes, from nearly flat to pointed lancet arches, multicurved trefoil arches, or ogee arches (pointed arches with reverse curves near their apexes).

architrave The lower or supporting section of an entablature. Above it are the frieze and then the cornice. Architraves are sometimes found above doorways.

ashlar Squared stones laid in regular courses with narrow joints to produce a smooth wall.

balusters The regularly spaced vertical elements of a fence or stair rail. Small columns are often used to support the railing.

balustrade A series of balusters supporting a railing.

banded column A column where horizontal bands of rustication alternate with smooth or fluted bands.

baroque Usually refers to the style derived from seventeenth-century architecture, painting, and sculpture associated with Rome and to some extent other cities in Italy. The style is characterized by extravagant ornamentation and dramatic spatial effects.

barrel vault A ceiling or roof arched in a continuous half-cylinder form.

bartizan A turret projected out from a wall on a supporting corbel.

bas-relief A sculpture that projects only slightly from a back-ground plane.

bay window A projection from the facade of a building containing windows and beginning on the ground, either square or polygonal in plan (see bow and oriel window).

berm Earth mound for weather protection, barrier, or landscape decoration.

blind arcade A series of arches attached directly to a wall and thus serving a purely decorative purpose. Characteristic of Romanesque architecture.

bow window Similar to a bay window except that it is curved in plan.

broach spire One of the most complex of spire forms, it was originally developed in wood but has since been copied in stone. An eight-sided spire is mounted on top of a square tower, producing four odd spaces that are filled in with small half-pyramids. Broach spires are often further adorned with windows topped with gablets.

bull's-eye window A round or oval window with circular center and radiating panes.

buttress A structural mass of stone, brick or concrete to reinforce a wall, particularly when an arch or vault is exerting outward pressure on the wall. Two buttresses at right angles to each other at a corner are **angle buttresses. Setback buttresses** are similar to angle buttresses but are set back from the corner.

campanile A freestanding tower built to hold a bell.

cantilever A structural element that projects beyond the wall beneath it.

capital The decorative focus at the top of a column or pilaster.

cartouche An ornamental frame often enclosing an inscription or symbol.

castellated Featuring castle architectural forms such as crenellation in a building that is not in fact a castle.

chamfered Beveled or cut at an oblique angle.

Classical A style derived from the architecture of ancient Greece and Rome.

clerestory An upper story projecting above the mass of a building and having frequent windows to bring light into the interior.

coffered Having a regular pattern of recessed panels: an ornamental ceiling treatment.

Colonial The style of architecture in the American colonies in the seventeenth and eighteenth centuries, derived mainly from English traditions.

colonnade A series of columns supporting an entablature.

colonnette A small column.

console A scroll bracket used to support an element such as a mantel or lintel.

contextual, contextualism An approach to design that emphasizes how a building or object relates to and fits into its surroundings rather than treating it as a pure form in a vacuum.

corbelling Stone or brickwork which steps out from the face of a wall to support a projecting element.

Corinthian The late Greek architectural order that is more elaborate than the Doric and Ionic styles. Corinthian capitals combine eight volutes (scroll-shaped ornaments) with acanthus leaves. Below the elaborate capital is a fluted shaft.

cornice The projecting top of an entablature in Classical architecture, or the top of the facade of a building or of a door or window.

crenellation A series of openings along a parapet for fortification.

cresting A decorative topping on a roof or wall, such as the ornamental iron cresting often found on the rooflines of Victorian houses.

crocket A Gothic ornament usually based on the leaf, used to decorate the ridges of spires, gables, and other elements.

cyma reversa A molding with a double curve in which the upper curve is convex and the lower, concave.

dentils The row of rectangular blocks arranged like teeth on the lower edge of a cornice.

diaper A repetitive pattern of small carved or painted ornament on a wall.

donjon In medieval castle architecture, the large central tower, the most protected area of the complex.

Doric The earliest and simplest of the Classical Greek orders.

dormer A window projection added to a sloping roof.

egg-and-dart molding Alternating ovals and double-pointed spears in high relief; sometimes called egg-and-tongue or egg-and-anchor.

engaged column A column that appears to be partially built into a wall, but retains its roundness, unlike a pilaster, which is flat.

entablature In Classical architecture, the entire assembly that is supported by columns and includes the architrave, frieze, and cornice.

entasis A slight increase in the circumference of a column toward the center. This was created in Greek architecture to fulfill the Greek ideal of beauty and perfection by correcting the natural optical illusion that makes a straight column appear smaller in the center.

exedra A large recess in a wall, usually semicircular in plan.

facade An exterior vertical plane of a building; often used to refer to the front elevation.

fanlight The semicircular or fan-shaped window above a door that provides light into a hallway or other room.

Federal An American architectural style beginning with the Revolution and continuing until the rise of the Greek Revival in the early nineteenth century. It was largely a continuation of Georgian stylistic ideas, but more restrained and simplified. It is characterized by simple flat facades with little ornament. Window sizes usually graduated from the large ground-floor windows to small third-floor windows, except some architects continued to place the tallest windows on the second floor in the Georgian manner.

finial The decorative top of a spire, gable, pediment, or other element.

Flemish bond A brickwork pattern in which the headers (short end) and stretchers (long side) alternate in each course to form a pattern that is decorative.

frieze The central part of the entablature between the cornice and the architrave; it is often decorated.

gable The triangular end of a wall under a roof formed of two sloping planes.

gablet A small gable, generally decorative, although it may contain a lucarne to admit light or air.

gallery A long room or hallway extending the length of a house, or an upper level in a church or theater.

gambrel A roofline with two different slopes, the upper being flatter and the lower being steeper.

Georgian The architectural style named for the period of the reign of the four Georges on the throne of England (1714–1830) but more truly neo-Palladian. It is an elegant symmetrical style with a large ornamental vocabulary developed by Andrea Palladio. Features include pilasters at corners, a portico or central pavilion with pediment and pilasters, fanlights, and Palladian windows.

Gibbs surround A lively checkered pattern of stone blocks around the jamb of a door or window under a triple keystone head; James Gibbs is credited with popularizing the device.

Gothic A medieval style of architecture developed in France and found primarily in northern Europe, characterized by pointed arches, vaults, and flying buttresses. The Gothic Revival reached the United States in the nineteenth century with romantic notions about reviving the ornament and atmosphere of medieval times.

Greek Revival The Greek Revival style developed in America between 1825 and the 1850s and represents a strong break with Georgian and Federal styles. It is based on Classical Greek architecture with bold simple forms. The elements of the Greek temple front—pediments and columns—are key components of the style.

header A brick which is laid so that only the short end is visible in a wall.

hipped or hip roof A roof form without gable ends, in which four planes slope up to the ridge.

"historic skirt" An approach that hides the lower floors of a new high-rise building behind a historic building or group of buildings to maintain the traditional streetscape while vastly increasing the density of use on the site. The approach was developed as a compromise between those who wanted to retain old low-rise buildings and those who wanted large-scale new development. It differs from the "facade wrap" in that the new development is set back a significant distance behind the historic facades with a roofline that looks authentic.

hood mold Developed in medieval architecture, it is a projecting molding over a door, window, or archway to protect the opening from dripping rain.

in antis Recessed into the face of a building, as a portico *in antis*.

infill Structures built to fill gaps in an existing architectural context.

International Style A style developed in the 1920s and later that attempted to eliminate historical and cultural references from architecture and to begin anew with simple forms and materials suited to contemporary technology and human needs; Le Corbusier, Walter Gropius, Mies van der Rohe, Marcel Breuer, and others were leaders of the movement.

Ionic In Classical architecture, a fluted column shaft is mounted on an Attic base and surmounted by a capital composed of two large scrolls (volutes) topped by a dentil cornice.

jetty A projection on the exterior of a building caused by an upper floor overhanging a lower floor.

lancet window A tall, narrow Gothic-style window.

lintel A horizontal supporting member that spans an opening.

lucarne A small window projecting from a roof and often surmounted by a gablet; particularly associated with Gothic architecture.

lunette A half-moon–shaped window or wall panel.

machicolation A picturesque parapet developed in medieval castles for defense. Stone or brick corbels support arched openings in the floor through which the enemy could be attacked from above. In nineteenth- and twentieth-century architecture the form is purely decorative and the openings are omitted.

mansard roof A steep, almost vertical roof, usually with dormer windows, enclosing the top floor, as in most Back Bay houses. The style came from Paris, where it was associated with the designs of the seventeenth-century architect Francois Mansart.

marquetry An inlaid pattern of stone, wood, or other materials.

modillion Ornamental brackets within the cornice of Corinthian and composite orders. Modillions are arranged in uninterrupted rows above the dentils but are more widely spaced.

mullion The major vertical member used like a rail to create large subdivisions of a window or door.

muntins The bars that subdivide window sash into small panes and hold the glass.

nave The major space of a church between the entrance and the chancel.

Neoclassical A style of architecture developed in Europe in the later eighteenth century based on the rediscovery of the architecture of ancient Greece and Rome.

oculus A round or oval window or opening.

oriel window Similar to a bay window, except that it is not supported from the ground but is projected from the wall, usually of an upper floor. Oriels are found throughout the Back Bay but are less common than the bay window.

Palladian window A window composition with a central arch supported on columns flanked by shorter side lights. The motif was popularized by the Italian architect Andrea Palladio.

parapet A low wall, often at the edge of a roof.

patera A round or oval low-relief decoration on a wall.

pediment A triangular expression of a gable roof, as in the Greek temple front; often used above doors and windows. A **broken pediment** eliminates most of the base of the triangle, while an **open pediment** is open on top, with center point missing.

piano nobile In Renaissance architecture, the principal floor with the most important formal rooms, one level above the ground floor; the term was adopted in later European architecture.

pilaster A flattened column attached to a wall for decoration.

pinnacle A miniature spire that is purely ornamental, often used on top of a buttress or gable.

porte cochere A roofed extension of an entrance which accommodates carriages to allow passengers to enter the building protected from inclement weather.

postmodern An eclectic style developed in the United States beginning in the 1960s, in reaction to the sterility of the International Style; elements from a variety of architectural vocabularies are used decoratively, often with great exaggeration.

putti Cherublike babies, often with wings, favored in Italian Baroque ceiling designs.

quatrefoil Gothic window tracery divided into four circular parts.

quoins The prominent stones at the corner of a masonry building.

reconstruction A room or building that has been rebuilt precisely as it was originally.

recycling Drastic adaption to new uses of a building once serving a different purpose.

renovation Alteration and repair of a building, retaining many of its original features but adapting them to new uses.

restoration A process of retaining all original materials and features in an old building and using historically correct methods in repairs to return it to a state as much like its original condition as possible. Nothing is adapted or altered in restoration.

"retro-Deco" Design of a contemporary building to look vaguely Art Deco in style with mannered surface decoration. Motifs are typically geometric, but they may also be stylized figural or floral forms; in any case, they are clearly surface applied rather than integrated with the structure.

roll molding A round molding of at least a half-circle in section.

Romanesque A pre-Gothic European style of architecture particularly associated with Italy. Its round arches and vaults were much appreciated by H. H. Richardson and incorporated into his own style.

roundel A circular ornament that differs from a patera in that it has no relief decoration. A roundel may be completely blank.

rustication A treatment of stone that emphasizes the joints.

segmental arch An arch composed of a circular segment of less than a semicircle centered on a point beneath the spring line.

spandrel The triangular area between two adjacent arches.

stela, stelae A vertical slab or pillar with incised inscription or decoration.

stilted arch An arch that appears vertically elongated because it is sprung from a point above the supporting posts or columns.

stretcher In brickwork, a brick laid so the long side is exposed.

string course A prominent horizontal band of masonry on a facade which sometimes projects.

superblock A large parcel of developed land in which several blocks are joined by the elimination of streets. A superblock avoids through-circulation to create a protected enclave.

swag An ornament that resembles draped fabric.

trabeated Constructed by the post-and-lintel system.

tracery The ornamental branched mullions particularly associated with Gothic churches.

transept The crosswise arm of a cruciform church.

trefoil Gothic tracery dividing an arch into three curved parts.

trompe l'oeil A painted or low-relief view intended to fool the eye and create a sense of distance or perspective grander than reality. The device was developed and perfected by Baroque architects and painters.

Tudor A picturesque style that originated in fifteenth-century England, characterized by half-timbered stucco or brick with half-hipped roof and leaded windows.

turret A small tower projecting above the roofline and derived from medieval castle architecture.

tympanum The triangular surface within a pediment.

vermiculated Having a mossy, worm-eaten, or spongelike appearance; a finish given to stone.

Victorian The long eclectic period of architecture more or less during the reign of Queen Victoria (1837–1901).

Vitruvian Any architectural ornament associated with the Roman architect, Vitruvius. The Vitruvian scroll is a series of wavelike forms.

voussoir A wedge-shaped stone used in forming an arch; the center stone is called a keystone.

Selected References

Amory, Cleveland. *The Proper Bostonians*. New York: E. P. Dutton, 1947.

Boston Landmarks Commission. *Central Business District Preservation Study*. Boston Landmarks Commission, monograph, 1980.

Boston Landmarks Commission. *Building and Streetscape Preservation Survey for Boston's Theater District*. Boston Landmarks Commission, monograph, 1979.

Boston Society of Architects. *Architecture Boston*. Barre, Mass.: Barre Publishing, 1976.

Bunting, Bainbridge. *Houses of Boston's Back Bay: An Architectural History, 1840–1917*. Cambridge, Mass.: Harvard University Press, 1967.

Bunting, Bainbridge, and Robert H. Nylander. *Report Four: Old Cambridge*. Cambridge, Mass.: Cambridge Historical Commission, 1973

Committee on the Visual Arts. *Art and Architecture at M.I.T.: A Walking Tour of the Campus*. Cambridge, Mass.: Committee on the Visual Arts, 1982.

Cushing, George M., Jr., and Ross Urquhart. *Great Buildings of Boston: A Photographic Guide*. New York: Dover Publications, 1982.

Drake, Samuel Adams. *Old Landmarks and Historic Personages of Boston*. Boston: Little, Brown, 1906.

Fein, Albert. *Frederick Law Olmsted and the American Environmental Tradition*. New York: Braziller, 1972.

Frothingham, Richard. *History of Charlestown, Massachusetts*. Boston: Little and Brown, 1845.

Harris, John. *The Boston Globe Historic Walks in Old Boston*. Chester, Conn.: The Globe Pequot Press, 1982.

Hitchcock, Henry-Russell, Jr. *The Architecture of H. H. Richardson and His Time*. New York: Museum of Modern Art, 1936.

Hunnewell, James F. *A Century of Town Life; A History of Charlestown, Massachusetts 1775–1887*. Boston: Little, Brown, 1888.

King, Moses. *King's Handbook of Boston*. Cambridge, Mass.: Moses King, 1878.

Kirker, Harold. *The Architecture of Charles Bulfinch*. Cambridge, Mass.: Harvard University Press, 1969.

Kirker, Harold and James. *Bulfinch's Boston 1787–1817*. New York: Oxford University Press, 1964.

McIntyre, Alexander McVoy. *Beacon Hill: A Walking Tour*. Boston: Little, Brown, 1975.

Miller, Naomi, and Keith Morgan. *Boston Architecture 1975–1990*. Munich: Prestel-Verlag, 1990.

Morison, Samuel Eliot. *One Boy's Boston 1887–1901*. Boston: Houghton Mifflin, 1962.

Newton, Norman Thomas. *Design on the Land: The Development of Landscape Architecture*. Cambridge, Mass.: Belknap Press of Harvard University Press, 1971.

Rettig, Robert Bell. *Guide to Cambridge Architecture: Ten Walking Tours*. Cambridge, Mass.: M.I.T. Press, 1969.

Sawyer, Timothy Thompson. *Old Charlestown*. Boston: J. H. West, 1902.

Southworth, Michael and Susan. *Topographic Histories of Boston Neighborhoods* (12 volume monograph). Boston: Boston 200 Corporation, 1973–1974.

————. *Ornamental Ironwork: An Illustrated Guide to its Design, History, and Use in American Architecture.* New York: McGraw-Hill, 1991.

Stebbins, Theodore E., Jr. "Richardson and Trinity Church: The Evolution of a Building." *Journal of the Society of Architectural Historians,* December 1968, Vol. XXVII, No. 4.

Tucci, Douglas Shand. *Built in Boston: City and Suburb 1800–1950.* Boston: New York Graphic Society Books, 1978.

Van Rensselaer, Mariana Griswold. *Henry Hobson Richardson and His Works.* New York: Dover Publications, 1969.

Victorian Boston Today: Ten Walking Tours. Boston: New England Chapter of the Victorian Society in America, 1975.

Weston, George F. *Boston Ways: High, By, and Folk.* Boston: Beacon Press, 1957.

Whitehill, Walter Muir. *Boston: A Topographical History.* Cambridge, Mass.: Harvard University Press, 1963.

Whitehill, Walter Muir. *Boston Statues.* Barre, Mass.: Barre Publishing, 1970.

Index

Numbers in bold face refer to street addresses

About the Authors

SUSAN AND MICHAEL SOUTHWORTH have practiced urban design, planning, and architecture in Boston and in the San Francisco Bay area, where Michael is a professor of urban design and planning at the University of California at Berkeley. Much of the Southworths' work has dealt with preservation of older towns and buildings and their adaption to contemporary needs, as well as with the design of urban discovery trails and information systems. Among the Southworths' award-winning projects were the conceptual plan for the Urban National Park in Lowell, Massachusetts, intended to revitalize America's first planned industrial community as an educative environment, and their mixed-use mill conversion design for the historic Boott Mill in Lowell. For Boston's Bicentennial they designed a citywide network of discovery trails and information kiosks. Other books by the South-worths include *Ornamental Ironwork: An Illustrated Guide to Its Design, History, and Use in American Architecture* (McGraw-Hill) and *Maps* (New York Graphic Society Books). Michael Southworth contributed to and edited *Wasting Away* by Kevin Lynch (Sierra Club Books) and *City Sense and City Design: Writings and Projects of Kevin Lynch* (with Tridib Banerjee, MIT Press).

Additions, Corrections, Comments

Readers who believe an important site has been omitted from the guide or who have other comments are invited to submit them to the authors for consideration in the next edition.

Please respond to:
Michael and Susan Southworth
The Globe Pequot Press
P.O. Box 833
Old Saybrook, Connecticut 06475